NIGEL CALDER

The English Channel

CHATTO & WINDUS
LONDON

Published in 1986 by
Chatto & Windus Ltd
40 William IV Street
London WC2N 4DF

ISBN 0 7011 3053 9

Printed in Great Britain by
Redwood Burn Limited, Trowbridge, Wiltshire

Contents

Illustrations follow pages 86 and 214.

Maps appear at the beginning of each chapter.

Author's Note

Many seafarers, scientists, and scholars have contributed information to this book, and any acknowledgement in the text or in the references barely expresses the gratitude I feel. The library of the Cruising Association has been a valuable resource. Thanks are also due to all who have sailed the Channel with me, and especially my wife, Lizzie, who does not look the sort to wrestle with a genoa in a squall but manages very well.

Dates. Between A.D. 1582 and 1752 calendars differed on the two sides of the Channel, because England continued to use the Julian or Old Style calendar long after France, along with other continental countries, had adopted the corrected and improved Gregorian or New Style calendar. Between 1582 and 1699 the discrepancy was ten days (e.g., July 19 in England was July 29 in France) and between 1700 and 1752 it was eleven days. The Gregorian calendar gives a better indication of the sailing season, so it is used here.

Measures. Distances over water are given in nautical miles, called here sea miles, where 1 international nautical mile equals about 1850 metres, or 1.15 land miles. A knot is 1 nautical mile per hour, or 1.15 land miles per hour. Ashore, distances are given in kilometres, where 1 kilometre equals 1000 metres, or 0.62 land mile. Heights, depths, and lengths of ships are given in metres, where 1 metre equals 3.28 feet, or a little more than a yard. A fathom, an obsolescent measure of depth, equals 6 feet, or 1.83 metres.

The English Channel

World's Bend

Welcome aboard. Your life jacket and harness are in the locker beside your bunk, and there are emergency exits forward and aft. In the unlikely event of the boat catching fire or crashing into Ushant, a white box thrown into the sea will magically transform itself into a life raft. We are cruising at an altitude of sixty metres over the continental shelf of Europe, with a ground speed of three knots.

Spacetime shrinks in a fog at sea, so you can scarcely tell *when* you are, never mind where. The waves don't know what century it is. They were the first prowlers on the Earth's surface, and the kaleidoscope of waves has never quite repeated the same pattern anywhere, in 4400 million years. Here and now, whatever that means, a moderate Atlantic swell has become syncopated as it feels the uneven shallows and tidal currents of a dangerous corner of the world.

All ships and boats are much the same, just ploughs for the water. Ours is a ketch, a two-masted sailing boat with the bigger mast in front, and she is built of glass and plastic. But whether your vessel is clad in skin or planks or steel makes little difference to what it feels like to be looking for the island of Ushant in limited visibility at dawn in summer.

The yacht is a time machine that lets us share the experiences of a hundred generations of seafarers. We are bound for the English Channel, the most fascinating stretch of water in the world. It is only a puddle, containing one part in 250,000 of the planet's salt water. The Gulf of St. Lawrence and the Gulf of California are much larger, while the fresh water in Lake Baikal in the Soviet Union could fill the Channel four times over. But in the stormy seas between England and France, events unfolded that shaped the modern world, and the Channel remains a wild frontier between two closely related peoples who by long tradition detest each other's manners and philosophy. It was the laboratory where modern nationalism was invented.

Nature governs human life in the Channel and along its shores. The geology created different kinds of lands on the two sides of the water, and provided harbours for fleets contesting the command of the oceans. In their battles, a change in the wind could alter the fate of nations. The fish first lured to sea the men who built rival trading empires that encircled the globe. Within the Channel, everyone has to defer to the impartial tides and currents.

Sightseers flock to the Channel shores, which are thick with the man-made fossils of past glories. The sea has offered unlimited chances for trading and smuggling, piracy and conquest. No one has kept the advantage for very long because the human and natural worlds keep changing. New findings of geologists, marine scientists, and climatologists illuminate the past, as do the discoveries of archaeologists, who have rich pickings in the Channel's harbours and wrecks.

Supertankers move in procession up the Channel and daily threaten to pollute the shores with oil. New maritime traffic systems, and even a special version of the English language, have had to be invented to cope with the shipping risks in the world's busiest seaway. To reduce their dependence on imported oil, the French are building large nuclear power stations on the cliffs, while the British are seeking oil beneath the bed of the Channel itself, and hope to use hot rocks under the coast to turn the sea water into steam. And where full-rigged frigates used to shadow one another, American, British, French, and Russian nuclear submarines play their all-too-earnest games of hide-and-seek.

In a small boat you can easily lose your way in the open spaces of the Channel, or spend a lifetime exploring all its bays. The oldest features of the coastline contain rock more than two billion years old; the youngest are beaches built in last week's storm. Beyond each major headland a different world opens, and the names of the ports read like battle honours from the Europeans' conquest of the sea and the world: Brest, Saint-Malo, Cherbourg, Caen, Rouen, Le Havre, Dieppe, Boulogne, Calais, Dunkirk. On the English side, all with tales to tell, are Falmouth, Plymouth, Brixham, Dartmouth, Southampton, Portsmouth, and Dover.

The people along the shores have long traditions of cross-Channel trade and rivalry. In the western Channel, rugged Cornwall and Devon face rugged Brittany. In the centre, blander Dorset is nearest to the Channel Islands, and Hampshire and Sussex are opposite Normandy. And at the far end, where the shores constrict the sea at the Dover Strait, Kent confronts Picardy and Flanders. The Channel is a jewel box of nature and history, and the seafarer can wreck himself just as well on peridot as on sand.

Yet from the western entrance of the Channel to the far side of the Dover Strait is less than 350 sea miles, or 650 kilometres,

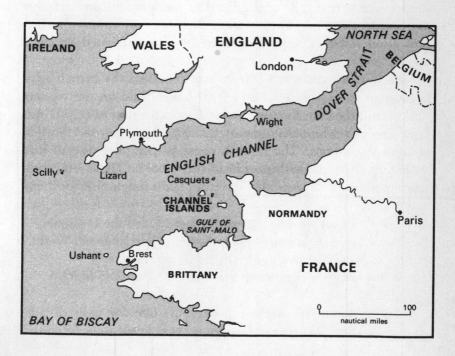

the distance from Washington, D.C., to Boston, Los Angeles to San Francisco, or Milan to Paris. Ships making fifteen knots can round Ushant and be through the Dover Strait twenty-four hours later. Most of the voyage on a direct course is out of sight of land. That suits the seafarer who knows that the land, not the sea, is where the dangers lie, and he is happy to glimpse only the few headlands and islands that project closest to the central axis of the Channel.

The flat-topped island of Alderney may loom up on the starboard side, but the long-haul navigator gives it a wide berth because rocks called the Casquets are evilly sited to the west of Alderney. The only glimpse of France before the Dover Strait may be Cap de la Hague on the Cherbourg Peninsula near Alderney. The next headlands to show themselves may be on the English shore to port: the white high-rise Beachy Head and the low, shingly Dungeness beyond it. Then France, curving abruptly northward, reappears ahead in the shape of Cap Gris-Nez, or Gray Nose. Steer between that and the white cliffs of Dover, watching out for broken water that tells of sandbanks, and you are through into the North Sea. The direct route is forbidden by modern traffic-separation schemes, but seamen in the past navigated by those marks.

On either side of the Cherbourg Peninsula the French coast falls away in large bays: the Gulf of Saint-Malo on the western side, and in the east, the wide Seine Bay extending to Cap D'Antifer, France's white analogue of Beachy Head. Beyond Antifer, Somme Bay opens. The English coast is straighter overall than the French coast, but with more headlands close in. The seventeenth-century sea song "Spanish Ladies" supplied a mnemonic for them:

> The first land we made, 'twas the head called the Deadman,
> Next Rame Head near Plymouth, Start, Portland, and Wight.
> So we sailed by Beachy, by Fairlee, and Dungeness,
> Where we bore right away for the South Foreland Light.

The seafarer knows these lineaments like the faces of mistrusted companions. He can recognize them in sunshine or squall, and remembers what off-lying rocks and tide rips lurk beside them. The details change with the passing centuries, but even a prehistoric navigator would recognize most of the present landmarks.

Our ketch, *Charmed* by name and nature, will follow the shores. When she has sailed eastward along the French coast from Brest to Dunkirk she will cross the Dover Strait and come back westward down the English shore to Scilly. The Channel is an untidy museum, with exhibits set out at random. They will speak for themselves in geographical rather than chronological order, but will convey a sense of what seafaring on the Channel is like, and the continuity of the timeless sea. Each stretch of salt water and coast will evoke a theme that may be prehistoric or ultramodern, or something in between, whether the Spanish Armada or Jesus Christ's grandmother.

If you want to see ships, let the ghosts populate the fog. With deliberate imagination you can hear the creak and splash of the oars of a galley financed by Signor Antonio, Shakespeare's Merchant of Venice, rowing for safety's sake in this light wind. Her crew would notice nothing anachronistic about today's waves, the set of the tide, or the weather. Summer fog was probably about as common four hundred years ago as it is now: one day in five. The seafarer knows when he is entering the Chops of the Channel, because the ragged waves tell him, and so does his sounding line.

A long cord with a weight on the end, for measuring the depth of water, was the pilot's chief instrument for thousands of years before the magnetic compass. The echo sounder has replaced the cord with ultrasonic pulses, and the ketch's electronic gadget shows at a glance that there are still sixty metres of water under the keel. What it cannot provide, as any sounding lead primed with animal grease would do, is the sample of the sand and broken shells from the sea bed that the Venetian galley captain certainly wants to inspect. The old seafarers knew the shape and composition of the sea bed as well as you and I know the hills and colours of the landscapes of home.

Not, of course, in the deep oceans. There you would need a cord five kilometres long to reach the sea bed. "Mine affection," says Rosalind in another of Shakespeare's plays, "hath an unknown

bottom, like the Bay of Portugal." The Venetian captain coming
north from Portugal had "no bottom" all across the Bay of Biscay,
which is an arm of the Atlantic Ocean. He would have "entered
soundings" yesterday, on the continental shelf of France—the
doorstep of northern Europe. Now his problem is to feel his way
in the morning mist around the corner of France without hitting
the rocks, and then turn northeastward into the English Channel.

Ushant is a loose tooth in the Chops, or jaws, of the Channel.
Europe opened its mouth 115 million years ago. The continents
were hugger-mugger before then. Portugal lay alongside the Grand
Banks of Newfoundland, and northern Spain butted against the
present continental shelf between France and Ireland. An embry-
onic English Channel, much older than the Atlantic Ocean, existed
as a rift valley between the islands of Cornwall and Brittany. It
resembled the present-day rift valleys of East Africa, where the
ground has subsided between opposing scarps, but it was flooded,
forming an inland sea. At the Spanish end, the rift valley of the
western English Channel made a T-junction with another rift valley slanting across it, which then grew into a true ocean basin.
When North America and Europe were beginning to tear themselves apart, the juvenile North Atlantic Ocean was uncertain which
way to grow between them. The Bay of Biscay was an experimental flourish. Spain fell away like a drooping Habsburg lip, and
the valley between Brittany and Cornwall was opened to the ocean
swell.

As the old shantymen sang: "From Ushant to Scilly is thirty-
four leagues." At three nautical miles to a league, it is indeed about
102 miles from here to the islands of Scilly, the loose teeth in the
English jaw of the Channel. That has been roughly the gape for
a hundred million years. When the rest of France dried out, Brittany became its western peninsula, dividing the English Channel
from Biscay.

The Spanish Armada came this way to liberate England from
the heretic Queen Elizabeth I and reunite the Church of God. Like
all northbound traffic making for the English Channel, the Duke
of Medina Sidonia and his fleet had to work their way past Ushant.
So here are more ghosts to overawe you at this quadricentennial

of the Armada campaign. A hundred warships of the first great maritime empire lay becalmed in the fog here on July 26, 1588.

The Armada had suffered extraordinary delays after leaving Lisbon two months earlier. The unhelpful and often violent weather perplexed the admiral, because God controlled the winds and the Armada was plainly doing God's work. Yet the summer of 1588 was unusually stormy and variable, even for the fickle seas of northwestern Europe. Weather charts reconstructed by modern climatologists show the centre of a depression tracking over Ushant, becalming the Spanish fleet, and then bringing northerly winds in its wake.

As a result, by the afternoon of that grey Tuesday in 1588, you would have seen the wind-balked ships of the Armada lumbering eastward here, seemingly heading for catastrophe on rocky Ushant or the Breton mainland beyond. The pilot in the flagship *San Martín* had figured this out for himself. At the sound of a gun all the ships turned unhandily to sail westward. If you had been a spy for Francis Drake, leader of the English naval defence in all but title, you would have noticed at once that the high-banked Spanish ships were making no progress northward, into the wind.

Drake and the English fleet had been down this way twice in the hope of meeting the long-advertised Armada. They mainly tacked to and fro in contrary winds, near Ushant. The weather dealt evenhandedly with the two fleets at this stage of their fencing. On July 17, with a fair wind, the English ships had charged towards northern Spain. The wind went around to the south, giving the Spanish their best chance to sail and perhaps slip past them, so the English had to run back past Ushant, to wait in their own waters.

On July 27, a full gale left the Armada scattered across the entrance to the Channel, between Ushant and Scilly. Better weather followed the next day, and by the afternoon of Friday, July 29, most of the Spanish ships were reunited off the Lizard peninsula, the southernmost tip of England, which lies almost due north of Ushant across ninety miles of water. An English vessel on patrol spotted some of the early arrivals at the Lizard and alerted the fleet at Plymouth.

The lonely monarch King Philip II of Spain ran his nation and empire by mail, from his desk at El Escorial in the mountains northwest of Madrid. He neither visited the great Armada that he conjured into being, nor dealt with its unwilling commander face-to-face. Some of his written instructions were ingenious, some prudent, some ambiguous, some foolishly precise. The oddest command of all, too clear-cut to be ignored by a dutiful fleet, was that the Armada, bound right up the Channel to the Dover Strait at the far end, should follow the English coast. Philip had heard that there were shallows and banks off the French coast, which was true enough, but any ship giving visible land and islands a clearance of several miles has deep water for most of the way up the middle of the Channel.

The king's hydrographic fears added a day's sailing to the distance that the Armada had to cover. They also made the fight convenient for the English, who could keep an eye on the Spanish fleet from the shore and resupply their ships from ports along the English coast. Shattered by shot and smashed by gales, only half of the Spanish ships that sailed confidently past Ushant returned southward to their homeland. As a result, the English felt more comfortable about setting up colonies across the Atlantic, in North American territories that the pope said belonged to Spain.

The Spanish, Portuguese, French, Dutch, and English peoples competed in trying to dominate the world by gun-carrying ships. In the process they defined their own nationhood. The defeat of the Spanish Armada tilted the scales in favour of the Protestants, at the origin of the English and Dutch nation-states. Both nations went on to create maritime empires out of all proportion to their numbers or the resources of the homelands, and they fought each other like sharks. The French were content to be spectators during the Armada. Later they tried repeatedly to wrest control of the seas from the Dutch and English.

England has lost its empire, and the nation that led the Industrial Revolution has become a net importer of manufactured goods. But it has left an indelible mark on the world. French historians are still puzzled to tell how the uncouth *anglais*—the people and their language—managed to upstage the more powerful and more civilized French. The most original of these historians, Fernand Braudel, has recently announced that the real struggle for domination was between the English and the Dutch, not the English and the French. It did not seem that way to the seamen for whom these waters near Ushant were a battleground for centuries.

Ushant is the world's bend, the turning point for shipping coming from the south on its way to the ports of northern Europe. Four ships an hour, day and night, alter course here, turning right to enter the Channel. As many going the other way swing left, towards Rio, Kuwait, or the Pacific. They pass well clear. In the old days, sailing vessels were advised not to come within sight of Ushant, even on a clear day. The prevailing winds and currents are liable to carry a slow-moving ship much closer to the shore than she intends. As a French proverb has it: *Qui voit Ouessant voit son sang*—"Who sees Ushant sees his blood." The new traffic lanes make prudence obligatory.

The French government, nervous of laden oil tankers that threaten to impale themselves on the rocks, has ordered all the kamikaze shipping to keep far out to sea. In order to satisfy the International Maritime Organization, the French lighthouse authority has had to invent an artificial Ushant. It takes the form of a deep-sea light tower 232 metres tall, fit to rise from the bed of the stormy sea thirty-five miles west of Ushant. The water there is 127 metres deep, so nearly half the structure protrudes above the surface, carrying radio and radar beacons as well as lights. The novel seamark, standing on a tripod of one steel and two concrete legs, helps navigators to keep in their prescribed lanes and avoid hitting one another or the Breton shore. With this innovation, the Créac'h lighthouse on Ushant loses its former status as France's westernmost welcome and warning to mariners.

Although Créac'h is hidden from view, the double blast of its diaphone confirms the presence of Ushant every two minutes. *Créac'h* means "hillock" in the Celtic language, but it was a favoured corner long before the Celts arrived. The lighthouse occupies the site of a tomb built of large stones in the megalithic phase of the Stone Age. Before there were pyramids in Egypt, seafaring peoples along these western shores of Europe were heaving large stones to make tombs, monuments, circles, and sighting stones, which served a strange blend of interment, phallus-worship, and astronomy. Twelve sea miles from here, near the entrance to Brest, they laid out more than a hundred stones in a double cross at Lagatjar, and even greater concentrations of megaliths survive down the Biscay coast.

Créac'h has stopped moaning. That means the visibility has improved near the island. The patchy mist is now scattered like the smoke of battle across the sea. If the ketch carried radar, Ushant would appear on the screen as what the British Admiralty's *Channel Pilot* calls "the open claw of a lobster." It habitually snatches imprudent or unlucky ships and grinds them into small pieces.

The sea bed has risen to little more than fifty metres below the surface, the contour where you start worrying if you cannot see anything. From that depth, underwater cliffs soar to break the surface as low-lying rocks at the tips of the lobster's claw. A short-range landfall in these conditions is like a lottery. What shall we see first? Will I like what we see? Or shall I have to stand on the brakes, which in a small boat means turning smartly out to sea?

A cloud a little thicker than the rest hardens abruptly into solid rock. A cluster of structures on top of a flattish rock makes a weird sight in the mist. The nearest structure quickly dresses itself in neat red and white stripes. It's the Nividic lighthouse.

Lampaul Bay is open south of Nividic and looks inviting in the morning sunshine. A tall rock in the middle of the long, narrow bay acts as a breakwater. At the far end of the harbour, the village of Lampaul is the capital of the Lilliputian empire of Ile d'Ouessant. The rocky mound at the ocean's edge is home for about 1500 people, but Ushant is a woman's island. Most of the men are absent as sailors and fishermen. Many have died at sea, and the wax crosses that memorialize them are supposed to guide their souls home to Ushant.

Women cultivate the almost barren soil and tend the sheep. Anthropologists say that many of the world's seafaring communities are matrilineal, because the women are left in charge of affairs and a sailor has more reason than most men to wonder whether his wife's child is really his own. By Ushantine tradition it is the woman who proposes marriage. The laws of France have modified many old customs, and so have the teachings of the Church, here represented in the spire at Lampaul—a useful leading mark if you want to enter the bay.

Lampaul's name is a corruption of *Lann-Paul,* meaning Paul's church. *Lann* is "church" in the Breton language and Old Welsh; in modern Welsh it has become *Llan. Lann* also figures in place names in Cornwall, the nearest piece of England, where Celts spoke a language very like Welsh and Breton. The *wall* in Cornwall means "Welsh." The sea has linked the Celts of France and the British Isles for more than two thousand years. Ushant is nearer to Ireland than to Paris, and Brittany has the same name as Britain. It was the Little Britain colonized by Celtic refugees—British Boat People fleeing across the Channel during the disturbances that followed the collapse of the Roman empire. Bretagne is the Frenchman's name for Brittany, and that is why he is obliged to distinguish his old enemy as *Grande-Bretagne,* or Great Britain. But the English are not British in this ethnic sense; nor, for that matter, are the French Gallic. Confusion becomes complete in the word *gallicisme,* which means the correct use of the French language. It would more suitably refer to the Welsh language, because the French name for Wales is Pays de Galles. When you trace ancestral roots hereabouts, you learn that everyone is a down-Channel or cross-Channel interloper. The Celts, and especially some of the Bretons of Brittany, will tell you that the English and French are not the only folk around with claims to nationhood.

Older human layers appear in the names of Ushant. It was *Uxisama* to the Gallic or Gaulish Celts who lived here before either the Romans or the British Celts came upon this outpost of Europe. The name means "highest," and must refer to the fact that Ushant stands a little taller above the sea than other islands nearby. The Romans, intruders from the south, called it *Uxantis,* and the English Ushant comes from that version. *Eussa* (Breton) and *Ouessant* (French) are variations imposed by later intruders from the north and the east. The Breton name is a pun, making it a sacred place for Heuzuz, the god of death.

The Saint Paul commemorated at Lampaul was not the Jew of Tarsus but his namesake, Paul-Aurelian. He arrived at Ushant from Wales soon after A.D. 500, as one of the wandering pilgrims regarded by the Bretons as the founding fathers of their faith. Long before Prince Henry of Portugal sent ships to find gold in Africa, the Celtic monasteries of western Britain dispatched *peregrini*, looking for souls to save, across the English Channel. As a result, the Bretons have many saints unheard of in Rome, and this Paul-Aurelian is reputed to have brought the Gospel to Brittany's far west.

He was more like a buccaneer than a priest. The Celtic saints had to be tough and fit to voyage across stormy waters. Their open boats were sheathed in animal hides. The saints carried weapons, and their hair was draped over their shoulders in Druid fashion. Arriving in Brittany, they would find a lonely island on which to settle and meditate before proceeding to the mainland. Paul chose Ushant as his forward base. From here he set off on his mission to northwestern Brittany. Some fifty miles along the coast from here, near the port of Roscoff, the market town of Saint-Pol-de-Léon was the seat of his eventual bishopric.

Pol and his fellow saints had to outwit the Celtic magicians and witches. The shores of Ushant, exposed to the sky and the wild sea, had more than their share of pagan rites. Among the pre-Christian Celts two main factions contended. In the cult of the mother goddess Ana, priestesses took a leading part, and a pair of hills near Killarney in Ireland are called Da Chich Anann, "the breasts of Ana." The other was the harsh, male-dominated Druid cult favoured among immigrants from Britain. The Christians did not enjoy perfect harmony, either. Heresies rocked the early Church, and there were preexisting bishoprics in Brittany, relics of the imperial Roman Church. The saints coming across the Channel simply ignored them.

Although the Roman Catholic Church recaptured Brittany, many compromises with the old Celtic religion show through. The Seven Brothers of the Celtic Pantheon have become the Seven Saints, the founding fathers of Brittany. Most startling of all, the Celtic mother goddess Ana reigns in Brittany in the twentieth century. She has been transmuted into Saint Anne, and the local clergy condones the legend that she was the grandmother of Jesus Christ. Anne-Ana went from Brittany to Palestine to give birth to the Virgin Mary, and Jesus came to Brittany to visit his granny before he departed for heaven. What potent spells the Celtic sorcerers still cast on those who live here!

Seamen of a hundred generations have drowned in the treacherous waters of western Brittany. A very modern phallus on the island's northern side, beyond the Créac'h lighthouse, has an inhabited bulb near the top and a flashing white light. That is Ushant's sea-traffic station, part of the surveillance centre called CROSS Corsen-Ouessant, which also coordinates search and rescue operations. Ushant possesses its own lifeboat at Lampaul, but there are no fewer than six other lifeboat stations within thirty miles. In 1983, in the area controlled by this CROSS centre, 571 people had to be rescued, and 43 were reported dead or missing. For the Celts, hell itself was cold and misty like the sea, and a ghostly night ship, *Bag Noz,* was skippered by the first person to die during the year.

Ushant is a part of Brittany's mosaic of igneous rocks, which only makes sense if you understand that we are sailing among the roots of mountains that formerly towered high overhead. About 300 million years ago, Brittany was the southern edge of Europe. Southern France was far away, a part of the great continent of Gondwanaland, which incorporated South America, Africa, and other southerly land masses. But the floor of the intervening ocean was diving to destruction under Brittany, and throwing up volcanic mountains like the present-day Andes of South America. Then the leading edge of Gondwanaland hit Europe's Breton bumper, and the wreckage made even grander mountains. In Brittany, 300 million years of erosion has taken the mountains away, and uplift has brought the granite to sea level. In the meantime, the tearing of Europe's fabric, when the Bay of Biscay opened, produced a ragged edge of land near the new continental margin. The endless dance of the continents has crushed, stretched, and sheared Brittany, leaving it crisscrossed by faults.

The island of Ushant is outlined by faults running roughly east–west and north–south. It consists of two blocks that have risen above their companions in the surrounding sea bed. Lampaul Bay marks the fault where the two blocks meet to make the lobster's claw. The fault created a line of weakness where erosion was able to carve out the bay. Ushant is a small scale model for the new geology of continents, in which the movements of blocks turn out to govern many features of the land and the sea bed. Other harbours of the English Channel lie, like Lampaul, in cracks between the blocks.

Fit for an Admiral?

The mosaic of granite paves a gap of ten sea miles between Ushant and the mainland of Brittany, and decorates it with small islands and large rocks. To approach Brest from the north a navigator must find the old fault lines where the water is deeper. That means closing with the mainland at Pointe de Corsen and then heading southward to the more prominent Pointe Saint-Mathieu, which guards the entrance to Brest harbour, France's main naval base.

If Ushant is like a lobster's claw, Brittany is the whole lobster, prodding the waters of the Atlantic. The arm made by these northern headlands and islands running out to Ushant is matched by a more withered arm some twenty sea miles to the south at Pointe du Raz, where tourists admire the violent sea in the Raz de Sein. That is a passage zigzagging towards the Bay of Biscay between the headland and a granite reef projecting twelve miles into the ocean and surmounted by the Ile de Sein, a habitable knuckle. Between the arms, the wide and deep water of the Iroise is the big-ship approach to Brest. The lobster's head, well retracted from the ocean, is the T-shaped peninsula of Crozon, built of sedimentary rocks sandwiched between the granite masses of northern and southern Brittany. Faults running east define the lobster's granite shoulders, and erosion has dug out huge natural harbours on either side of Crozon.

Pointe du Raz keeps growing because southern Brittany is sliding westward along one of the main faults. By the standards of major earthquake zones, the shocks here are trivial. An earthquake near the Raz in 1959 caused a panic at a chicken farm, and five dozen birds killed themselves. The most notable damage was done long ago, farther east along that fault, when an earthquake toppled and smashed the greatest pillar of the megalithic builders: a 350-ton monolith that formerly stood twenty metres tall. Northern Brittany is also on the move, and the second main fault runs eastward from Pointe de Corsen, past the city of Brest. Lesser faults have created plenty of small anchorages in the approaches to Brest. One of them squares off the coast that runs south to Pointe Saint-Mathieu along the Four Channel, which *Charmed* has been following.

The Breton name for Pointe Saint-Mathieu was *Pen-ar-bed,* "the end of the world." A tall, red-topped lighthouse and a ruined abbey now decorate it, together with the French navy's radar and signal station. From here to the Rade de Brest is a splendid sail of ten sea miles. Granite cliffs sixty metres high make a succession of headlands on the northern shore, rough hewn by the cross-faults. An old fort stands beside Bertheaume Bay, and another red-topped lighthouse occupies a spear of low-lying rock projecting from the headland of Petit Minou.

The regulations say that yachts must keep well to the right of the main channel, so our ketch passes close to a yellow buoy with a black stripe that marks Les Fillettes, or the Little Girls. These are the first of a row of rocks that lie in wait for careless sailors, right in the middle of the entrance to the Goulet, where the high ground of Crozon closes in from the south to make a gullet about one mile wide and three miles long.

Beyond the Goulet lies the Rade de Brest, where fifty square sea miles of water offer an anchorage fit for an admiral. Nature seduced the French navy into making Brest its main base for confronting the English. A Little France was planted here in half-alien Brittany, to build and service the warships. The Bretons, the finest seamen in Europe, manned the rigging. But Brest was strategically flawed in the era of sailing ships.

The geological faults decreed that the great harbour should open towards the west. The Earth's rotation ensured that the prevailing winds in these latitudes blew from the west. Brest was a trap, and nature helped to keep Napoleon's navy locked up here, at the climax of the contest between the British and the French for the control of the seas.

French fleets coming out of Brest alarmed the British often enough. The one that most affected the course of history left here in March 1781 to help the American rebels who were plaguing the old enemy. The French navy was bent on revenge. In a November gale off southern Brittany, some twenty years earlier, the British had hounded its warships onto the rocks, and Bretons mourned their seamen. In that disastrous war the French lost India, Canada, and other colonies to the British. In 1779 a refurbished fleet sailed from Brest for an invasion of England. They were to shepherd forty thousand troops across the Channel from Saint-Malo and Le Havre to Portsmouth. Bad weather and shipboard disease defeated that enterprise, and attention switched to America, where the British were smothering the United States at birth.

The rebels begged for help, and 6700 French troops set sail

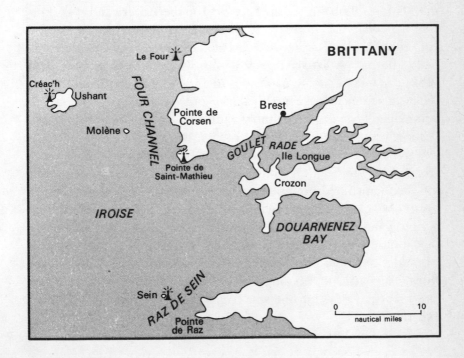

from Brest for Newport, Rhode Island, in May 1780. They roughly doubled George Washington's army. In the following year a strong fleet commanded by the Comte de Grasse left Brest to cross the Atlantic, and the French navy's finest hour had come.

The Comte de Grasse went first to the West Indies to capture the island of Tobago and collect more troops. A frigate brought him an urgent message. The French and American armies were ready to attack one or another of the main British armies, in New York or Virginia, but they needed de Grasse to deal with the British navy. By replying that he would sail at once for Chesapeake Bay, de Grasse chose the theatre in which the outcome of the rebellion was to be decided. At the Battle of the Virginian Capes, on September 5, 1781, the leading British ships were badly shot up by the corps of gunners that had been training in Brest for fourteen years. The British fleet withdrew to New York, and a British army was trapped without supplies or reinforcement. It surrendered at Yorktown six weeks later.

For all this effort the French gained little for themselves except the island of Tobago. Their support for the American rebels created a new hydra head of Englishness, in which the benighted culture of the Anglo-Saxons flourished more vigorously than ever. Even the navy's satisfaction was short-lived. Back in the West Indies, de Grasse had to surrender in a battle with the British fleet, when the French lost ten ships and fourteen thousand men. The war helped to make the country bankrupt, and the American Revolution set the example for the French Revolution.

When a new war broke out with Britain in 1793, four years after the Revolution, the French ships appeared to be a good match for the British. Although fewer in numbers, they were bigger, better built, and armed with heavier guns. But revolution was hard to handle in the navy. Democratization, long overdue, meant that junior officers found themselves promoted as captains and admirals, and merchant skippers were given command of warships. The patriotic zeal that carried the French revolutionary army like a storm across Europe was frustrated in the navy by a lack of experience.

At a December dusk in 1796, thirty warships and twenty

transports set off with twenty thousand troops for an invasion of Ireland. An easterly wind took them through the Goulet. To avoid a British fleet lurking near Ushant, the French admiral in *Fraternité* had ordered his ships to use the southern exit, the Raz de Sein. He changed his mind when the wind started blowing from the south, and headed out through the main channel, the Iroise. Many of his ships made no sense of his signals.

One of them hit the rocks and fired her guns as a signal of distress. To make the confusion total, the British frigate *Indefatigable* used the cover of darkness to sail into the Iroise and put on a fireworks show of gunfire, blue signal lights, and a blaze of rockets. The French captains were bewildered. Some ignored the crazy scene and wriggled out through the Raz, in accordance with their original orders. The last laugh but one was with the French because, scattered in small groups, they eluded the British fleet. But blizzards prevented the landing in Ireland.

The Goulet leads *Charmed* towards the chunky, fortified Pointe des Espagnols, opposite Portzic with its modern oceanographic laboratory. The city of Brest stands on the northern shore beyond Portzic. It is fronted by the large breakwaters of the naval base, with grey warships lying inside them. To visualize Brest at the time of the French Revolution, you have to erase the breakwaters and focus on the Penfeld River. That was the original harbour, used by Celts and Romans, and a medieval castle survives at its mouth near the modern lifting bridge. The navy has always used the Penfeld's western bank for its installations, and only French visitors are allowed to go there. Buildings more elegant than anything to be seen today stood on both the naval and civilian sides of the river.

The Revolutionary and Napoleonic wars spanned eighteen years, with only two short breaks. During most of that time there were British warships off Brest. To begin with they were only frigates, but later the British fleet remained at sea off Ushant winter and summer, in a patient demonstration of seamanship. When the wind blew hard from the west, the British ships beat their way out into the Atlantic, or even ran for shelter in Tor Bay on the English coast, confident that the French could not leave harbour against the wind. But whenever the weather was suitable for a breakout, the blockading fleet closed to within sight of the French shore.

Boredom was the chief enemy as the ships tacked to and fro. The crews had to remain alert to anything the French might try, and also keep themselves off the rocks. While they hung about dangerous waters that most seafarers left as quickly as possible, they had interminable practice in handling the complicated machinery of large, windpowered ships. Sloops and frigates operated as close inshore as impudence allowed. In 1801, in the approaches to Brest, one of the frigates was an unknowing target for the American inventor Robert Fulton in the oar-driven submarine he hoped to sell to the French government. Although Fulton and his crew rowed feverishly, they did not get close. Blockade-running coasters, *chasse-marées* ("tide chasers"), would sometimes slip into Brest at night on the flood tide, between the rocks near the Crozon shore, but the blockade forced the French to build a canal to Brest, to carry supplies to the fleet.

In 1805 the conquest of England was Napoleon's first priority. The main responsibility lay with the fleet at Brest, and its commander, Honoré-Joseph-Antonin Ganteaume. The duty of preventing the adventure belonged to William Cornwallis, who was in charge of the Channel Fleet blockading Brest. Cornwallis was known as Blue Billy because of his determination to remain at sea. If a gale forced his ships to run for shelter and replenishment in Tor Bay, the fleet was no sooner anchored than the flagship *Hibernia* would run up the blue signal flag denoting imminent departure.

The preparations for the invasion were grandiose. Shipyards from the Netherlands to western France built nearly 2000 barges to carry 100,000 troops, complete with their guns and horses. The naval plan required all the fleets, from Brest, Rochefort in Biscay, Ferrol in Spain, and Toulon in the Mediterranean, to break out and rendezvous in the West Indies. The idea was to draw the British fleets to the wrong side of the Atlantic and to mass the French and Spanish ships for a dash back to the undefended English Channel.

Horatio Nelson had a less certain grasp on Toulon than Cornwallis on Brest, because he was always hoping to lure the French out to fight. As a result the French ships from Toulon, commanded by Pierre-Charles Villeneuve, accomplished the first part of the plan. Nelson chased them to the West Indies, only to hurry east again when he guessed they were returning to Europe. On July 22 an inconclusive battle took place in fog off northern Spain, between a British force under Robert Calder and Villeneuve's stronger fleet. Calder was court-martialled for capturing only two ships. Villeneuve received exhortations from Napoleon to free the fleet from Brest and sweep all before him.

If you give us control for three days, nay, even for twenty four hours, your task will be done: all is ready, Europe waits breathless on this great event. [Trans. D. Howarth.]

Villeneuve chose instead to retreat to southern Spain, and the Brest fleet stayed put. During these alarms, the British blockading force was reduced to fifteen ships of the line as compared with twenty-five in Brest. Ganteaume thought he could shoot his way out, but he was forbidden to sail because a major naval battle was not what Napoleon had in mind. While the British sacked Calder for failing to wipe out a superior force, the French would not let Ganteaume take his chance against a weaker one. Different attitudes to sea power, evolved in hundreds of years of warfare in the English Channel, decided the outcome.

The only way the French admiral could leave Brest unscathed was to pray for a gale that would drive the British ships into the Atlantic while allowing his own ships to leave harbour. The odds against such weather were long indeed: easterly gales are almost unheard-of at Brest in summer. Napoleon's orders remain as baffling today as they must have been to Ganteaume at the time. The plan to conquer England relied on a freak wind.

On August 22 Ganteaume made a bid to leave Brest. He began moving his fleet out through the Goulet, and assembling it in Bertheaume Bay, or "Berthon" as the unschooled English called it. Cornwallis's ships then defied the shore batteries to come in closer than ever before. As he was still not allowed to fight, the French admiral could only return to harbour. A French satirical rhyme of the time ran as follows:

> Here lies the Admiral Ganteaume,
> Who in an east wind thought it best
> To sail from Brest towards Bertheaume.
> But when the wind was from the west
> He turned and sailed back home to Brest.
> [Trans. adapted from D. Howarth.]

A week later the truth dawned on Napoleon that Villeneuve was timid and Ganteaume was never going to get out. The emperor ordered the Grand Army to march from the English Channel to the Danube, where British diplomats had stirred up trouble for him. The small craft of the invasion fleet were docked, and their crews disbanded. The attack on England had been called off. The blockading fleet's task lacked the drama of a major sea battle like Camperdown, where the British had crushed the Dutch eight years earlier, but it decided the final contest at sea between the British and the French. The American naval historian Alfred Mahan wrote:

> Never in the history of blockades has there been excelled, if ever equalled, the close locking of Brest by Admiral Cornwallis, both winter and summer, between the outbreak of war and the battle of Trafalgar. It excited not only the admiration but the wonder of contemporaries.

Trafalgar only confirmed the victory, when Nelson's fleet captured half of Villeneuve's in the battle off southern Spain on October 21, 1805. Most of the prizes sank in a storm that followed, taking many wounded men with them. Nelson died in the battle, and Villeneuve wished he had. When the British sent him home a few months later, he landed in Brittany and found he was so despised that he killed himself. Ganteaume took Villeneuve's place as commander at Toulon.

In accordance with the meteorological odds, the advantage of the weather came at last to the fleet in Brest in December 1805, and eleven ships of the line, with supporting frigates, evaded the British blockade and set off for transatlantic raiding. All but three came to a sticky end. *Vétéran,* returning home to France, encountered a British warship that chased her into Concarneau, a fishing port on Brittany's south coast. Concarneau was far too small for a ship of the line, and *Vétéran* was stuck there for three years—a nuisance for the fishermen and a humiliation for a navy that, less than thirty years before, had beaten the British during the American Revolution.

Americans remembered their debt to the French when they joined in World War I in 1917. The French, the British, and the Americans were all on the same side for a change, fighting the Germans. Many of the American troops came past Pointe Saint-Mathieu, going the opposite way to de Grasse's. They arrived in Brest in commandeered German passenger liners, and the band played "The Gang's All Here." Again, a transatlantic intervention proved conclusive.

A flotilla of millionaires' steam yachts, hurriedly adapted to antisubmarine warfare, appeared at Brest in July 1917 to support the French navy in the Brittany Patrol. Manned by the raw gobs of the U.S. Navy, they made a curious sight with their fancy clipper bows and their dazzling camouflage paint. In the Restaurant des Escargots a seaman just ashore from the yacht *Emeline* was heard to remark, "War sure is hell when it reduces a country to eating snails." There were naval misapprehensions too: the porpoises mistaken for submarines, the floating mine that turned out to be a dead pig.

By the end of the war, the Americans manning the yachts were as thoroughly acquainted with the hazards of western Brittany as the British blockaders had been. Ushant was where they met the transatlantic convoys and hoped the U-boats were not doing the same. The American yachts also led convoys southward in darkness, by the inshore zigzag through the Raz de Sein. One yacht was torpedoed by a U-boat, but two were lost by shipwreck and collision.

In wartime, all but a very few of the lighthouses and lighted buoys were extinguished or darkened, which made the pilotage all the more tricky. A latter-day Paul Jones of the yacht *Emeline,* H. Wickliffe Rose, entered Brest in an American destroyer a few weeks after that war ended, and described his astonishment at the blaze of lights.

> All the beacons unused during the war were now glowing and flashing, and the entrance to Brest which we had navigated a hundred times before was as bewildering as a strange coast. Carefully we identified our old friends among the lights and found our way through the Goulet into the harbour.

Brest was in Nazi hands a generation later, and German seamen found it was their turn to learn the way past the Little Girls. On a moonless night in February 1942 a battle fleet had to do it by dead reckoning, because a smoke screen covered the Goulet after a British air raid on the naval base. The battle cruisers *Scharnhorst* and *Gneisenau,* together with a cruiser and six destroyers, came charging out of Brest by direct orders of Adolf Hitler, in a bid to dash home via the English Channel. They reached the Dover Strait before the British realized they were out, and would have arrived in Germany unscathed if both battle cruisers had not been badly damaged by magnetic mines laid by the British air force. *The Times* of London thundered: "Nothing more mortifying to the pride of sea power has happened in home waters since the seventeenth century."

U-boats slipping out of the bomb-proof submarine pens just west of the Penfeld River were a far graver threat than the battle cruisers. Winston Churchill commented that the Germans should have staked everything on the Battle of the Atlantic. It was a savage competition in drowning. At the end of 1942, newly built U-boats were arriving in Brest and other Breton ports at a rate of one a day, compared with losses of three U-boats a week. The U-boats were sinking four ships a day on average, but American shipyards were catching up with even that appalling rate of loss. The score tipped heavily in the Germans' favour in March 1943 in the biggest of all convoy battles, when twenty-one ships were sunk against the loss of only one U-boat. Then the balance suddenly tilted the other way. In May 1943, forty-one U-boats failed to return to base. During the next three months not one Allied merchant ship was sunk on the North Atlantic convoy routes, while U-boats were being destroyed at a rate of six a week.

Not until long after the war did the truth emerge, that the Battle of the Atlantic was really a competition in code-breaking. The U-boat successes early in 1943 came about because the Germans had broken the British naval ciphers. Meanwhile the British were reading the top-level German naval ciphers, and the abrupt change of fortunes in May 1943 signified that they had begun to find out exactly where the U-boats were heading.

Brest is now the base for France's strategic nuclear force. The black submarines like giant whales that pass through the Goulet wearing the French tricolour are far more awesome instruments of destruction than the old U-boats. On their patrols to undisclosed corners of the ocean they are constantly ready to launch missiles tipped with H-bomb warheads, on command from the president of France. Missile-carrying submarines have replaced wooden ships of the line, armoured battleships, and aircraft carriers, as the primary naval weapons.

The modern submarine pens occupy a large square building on Ile Longue, which lies outside the oyster beds in a corner of the Rade, four miles south of the breakwaters of Brest. If you sail closer than five hundred metres to this "Long Island," you are liable to be blown up in a minefield. And should you think of taking a swim there, the marines may not hesitate to toss a hand grenade into the water. These are commonplace facts of life in the era of nuclear weapons.

Thoroughly uncommon, though, is the French attitude to nuclear weapons. The missile-carrying submarines slipping routinely in and out of Brest assert the French ideal of independent nationhood in the nuclear era. The British have missile-carrying submarines as well, based in western Scotland, but these carry

American-made missiles. The first British nuclear-powered boat had an American reactor. The British are the only people in the world openly helped by either of the superpowers to acquire strategic weapons systems for nuclear war. The proposed re-equipment with the American Trident II missiles shows that the special relationship continues between the English-speaking countries. The French have been far more self-reliant. Not only their bombs but their missiles are entirely home-made, and France has also become the leader of European space-rocket technology. The French invented their own reactors for powering their nuclear submarines.

In the peculiar geography of nuclear strategy, the Ile Longue is now much more important than Paris, but French theories of nuclear deterrence have the Parisian hallmark. They manage to be startling and baffling at the same time. While the British are sheepish about their nuclear weapons and assign them to the NATO alliance, France is not even a full member of NATO. In nuclear diplomacy, too, the French are unabashed mavericks who refused to sign the Test-Ban Treaty or the Non-Proliferation Treaty.

During the reign of Charles de Gaulle as president of France, some military theorists near to him favoured a posture of *tous azimuts,* "all directions," meaning that France might find itself at odds with the British or the Americans. De Gaulle did not go as far as that, and when he pulled France out of NATO in 1966 he claimed still to be an ally of the U.S. and his European neighbours. But he insisted that France should not accept the status of a lesser power, and sought better relations with the Russians.

De Gaulle was thoroughly sceptical about alliances in the nuclear age, and especially about American promises to defend western Europe against nuclear attack. Nuclear war, as the French envisage it, will be a matter of *sauve qui peut*—every nation for itself. They do not want their lives and liberties destroyed in a nuclear shoot-out between *les anglo-saxons* and the Russians. But their famous logic becomes tortured and stretched when they deny that they are setting an example, such that every nation on Earth might want to acquire its own independent force of missile-carrying submarines. Perhaps even the Bretons, who play their traditional part in manning the French *force de dissuasion.*

The supposedly hostile submarines in these waters are, nowadays, Russian. Air photographers of the Skyfoto company, based at Dungeness on the English coast, make it their business to take pictures of all the shipping in the English Channel. They frequently snap Soviet warships passing through, although they don't like it when anti-aircraft missiles swivel around in their launchers, tracking their small Piper Seneca. Skyfoto sees about two Soviet submarines a month, going up- or down-Channel on the surface, where they are supposed to be. The navies of France, Britain, and the U.S. are more concerned when the Russians are submerged.

So are the fishermen, for whom submarines of any nationality pose a threat even in peacetime. Between 1982 and 1984 three French and Irish fishing boats were sunk in fair weather in Irish waters, with the loss of sixteen lives, apparently as a result of British or American submarines becoming entangled in their nets. In the Channel, in the summer of 1984, the British trawler *Joanna C* found herself being dragged around in circles off the coast of Devon in the middle of the night. With a guilty conscience, the British navy told the skipper by radio to cut his nets. As a result, the navy had to pay him compensation even when it turned out that no friendly submarine was in the area at the time. A submerged Soviet submarine was evidently on an intelligence mission outside the British naval base at Plymouth, in the course of the endless shadow-boxing that passes for peace in our time.

The Russians presumably nose about off Brest, keeping an eye on their fellow submariners from France. And the U.S. Navy may be out there too, doing the same thing. After all, the American secretary of state did warn the French defence minister, back in 1962: "If you target your nuclear force independently, we shall target it with ours."

Accidental Oil

The lumpy Four rock and its lighthouse mark the northwestern corner of Brittany, where smaller rocks crowd the water in front of the hazy cliffs. Some of the youngest granites of Brittany, just 280 million years old, cap the coast and turn eastward at Portsall. Large grains make the rocks easy to erode, enabling the sea to devastate the coastline. The ruins appear in serried ranks in the Argenton rocks, in larger irregular lumps in the Portsall rocks, and farther east towards the Ile Vierge they form miniature islands half a kilometre wide.

This is *aber* country, decorated by the diminutive fjords of Aber-Ildut, Aber-Benoît, and Aber-Wrac'h. If you approach the *abers* from the landward side, you find yourself descending sharply from the low plateau of Brittany to shallow arms of the sea surrounded by trees. From here, the shoreline zigzags eastward. Lying about a hundred sea miles away, almost at the far end of Brittany, Saint-Malo is the first major port after Brest. The approach to it is marked by the one really distinctive headland, Cap Fréhel. The intervening coast is more inviting to fishermen and yachtsmen than to freighters. There are plenty of small harbours and estuaries concealed behind seemingly impenetrable barriers of rocks. The few coastal towns—Morlaix, Lannion, Saint-Brieuc—with populations of twenty to sixty thousand people, seem like metropolises by comparison with the small villages that are typical of the region. On this confusing and often alarming coast, islands provide the best landmarks. Ile Vierge, the English Channel's Virgin Island, is no island paradise, but a useful crag for supporting a large lighthouse. Ile de Batz, marking the port of Roscoff and the entrance to the Morlaix River, serves the same purpose, and is slightly more habitable.

Northern Brittany possesses the least developed coast of one of France's poorer provinces. Earning a living from the sea begins with the shellfish: scallops, lobsters, crayfish, crabs, and so on. Oysters and mussels grow under human supervision in sheltered estuaries and bays where they can still feel the tidal currents that bring them nourishment. By the time they are harvested and brought ashore, the oysters have been trained to think that the tide has gone out, so that they close tightly, hold some sea water, and keep themselves fresh for the table. The Morlaix estuary and Cancale, near Saint-Malo, traditionally rank among the Channel's prime centres for oysters, but the Cherbourg Peninsula surpasses them. Mussel cultivation near Saint-Malo has become big business in the past few decades. Seaweed harvesting on the beaches, an ancient

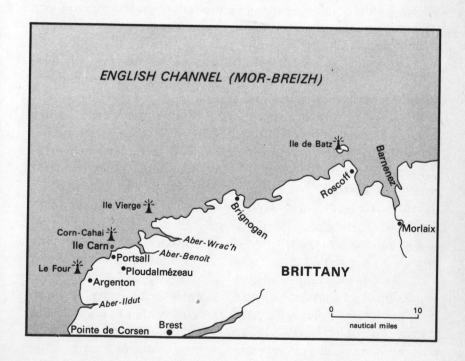

occupation, provides local farmers with natural fertilizer for their artichokes, onions, and spring greens. In a few places a modernized seaweed business supplies alginates to the food and chemical industries.

The *Ar-mor,* the Celtic "land of the sea," gave Brittany its Roman name *Armorica.* Inland is the *Ar-goat,* the "land of forests," but the trees have mostly gone, leaving either open moorland or cultivated land. The soil is stony but fertile once you get beyond the reach of the salt sea spray that poisons it. The Ice Ages dusted Brittany with loess, soil created from rock that was ground into windblown flour by the glaciers. Recent felling of trees and the enlarging of old fields have accelerated the erosion of the soil.

This northern shore is gaunt, without the grandeur of rocky Norway or Maine. In summer, like migrant birds, the tourists bring multicoloured shirts and bank notes here, but they prefer the less forbidding and warmer southern coast of Brittany, where many well-heeled Parisians have built second homes. The salt seems to have preserved the north against infection by the modern world. Underdevelopment is peaceful and picturesque, and you can recapture the past more easily here than on any other stretch of the English Channel shore.

The route for the day goes by way of Portsall, towards Roscoff. (At sea you should not say you are going "to" somewhere, because who knows what wind and weather will do? "Towards" avoids hubris.) And any appreciation of the scenery from a small boat is overprinted by quiet terror. The rocks you can see are not the problem; concern yourself rather with the submerged rocks strewn like a natural minefield stretching three miles from the coast. The currents that sluice between them make it difficult to follow a safe route, even if you know where it is. Yet the rocks that force passing ships to keep well clear of Brittany provide shelter for small harbours, and leading marks help rock-hopping boats like ours to pick their way between the reefs and the shore.

The idea of leading marks is old and simple. Keep two fixed objects lined up ahead of you and you are bound to travel straight. If the nearer one sidles off to the left, you steer left to correct your course. The objects may be natural or unintended marks—trees, hills, buildings—but often in the English Channel they are pillars on rocks or brightly painted slashes on the shore or flashing lights, put there on purpose to guide boats clear of rocks and shoals. The system falters when mist obscures the shore. It frequently does so in Brittany, because of the agitation of the sea by the tides.

Out in the Atlantic, summer sunshine creates a lid of warm water, blue and transparent, covering the ocean. Fifteen miles west of Ushant strong tidal currents flowing over the sea bed become turbulent enough to mix the sea, from top to bottom. The sea surface becomes cooler, and also greener and less transparent, because the water coming to the surface is rich in natural fertilizers that nourish blooms of small plants. The onset of mixing creates a cold front in the water, which satellites, computers, and research ships can trace across the Channel. Because the tidal currents are weaker on the English side, the front slants northeastward, from Ushant to Portland.

From the warm side to the cold side of the front the density of small plants increases fivefold in a distance of a few miles, or even fiftyfold in eddies where superblooms create a chocolate-coloured scum on the water. Silt churned up by the tidal turbulence plays a part in making the Channel water murky. And the air, too, becomes misty when moist air from the ocean encounters the coastal waters chilled by the tidal mixing. Knowing the theory does nothing to improve the visibility when the seafarer trusts his life to picking out the right rocks in the mist, and steering by them.

In the medieval story of Tristan and Iseult, the Irish lady Iseult, Queen of Cornwall, comes this way bound for Portsall Bay, which lies behind the small headland on our starboard bow. Her pilot presumably uses the same rocks as we do for leading marks, and is now passing south of Bosseven rock and the Ile Vert. Iseult's lover, her husband's nephew Tristan, is dying of a poisoned wound for which only Iseult has the antidote. The ship is using a white sail. That was the arrangement if Iseult agreed to come; otherwise the sail was to be black. Watching from the headland, Tristan's wife sees the ship approaching and hurries off to lie to him. She tells him the sail is black. As a result, Tristan has given up the ghost by the time Iseult reaches his bedside.

This legend and others surrounding King Arthur and his knights sprawl untidily around the Celtic world. The Celtic-British wizard Merlin is said to be trapped for ever by the Lady of the Lake in the Breton forest of Brocéliande, which lies over towards Rennes, the capital of the province. If so, Merlin has languished there for only a millennium and a half, which is a short time in the human occupancy of Brittany.

In Portsall Bay you can feel trapped in a cul-de-sac of rocks. Even a couple of hours past low water the boats in Portsall harbour lie tilted on the sand. A row of small islands offshore are revealed as hillocks on a reef half a mile long. You can see how early navigators used the fall of tide to inspect the sea bed and make a mental chart of rocks that are covered at high water. Another Breton tale concerns the young woman who confidently told a suitor that she would never yield to him—no, not till the rocks vanished from the sea. He waited patiently for an exceptionally high tide.

There is a way out to the north, on new leading marks. You must keep two obelisks on the shore astern exactly in line in order to follow a very narrow channel past the next headland. At the bottom of the tide it would be impossible, because some of the rocks now under the ketch's keel break the surface then. By this route the time machine reaches Ile Carn, a small island connected to the shore by shallows, so that visitors on the shore can walk out to it when the tide is down. The name means "cairn," and the humps are chamber tombs built of large stones around 4100 B.C., when people went to considerable trouble to bury their dead in style. Ile Guénnoc, by Aber-Benoît, is another megalithic mausoleum.

Less than two sea miles offshore from Carn, the white octagonal lighthouse of Corn-Carhai tells ships to keep clear of the Portsall rocks. A few hundred metres from it lies one that didn't: the split and rusting hull of *Amoco Cadiz*. The wrecking of that supertanker in 1978 was the most traumatic event in Brittany since the end of World War II, and its aftermath tells you more about Breton pride in the late twentieth century than any amount of polemics.

On March 16, 1978, the supertanker rounded Ushant on her

way to Lyme Bay on the southern coast of England. *Amoco Cadiz*, 334 metres long and wearing a Liberian ensign, was carrying 220,000 tons of crude oil from Iran. She was moving steadily through the rough water of a southwesterly gale, well north of Ushant, and sixteen sea miles west of here. She had to turn to avoid another ship, and her rudder jammed, full over to port. That was at 9:46 A.M., Greenwich time. Rather than motor in anticlockwise circles and risk collision with other ships, the captain stopped the engine. The engineers wrestled unsuccessfully with the steering gear for an hour and a half. The gale veered to the northwest, blowing towards the shore, and the ship was doomed. The tugboat *Pacific* had a towing hawser aboard by 2 P.M. but *Amoco Cadiz* had already been carried like a drifting rowing-boat six miles nearer to danger.

For two hours the tugboat reduced the giant ship's drift towards the shore, but then the hawser broke. The captain of *Amoco Cadiz* ran his engine full astern. The ship weathercocked with her stern to the wind, and the engine helped to check her drift. The tide turned and the current set towards the northeast. At 7 P.M., with night approaching, the engine was stopped to allow the tugboat to try passing a new hawser aboard. Wind and tide then took full control of the supertanker, driving her stern first at two knots towards the Portsall rocks. She dropped one of her anchors, but the pressure of wind and tide on the huge vessel snapped off the anchor's flukes. The second anchor was not released, and the ship continued to drift.

In vain the Corn-Carhai lighthouse flashed its triple warning every twelve seconds. The new hawser from the tugboat was at last secured aboard at 8:55 P.M., but less than ten minutes later the supertanker bounced on a rock and began to leak. She continued to drift, and at 9:30 the ship was done in by a rock near the Corn-Carhai. The granite tore out her bottom and flooded the engine room. The people were lifted off by helicopters of the French navy during the stormy night, while waves broke on the wreck and crude oil gushed from the cargo tanks. The crew's ordeal was over; Brittany's was about to begin, and the shipwrecked sailors were greeted not with pity but with anger.

There were many recriminations afterwards about the captain

who had telephoned the American owner to ask his permission to accept the tug's offer of assistance and the crew who seemed unsure how to operate the anchors. French officialdom worked itself into a bureaucratic rage, and the rearrangement of the shipping lanes off Ushant, marked by the new offshore structure there, was a long-term result of the stranding of the *Amoco Cadiz*. The most reflective comments from seamen concerned the lack of adrenaline secretion, when the steering failed in a gale off one of the nastiest coasts in the world. In their great slab of a ship, with their faces and eardrums protected from the wind, captain and crew seemed almost unaware that they were in mortal danger. Precious hours and sea miles were lost in tinkering and indecision.

The loss of *Amoco Cadiz* also demonstrated the unreliability of a ship twenty thousand times larger than a yacht. If our ketch's steering gear failed, you could rig up something in a matter of minutes. If her anchor broke, there is a spare within easy reach. She has alternative methods of propulsion, of navigation, of boiling a kettle. Yet one of the largest ships in the world, carrying a valuable cargo, seemed to be lacking in options.

The smell is what Alphonse Arzel remembers most vividly. As the mayor of this district, called Ploudalmézeau, he was reading in bed when the maritime authorities phoned to tell him of the wreck. The onshore wind carried the odour of the crude oil inland from a distance of four kilometres, and as Mayor Arzel hurriedly dressed it pervaded his house. The smell was overpowering by the time he reached the shore, where the tug was going through the motions of trying to free the stricken supertanker without wrecking herself. In the darkness he saw that the ship was well and truly stuck, and the stench told him he had a major pollution disaster on his patch. *"On va faire un procès, cette fois,"* Arzel thought. "This time we really will sue them."

It was not the first tanker disaster in Brittany. In 1976 there had been two: *Olympic Bravery* wrecked on Ushant, and *Boelhen* around the corner in the Bay of Biscay. Their pollution of the beaches was not quite bad enough to put the Bretons on the warpath. The British had *Torrey Canyon* on their rocks off Scilly in 1967, with 119,000 tons of Kuwaiti oil, much of which polluted

English and Breton beaches, yet the legal consequences were muted. *Amoco Cadiz* was carrying almost twice as much crude as *Torrey Canyon.*

When dawn broke, the "chocolate mousse," the floating emulsion of oil and water, was already coating the beaches of Portsall Bay. It daubed the megalithic islands of Carn and Guénnoc like a mindless vandal. During the next two weeks, the seas whipped by the March winds ground *Amoco Cadiz* on the rocks, tearing the giant ship until virtually all of the oil oozed out. Years after the event, black lumps like asphalt are still to be found on the Breton shores. Dig in the *abers* at low tide and you will find the *Amoco Cadiz* oil as a geological stratum, less than a metre below the surface, with rainbow-streaked water oozing into the trench. At the time, it smothered the oysters.

It is two days' sailing, towards Roscoff and then onward beyond Ile de Bréhat, to escape from the stretch of coast polluted by the oil slicks as they were driven eastward by the wind. The *marée noire,* the "black tide" from *Amoco Cadiz*, brought only filth and misery to the fishermen and villagers of northern Brittany.

The most harrowing sight was of dead and dying sea birds. The sandy beaches, where the tourists are sunning themselves today, became dumps for the supertanker's oil. The Ile de Batz up ahead, where Saint Paul supposedly fought a lion, suffered the same insult. So did Roscoff nearby, a port famous for its former smugglers and its active marine biology laboratory. The rock-strewn estuary leading from Roscoff towards Morlaix stank like a gas station. The famous oysters of Morlaix that were not killed outright became too contaminated to eat and had to be destroyed.

A boom in seaweed followed the slaughter of limpets, because those humble animals of the intertidal zone normally keep it under control. Workers at the modern seaweed plant near the shingle spit of Talbert, far to the east, noted the extravagant growth after *Amoco Cadiz*. Fishermen in oil-stained boats found themselves harvesting the biggest shrimps that anyone could remember, when the checks and balances of the Channel's ecosystem broke down.

A shift of the wind also carried oil from *Amoco Cadiz* west and south, to envelop Low Brittany: it invested Ushant, spread its iridescent carpet over the Iroise off Brest, and penetrated the Raz de Sein. The French government sent the army to Brittany to help clean up the mess, and stretches of the beach were simply shovelled away into trenches lined with polythene. Volunteers came to lend a hand, but for want of any proper organization many went away again. There often seemed little that anyone could do. In the *Torrey Canyon* disaster across the Channel, detergents had often harmed marine life more than the oil itself. In six months' operations, 25,000 tons of oil were removed from the Breton beaches by human effort.

The sea did most of the work of purging the shores and waters. So thorough was its cleansing action that a stranger might visit the shoreline today and not know anything had happened. Only in the *abers* and other silty inlets where the tide is attenuated are nature's efforts obviously incomplete. What happened to the oil? More scientific study has gone into the *Amoco Cadiz* disaster than any other oil spillage, with French, British, American, and Canadian researchers joining in. As a result, there are detailed figures telling how the oil disappeared.

The stench was a sign of dispersal. During the first month after the spill, 67,000 tons of oil simply evaporated. Micro-organisms in the sea digested some 10,000 tons, as reckoned by the oxygen they consumed in their sturdy biochemistry. About 30,000 tons became thoroughly mixed into the sea water. Some of the oil, about 18,000 tons, settled into the sediments of the sea bed, below the low-tide mark. Altogether, 62,000 tons finished up ashore, between the low-tide and high-tide marks. Of the 46,000 tons unaccounted for, some may have been destroyed by the photochemical action of sunlight, but most of it probably dispersed in the form of surface slicks and tar balls.

The waves, tides, and micro-organisms went on removing the oil. Five months after the spill, three quarters of it had gone from the subtidal sea bed. After two years, off the more exposed parts of the coast, the sea bed was more or less clean. The visible oil in the intertidal zone disappeared faster, aided by the efforts of thousands of troops and workers, who took care of about forty per cent of it. Most of that oil would have gone without human intervention, but it would have been a brave man who said so at the time.

You can welcome the evidence of nature's capacity to purify a polluted environment, without minimizing the dreadful effects of the oil on the ecology and economy of the coast. The oysters had gone, and poisoned flatfish had trouble with their reproduction. On some shores, the clams, amphipods, and other intertidal animals were wiped out, and worms swiftly filled their niches. Within three years, though, the marine animals were showing their resilience, and life along the Breton shore gradually returned to normal. That was despite another outrage, in March 1980, when the tanker *Tanio* broke in two and spilled a further 7000 tons of oil off the afflicted coast. By then the Bretons were well embarked on their legal battle over *Amoco Cadiz*.

"Un procès, cette fois." Mayor Arzel, now a senator as well, is a stocky, big-jawed, bespectacled man who led the Bretons in their fight for compensation, which may well take them ten years, all told. Although the French parliament set up two commissions of inquiry into the *Amoco Cadiz* disaster, the politicians of Brittany did not believe that the national government would take strong enough action against the polluters, and might even try to discourage the Bretons from pressing their own claims. "Left to the State, it would have taken for ever," Arzel said.

The Bretons turned down an offer of the services of government lawyers. They decided that, for the first time ever in France, a group of local communes should pursue a foreign case, using their own lawyers. They would form a *syndicat mixte* consisting of seventy-six communes of coastal Brittany, together with groups representing fishermen, estate agents, hotel keepers, and conservationists. The politicians would sink their party differences: In national politics Arzel supported President Giscard, but his deputy was a follower of Mitterrand. The huge legal costs would be met from local funds.

Fifty-five Breton mayors walked together down the street in Chicago to see their case launched at the courthouse in May 1982. The judge said he hoped they would be satisfied with American justice. It was the most complex maritime case ever to come before a court. One powerful plaintiff was the French government, acting for itself against the Chicago-based Standard Oil of Indiana and its offshoot, Amoco International. Another was Petroleum Insurance, of Britain, who had insured the cargo. The Shell Oil Company added Amoco Transport of Liberia to the list of defendants, together with the owners of the German tugboat. The Bretons sued everyone in sight: all of those mentioned so far, and also the Spanish builders of *Amoco Cadiz* and the American Bureau of Shipping, which certified the supertanker's seaworthiness. The Bureau settled out of court, and its payment went towards the Bretons' legal costs.

The Bretons' claim took the form of detailed dossiers prepared by each commune, itemizing the damage done and bills paid in the aftermath of the wreck. Their lawyers pierced the legal defences of multinational companies that scatter subsidiaries in various countries, and use ships wearing flags of convenience. The effects on international law and commercial practice will go far beyond the case of *Amoco Cadiz,* and even beyond the realm of shipping. The Bretons prevailed against a powerful adversary, castled in the Standard Oil Building beside Lake Michigan. At Easter 1984, Judge Frank MacGarr of Chicago had ruled that Standard Oil of Indiana was liable for the damage done by the wrecking of the *Amoco Cadiz*. Sums of $300 million or more were being mentioned. *"Mais ne nous laissons pas griser,"* Senator-Mayor Arzel said to his colleagues: "Don't let it go to our heads." It was sound advice—two years later they were still awaiting the final outcome.

The legal victory of the coastal communes of Brittany and their mayors asserted regional rights in the age of nation-states. Yet the Breton action had very little to do with Breton nationalism as it is advertised by the nationalist politicians who want autonomous Breton control of Breton affairs, in a decentralized "Europe of a Hundred Flags." As a matter of courtesy, and to poke fun at the French, many British yachtsmen fly the black-and-white flag of Brittany during their visits to these waters.

In Brittany itself, Yann Fouéré is a nationalist leader of long standing. After World War II he fled to Wales to avoid prosecution when nationalists were widely suspected of collaborating with the

German occupiers. That was the second French crackdown on Breton nationalists; the first was in Napoleon's time. Fouéré looks more like a schoolteacher than a desperate rebel, and at his farmhouse near Saint-Malo he gave me a brisk lesson on the case for regional autonomy.

The nationalists regard the underdevelopment and relative poverty of Brittany as a result of misrule from Paris. Fouéré cites the "law of peripheral neglect." According to some economists, regions prosper or wither according to their distance from the centre of decision-making. France has a quarter of its population concentrated within fifty kilometres of Notre-Dame in Paris, and seems to Fouéré a textbook example of this law. He sees France as a highly centralized colonial state, in which the hyperdeveloped "Superfrance" of Paris positively wants to keep Brittany underdeveloped, as a source of cheap labour and food, and as a pleasant place for a Parisian's vacation. When Breton nationalists point to the United States as a model of decentralized government, the reply comes from Paris: "Ah, but the United States is much bigger than France." When they offer Switzerland as another model, the rejoinder is: "Ah, but Switzerland is much smaller than France."

"France was never sea-minded!" The complaints of many generations of Breton seamen resound in Fouéré's exclamation. What exercises him is the wealth of international seaborne trade passing through the English Channel, which is known to Bretons as the Mor-Breizh, the "Breton Sea." Why does little of this wealth rub off on Brittany, except in the form of oil pollution? Fouéré allows himself a little nostalgia. In the fifteenth century, independent Brittany had two thousand ships, which traded in the Baltic and the Mediterranean, and often carried cargoes for the Spanish and English. Twentieth-century Norway is, for Fouéré, an example of what Brittany might have been, if left to its own devices. Norway, too, is a rugged country at an extremity of Europe, and its population is scarcely greater than Brittany's, yet Norway's merchant fleet is the sixth largest in the world, and twice as big as France's.

The fact remains that the Breton nationalists have had little political success, either in elections or more forceful demonstrations. Breton farmers share in the agrarian militancy about prices, quotas, subsidies, and taxes familiar in other parts of France, and they like to terrorize officials. The Bretons also resisted plans to site a nuclear power station near the Pointe du Raz. But few of the protesters are Breton nationalists. Nothing in Brittany compares with the sporadic electoral achievements by Welsh and Scottish nationalists in Britain, still less with the Irish nationalists' success in ridding most of their island of British rule. All of the deputies elected to the French National Assembly from Brittany belong to the socialist or conservative coalitions of France.

Nationalism has two opposite faces. French and British nationalism united different tribes and regions into centralized nation-states. The other face of nationalism wants decentralization, and asserts the right of regional or tribal groups to control their own affairs. In Brittany, that might mean loosening the ties with France. But to speak of autonomous Brittany implies yet another nation-state, wanting to put its flag alongside a hundred others in Europe. The decentralization latent in Brittany would inevitably involve even smaller units.

Where Breton traditions and languages have not been entirely swamped by French culture, they proclaim the independence and diversity of small districts, rather than a united Brittany. A Breton anthropologist has counted sixty-six distinctive forms of traditional dress. The ceremonial lace hats worn by women in different towns and villages made this deliberate diversity highly visible, while speech made it audible. The Breton languages resemble Welsh and the extinct Cornish language, but there are really four of them, and every village had its own dialect, signalling uniqueness. Efforts by academics to preserve the Breton language have smudged the languages actually spoken by elderly people.

Local action produces results. For example, Morlaix's Chamber of Commerce willed Brittany Ferries into existence, to carry tourists and their cars to Roscoff and Saint-Malo from England and Ireland. After the *Amoco Cadiz* disaster, the demand for compensation came not from a Breton pseudo-state, but from a coalition of coastal villages, pushing to the limit their right to independent action permitted by the French constitution. Their ad hoc union resembles Switzerland, which, with just the same geographic area as Brittany, is a voluntary federation of communes that was never a true nation-state. Every village has its own flag, and the Swiss use four official languages. In a world of centralized states armed with nuclear weapons, perhaps the slogan should not be "Europe of a Hundred Flags," but "Brittany of Fifteen Hundred Villages."

After a slow passage in light winds, darkness rules out the shortcut to Roscoff, between Ile de Batz and the mainland. Instead, the ketch drifts on the tidal current past the seaward side of the low island, which is silhouetted against the loom of Roscoff's street-lights. Then the task is to make sense of the many lighthouses and winking buoys in the eastern approaches, which at first sight are more confusing than helpful. Heading eventually for the right ones, the boat creeps into Roscoff's deep-water anchorage, in the new harbour where Brittany Ferries brings car people from England in the small hours of the morning.

Someone Else's Stones

A moderate breeze from the northeast has the ketch bowling along at six knots from Roscoff. She is leaning over as yachts will when they are pointing as near to the wind as possible, with the sails hauled close in. Sailors find it exhilarating, but passengers grumble about living on a tilt and about the spray coming over the bow when the boat nods into the waves. They also worry that the boat will capsize, and skippers have to explain about the heavy lump of iron in the keel that prevents it.

Morlaix Bay, a broad hollow in the shore where three rivers bring fresh water to the English Channel, is a maze of safe channels between underwater plateaus and miniature islands. On the eastern side of the bay, where the Térénez River emerges, a small peninsula called Barnenez supports about a dozen megalithic tombs built around 4000 B.C. When archaeologists discovered them in the 1950s they looked like untidy heaps of rough-hewn blocks, but it soon became clear that some of the tombs had been imposing structures faced with stone. The first architects used the local green rock of volcanic origin, but their successors used light-coloured granite from an island six hundred metres offshore.

Notice the different meanings of "rocks." To the passing navigator, the rocks in the sea are hazards to be skirted. For a local fisherman the same rocks may be good places to go fishing, and they are also familiar features of the seascape that guide him safely through the intervening deep water. But rocks, in another sense, are the fabric of the Earth, and the geologist finds his samples more often on the land than under the sea. To him, whether the granite is dangerous or not is a detail. He is more interested in the way it was formed from molten material deep underground during a collision of continents, when high ground occupied the present watery realm. Modern seafarers are seldom bothered about geology, beyond asking whether the sea bed is rocky, sandy, or muddy, and whether an anchor will hold in it. Those who sailed here in the Stone Age were experts in both departments. They were sensitive to the quality of rocks and stones. Ashore, they selected them as raw materials for making tools and weapons, and like more recent architects they kept an expert eye open for good stones with which to build.

A green beacon is the cue to turn out to sea. Our ketch swings into the wind and continues round to the north, with her headsail hauled in for the new tack. The beacon marks a rock called Pierre Noire, or Black Stone. The *Channel Pilot* lists some twenty Black Rocks, Pierres Noires, and variations thereon. Many rocks of the

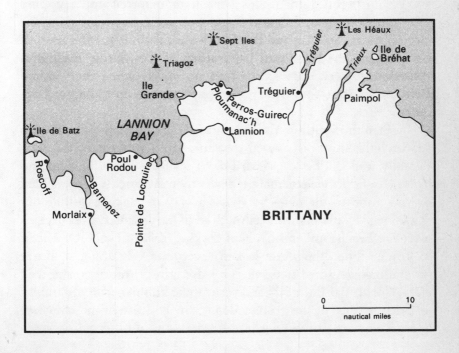

coast finish up black, even though they may be made of brown or green or pink material, because they are covered by black lichen. This lichen harbours small symbiotic marine plants and is better able to thrive in a difficult salty and tidal environment than any other plant or animal. It is so humble that many naturalists disdain to mention it, but in fact black lichen is the most obvious sign of life at the water's edge. You can see it from well out at sea as a black tide mark running along all the cliffs and rocky shores. It has nothing to do with oil pollution.

Nor are supertankers the only felons of the Breton shore. In Lannion Bay, the conical summit of Pointe de Locquirec away to the east is a reminder that the gourmets have eaten one handsome animal of the intertidal zone almost to extinction. The purple sea urchins *Paracentrotus lividus,* known locally as *les violets,* were coveted for their roes, so much so that the most inaccessible rock pools of Locquirec are among the very few places where they survive. They used to thrive in enormous numbers in Morlaix Bay. In the 1930s the leading expert from the marine biological station at Roscoff, Edouard Fischer-Piette, reported ample supplies of urchins on various reefs at Locquirec and farther east along the Breton shore. So Alan and Eve Southward from Roscoff's English counterpart, the Plymouth Laboratory of the Marine Biological Association, were puzzled to find no *violets* when they visited Brittany in 1974—until they came upon a few in hiding at Locquirec.

When the Southwards investigated the downfall of the Breton sea urchins, they discovered that in 1929 a fisherman had accidentally trailed a net overboard close inshore. When he hauled it up, he found *les violets* entangled in it by their prickly spines. That did no good to the net—but what a way to make a fortune out of old nets! It was a far brisker method of harvesting the sea urchins than the beachcomber's habit of forking them up one by one at low tide. When the secret leaked, everyone was doing it, if not by trailing weighted nets, then by dredging. Production peaked after World War II, but the indiscriminate killing of young urchins and disturbance of the grounds led to the collapse of the industry. Sea urchins are now under human pressure in other parts of the world, which is a pity. Besides being handsome and tasty, they clean the rocks and help to keep the seaweed under control.

At Poul Rodou, a little west of Locquirec, strange white rocks on the beach are penetrated by zebra stripes of black basalt. Those rocks are about 2200 million years old, or just half the age of the Earth, and last froze at a time when the only inhabitants of the planet were bacteria. You can trace a belt of rocks of the same age northeastward across the sea to Guernsey and Alderney in the Channel Islands and the tip of the Cherbourg Peninsula. Icart Bay in Guernsey gave its name to the Icartian belt.

Around 650 million years ago, new volcanic and granite rocks began piling up around Icartia. During a period of about a hundred million years they created a broad block called Cadomia. It runs through northeastern Brittany and Normandy, and then, deep underground, across Europe. Brought to daylight here, on the French side of the western English Channel, are pieces of Europe's basement, which has gradually grown throughout the history of the Earth.

Continental basement of the same age as Icartia—more than 2000 million years old—runs beneath southern England, fronting the Channel, but it is buried by younger rocks. Like Icartia, it seems to be a sliver broken loose from some other old continent and then embedded in rocks of Cadomian age, around 600 million years. According to the latest geological ideas, England and northern France were part of a Cadomian continent that collided with northern Europe and North America about 450 million years ago. The basement of the English Channel is of Cadomian age, and the flooded region in the western Channel corresponds with a sandwich of Cadomian rocks, between the much older Icartian slivers of southern England and northern France.

Later collisions attached the central and southern zones of Brittany, making the province a hotchpotch of rocks of different ages. The most spectacular disturbance appears at the far end of Lannion Bay. In front of the white domes and dishes of a space telecommunications centre, a swarm of islands lines the shore, of which Milliau and Ile Grande are the largest. Farther out to sea are the Triagoz or Treaclepot rocks, and the Sept Iles away to the east. Facing the Sept Iles are the headlands around Ploumanac'h. For a navigator these are the main navigational features of a strange pink world, the Breton Corniche. Geologists, tourists, and yachtsmen all love the place, and the Sept Iles are a sanctuary for gannets and puffins.

The Corniche is a lump of granite known as the Ploumanac'h massif. It froze 300 million years ago, and later pushed its way up through the crust like a hydraulic ram. The centre is Ile Grande, and concentric rings of the intrusion surround it like a target, from Milliau in the west to Pors Rolland in the east. The outer ring contains perthite, coloured pink by iron, and consists of large grains that make it very vulnerable to erosion. As a result, nature has made extraordinary shapes in the rocks on the shore, including the Death's Head of Tregastel and Napoleon's Hat and the Tortoise at Ploumanac'h. They look like Henry Moore sculptures.

Nature's way with stones must have helped to inspire the people who erected megalithic tombs and standing stones, on the Ile Grande and all around the Corniche. The oldest in this district are passage graves on the Sept Iles. Megaliths have kept cropping up along our route on the way from Ushant. Many people still imagine that the structures made of massive stones have something to do with the Celts. The Celtic priests made use of these pre-existing sites of mystery and ritual, but they were no more related to the megalith makers than New Yorkers are to the pyramid builders of Mexico. From an ethnic point of view the megaliths were someone else's stones.

The Breton archaeologist Pierre-Roland Giot excavated several of the megalithic sites, including Barnenez and Ile Carn. In 1959 the central tomb of Carn became the first megalithic tomb in Brittany to be dated by the radiocarbon method. The first verdict from the radiocarbon lab was that the structure on Ile Carn was built around 3300 B.C. Later corrections to the radiocarbon timescale make it 4100 B.C. Megalithic graves elsewhere in Brittany, including the Sept Iles, also turned out to be extremely old. The radiocarbon dates blew sky-high the archaeological theory that the habit of building with massive stones was learnt from the supposedly more advanced civilizations of the eastern Mediterranean. The time that separates us from the early megalith builders is more than twice as long as the interval since the first Celts came to the Channel shores.

An experiment a few years ago by archaeologists in France tested how much effort was involved in moving huge pieces of rock for building. A concrete block of thirty-two tons, corresponding to the capstone of a typical megalithic monument, was successfully moved by about 200 people working in a team, with 30 of them manipulating tree trunks as rollers and levers, and 170 pulling on ropes. The effort, in other words, was large but not unimaginable, provided people thought it worthwhile.

Why did they bother? There can be no simple answer, because even around the Ploumanac'h massif the megalithic structures vary in age by a thousand years, and in nearby parts of Europe the span is even greater.

The oldest megaliths of all are to be found along the northern shore of Brittany, and in the nearby Channel Islands. A tomb on Guernsey, less than sixty sea miles from the Breton Corniche, dates from about 4500 B.C., and may be the oldest stone building in the world. You cannot enter the minds of the people who lived beside the Channel long ago, but you can read the archaeological record carefully. Then you find that architectural megalomania began at the time of another major event, the arrival of the first farmers at the coast.

The farmers were not the earliest inhabitants of the Channel shore. Modern, talkative human beings like ourselves first lived as hunter-gatherers. They invaded France about thirty-five thousand years ago and extinguished their cousins the Neanderthalers. But the northern coast was uninviting. The English Channel was empty at the time, because an ice age was locking up much of the ocean's water in ice sheets. At the climax of the Ice Age, around eighteen thousand years ago, this region was a frigid desert, and the nearest trees were in the south of France. When the thaw came, hunters moved north into vacant territory. By 9000 B.C. they were hunting reindeer beside the Seine River and living in tents of reindeer skin. They followed the game onto the dry beds of the Channel and the North Sea, and the trees came after them. Ice sheets and glaciers still buried Scandinavia, Scotland, and the northern North Sea.

The Ice Age had ended by 8000 B.C., in a blaze of hot summers in the northern hemisphere. The sea level was still low, but it gradually rose as the ice sheets melted. As grassland gave way to forest, and the pressures of skilful hunting intensified, the big animals of the Ice Age became largely extinct. The people adapted to catching smaller game, herding big game, and fishing. In the North Sea they hunted seals, presumably from boats. On Brittany's south coast they gorged themselves on mussels, winkles, limpets, oysters, and scallops. Archaeologists find the shellfish mixed with bones of fish, wild duck, and penguin, and some land animals were also on the menu. On the English side of the Channel, hunters used the fine white building stone of Portland to pave the floors of a shelter and construct a cooking pit in about 5000 B.C. They ate winkles and limpets, and may also have used picks to dig up the roots of plants. Many other campsites must now lie under the sea, because the water nosed up the Channel and nudged the people onto higher ground. These first claimants continued their hunting-and-fishing life for four thousand years.

Everyone else was an intruder. First to arrive on the shores of the English Channel, about 4500 B.C., were the modest agents of the neolithic revolution. They were farmers of the earliest kind— horticulturalists with hoes. With their special skills, seeds, and livestock, they had spent five thousand years hoeing their way slowly across Europe from the Middle East, along the belts of easily worked loess soil. They greatly outnumbered the hunters of Europe, and you can imagine the farmers sometimes displacing and sometimes marrying the hunters. Their Middle Eastern ancestry seems to have been progressively diluted with hunter-gatherer genes as they worked their way westward. When they reached the Channel, some of them crossed it in simple boats and started farming in England.

Meanwhile, the megalithic phenomenon began on the French side. The native hunters could have started the stone-hauling as a protest at finding their last hunting grounds under threat, but most experts imagine that the farming people themselves invented the megalithic monuments. Why should the sight of Channel surf provoke an effort unthought of in the slow migration across Europe? The British archaeologist Colin Renfrew thinks it was a response to running out of land. The farmers' westward spread, driven by the pressure of ever-growing populations, came to an end at the sea. They could no longer send surplus population into new territory, and needed tighter forms of social organization than during the easygoing expansion. Heaving on ropes and putting up stone monuments promoted teamwork, and the resulting monuments asserted a group's claims to the available territory.

If Renfrew is right, you can see the English Channel and the Atlantic shore of Europe in a new light: as the termination of an ancient frontier existence. The Pacific coast of the United States halted the westward spread of farmers during the nineteenth century, and future archaeologists may say that the American response was to build space rockets. In effort and symbolism, the space programme seems to Renfrew a modern analogue to the megaliths of prehistory.

In Brittany the stonework was meant to impress. It foreshadowed the stone buildings that became emblems of power, religion, and statehood, such as you will find in Paris and London. But lighthouses, too, are built of large stones. Seagoing fishermen would have seen the megalithic monuments near the shore, and found them useful landmarks. One motive for setting up freestanding stones, the menhirs, **might have** been to create beacons and leading marks on purpose.

The great broken menhir on the southern shore of Brittany, formerly twenty metres tall, is a candidate for that interpretation. It must certainly have helped seafarers to find their way among particularly treacherous rocks and islands. As astronomical instruments, too, the stones seem to have been used to study the motions of the Moon—a matter of great consequence for sailors wanting to understand and predict the tides and currents of these dangerous waters.

Between the first farmers and the Celts, several waves of new technology came this way. Ox-drawn ploughs, milking cows, and woolly sheep transformed farming methods. Then tamed horses arrived on the Channel shore, and metalworking in copper and bronze put an end to the Stone Age.

One group of newcomers involved in these innovations consisted of the early Indo-Europeans. They were militant cowboys, complete with horses, who broke out from a homeland near the Volga River about 3000 B.C. and spread far and wide. They were male-dominated, they revered their horses and cattle, and they glorified war. Most of the peoples who figure in later European prehistory and history—Greeks, Celts, Romans, Germans, and so on—spoke Indo-European languages. As to the first arrivals at the English Channel, the simplest theory is that the earliest Indo-Europeans came here about 2300 B.C. They can then be identified with the Bell Beaker people, who made fine pots with thin walls. During the subsequent centuries, seaborne traders were travelling along and across the Channel, carrying gold from Ireland and amber from the Baltic.

The Celts originated as a Rhine Army of Indo-Europeans who adopted and developed the new technology of iron smelting, starting about 800 B.C. They spread their iron industry and their language across Europe, east and west. The Iron Age in the English Channel region began around 600 B.C. with the arrival of the Celts in northern France. They conquered England after 500 B.C. By the time written history began with the coming of the Romans, the Celts had been fully in charge of the Channel for several centuries.

The original Gaulish Celts learnt to speak Latin and they have left no obvious linguistic trace in Brittany, except in some place-names. The present inhabitants of the province claim genetic as well as linguistic descent from the British Celts displaced across the Channel around A.D. 500. After a thousand years they lost their independence to the French, who represented ancient rivals of the Celts—the Germans. Both the French and English are the Johnnies-come-lately of the English Channel.

·   ·   ·

For seafarers, erosion of the Breton Corniche has hollowed out the shallow harbour of Ploumanac'h, studded with pink rocks. Through a narrow opening to the small pink cove of Pors-Kamor, beside the pink Mean Ruz lighthouse, the lifeboatmen of Ploumanac'h make their exits and entrances in their thirteen-metre *Jean Denoyelle*. The gap is only thirty metres wide, and they go out in storm-force winds. They are responsible for the stretch of coast from Batz to Bréhat. They are local men—a fisherman, a stonemason, and so on—ready to be summoned from their work or their homes at any time to risk their lives because others have risked theirs. In the past ten years they have saved or helped seventy people and forty vessels. Their president, a former Air France pilot, complains that most of their calls are now to rescue the board sailors who are enticed out on a fine day, not realizing that the currents and weather of this coast have to be treated with respect. The lifeboatmen were not on call in A.D. 300 or thereabouts when a Celtic ship of the Roman era wrecked herself on the rocks nearby. The lead ingots that she carried, marked with strange inscriptions, were found in 1983 by a Breton skin diver, Loïc le Tiec.

Beyond Ploumanac'h and the neighbouring seaside resort of Perros-Guirec, the ketch enters the geological realm of Cadomia, and 600-million-year-old granite lines the shore. A regiment of rocks with sharpened spears parades off the Pointe du Château. Around the corner is the Tréguier River, a deep-cut valley where the fields come down to the high-water mark. It leads to Tréguier, a quiet medieval town where Yves Helori administered justice so benignly in the thirteenth century that he was made a saint. That must be a record for a lawyer.

At the last corner before Ile de Bréhat, a lonely lighthouse, two miles offshore, reminds ships to keep clear of the reef of Les Héaux. Bréhat stands at the mouth of the Trieux River, Tréguier's twin. The island is famous for its frost-free climate and its subtropical vegetation, including figs. It offers an anchorage sheltered from the northeasterly wind where you can fall asleep on your narrow bunk listening to the tinkling of the restless current against the hull and dream of hauling stones to impress the neighbours.

The Tides of Saint-Malo

At Bréhat, the Breton coast makes an almost right-angled turn towards the southeast. Erosion has hollowed out the shore to create the English Channel's largest bay, the Gulf of Saint-Malo. Cap de la Hague, the other gatepost of the Gulf of Saint-Malo, lies sixty-seven sea miles away to the northeast, at the tip of the Cherbourg Peninsula, which belongs to Normandy. The Norman coast runs southward to meet eastward-trending Brittany at the apex of a watery triangle, near the sacred conical rock of Mont Saint-Michel. Saint-Malo itself, the chief port of northern Brittany, lies a little nearer, but it is well tucked into the corner of the gulf. Relics of vanished territory clutter the triangle with rocks and islands. The Channel Islands are the largest and most habitable of them, and the Casquets near Alderney are the most troublesome rocks for Channel traffic.

Crisscross faults weakened the old shoreline and mapped out the features that survive. The island of Bréhat itself is separated from the shore by a small fault. And the Gulf of Saint-Malo starts emphatically at Bréhat because, just two sea miles east of the island, a more important fault runs southeastward. Geologists exploring the sea bed have found displaced rock formations showing that western Brittany has moved three kilometres northwestward, relative to eastern Brittany, along this fault. It defines the coast down to the port of Saint-Brieuc, and then intersects a fault that turns the coast through another right angle, leading to the headland of Cap Fréhel, the chief landmark on the way to Saint-Malo. It is lopped off at its end by yet another crossing fault. This coastline is cubist sculpture, and Fréhel is the masterpiece.

The headland projects decisively into the Gulf of Saint-Malo and stands seventy metres high. A modern lighthouse rises another thirty metres above it. With its steep cliffs and flat top, Fréhel makes an easily recognizable landfall for ships coming from England or the west. Fingers of rock like a clenched fist project from beneath the lighthouse, with dark hollows between them, and an isolated stack of rock, Amas du Cap, protrudes from the water like an upturned thumb.

The parapets of Fréhel are made of plum-coloured sandstone, roughly 400 million years old, capped with this season's grass, heather, and gorse. Primroses grow in spring in the crevices of the fist, and on the summit, honeysuckle and violets. It is always surprising to find such flowers in places where onshore gales shake the ground and create fountains of spray. Groomed by the rabbits, the vegetation has the appearance of hair cut *en brosse*. The fine-

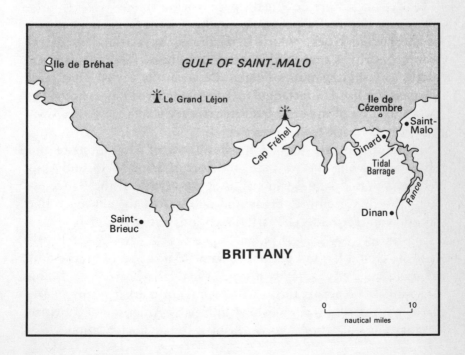

grained sandstone has an almost lithographic quality, and the strata tilt gently to the west, giving an overall effect like papier-mâché, as if the cape were made of many layers of paper, and then cut with a knife.

The square tower of the lighthouse was built in 1947, with no expense spared, using granite from the far end of Brittany. The Germans were paying part of the cost as a matter of post-war reparations. It is set quite far back from the end of the cape, where a small granite tower houses the loudspeakers of the fog signal— a double blast every minute in thick weather. The inevitable Nazi gun emplacement, now demolished, is still visible in its ground plan. The remains of an old lighthouse stand beside the modern one. From the Restaurant de la Fauconnière, perched on the eastern clifftop, you can watch the gulls of the Fauconnière, a set of stacks rising from the water like an avian Manhattan, with dozens of birds gliding and squabbling thirty metres above the sea. The guano of many generations of birds discolours the tops of the stacks, like cream on the plum. Fréhel is altogether so magnificent, it looks as if it were designed by a Frenchman.

From Cap Fréhel proper, a small bay leads to the next corner of the faulted block, which is decorated by a round medieval tower. Nearby is a megalithic standing stone no taller than a man, locally called Gargantua's Finger. Between the Fréhel block and the next headland, a rectangular fault-engendered bay is noted for the cultivation of mussels, but salt-resistant plants are busily winning the bay back from the sea.

The distant prospect of the headlands of Saint-Lunaire and Dinard, showing the way into the port of Saint-Malo, quickens a sailor's pulse. Saint-Malo stands at the mouth of the Rance estuary. Ile de Cézembre, broad and tall, guards the approach like an off-lying fortress. The island's curious name comes from the Gaulish Celts' *Segisama briga,* or "highest rock." As the ketch sails past the Grand Jardin lighthouse, Saint-Malo appears on the port bow as a small city radiating history. On the starboard bow, facing old Saint-Malo across the estuary, is the up-market resort of Dinard, transformed from a fishing village by American and British visitors pursuing the Victorian fashion for seaside vacations.

The medieval core of Saint-Malo occupies a compact peninsula washed by the English Channel's tides. It was lovingly restored in gleaming stone after World War II, having been devastated when the German army held out against the Americans for two grim weeks in August 1944. The car ferry coming out on her way to England confirms that the port is still in business. And a glance at the ramparts, towers, and spires tells you that Saint-Malo has been an important base for maritime trade and sea power for a thousand years.

Saint-Malo was an island when it was first occupied in the eighth century A.D. as a refuge from the Viking pirates. In 1144 the local bishop moved to Saint-Malo from nearby Alet and fortified it. For four centuries Saint-Malo prospered as a port of the independent Duchy of Brittany. The Channel traffic emanating from here helped to link the peoples of Brittany, France, and England in a nervous relationship, at a time when Breton independence was in doubt and the French and English were at critical phases in their pursuit of nationhood.

Of all the people who ever came to Saint-Malo to embark for a Channel crossing, the most reluctant was an eighteen-year-old lad from Wales called Henry Tudor. The year was 1475, and Henry was accompanied by emissaries from England. They had fetched him from the glittering court of Duke Francis II of Brittany, where he was a fugitive, in order, as they said, that he should marry the English king's daughter. He knew that he was going to be murdered. Henry had a tenuous claim to the English crown in an era when high politics was a game of displacing one unlawful king by another. Four years earlier, in the long-playing family feud among England's royalty—York against Lancaster, white rose against red—the white rose won. Henry was heir to the House of Lancaster, and he fled in the care of an uncle. They sailed from Wales, aiming for the French royal court, but the perverse weather of the English Channel deposited them in Brittany instead. To the paranoid English king, Henry Tudor remained, politically if not genetically, "the last imp now left of Henry VI's brood."

What was young Henry to do when he came to Saint-Malo in the clutches of the Plantagenet agents? He feigned illness. Then the Bretons realized, almost too late, that the cheerful picture of a royal wedding was just a cover for an intended assassination. The duke's treasurer came hurrying down the road from Nantes. He distracted the English officials, no doubt with the help of Muscadet wine, while his servants spirited Henry away to a safe house somewhere in Saint-Malo.

The Bretons must have liked the Welsh lad, and had a capacity for devious political thinking, or else it is hard to see why they offended powerful England to save his life. The emissaries sailed away with nothing more than a promise from the Bretons that Henry would not be allowed to make mischief. He was duly imprisoned in a succession of Breton strongholds. In 1483 a new English king, Richard III, tried again to winkle Henry out of Brittany, but he found that the young man was now a significant pawn on the European chessboard. The French king insisted that Henry be handed over to him, and the Duke of Brittany claimed that he needed English archers to resist that demand.

Eminent Englishmen opposed to Richard III were in treasonable correspondence with Henry in Brittany. Duke Francis lent the young pretender fifteen ships and a force of perhaps five thousand men for an invasion of England. Henry set sail with his Breton army in October 1483. His arrival was supposed to be co-ordinated with rebellions in Wales and various parts of southern England, but everything went wrong. A rough night at sea scattered his fleet, and Henry arrived at dawn on the English coast with only two ships. Nor was he at Plymouth as intended, but at Poole, where the shore was guarded by the king's troops. When a boat was sent ashore to identify them, astute soldiers tried to persuade the sailors that they were rebels, and invited Henry to land. Suspecting a trap, Henry sailed back across the Channel. He landed in Normandy and marched his troops home to Brittany, where refugees from England and Wales told him the rebellions had failed.

The English king incited his sea captains to attack Breton ships and ports. But then he made a secret deal with Brittany's chief minister. In exchange for Henry, he would supply the archers that the Breton army wanted. Henry escaped again. Disguised as a servant, with Breton troops hard on his heels, he slipped across the frontier into France. The French king was a teenager who took his orders from his twenty-two-year-old sister, Anne, and she had her eye on the conquest of Brittany. Monsieur Tudor was to be the means of stirring up civil war in England, as a diversionary tactic. Let the English archers fight one another instead of helping the Bretons in their hour of need. Nor would the expedition cost very much, because it was not meant to succeed.

So it came about that Harfleur in Normandy, rather than Saint-Malo in Brittany, was the Channel port from which Henry Tudor launched his second invasion attempt, under French instead of Breton auspices. In August 1485 Henry left Harfleur with a small fleet, a few guns, and about three thousand troops. Only one in ten of them were English; the rest were Norman, Breton, and Flemish mercenaries under a Breton general. The task force set off in light winds right down the English Channel, around Land's End, and northward to Wales. Henry Tudor had good reason for sailing all the way to Wales for his landing. He had Welsh ancestors and a Welsh surname, and had spent his childhood in Wales; possibly he had never even visited England until he invaded it to claim the crown. The Welsh bards had identified him as the deliverer who would at least soften the English rule of their Celtic land.

Henry played it both ways. In Wales he was a Welshman, but he claimed the English crown as an Englishman of royal birth. It was a Celtic conquest, all the same. Henry marched unopposed through Wales and picked up enough Welsh troops to give him the confidence to cross the Severn River into England. A few English troops joined him, but it was with a largely alien force that he faced the English king. Shakespeare, with his gift for seeing everyone's point of view, lets Richard III disparage Henry's army as "a scum of Bretons" and "overweening rags of France." The invaders killed Richard in the heart of his kingdom. Henry the Conqueror was crowned King Henry VII. He married a king's daughter after all, to unite the red rose and the white, and he founded the Tudor dynasty. Queen Elizabeth I was his granddaughter.

Meanwhile, French expansionist schemes had been served. Two days after Henry landed in Wales, the Bretons were bullied into signing a bad treaty. England's new king could not prevent the subsequent assimilation of Brittany by France, and it altered the strategic map of the English Channel to France's great gain. Disaster came to the Bretons on July 28, 1488. Sixty kilometres from Saint-Malo, on the Couesnon River dividing Normandy and Brittany, the French army stormed a key fortress. The Duke of Brittany capitulated. He died soon after, leaving his twelve-year-old daughter at the mercy of the French. Three years later the Duchess Anne was married to the French king. It was a bad time for the Celts: a noncommittal Welshman sat on the English throne, but a Frenchman ruled in Brittany.

In the year after the Duchess Anne's more or less forced marriage, Columbus discovered the West Indies for Spain. Saint-Malo was the only decent port between the Seine River in Normandy and Brest at the far end of Brittany, and it played a big part in the French quest for a maritime empire. The pope had divided the world between the Spanish and the Portuguese, but King Francis I of France asked what clause in Adam's will sanctioned that partition. Breton fishermen had found their way to Newfoundland and the Grand Banks by 1514. From Dieppe in Normandy, in 1524, the king dispatched the first official French transatlantic expedition, under Giovanni da Verrazano, which discovered New York. From Saint-Malo, Jacques Cartier set sail with two ships on April 20, 1534, under orders from the king to look for a possible route via the North American fishing grounds to the Pacific Ocean.

So it came about that this sailor from Saint-Malo gave Canada its name, from the Huron word for "village." But Cartier also managed to give the place such a bad reputation that colonization was set back for more than half a century. On his 1534 expedition, he found the Gulf of St. Lawrence, and came home with a couple of Indians. Next year Cartier set off once more with three ships, and his Indian prisoners guided him up the St. Lawrence as far as the rapids at Montreal. After a severe winter, the survivors kidnapped more Indians and returned home with the theory that rivers beyond Montreal might emanate from Asia. In 1541 Cartier sailed proudly out past Ile de Cézembre yet again, to establish the very first colony of northern Europeans in North America. Another Canadian winter, and friction with the Iroquois, drove him back to Saint-Malo with what he thought were gold and diamonds. They gave rise to the French adage "As false as a Canadian diamond." Not until 1608 did Samuel de Champlain, sailing from Normandy, finally establish a permanent settlement at Quebec. The French had missed the chance of stealing a march on their English rivals.

The *corsaires,* or privateers, are the most obtrusive ghosts of the Rance estuary. Saint-Malo's architecture reflects the wealth that privateering brought to the shipowners. The English, themselves no saints at sea, regarded the port as a nest of pirates who cruelly ravaged their merchant shipping in times of peace as well as war. From the French and Breton viewpoint, the seafarers were heroes who brought riches and naval glory to the *Cité corsaire.*

Such matters were always subjective and legalistic. From the thirteenth century to the nineteenth, a piece of paper from a king converted a pirate ship into a private warship by authorizing her captain to prey on the shipping of the king's enemies. This was a grey area, where a monarch might invest privately in an expedition without it being quite official. The declension went like this:

> I am a privateer
> You are a buccaneer
> He is a pirate

The Church, enriched by the insurances on their souls paid by the owners and captains of privateering vessels, duly found theological authority for their trade. It even regularized the sex life of the *corsaires* by declaring that their marriage vows applied only on the homeward side of Cap Fréhel.

Out of hundreds of *corsaires,* the two most venerated by the French were Jean Bart, who hailed from Dunkirk in the Dover Strait, and René Duguay-Trouin, a native of Saint-Malo. Both of them made separate and dramatic escapes across the Channel from

Plymouth to Brittany in small boats. Bart and his ship *Railleuse* were captured by the English in a battle off the Casquets in 1689. A Flemish captain smuggled a file to him in his prison in Plymouth, and Bart rowed himself and four companions to Erquy, just west of Cap Fréhel. Five years later, when Duguay-Trouin was captured in *Diligence,* the English had not learnt their lesson. He turned all the charm of a twenty-one-year-old Frenchman on the good-looking wife of a local merchant. With her help, he bought a longboat from a Swedish ship and sailed cheerily out of Plymouth with four fellow prisoners. He fetched up in Tréguier.

The romantic view of the *corsaires* is not unwarranted. They were excellent seamen, as they had to be to survive among the rocks and violent tides of the Gulf of Saint-Malo. They were gallant fighters too. Duguay-Trouin was credited with capturing or sinking 188 ships, of which twenty-eight were warships or enemy privateers. He once borrowed thirteen warships from the king of France, seized Rio de Janeiro, and ransomed the city back to its Portuguese owners.

Yet the *corsaire* business was a pitfall for the French. Instead of competing seriously with the English and Dutch for mastery of the sea, they were too eager for the quick returns of commerce raiding. The French navy lost many of its best seamen and potential commanders, who opted for the privateering life.

If you are looking for French maritime glory here, remember also Louis-Antoine de Bougainville, who first colonized the Falkland Islands in the South Atlantic in 1763. Their Spanish name, Malvinas, comes from the French name Malouines, meaning the Saint-Malo islands. Bougainville also set off from Saint-Malo to sail around the world, in 1766–69. He gave his name to one of the Solomon Islands in the Pacific, as well as to a scarlet tropical flower.

The Rance estuary, a kilometre wide, follows straight along an old fault line for thirteen kilometres inland, with bays offering anchorages among gracious hills. Then the river bed turns away from the fault and narrows. Shallower boats than *Charmed* can follow a winding but navigable route to Dinan, another medieval fortress town, standing on a plateau seventy-five metres above the water. The boats can then climb over the Breton hills and down to the Bay of Biscay, by way of the Canal d'Ille et Rance and the Vilaine River. But even to start entering the Rance estuary nowadays, our ketch has to go through a lock in a barrage that straddles its mouth.

The barrage belongs to the *usine marémotrice,* the Rance tidal power station, which began operating in 1965. The Channel tides have driven waterwheels for nine centuries or more, but the Rance was chosen for the first large-scale exploitation of tidal energy anywhere. The tides are vigorous all over the Channel, but in this corner of the Gulf of Saint-Malo they are exceptional. The average difference, or range, between low and high water is 8.4 metres, compared with the couple of metres that is typical for other coastlines of the world. Sometimes the range at the mouth of the Rance is 14 metres. When you anchor here you need to let out plenty of chain or rope if you don't want to drift away when the tide rises.

The range of the tides is more formidable on the French coast than on the English side of the Channel because of the Earth's rotation. All moving objects in the northern hemisphere, including the air of a wind or the water of a tide, swerve to the right of their intended course. So the flood tide, going up-Channel, tries to press towards the French coast, creating higher high tides. The ebb tide flowing down-Channel draws away from the French coast, making low water lower. In the Gulf of Saint-Malo, the Cherbourg Peninsula lies across the path of the flood tide and abruptly reduces the width of the Channel by half. You can think of the rising water coming up the Channel as a wave. When it hits the barrier of the Cherbourg Peninsula, the wave bounces back from it, intensifying the tides in the Gulf of Saint-Malo.

Nature's offer of strong tides was combined with inviting geography. The long and wide estuary of the Rance was a ready-made pound for storing water. Just three kilometres inland from Saint-Malo, the seascape also provided a convenient pair of headlands facing each other across the estuary, with the island of Chalibert between them. When French engineers decided to show the rest of the world how to tap the tides, the Chalibert site chose itself.

The 800-metre barrage rises as a concrete wall in front of us, and a line of small buoys guides the ketch towards the lock at the western end, clear of the turbulent zone where water rushes through the central section of the barrage. A signal of black-and-white cones shows whether the water is flowing upstream or downstream through the barrage. Beyond it, the tides still rise and fall with the passing hours, as they have done for thousands of years. But the skipper has to collect special tables from the lock keepers because the tides of the Rance estuary are now set by human beings and their computers. The times of high and low water inside the dam can differ by as much as two hours from the natural tides outside. The water may stay high or low for longer than you would expect, and then change its level with a whoosh. At the wrong place and time, the ketch could be afloat one moment and high and dry fifteen minutes later.

In the oldest and simplest concept of tidal power, you allow the rising tide to fill a basin; then you close the sluice gates, and when the tide falls you let the impounded water run out through a waterwheel. The engineers of Electricité de France were more subtle, and installed water turbines that respond to relatively weak currents of water flowing through them in either direction. The puzzle is then to figure out the most efficient way of using the natural tides of the Gulf of Saint-Malo as they rise and fall outside the barrage. The operators can block the water or let it flow freely. Or they can cause it to run through the turbines and generate power. They can even use the turbines as pumps to drive the water in either direction.

There is a ceaseless trade-off between extracting energy now and building up the difference in water level between the two sides of the barrage, which means more energy later. Ideally, the barrage would supply power that fluctuated according to public demand, which varies with the time of day and is therefore geared to the Sun. But the tides follow the Moon, and the timing and range of the tides varies from day to day. That is why the operators need a computer to optimize the flow of salt water.

The twenty-four turbogenerators built into the dam are rated at 10 megawatts each, or 240 megawatts in all. After all the juggling with the water levels, they give a combined output that averages about 60 megawatts year in, year out. That is not much for a modern power station, but it is useful enough, and after twenty years it has not been matched, even though tidal power figures in everyone's lists of clean and renewable sources of energy. Much grander projects include the American and Canadian proposals for the Bay of Fundy, and a British scheme for a barrage across the mouth of the Severn River, but high interest rates have not been encouraging. Even the French have held back from damming off Mont Saint-Michel Bay, just east of the Rance River, which could in principle give them 10,000 megawatts of power from the English Channel tides.

Never a Barrier

The shore of the Rance estuary, between the tidal barrage and Saint-Malo, is dominated by a rocky peninsula named Alet. A lump of Cadomian granite, 550 million years old and half a kilometre wide, pushes its steep cliffs into the estuary. Alet was adapted by the Nazis into a modern fortress, and you can still see shell damage and rusting antiaircraft guns from the battles of 1944. Connected to the mainland by a causeway only one hundred metres wide, it is a natural stronghold.

When Saint-Malo was an uninhabited rock, Alet was a thriving port. Before the Romans came to Brittany, Celtic traders were setting out from the Rance estuary bound for the English shore, more than a hundred sea miles away. For anyone wanting to understand the origins of the nations, the most important news from the archaeologists is that the English Channel was never a barrier between France and England. This contradicts the belief of many landlocked historians.

Even in the Stone Age, people crossed to and fro with crops, animals, new gadgets, and ideas about moving stones. The occasional cross-Channel excursions of those days hardly rated as trade. While thousands of neolithic axes made of Breton stone have been found in Normandy and elsewhere, precisely six are known from southern England. In the opinion of the Breton archaeologist Pierre-Roland Giot, routine seafaring across the widest parts of the English Channel had to wait for the advent of bronze tools for use in boatbuilding.

An ancient wreck found near the shore of Devon, 115 sea

miles northwestward from the Rance, tells of commercial shipping in the Bronze Age. What the diver Philip Baker discovered in 1977 was much less than a timbered hulk. Of the vessel that came to grief on Moor Sand near Salcombe, all that remained were bronze items from her cargo—swords, axes, and blades. Their design dates them to about 1100 B.C. Another cargo of bronze of similar age turned up at the other end of the English Channel, five hundred metres from the foot of the Dover cliffs. The tally of about 350 bronze items, mainly weapons, made the Dover shipwreck by far the largest Bronze Age hoard known in England. The Dover and Moor Sand wrecks also provide the earliest prehistoric collections of objects that were in transit across the Channel.

A diving archaeologist from Cambridge, Keith Muckelroy, investigated both cargoes. Before he died in 1980 at the age of twenty-nine in a diving accident, he had concluded that these were cargoes of scrap bronze on their way from France to England for recycling. As Muckelroy wrote:

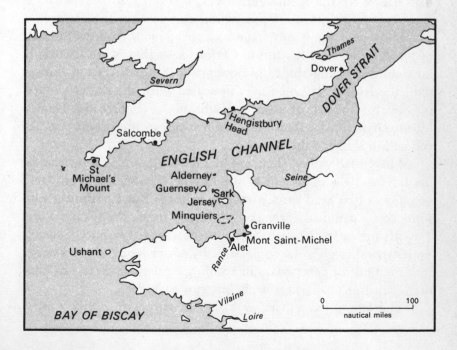

In the later second millennium B.C. there existed vessels of size and quality sufficient to transport bulk materials across the Channel, probably at regular intervals, and certainly guaranteed of receptions which warranted the organization of Bronze Age shipping by a community or segment of a community.

Prehistorians had imagined that any traffic across the Channel during the Bronze Age would use the shortest sea route, at the Dover Strait, where you can see one shore from the other. The Moor Sand wreck shows that seafarers were bolder than the experts supposed. A natural point of departure from the French side would have been Guernsey in the Channel Islands, a distance of almost seventy sea miles. The vessel that finished up as the Dover wreck seems to have set out from the Seine River in Normandy and had covered about 120 sea miles.

A sword from the Moor Sand wreck, in almost perfect condition, was of a design originating in northern Italy. Muckelroy imagined a scrap dealer collecting, from a tribe in France, alien bronze objects that they did not care for. He speculated that raw materials were the main alternatives to bronze in cross-Channel cargoes: timber, stones, hides, wool, and perhaps foodstuffs.

How were the Bronze Age boats propelled? Andrew Sherratt of the Ashmolean Museum in Oxford says they were rowed. In his opinion, sailing ships did not appear in northwestern Europe until the Iron Age, when they appeared with the potter's wheel in "the bow wave of Roman civilisation." Before the Roman legions arrived, the Rance estuary became an important port for the sailing ships of the Iron Age.

This broad valley, sheltered by green hills and granite islands, lies far from the main axis of the English Channel, and reluctant voyagers often head for Cherbourg instead. But Cherbourg's location on a peninsula projecting halfway across the Channel was a disadvantage in the days before mechanized transport. Sensible traders tried to go as far as possible by water, and a day's passage into the Gulf of Saint-Malo in a sailing boat took them 120 kilometres nearer to markets in the interior of France.

The Rance River itself was also an attraction. Only a select few, out of the dozens of excellent harbours and anchorages in the Channel, ever became major ports. The test was inland transport, and the rivers mattered most. The ideal port stood near the mouth of a great river that gave access to large territories, for goods carried by boat or raft. The Rance River is not very long, but vigorously tidal, and it carries boats effortlessly upstream or downstream twice a day. A short overland portage brought traders and travellers from the Rance to the Vilaine River, which issues into Biscay, on Brittany's southern shore.

The regional organization of ancient trade was like today's drug traffic. The pusher on the streets in London or Paris obtains his supplies from a local wholesaler, who may get them ready-processed from Sicily. Few Sicilians will have visited the remote villages of Pakistan where the crop grows. Dealers know only their immediate suppliers and customers, and the price soars as the drug moves from producer to addict. So it was with wine, slaves, and metals in prehistoric Europe. During the last thousand years B.C., Brittany traded directly with southwestern England, and also with regions to the south, centred on the Loire and Garonne rivers running into the Bay of Biscay.

Italian wine found its way to the shores of the English Channel several decades before the Roman legions, and reinvigorated the trade routes. Barry Cunliffe of Oxford University has traced wine travelling from Italy to England. It went first to the early Roman colony of Narbo, modern Narbonne, on the Mediterranean shore of France. From there a trail of distinctive wine pots, known as Dressel amphoras, leads across southwestern France to the Garonne River and the Biscay shore. The wine industry of the Bordeaux region began when people living there decided to produce wine instead of merely transhipping it. The Italian wine went onward to southern Brittany, and eventually to Alet, where it was shipped across the English Channel.

The telltale Dressel amphoras show up again at Hengistbury Head in Dorset, together with Mediterranean glass. The Alet–Hengistbury route was the main link in trades that ramified on both sides of the Channel. At Hengistbury the traders filled their ships for the return crossing to Alet with exports gathered from southern and southwestern Britain. These included iron and other metals, and perhaps also grain, hides, woollen textiles, and slaves.

Breton archaeologists have unearthed a pre-Roman town at Alet, consisting of a jumble of wooden houses and workshops. They have found pits for storing grain, querns for grinding it, animal bones, and large quantities of limpet shells, though not the oyster and mussel shells that figure so numerously in the garbage of Saint-Malo today. Industry is represented by iron slag and iron products, and by stocks of copper-silver alloy that may have been used for minting coins. There is also jewellery and the usual collection of broken pots. The first town of Alet flourished for about a hundred years, from the end of the Celtic Iron Age into the early Roman occupation. It was built in about 80 B.C. by the Coriosolites, whose capital city was near the village of Corseul, twenty kilometres away, across the estuary from Alet.

Dozens of Coriosolite coins have turned up in southern England, notably at Hengistbury. Like Alet, Hengistbury is a small, defendable peninsula beside a harbour. Although goods passed in both directions across the Channel, a lack in Brittany of Celtic coins from southern England indicates that the shipping was based on the Rance River, rather than on the British side. So you can visualize Coriosolite ships sailing from the Rance estuary, out past the undeveloped islands of Saint-Malo and Cézembre. They faced a crossing of 140 sea miles, largely out of sight of land, to reach their emporium at Hengistbury Head. They often anchored at Guernsey in the Channel Islands to wait for favourable winds or tides. They did so by permission of the Veneti, who were masters of the seas and islands of the western English Channel.

In the first Roman account of seafaring in the English Channel, Julius Caesar said of the Veneti:

They have the largest fleet of ships, in which they traffic with Britain; they excel the other tribes in knowledge and experience of navigation; and as the coast lies exposed to the violence of the open sea and has but few harbours, they compel nearly all who sail those waters to pay toll. [Trans. S. A. Handford.]

Caesar also told how the Veneti made their strongholds on spits and headlands, and exploited the tides in their defence. And he described the ships that sailed in these waters two thousand years ago.

> The Gauls' own ships were built and rigged in a different manner from ours. They were made with much flatter bottoms, to help them to ride shallow water caused by shoals or ebb-tides. Exceptionally high bows and sterns fitted them for use in heavy seas and violent gales, and the hulls were made entirely of oak, to enable them to stand any amount of shocks and rough usage. The cross-timbers, which consisted of beams a foot wide, were fastened with iron bolts as thick as a man's thumb. The anchors were secured with iron chains instead of ropes. They used sails made of raw hides or thin leather, either because they had no flax and were ignorant of its use, or more probably because they thought that ordinary sails would not stand the violent storms and squalls of the Atlantic and were not suitable for such heavy vessels. [Trans. S. A. Handford.]

The campaign that brought the Romans to the shores of the English Channel was made easier because the Gaulish Celts were always squabbling among themselves. Tribes would help the invaders if it gave them an advantage over old rivals. By 57 B.C., Caesar had dealt with the Belgae of the Dover Strait region, while young Publius Crassus occupied Brittany and was preparing to attack Aquitaine on the Biscay shore. The conquerors felt confident enough to mark the mastery of Gaul with celebrations in Rome that went on for fifteen days. But next year the Celts of the west rebelled: When Roman officials came to buy food, the Veneti seized them as hostages. The Coriosolites followed suit.

Caesar realized that the Veneti would have to be beaten afloat, and he had warships built on the Loire River. While legions ashore repressed the Coriosolites, Decimus Brutus brought out the new fleet of rowed galleys to do battle with two hundred Celtic ships off Brittany's southern shore. The conventional method of attack by ramming had little effect on the Celts' oak hulls. The most effective Roman device was a hook for grappling the rigging and making the sails fall down. As each Celtic ship came to a standstill, two or three Roman galleys could overwhelm her by boarding. Against the odds in Brittany, the wind died. The oar-driven Roman warships could then pick off the becalmed ships one by one. As the Veneti had committed all of their warriors and ships to this battle, it was a disaster for them. The survivors were sold into slavery. A race of doughty seamen accustomed to storms was extinguished by a rare calm. "Nothing could have been more fortunate for us," Caesar commented.

Life at Alet continued in its Gaulish style for more than sixty years until, around A.D. 20, the wooden buildings were razed by imperial diktat. The Romans replaced them with a planned town of stone-built houses roofed with red tiles. They also built docks twenty kilometres up the estuary at Taden, near Dinan, which was then the head of navigation on the Rance River.

"To navigators bound for the docks of Taden, the Gallo-Roman town of Alet would have looked like a red checkerboard." So says Loïc Langouët of the University of Rennes, the man who has done most to bring ancient Alet back to life. He is a physicist who is also a diver. Langouët's search for ancient Alet began with a stylized Roman road map, six metres long, which showed a road terminating at the coastal station of *Reginca*. That is a pre-Roman name for the Rance. *Reginca* was adopted by the Romans to apply equally to the river and the port of Alet on its estuary. Since 1971, much of Langouët's energy has gone into establishing the antiquity of Alet and its importance in the history of the English Channel.

In one respect, Langouët started too late. The engineers building the tidal power station dredged much of their sand and gravel from a bank between Alet and the barrage. In the process they removed large pieces of the coastline of two thousand years ago. When the station began producing electricity, the computer often prescribed opening the sluices in the barrage when the tide had half risen. The rushing water decapitated another historic sandbank, immediately south of Alet. Many ancient artefacts may now be locked inside the concrete of the tidal barrage, or lie broken and scattered at the river's mouth.

The building of the barrage in the 1960s coincided with a worldwide surge of interest in amateur diving, and treasure hunters searched the bottom of the Rance estuary. Many of them turned in their finds as soon as a proper archaeological laboratory was set up on Alet in 1975. A diesel-powered catamaran served as a diving boat, and Langouët called her *Canalchius,* "the rock of the Channel," the Gaulish name for the rock on which Saint-Malo stands. The tidal power station continues to dominate the archaeological programme at Alet, because diving is possible only when the turbines rest for an hour or two at the top of each tide.

Langouët made his key discovery underwater on the southern side of Alet, near the fourteenth-century Tour Solidor. He identified a lozenge-shaped water tank, and a multiple water pump built of wood and weighing more than a ton. This equipment dates from around A.D. 100, and its purpose was plainly to supply ships with fresh water. A small canal led water from a spring on the peninsula down to the tank; the pump delivered it up to the ships. *Up* is the important word. If the shoreline was the same then as it is now, the pump would have been covered by five metres of salt water at high tide.

Evidently the Rance estuary had a different shoreline two thousand years ago. Langouët reasons that the recently destroyed sandbanks were remnants of a long, unbroken levee that remained above sea level, and was trimmed and straightened by the tidal currents. The present bays on either side of Alet were marshy terrain below sea level. That made Alet the obvious landing place, where you could walk inland without getting your feet wet. If the port was on the beach near the southwestern tip of Alet, the siting of the freshwater machinery behind the bank makes good sense; so, at last, does a sea-bed cemetrey found beside Alet in 1846.

The traders and fishermen simply beached their boats on the river bank, and the great tides made that a simple operation. The site was protected from storms in the English Channel by the clutter of rocks and banks offshore, and the tidal currents could speed the mariner on his way, whether out to sea or up the estuary towards the heartland of Brittany. For more than four centuries,

Alet's old shoreline seems to have served very well. It would have been a suitable place for goods and passengers to transfer between seagoing ships and the shallower barges of the river traffic.

A better harbour came into existence around A.D. 350, towards the end of the Roman era, when the ancient levee was breached just south of Alet. The feet of all those sailors and towns-folk tramping to the beach might have worn down the bank to a level where an exceptional tide could break through. However it came about, the breaching of the bank created a completely different harbour. The rocky inlet known today as Port Saint-Père replaced the vanished beaching area. The marsh south of Alet, scoured by the tide, became an anchorage where dozens of ships could lie.

By then the Roman empire had been crippled by devastating epidemics, and Christianity offered consolation to the sick and the bereaved. Saint Martin, the chief founder of Christianity in Roman Gaul, established a cathedral at Alet around A.D. 380. Taking advantage of the empire's weakness, German pirates ran amok in prosperous towns and villas along the Channel shores of Roman Gallia and Britannia. British Celts began fleeing to Brittany. That is how Langouët explains a massive importation of the characteristic pottery of Southampton into Alet during the fourth century A.D.

Brittany was not safe from the pirates, either. The Romans built a fort on the Solidor rock at Alet and manned it with five hundred Martians—infantry and cavalry of the Mars regiment. This was just one of a chain of forts that sprang up at the time. Three were on the Biscay shore and one was at Brest, but the greatest rash of forts was around the Gulf of Saint-Malo: at Cherbourg and Alderney in the north, at Coutances and Avranches on the Cherbourg Peninsula, and at Alet itself. Evidently the German pirates found rich pickings in this corner of the Channel.

The people of western Gaul revolted against the Romans in A.D. 410, and within ten years the Martian garrisons had left. The inhabitants paid for their freedom by an abrupt economic decline. Then they found themselves overwhelmed by their Celtic cousins from Britain, as the refugees became conquerors. One of the new-

comers, Prince Juduual, recognized the strategic importance of
Alet and rebuilt the town in A.D. 575. And when, in that same
century, the Welsh priest Saint Maclou landed on Ile de Cézembre,
he was able to walk to Alet along the remnants of the old sandbank.
He became Bishop of Alet and bequeathed his name to the much
younger city of Saint-Malo.

The offshore rocks that shelter the Rance estuary were always a
hazard for visitors by sea. Our ketch carries a library of charts,
pilot books, and tidal data that help her to find her way out among
the rocks, but large ships have to use the services of the local
pilots. In medieval times Breton pilots enforced their rights at the
point of the sword or the gun. But they had their responsibilities
too. These were set out in the oldest-known printed pilot book
from northern Europe, *Le routier de mer*. It was published in Rouen
some time between 1502 and 1510, and was probably written by
a Biscay man, Pierre Garcie. To his information about tides and
courses to steer, Garcie appended the twenty-six *rôles d'Oléron,*
which in 1266 codified international laws of shipping in northwestern Europe. The law relating to pilots translates as follows:

> A pilot undertakes to guide a ship to Saint-Malo or another place.
> If he fails and the ship perishes because he did not know the way,
> and the merchants suffer loss, he is bound to pay the damages
> if he can. And if he has not the means to do so he must have his
> head cut off. And if the master or any of the seamen or any of
> the merchants cut off his head, they are not liable to make amends.
> But all the same they ought to make sure before doing so whether
> or not he has the means to pay. This is the judgement.

On leaving Saint-Malo, one's first decision must be: which
way around the Minkies? The Plateau des Minquiers is a drowned
twin of the island of Jersey, growing seaweed instead of tomatoes.
It throws a wilderness of rocks fifteen sea miles wide across the
bow of any ship trying to sail north from Saint-Malo. Many of
the rocks are uncharted. In theory you can sail right through them,

with what the pilot books call "local knowledge," but it is better to turn left and avoid the Minkies altogether.

Garcie's old *routier* would have you turn right. He gave courses starting northeastward to the Iles Chausey, and thence north to the island of Jersey and on to Cap de la Hague. That route, east of the Minkies, looks the straighter way, but it is fraught with rocks that Garcie did not specify. The western shore of the Cherbourg Peninsula runs northward for sixty-seven sea miles from Mont Saint-Michel to Cap de la Hague, and the *Cruising Association Handbook* describes it as:

> an inhospitable and rocky coast, exposed to winds from between west and north. There is no sheltered anchorage. The marks are difficult to identify . . .

On the chart the region looks like a snare thrown into the English Channel, athwart the prevailing winds and spiked by nature with obstacles for killing sailormen. That westernmost coast of Normandy resembles Brittany geologically, having been assembled in the same collision of microcontinents, but there are no bolt holes where a hard-pressed skipper might find refuge. It is like Brittany without the harbours. The only port that does not dry out entirely at low tide is Granville, near the southern end, but to reach it you have to wait for high tide to cross a wall of rock.

Visit it all from landward and you will find an enchanting stretch of coast, starting with Mont Saint-Michel, "the pyramid of the sea." It is the jewel of the French tourist industry. The traces of megalith builders and Celtic priests have been erased by the Christians, whose pilgrims have been going there for nearly thirteen centuries. The pointed lump of granite is topped by a fortified abbey that grows symmetrically out of the rock and carries its culminating spire 150 metres above sea level. The habit of dedicating churches on hilltops to the Archangel Saint Michael traces back to a cult that began in Italy in the fifth century, when the Archangel reportedly appeared to a shepherd on a mountain.

An amazing sight from the ramparts of the abbey is the rising tide galloping in across a flat beach twelve kilometres wide to embrace the island. But Mont Saint-Michel itself is best seen from a distance, from Avranches, the medieval city across the estuary of the Selune River. Almost as eye-catching as Mont Saint-Michel is the medieval fortress at Granville, where a natural castle of rock juts into the sea. The man-made ramparts of the old town command the harbour, the beaches, and the sea towards Chausey. It is screened by rocks that were moved and scratched by glaciers 440 million years ago.

A boat coming out of the Rance at a convenient time, when the water is high, meets tidal currents that carry her westward. The easiest course therefore leads west of the Minkies. From there we shall head for Guernsey. The prehistoric seamen bound from Alet to Hengistbury are likely to have come this way. The first principle of sailing in strongly tidal waters is to make the currents work for you, instead of trying to fight them. Even if that means going off the direct course, it is faster in the long run.

On Loïc Langouët's Roman road map, the Channel Islands are shown schematically as *I. Lenur*. The "I" just means *insulae* or "islands" in Latin, but *Lenur* is an old Celtic word for "moorings." Pottery of identical kinds found on Guernsey and the French and English shores confirms the island's role as a prehistoric staging post. Some of the pottery was made in Guernsey.

How did the seafarers find their way? No trader would entrust a valuable cargo of scrap bronze or Italian wine to an incompetent skipper. The invasions and warlike migrations that carried new blood, cultures, and forms of government across the sea would have literally foundered without good navigation. A pirate would be comical, not frightening, if he kept getting lost.

The magnetic compass arrived in Europe from China only seven hundred years ago. The skippers coming this way in prehistoric and most of historic times made routine passages to Britain without it. They followed the Channel Islands as far as they went, and then launched themselves into the wide-open spaces of the English Channel. From Alderney to Hengistbury is more than sixty sea miles. Bronze Age seafarers were making Channel crossings of more than a hundred miles three thousand years ago.

A skipper would have sailed his route often before, as an apprentice, and would have a mental chart. The task consisted of identifying enough signs along the way to avoid dangers and reach the destination. If he went into unfamiliar waters, the skipper hired a pilot. He would use navigational mnemonics in the form of stories, such as Homer's *Odyssey* for the Mediterranean and Norse sagas for northern waters. But little of what the skipper and his pilots knew was ever written down, even if they were literate.

Instead they used all their senses and many branches of memory. They knew the waters where they sailed far more intimately than those of us who do it by buoy, book, and compass. The skipper noticed the colours of the shore, the rocks, and the seaweed, and whether the water was grey, green, blue, yellow, or alarmingly white. He registered the smells off the land, the shouts of the birds in their clifftop colonies, the murmur of distant breakers. A modern sailor concentrates on the lighthouse at a headland, but his predecessor studied the scenery of the headland and knew its humps, valleys, and woods from every safe direction.

The bottom of the sea was familiar too. In the skipper's mind, the slopes, ridges, and hollows of the sea bed were as plain as if the water had been drained away and he had tramped all over it. His mentor was the sounding lead. A leadsman near the bow threw the weight into the water ahead. When the long cord became vertical and just taut, as the ship caught up with the weight, marks on the cord told the depth of water. Grease on the base of the lead picked up samples of sand or gravel or broken shells from the bottom of the sea. If the bottom was muddy or clayey, a piece of fabric could be used instead. The skipper would examine each sample like a medieval doctor with his patient's urine. His eyes would take in the colour and general appearance of the material and his fingers would feel its texture; he might sniff it and even taste it. "Ah," he would say, "we shall be in Guernsey by nightfall." To his passengers it seemed like witchcraft.

In Garcie's *routier* of the early sixteenth century you read items like this:

If you have sixty or sixty-five fathoms you will find fine sand, speckled with pink, and will be at the coast of Ushant. . . . Two or three leagues from the Casquets you shall find forty fathoms and big black chipped stones.

Marine scientists can explain why the sea bed offers such signatures. The supply of sand, gravel, and broken shells reflects the local rocks and shellfish populations. Garcie's pink speckles off Ushant correspond with the pink granite of Brittany. Where tidal currents are strongest, the water carries away mud and sand and fine-ground shells, leaving heavy lumps of gravel or even bare rock. The "black chipped stones" near the Casquets are the residue left by the strong currents of the central region of the Channel.

What we call compass directions, our forefathers called winds. Several notions were wrapped together, starting with the direction from which the wind blew. The mind leapt at once to possible destinations that lay downwind or on courses off the wind that a boat might sail. These were matters to be known without a chart. The early sailor studied the feel of the wind, which could help him to identify it, and give a sense of its direction. For example, in northwestern Europe, winds from the north are cold, and southwesterly winds are warm and moist, while easterly winds are dry, warm in summer and cold in winter. Personifying the winds as truculent creatures helped the ancient mariner to remember their characteristics at different seasons and make weather forecasts. In the autumn, the east wind of the Vikings put on a cloud-covered hat, while the northwest wind, lamenting the loss of his beautiful summer sunset, knitted his brow and threw out hail, thunder, and lightning.

In clear weather, the surest indicators of direction were the stars and the Sun. In the tropics, a procession of stars moves overhead as if on a conveyor belt. As you come away from the equator into cooler latitudes, the polar stars appear more prominent and you notice, as Homer did, that the constellation of the Great Bear "never takes a bath in the sea." The conveyor belt becomes a wheel. The polar stars revolve around a fixed point in the sky, indicating north, while the southerly stars ascend in turn to a highest point in the sky, indicating south.

The Pole Star, Polaris, is at present closely aligned with the Earth's axis, and you could steer a course by keeping the bow at a constant angle to the star, using a long stick held at arm's length. In Roman times, the bright star nearest to the pole, Kochab in the Great Bear, was almost ten degrees off. If you had steered resolutely by Kochab, you would not have done too badly, because as the night progressed the star revolved around the pole, and the errors would tend to cancel out. But seafaring peoples probably had a good idea of where the true pole lay, in the hole in the circumpolar sky.

The directions of sunrise and sunset vary with the seasons, but the direction of south, where the Sun is at its highest and shadows are shortest, remains a reliable direction. If you had to steer by the Sun, without modern instruments, you could make a simple solar compass the day before sailing, marking the directions of sunrise and sunset, with south midway between them, and rely on your sense of time to turn it at an appropriate angle to the Sun at each hour of the day.

No helmsman can steer a boat with perfect precision, and in the heyday of oceangoing sailing ships, compass courses were set within five or six degrees. In fifty sea miles, an error of six degrees puts you about five miles off your ideal course. A prehistoric seafarer would be doing well if he arrived that close to his objective. A glimpse of a recognizable headland would then tell him how to correct his course. Or he could aim off, going deliberately east or west of his destination, so that he was in no doubt which way to turn when he reached the far shore.

When cloud obscured the stars or the Sun, a helmsman could continue for a short while by assuming that the wind direction stayed the same. The directions of the waves, and especially swells coming from the ocean, would have been a surer guide. In the western Channel, the swell generally comes from the southwest or west.

The Polynesian navigators of the South Pacific use the swell for holding their course in midocean, and can even detect the presence of invisible land by its effects on the direction of the waves. The problem is to sense, not the local waves that make the boat lurch about, but a slow rise and fall that underlies them all. The most sensitive swell detectors are the testicles. The navigator lies down, preferably in a cabin away from all distractions, and when he can distinguish the particular swell in which he is interested, he calls out to the helmsman which way to steer. The militant feminists who have rewritten a famous Bible story as "Norah's Ark" may have to allow some differences between the sexes in navigational technique.

Noah used another venerable aid, shore-sighting birds, when he released a raven and a dove to look for land. If the bird returns to the boat, it is reporting that no land is in sight. But as you near the target coast, the bird will fly off ahead, showing the way. Many a raven was let loose in the English Channel for this purpose. Free-range birds were useful too. Growing numbers of shore-based sea birds were a sign of land, and their homeward flights told the navigator where their nesting grounds lay. Out at sea, other birds following migration routes drew arrows in the sky, pointing far beyond the horizon. Irish monks may have discovered Iceland by following the geese heading there in the spring. In this way, many apparent miracles of early navigation and discovery become almost self-evident.

When all the natural aids to navigation have been added to-gether, there remains the magic factor provided by the brain. Keith Oatley, a psychologist at the University of Sussex, is impressed by the human ability of maintaining a mental map, knowing one's position and course within it, and using all possible cues to check and update it. Prehistoric navigators cultivated this skill, and the Polynesians still do so. "The accuracy of non-instrumental navi-gation," Oatley says, "could perhaps be made comparable with that using charts, distance-measuring devices, and compasses."

The ketch has safely bypassed the Minkies, and Jersey is abeam. The Channel Islands and the rocky plateaus that make the Gulf of Saint-Malo a tricky place to sail are sketched out by geological faults. Like the mesas and buttes of the American West, they are lumps that have resisted the erosion that left most of the Gulf below sea level. The islands are elderly pieces of granite, and comparatively deep water between them corresponds with shat-tered and eroded fault lines. The eastern side of Jersey connects with the Norman shore; geologically, it is a peninsula, the neck of which happens to be awash. The faults are still active. On April 15, 1773, for instance, the streets of Jersey Town (St. Helier) were crowded with people rushing out of their homes in alarm, and the earthquake produced much the same reaction in Saint-Malo.

Think of the Channel Islands as dry blocks that stand among the crisscross faults of the Gulf of Saint-Malo like the black squares of a crossword puzzle. Jersey, to the east, appears to be an almost flat slab, some seventy metres high. Guernsey, to the north, looks much the same, but the islands are not as flat as they seem from a distance. Ashore, you will find undulating hills sloping down to beaches and harbours at many places. Guernsey is a bustling island, and Jersey is even brash.

By contrast Sark, east of Guernsey, is smaller and taller than the other islands and daunts the boat-borne visitor with frowning cliffs on every side. Settlers had to tunnel through the cliffs to establish Sark's small port of Creux. Sark is the quaintest and quietest of the islands, ruled in a semifeudal fashion by a *seigneur*. Automobiles and bitches are banned.

Two breakwaters define the entrance of Guernsey's Peter Port, and right between the pierheads where all the boats and ships have to pass, the powerful propellers of modern ferries plying from England uncovered the hull of a wreck from Roman times. It was discovered by Richard Keen, who was diving there on Christmas Day, 1982. The massive oak structure turned out to belong to a sailing ship dating from about A.D. 190. Sadly, the propellers that dug out the wreck also exposed it to damage. By 1985 two thirds of the hull had been destroyed, and a team of fifty divers led by the nautical archaeologist Margaret Rule hurried to save what was left by bringing it up piece by piece for preservation ashore.

The vessel was a merchant ship built in the Celtic tradition. She was carrying a flammable cargo of pitch, and there was a fire on board when she came to grief. Molten pitch penetrated between the planks and held them together when the massive iron nails rusted away in the wreck. The iron hardened the silt like plaster around the ship, so parts that have been destroyed are preserved as casts showing even the grain of the wood. The divers also recovered her key item of navigational equipment: a sounding lead.

7

Towards Barfleur

Eleanor's Empire

Except when the summer vacationers invade them, Guernsey and
Jersey are worlds apart—from each other as well as from the rest
of humanity. Both have many fishermen and fertilize their soil
with seaweed. Both have been proud of their dairy cattle, the
Jersey and Guernsey cows, and of their sweaters—jerseys and
guernseys. Nowadays they are both islands of glass, with many
greenhouses producing tomatoes and flowers for export. Despite,
or perhaps because of, their many similarities, Jerseymen and
Guernseymen show as much mutual disdain as the English and
the French.

The British flag flies on the castles in both Jersey Town and
Guernsey's Peter Port. Separated by only fifteen miles of sea, the
bailiwicks of Jersey and Guernsey nevertheless have separate governments, with their own laws, coins, postage stamps, and customs posts. Guernsey controls a small maritime empire including
Jethou, Herm, Sark, and Alderney far to the northeast, the third
largest of the Channel Islands. The only jewels in Jersey's imperial
crown are the Ecrehou and Minquier rocks.

This posturing would be laughable but for the severity of the
seascapes and the violence of the currents, which make seaborne
invasion difficult. As a result the Channel Islands, or Iles Anglo-
Normandes, as the French call them, remain as British footholds
in the geographic territory of France. The ties are loose. Jersey
and Guernsey have lieutenant-governors appointed by the Queen
in London, but the British made no attempt to stop the Nazis

occupying the Channel Islands when France fell in 1940. They could hardly presume to tax the islanders. Jersey and Guernsey are, in fact, tax havens, drawing rich Britishers to establish legal residence here. For ordinary folk, the low prices of spirits and tobacco proclaim the virtual independence of the Channel Islands.

Many of the islanders have French-sounding names, and even preserve dialects of Norman French, so you would be quite mistaken to think of them as English colonists. The Channel Islands are relics of the Angevin empire, which was centred in France but opposed to the French kings. It flourished eight hundred years ago. England was part of the Angevin empire, too, and when the French destroyed it, England and the Channel Islands were the pieces that escaped. They maintained a liaison ever after.

From Guernsey, the ketch launches herself into the tidal spate that will carry her toward Alderney, and then catapult her through the Alderney Race. The object gleaming white in the hazy sunshine, away to the north, is not a ship, but the Casquets rocks, as in caskets or coffins. They rank high among the English Channel's assassins. A lighthouse rises like a smokestack, and the stumps of two other lighthouses give a fair imitation of a ship's superstructure. Nowadays, lighthouses are solitary towers, and they use modern machinery to generate characteristic sequences of flashes, so that you can tell them apart. When lighthouses ran on coal fires, the only way to distinguish one from another was by the number of lights. So there were formerly three lights on the Casquets. They did not prevent a British flagship wrecking herself there in a gale in 1744, with the loss of 1100 lives. If you should ever see the Casquets and Alderney from the air, the mass of islands, rocks, and shallows and the tidal turbulence plainly visible in the water around them might put you off sailing here.

From sea level, big rocks such as Burhou seem like friendly landmarks. If you wanted to go ashore in Alderney, you would turn into the Swinge between Alderney and Burhou to find the harbour on the north side of the island. The harbour is a machine for feeding the island of Alderney in small pieces into the eight-knot currents of the Swinge. An odd-looking train chuffs down the breakwater, bearing stones in quantities that would have amazed

the megalithic builders. When the Admiralty in London decided
to build a breakwater more than a kilometre long out into the
Swinge, the islanders shook their heads. By 1864 the breakwater
was complete, a triumph of Victorian engineering. By 1872 most
of it had been swept away. To maintain even the half breakwater
that survives as anything better than a man-made reef requires a
hundred tons a day of Alderney stone to be offered as a sacrifice
to the god of the Swinge.

As you scurry past the rocks and cliffs of Alderney's southern
shore, French headlands appear on the far side of the Alderney
Race. Away to the south is Flamanville, which carries a nuclear
power station. More nearly ahead are hefty Jobourg, and the dying
fall of Cap de la Hague, at the corner where the Cherbourg Peninsula has been sawn off by a fault in the floor of the English
Channel. Blame the peninsula for the tidal torrent. It causes the
water in the Gulf of Saint-Malo to heave up and down extrava-
gantly, and water spills around this corner. It reinforces currents

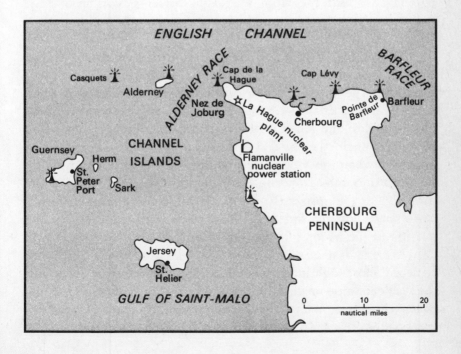

that in any case flow faster here, midway along the English Channel, than they do at either end. Near the French shore the currents can reach ten knots, twice as fast as sailing boats normally travel. For prehistoric seafarers the Alderney Race must have seemed like the supernatural engine of the sea. The pitching is no less violent when you know that the tides are matters of physics and geography.

The strongest tides occur when the Sun, Moon, and Earth are all roughly in a line and the Sun reinforces the Moon's tidal force. They occur around the time of Full Moon and New Moon, at intervals of roughly two weeks, and their name, spring tides, has nothing to do with the season of the year; they are "springing" in the sense of leaping. The lowest as well as the highest water levels occur during the periods of spring tides; in other words, the range of the tides is greatest then. For the weakest tides, called neaps, the visual signal is the First or Last Quarter, when the Moon's orbit has carried it to a position at right angles to the Earth–Sun line, so that we see it half lit. The Sun's tidal force is then at odds with the Moon's, and the currents swirl around the Channel Islands less alarmingly at neaps, when the Sun tames the water.

The timing of the tides changes from day to day, and also from place to place. Electronic computers had to be invented before tidal experts could be reasonably sure they understood what happens in the English Channel. The skippers of prehistory had no tide tables, and relied instead on always knowing the position of the Moon in the sky. They had simple rules of thumb. For example, when the Moon is due south, the tide is at its lowest in the Gulf of Saint-Malo, and the Alderney Race is flowing in the direction of Guernsey. By the late Middle Ages printed books were specifying the time of high water at various places by the bearing of the Moon on a magnetic compass.

A great deal of old seafaring art was lost when compasses replaced shore-sighting birds and a knowledge of the swell and the sea bed. Some medieval skippers spurned the newfangled compass, which was not strictly necessary even for crossing and re-crossing the oceans. The switch from traditional to scientific methods of navigation took several centuries to complete. It was costly in lives as well as pride, because the new techniques had hidden snags. One famous man of science tried strenuously to put them right.

In July 1701 a three-masted sailing ship, a diminutive English warship, was lying to two anchors in the middle of the Alderney Race. The ship was *Paramore;* her captain, the astronomer Edmond Halley. He was engaged in the first scientific survey of the tidal currents of the English Channel, but here they were proving almost too much for him. When *Paramore* tried to reach the island of Alderney, she was brushed aside by the Race. The crewmen weighed anchor as the current slackened, and they were shocked to find one of the anchors twisted by the force of the tide. The strength of the current, measured by an old-fashioned log, was recorded in the captain's log as "better than five knots."

Paramore then headed for Jersey, but another current picked her up and propelled her toward the Ecrehou rocks. That might have been the last we heard of Halley, but in the nick of time the southerly wind freshened, the current slackened, and *Paramore* clawed her way at sunset into a bay on Jersey. The next day Halley related in his log: "I went to Jersey town to get me a pilot acquainted in these parts."

Halley and *Paramore* toured the English Channel for four months. In the international spirit of science, he made sure that his orders said his work was meant to improve navigation in the Channel for the benefit of "the subjects of His Majesty or other Princes trading into the Channel." He was instructed

> to proceed with the said vessel and use your utmost care and diligence in observing the course of the tides according as well in the midsea as on both shores as also the precise times of high and low water, the set and strength of the flood and ebb, and how many feet it flows, in as many, and at such certain places, as may suffice to describe the whole.

Paramore was about twenty metres long, less than twice the length of our ketch. She was a pink, a vessel of a Dutch type with a flat bottom and bulging sides. In writing to his chum Isaac

Newton, Halley was pleased to call her "my frigate." Although *Paramore* was a humble vessel, her first captain had been Peter the Great of Russia. During a visit to England, the czar studied ship-building on the Thames, where *Paramore* was built, and he bor-rowed her for sailing experiments in 1698.

Halley's first voyages in *Paramore* were to the North and South Atlantic, in 1698–1700. Two English merchant ships mistook *Par-amore* for a pirate ship and fired at her. Then Halley's crew began to mock him. His navigation would have been impeccable, but he may have lost face by not knowing a preventer from a par-buckle. His lieutenant told Halley in front of the crew that he was "not only uncapable of taking charge of the pink, but even of a longboat." The lieutenant was court-martialled when the ship re-turned to England, but the presiding admiral, Clowdisley Shovel, was lenient with him, observing that "there may have been some grumbling among them as there is generally in small vessels." Nevertheless, Halley persevered in his naval career, with fresh crews.

The voyages of *Paramore* were epoch-making. They estab-lished the idea of scientific expeditions, which the British navy continued with James Cook, Charles Darwin, and other voyagers. And Halley delivered important results. He was the most versatile experimental philosopher of his time; Halley's Comet has drawn attention away from his other interests, which ranged from dew formation to life expectancy. In marine science he did pioneering work on the trade winds, the saltiness of the sea, and the silting of harbours; also on the design of diving bells, which he tested himself under twenty metres of water off the Sussex shore of the Channel, where he passed the time identifying the fishes. Halley's Atlantic missions in *Paramore* charted the magnetic variation. This is an awkward discrepancy between magnetic north, shown by the compass, and true north as defined by the axis of the Earth's spin.

Halley first measured the magnetic variation when he was a schoolboy in London, and he was fascinated all his life by the variation of the variation. It changes from place to place, and also from year to year. As a result of his voyages Halley produced the

til ye come in to iiij. fadam deep and yf it be streny
frounde it is betwene hu schant and cisse in the entre
of the chanel of flandres and soo goo youre course
til ye have sixti fadam deep. than goo est northe est
a longe the see. + c.

A fifteenth-century ship approaching the English Channel from Spain used a
sounding lead to measure the depth of water. The directions to seafarers read:
". . . till you come into four-score fathoms deep and if it be streamy ground it
is between Ushant and Scilly in the entry to the Channel of Flanders and so go
your course till you have sixty fathoms deep, then go east–north–east along the
sea." (Hastings MS Sailing Directions, c. 1470.) *(Society of Antiquaries of London)*

The "streamy" or turbulent waters of the western English Channel between Brittany and southwestern England show up cool and white in a satellite image which registers surface temperatures. The contrast with the warm (dark-shaded) surface water of the Atlantic Ocean to the left is due to mixing of the layers of the sea by strong tidal currents in relatively shallow water. *(Robin Pingree/P. E. Baylis)*

Mayors from the coastal communes of northern Brittany marched to the Federal courthouse in Chicago in 1982 to demand compensation for their worst oil pollution disaster, caused by the wreck of the supertanker *Amoco Cadiz* four years earlier. Their leader, Alphonse Arzel, is on the right, below the stop light. *(Maire Jean Larribau, Trégon)*

(*Opposite*) Crude oil spilled from shipwrecked tankers has repeatedly afflicted the rocky coast of northern Brittany. Although great effort goes into cleaning the rocks and beaches, most of the oil is eventually eliminated by natural processes. *(John Hillelson Agency/Raymond Depardon)*

The peninsula of Alet, in the estuary of the Rance river in Brittany, was a focus of cross-Channel trade two thousand years ago, when Saint-Malo (in the background) was still an uninhabited island. Diving archaeologists have discovered port installations on the near side of Alet. *(Doucet-Dinard)*

(*Opposite*) Cross-Channel invasions, 1066 and 1944. The scene from the Bayeaux Tapestry shows men and horses of William the Conqueror's army en route from Normandy to dislodge King Harold of England. In the photograph taken on the beach at Arromanches on the day after D-Day, American artillery was arriving in Normandy from England to help expel the Nazi occupiers. *(Michael Holford Library* and *Imperial War Museum, London)*

The four domes of the Paluel nuclear power station make a new landmark for seafarers on the chalk cliffs of Normandy. Each houses a 1300-megawatt reactor, and the English Channel provides cooling water for the turbogenerators. Paluel is one of five nuclear power stations on the Channel shores. *(Denis Poidvin/Electricité de France)*

At Sangatte in northern France, in 1983, a sea-bed machine crawled out of the water after digging a trench for a cross-Channel power cable. Electricity generated by French nuclear stations reaches England by this route. *(C. E. G. B. Transmission and Technical Services Division, Guildford)*

The first airborne crossing of the
English Channel was accomplished
by Blanchard and Jeffries in 1785, in a
hydrogen balloon. They had to
jettison most of their gear and
clothing to maintain sufficient height
to reach Calais.
(Mary Evans Picture Library)

A nineteenth-century proposal for
linking France and England with a
tunnel under the Dover Strait, due to
Aimé Thomé de Gamond, visualized
an artificial island in mid-Channel.
For nearly two centuries of talk the
British preferred to be seasick, and
twice halted the tunnelling
operations.
(Mary Evans Picture Library)

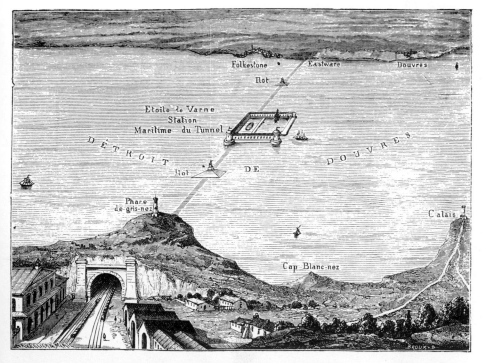

The culminating battle in 1588, between Spain and England, took place off Gravelines in the Dover Strait. This contemporary illustration shows the French and English coasts in the background, left and right. *(Mary Evans Picture Library)*

The sandbanks off Dunkirk show clearly in a radar image from the Seasat satellite. They created routing difficulties for the ships that rescued 350,000 British and French troops in 1940. Also visible, left of centre, is the breakwater of Port Est, where most of the survivors embarked.
(Seasat/Royal Aircraft Establishment, Farnborough)

first comprehensive maps of variation. He had hoped that they might provide a way of determining a ship's longitude in the North Atlantic. That they did not, but they launched geophysics as a science. In the 1960s the research on the Earth's magnetism that Halley started in *Paramore* arrived at its grandest conclusion: that during many intervals of geological time the magnetic north pole was near the geographic *south* pole. This led directly to the proof of continental drift and a revolution in geology.

In the Channel Halley studied magnetic variation as well as the currents, and he surveyed the shores by astronomical methods. This work was overdue. Halley published a broadside to alert seafarers to his discovery that the rocky islands of Scilly, at the western end of the Channel, lay five to fifteen sea miles south of the position shown in most charts and books of the time.

This mistake mattered less when the local magnetic north lay east of true north, as it had done until 1656, the year of Halley's birth. Before then, anyone approaching from the Atlantic was likely to be steering south of his intended course and so might enter the English Channel south of Scilly, even though it was wrongly charted. But as the variation changed to the west, more and more ships found themselves arriving north of Scilly, "not without great danger and the loss of many of them," as Halley remarked. Captains spoke of a mysterious indraft of the tide until Halley solved the puzzle. He did not save the life of Clowdisley Shovel, who presided at the court-martial of Halley's lieutenant. Admiral Shovel's fleet was returning home from the Mediterranean in 1707 when his flagship and three others were wrecked on Scilly by faulty navigation.

The Casquets, east of Alderney, figured in the same broadside when Halley corrected the so-called Channel Course. This was the course that allowed a ship to leave the English coast at Dungeness at the eastern end and pass right down the Channel, to arrive at a safe position north of Ushant. By tradition, this course was west-southwest (247.5° magnetic, in modern terms), but by 1700 the change in magnetic variation meant that ships steering that course from Dungeness were heading about 240° true, straight for the Casquets. Halley blamed recent shipwrecks at the Casquets on the neglected compass error, and urged a change to west by south (258.75° magnetic) for the Channel Course.

The currents were Halley's main concern in his Channel cruise in *Paramore*. On his earlier voyages he had been fascinated by the way the tidal currents sometimes helped and sometimes hindered his efforts to get down-Channel and out into the Atlantic. He wanted to produce the first scientific chart of the currents, the forerunner of the tidal atlases used today. It meant anchoring at many chosen locations to observe the currents. As he wrote to the Admiralty in London, from Dartmouth in Devon:

> The frequent weighing my anchors in so deep water has been very hard service to my small company, but the greatest difficulty I find, is from the frequent gales of wind . . . which, in this month of August, have forced me four several times into harbour.

What Halley observed, each time he anchored, was the time when the eastgoing currents went slack, before turning to run toward the west. This was the moment when a sailing ship, trying to battle out of the Channel against contrary winds, should weigh anchor to benefit from the westgoing tide. "When," in a tidal regime, meant how long before or after the time when the Moon was due south.

In four months' work Halley sought to replace the sailor's half-instinctive appreciation of the Channel tides by scientific data. The resulting chart was a masterpiece of presentation, and eighteenth-century pilot books copied it. As a portrait of complex currents it is inadequate. Those of the Channel Islands and the Gulf of Saint-Malo are represented by only three arrows, pointing roughly east, which is misleading. Halley also failed to realize that the currents are out of phase with the turn of high water. But if you simply want to know when the tidal currents turn, Halley's chart will serve today. For the Alderney Race it shows the current running eastward until nine hours after the Moon passes due south. As that was seven hours ago, the current speeding us past Alderney has a couple of hours still to run before it falters.

The French call the Alderney Race the Raz Blanchard. The grey lighthouse of Cap de la Hague stands on a rock among foamy shallows a mile offshore. A smaller black-and-white tower marks the outer end of the shallows, and that is where the current rushing up the French coast reaches its highest velocity. In fact, the ketch begins to feel its northward set driving her crabwise out of the Race. A giant chimney ashore belongs to the nuclear reprocessing plant of La Hague. As it comes into line with the beacon tower of La Plate, the boat is around the corner, out of the Gulf of Saint-Malo and back in the main valley of the English Channel.

The coast of the Cherbourg Peninsula is cleaner than Brittany's, with fewer rocks breaking the surface offshore, but that deprives it of natural breakwaters which might give shelter to ports and anchorages. An exception that proves the rule is Omonville, a few miles beyond Cap de la Hague. A reef projects from the shore and protects a small anchorage. Divers have found the remains of a small merchant ship wrecked off Omonville in Edmond Halley's time. She was carrying a cargo of peat and glass.

The port of Cherbourg has one of the grandest harbours in the English Channel, but it is man-made. Cherbourg began as a village at the mouth of the Divette River, opening into a bay where offshore islands offered some shelter. From a strategic viewpoint it could not be better placed, in the heart of the Channel and just sixty miles from England's Isle of Wight. But it was open to northerly gales, and not a place to harbour battle fleets before the breakwaters were built.

One man who saw the need for a base at Cherbourg was the military engineer Sébastian Le Prestre de Vauban. He designed impregnable fortresses that still astonish tourists all the way from Luxembourg to the islands of Biscay. In the years around 1670, as France's navy grew, its bases at Toulon in the Mediterranean, Rochefort in Biscay, Brest in Brittany, and Dunkirk in the Dover Strait, were all developed under Vauban's guidance. Arguments raged about Cherbourg, where Vauban conceived an expensive fortified harbour. There is nothing new about pork barrelling, and courtiers who favoured Le Havre on the Seine persuaded Jean-Baptiste Colbert, Louis XIV's chief minister, to cancel the Cherbourg project. With hindsight, that was the moment when the French turned their back on the sea.

Building eventually began at Cherbourg in the mid-eighteenth century, but the British knew Cherbourg's strategic potential and destroyed the harbour works in a raid in 1758. The main break-waters were started in 1776, but the Channel's storms and currents undid the work almost as fast as it was accomplished. When Na-poleon visited the town he promised to repeat "the marvels of Egypt" there, but that was the trouble. The scheme was too gran-diose for rapid completion, and Napoleon's fleet for the invasion of England had to languish at Brest. Seventy-seven years elapsed before the man-made port was formally opened in 1853.

The engineering feat speaks for itself. The massive break-waters, five kilometres long and with two entrances between them, have subdued a piece of the Channel. Forts and lighthouses stand on the breakwater heads. An inner breakwater protects the docks and shipyards, and the terminals for ocean liners and Channel ferries. In a system of Chinese boxes, yet another breakwater makes the yacht harbour totally sheltered close to Cherbourg town.

In World War II Cherbourg was the first major port liberated by the American army after the Normandy landings in 1944. The Germans blew up everything in sight, and sank ships and laid mines in the harbour. Once cleared, Cherbourg became a major supply route. PLUTO, the "pipeline under the ocean," ran here from the English shore, carrying fuel for George Patton's tanks, which liberated Brittany and then encircled the Germans in Nor-mandy. The town was ravaged, too, but unlike other Channel ports that suffered the same fate, it had little character before or after.

Bound east from Cherbourg, the ketch must clear a string of rocks that extends for two sea miles from Cap Lévi, and then avoid the turbulence off the Pointe de Barfleur, where the Cher-bourg Peninsula turns sharply south at the entrance to Seine Bay. The currents of the Barfleur Race pour around the corner in either direction. Fairly high ground around Cherbourg falls away towards the east, and the lighthouse of Barfleur pops out of the sea when you first see it. It stands on a small island in the Gatteville reef that projects from the headland, prolonging the downward slope of the shore. The Barfleur corner is a knob of granite some 300 million years old. The lighthouse, grey with a black top, is a noble structure seventy metres tall.

As the ketch rides the current around the headland at a cautious distance the harbour of Barfleur becomes visible. The Norman bell tower in the small town has rung the changes of more than eight centuries.

Two episodes in the Barfleur Race helped to shape the histories of England and France. The more recent event was a battle between the French and the English fleets in 1692, which culminated a little farther along the coast. The other was a shipwreck more than five centuries earlier, with extraordinary dynastic and imperial consequences.

The year is 1120, scarcely more than half a century since Duke William of Normandy conquered England. His son Henry I is now king, and his grandson William is in line to succeed. Seen from this side of the Channel, England belongs to Normandy, rather than the other way around. The king and his court often commute across the water, and for people of Viking stock the journey is trivial, even in November. King Henry has just set off from Barfleur for Southampton, and his ships have disappeared to the north. Prince William, eighteen years old, has lingered in the town, enjoying a party with his young relatives and friends. *Blanche,* the White Ship, is waiting in the harbour, and her skipper, Thomas Fitz-Stephen, is trying to hurry the partygoers aboard. He has promised the king to catch him up, and night is falling.

At last *Blanche* comes skimming like a water beetle out of Barfleur, into the gathering darkness. The oarsmen are rowing hard. Counting passengers and crew, there are perhaps three hundred people aboard. The lanterns are lit and the party continues, with singing and dancing. Fitz-Stephen is an experienced skipper, and he may be trying to dodge the worst of a contrary current in the Barfleur Race by keeping close to the Pointe de Barfleur. There is no lighthouse, and the lights of the revellers are spoiling his night vision. Perhaps he has shared too much of his passengers' wine. Whatever the reason, *Blanche* stops with a jolt and a splintering of oars as she slams into the granite of the Gatteville reef. Water as chilly as death gushes through sprung planking in the ship's port side.

While the crew try to push her off the rocks with boathooks, Fitz-Stephen decides that his first duty is to save the future ruler of Normandy and England. He gives orders for the ship's only boat to be launched. He puts Prince William into it and tells the boat's crew to row for the shore. But the prince's half sister, the Countess Maria de Perche, shrieks that he should not abandon her so barbarously. William orders the boat back to the stricken *Blanche*. Passengers and crew stampede toward their only possible means of escape. All discipline gone, they leap into the boat and sink it. Prince, countess, skipper, and all, die in the dark water of the Barfleur Race. Only one man, described as "a rustic person," manages to cling to the ship's mast all night, and lives to tell the tale.

To put the wreck of the White Ship in perspective, think of it as a shipload of young Sicilian *mafiosi* going down in the Messina Strait. The self-appointed nobility of feudal Europe carried on a wholesale protection racket. They acquired territory where they could extort labour from the serfs and taxes from free men. The racketeers were styled dukes or barons or knights. They had metal suits and armoured horses in place of bulletproof vests and cars, and troops of archers served them instead of machine guns. Powerful lords ran extended households as if they were godfathers to their hoodlums. They were keen that their own families should inherit their territories, but siblings and children kept demanding larger pieces of the action.

For the medieval bullies on horseback, treason was a fine art. Support the right boss and there might be plenty of loot; change sides and your reward could be a county. But if you backed the wrong king-killer you were liable to die in battle or on a scaffold. Half of France or England could change hands and it would be a matter for only a passing comment. To peasants and sailors it made little difference who was collecting the taxes or demanding military service. They died in battle by land and sea with little notion of what they were fighting for. Loyalty was addressed to individual lords, and perhaps to a king, but not to a nation.

The death of young Prince William on the Gatteville reef left the Anglo-Norman mafia in disarray. His sister Matilda was next in line for the crown, but many lords disliked the idea of a god-mother. Nor were they happy about the Angevin connection. Her father had shrewdly married Matilda, against her wishes, to the Count of Anjou, who controlled independent territory on the Loire River and other lands nearby. His father had been a crusader and king of Jerusalem, so the little matter of the English Channel was no bar to ambition. The family nickname was Plantagenet, from the broom plant (*genista* in Latin), which is a hardy shrub.

Anjou became the heartland of the Angevin empire after a conquest that would have impressed Al Capone. It started badly, when Matilda's father died and the Anglo-Norman barons gave the crown to a male cousin. The Count of Anjou thereupon seized Normandy, and Matilda herself was soon on the warpath to claim the English throne. She sailed with an army to Arundel in Sussex, where she landed on September 30, 1139. A long civil war ensued, and Matilda came within an ace of seizing the crown. In 1147 her fourteen-year-old son Henry led a small expedition from Normandy to lend his working mother a hand. But in the end she failed, and had to flee across the Channel.

The hopes of the Plantagenets began to focus on Henry, a freckled teenager. He was named Duke of Normandy, and when his father died he inherited Anjou. In 1152, at the age of nineteen, Henry married Queen Eleanor of Aquitaine. She was eleven years his senior and one of Europe's most beautiful and formidable women. Eleanor had just been divorced by Louis VII, king of the Franks, because of her highjinks in Antioch when she accompanied him to the Holy Land during a crusade. (Louis should have stifled his jealousy, because he divorced half the territory of geographic France.) Eleanor's lands included the entire west coast from Brittany to the Spanish frontier, and a swathe extending across southern France almost to the Rhone River. When she married Henry, their joint territories extended from the Channel to the Mediterranean, with England still to play for.

In January 1153 young Henry set off to invade England with

a force of thirty-six ships and three thousand mercenaries. They landed at Wareham in Dorset. When some of the troops plundered a monastery, Henry sent them home in disgrace, and many of them drowned in a Channel storm. But Henry forced the king in England to name him as his successor, shortly before he died. On December 7, 1154, Henry brought Eleanor here to Barfleur harbour, and together they set off across the Channel to be crowned king and queen of England.

As Henry II, the conqueror became the terror of the Celts of the British Isles. He drove the Scots out of northern England and subdued Wales. He encouraged Anglo-Norman adventurers to invade Ireland, from 1166 onward, and so began the English presence in that Celtic island. Once he had extended the Angevin empire to the Scottish border, Henry II spent most of his reign on the French side of the Channel. He was in Normandy when, in 1170, he exploded in rage about the conduct of Thomas Becket, the popular archbishop of Canterbury. The knights who slipped away to murder Becket in his cathedral had to cross the Channel in winter to get there. It was in Avranches, near Mont Saint-Michel, that Henry made his penance for that crime, barefoot in the cathedral square.

His chief bequest to England was a system of justice that relied on common law, and restored trial by jury as the way of deciding cases. Henry also clarified the law governing wrecks, although his ruling that a ship was not to be deemed a wreck if there were any survivors became an incitement to murder on the beaches. Henry invited German merchants to London to promote seaborne trade, and from their nickname "Easterlings" comes the name of the pound sterling.

Queen Eleanor's gifts to Norman and English seamen were the *rôles d'Oleron,* codifying sea law, and also safe trading with the Biscay shore of Aquitaine, especially with the wine country of Bordeaux. She bore five sons and three daughters for Henry, and during her enforced domesticity she cultivated gracious living. Her court at Poitiers became a centre of poetry and music. Troubadours from the south brought their songs of courtly love, and Celtic tales of King Arthur's court, idealizing chivalry, found a ready audience at the heart of the Angevin empire.

Reality was more sordid. Henry was an incurable womanizer, and in 1173 the wrathful Eleanor encouraged her sons to launch a revolt against their father. Henry stamped it out. Again he shipped Eleanor across the Channel, but this time for imprisonment in England. She was in custody for fifteen years, until Henry's death. By then she was in her seventies, but that was when the most strenuous period of Eleanor's life began. When her reckless son, King Richard the Lionheart, disappeared down-Channel to go crusading, she struggled almost unaided to keep her sprawling empire intact.

Eleanor had been too fertile. While her daughters were married off to German, Spanish, and Sicilian princes, her sons quarrelled over their inheritance. Philip II, the king of the Franks, was keen to hasten the decline and fall of the Angevin empire, and he conspired with King Richard's brother John. When John became king in his turn, Philip claimed to be his master. Eleanor fought her last campaign against one of her grandsons, near Poitiers in 1202, when she was eighty years old. She died in a monastery two years later, knowing that Philip was menacing Normandy, and Anjou itself. The Angevin rocket, launched when the ship *Blanche* sank on the Gatteville reef, was crashing.

The French picked up the pieces, and within a hundred years France began to approximate to its present scope. The English presence was reduced to enclaves on the Biscay shore, around the Somme River in the north, and in the Channel Islands. By then the cross-Channel ambiguities were resolved. Two distinct kingdoms were washed by the narrow sea: England to the north and France to the south. Eventually the only trace of Eleanor's empire was the Channel Islands.

If you ask an Englishman who last captured his country from the sea, he is likely to say at once, "William the Conqueror." He means the Duke of Normandy who, with his *mafiosi,* took possession of Anglo-Saxon England. According to a deep-rooted myth, the Channel and the navy have kept England safe from foreign invasion ever since. It is not true. William of Normandy landed a French-speaking army at Hastings in Sussex in 1066, killed the king, and made himself King William I of England. In 1153, Henry of Anjou took a French-speaking army to Wareham in Dorset, cowed the king, and became King Henry II of England. Then Henry Tudor sailed from Normandy to land at Milford Haven in Wales in 1485, with yet another French-speaking army. He killed the king and was crowned King Henry VII of England. Finally, in 1688, William of Orange disembarked a Dutch-speaking army in Tor Bay in Devon, drove the king into exile, and was hailed as King William III of England.

By my reckoning, that makes two Williams the Conqueror and two Henrys the Conqueror. The Channel was never a natural barrier to invasion, and it became something of a moat only if warships were in firm possession of it. Otherwise it was a bridge by which invaders could deliver a surprise blow anywhere along the English shore. If you wonder why two Henrys and one William escaped the fame or opprobrium of conquerors, the explanation is that they made an effort to win the hearts and minds of the English people. They encouraged commentators to depict their predecessors as villains, and the change of regime as a blessing. In short, they handled their public relations better than William the Conqueror did.

On the hills of this corner of Normandy walks the ghost of the English king dispossessed by the last of those invaders. He came here to try to get his kingdom back, and the second Tale of Old Barfleur explains what happened.

8

Towards Saint-Vaast-la-Hougue

Rooke's Bonfire

With the Barfleur lighthouse still plainly in sight, *Charmed* coasts southward to the next headland, the Pointe de Saire. Beyond it, the anchorage of Saint-Vaast-la-Hougue completes the panorama for the naval battle at Barfleur. Offshore, Ile Tatihou supports a curious tower with an asymmetric knob. The fishing village of Saint-Vaast is famous for its oysters, and only the modern buoys and yacht marina interfere with the seventeenth-century view.

When King Louis XIV of France declared, "I am the State," he asserted the traditional rights of a warrior king in a centralized bureaucracy of the modern style made necessary by the soaring cost of weapons and defences. The Bourbon "Sun King," who reigned for seven illustrious decades (1643–1715), made France unbeatable by land, and enlarged its territories. He was much less successful at sea, and one of the reasons was the failure to develop Cherbourg. His administrators created a fleet of more than a hundred splendid ships of the line, and lavished money on other bases, but left them without a good harbour in western Normandy. Along 150 sea miles of coast, between the Rance and the Seine, the warships had nowhere to go where they could lie in all weathers.

For want of any better port on the Cherbourg Peninsula, the French adopted Saint-Vaast-la-Hougue as a base for an invasion of England in 1692. It seemed to be their best chance ever. Two years earlier, the fleet commander Anne-Hilarion de Tourville beat an Anglo-Dutch fleet at the Battle of Beachy Head. Having won command of the Channel, he could think of nothing better to do with this awesome advantage than to annihilate the minor port of Teignmouth in Devon. But now Tourville was charged with escorting an army to England.

The aim was to put King James II of England back on the throne, from which he had been forcibly deposed in 1688. Like all deposed kings, James II had a bad press from those who toppled him. He was too candid for a politician. James Stuart grew up during England's last civil war, and he was fifteen years old when his father, King Charles I, was beheaded in London by Oliver Cromwell's republican regime. James escaped across the sea disguised as a woman, and then served in the French army. When he was only twenty-six, and dressed in the patched-up clothes of a soldier of fortune, his reputation as a daring and astute leader ran so strongly in the courts of Europe that he was offered the post of High Admiral of Spain and Prince of the Sea, at a high salary. Only his elder brother's sudden restoration to the English throne prevented him taking the job.

It was as Duke of York and Lord High Admiral of England that James greeted his brother at Dover as King Charles II in 1660. For the next quarter century he continued as Charles's loyal lieutenant. As Lord High Admiral, James commanded the English fleet in two battles against the Dutch in the North Sea. His energetic naval administrator ashore was Samuel Pepys. Afloat, one of his favourite admirals was William Penn.

New York is named in honour of James because, as Duke of York, he dispatched the English frigates that captured Dutch Nieuw Amsterdam in 1664. When the territory was subdivided, New Jersey acquired its name from Jersey in the Channel Islands, where James had taken refuge and been accepted as governor for a brief period during his exile. Pennsylvania was named for Admiral Penn and not, as many people imagine, the admiral's Quaker son who went to live there. The territory was given to William Penn Junior instead of the back pay owing to the admiral at the time of his death.

James caused a scandal by becoming a Catholic, when England had been militantly Protestant for more than a century. Even so, he became King James II when his brother died. Within four years a Protestant son-in-law, the Dutch Prince William of Orange, took England from him.

At the first attempt, the Dutch ships were flung back to their base by a westerly gale. The admiral commanding the English fleet massed in the Thames estuary did not believe the Dutch would hazard all their hopes at sea, with winter coming on. He wrote to King James: "Your statesmen may take a nap and recover, the women sleep in their beds." But the Dutch prince was in a hurry, winter or no, because James had a son and heir. The new baby destroyed any legal claim to the English throne that William might have had as husband of James's daughter. He had to act swiftly if he was to seize England by force before James had soothed his discontented Protestants.

The Dutchman was prepared for great battles by sea and land. He embarked an army of fifteen thousand men in five hundred transports. The Dutch troops were reinforced by some of the toughest mercenaries in Europe: Brandenburgers, Swedish cav-

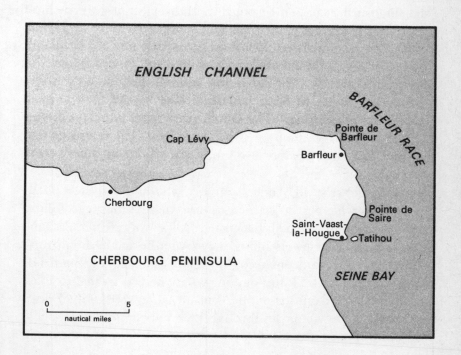

alry, and Swiss musketeers. Escorting the transports were fifty-two warships. In command of the Dutch fleet was Arthur Herbert, an English admiral who had disguised himself as an ordinary seaman to take a treasonable letter from certain Protestant aristocrats to William in Holland, asking him to come to their rescue.

Samuel Pepys, as secretary to the Admiralty, persuaded the English fleet to set sail, two days before the Dutch Armada left Helvoetsluys for the second time, early in November 1688. But the wind was blowing from the east, trapping James's navy in the Thames estuary, while letting the Dutchman sail where he pleased. Protestants called it the Protestant Wind. The armada headed first towards northern England, and then turned southward towards the Dover Strait and the English Channel. The English fleet was still beating its way out to windward, among the sandbanks of the estuary, while the people of Dover were watching the massed Dutch ships bowling downwind to an unknown destination.

A single Dutch transport, carrying two hundred troops, was caught by a frigate, but otherwise the invaders escaped scot-free. The English fleet passed through the Dover Strait a day behind them. On November 5, 1688, the Dutch fleet arrived off the Devon coast. A navigational error put it on the wrong side of a headland, but the Protestant Wind obligingly shifted and carried it into Tor Bay for the landing. The defending admiral, becalmed 150 miles to the east, wrote to King James: "I take myself for the most unfortunate man living." The Dutch army spent two days disembarking at Tor Bay, unopposed by sea or land. The campaign that followed was bloodless, because Protestant officers in James's army were reluctant to fight.

With Pepys's aid, James sent his wife and son secretly to France by yacht, but he warned no one that he meant to follow them. As a result, Kentish fishermen had a rare catch: a Catholic refugee laden with jewels and money. After he had been untrousered and robbed, someone recognized him as the king of England. James was packed back to London, where he was treated to a last show of loyalty from the public. But on December 18 the Prince of Orange drove victorious through Piccadilly amid pealing bells, and James slipped away down-river by barge. This time he made good his escape to France. In exile once again, James was deemed to have abdicated his throne.

The fifty-eight-year-old monarch in exile who inspected the army drawn up at Saint-Vaast was not the dashing general he had been in his twenties. James had become indecisive. For the invasion of England he shared in a triumvirate with two Frenchmen; it was command by committee. Even so, as a naval expert, James should never have agreed to the clumsy strategy dreamed up in Paris. It required Admiral Tourville to work a miracle against the combined Dutch and English fleets.

In the competition for maritime empires between the Netherlands, England, and France, fleeting naval alliances were made whenever one party seemed to become too strong. Earlier, the French and English had fought the Dutch together. Now it was the Dutch and English against the French. Later on, it would be the Dutch and French against the English. The contest forced the rapid evolution of modern nation-states. The French fleet answered to a centralized autocracy, and the Dutch to a federal plutocracy of wealthy merchants. When William of Orange took James's crown, it was on the understanding that he must do what the English Parliament told him to do. The English, like the Dutch, were on the road towards an illogical but durable compromise, the democratic monarchy.

The invasion plan called for Admiral Tourville to bring the French navy around from Brest to Saint-Vaast, where it was to embark thirty thousand infantrymen and take some storeships under its wing. Then the fleet was to proceed across Seine Bay to Le Havre, where transports were waiting, laden with cavalry and guns. Only then would the whole French armada head across the English Channel. Tourville was sailing under protest, leaving behind twenty ships that were not ready in time. James and the French expedition commanders at Saint-Vaast-la-Hougue learnt too late that the English and Dutch fleets had joined forces to quell the invasion. Together they were at least twice as strong as Tourville's force.

Ten boats were sent out with orders for Tourville to turn back, but all of them failed to reach him. The commanders could only ride the rocky road to the Pointe de Barfleur and look anxiously out to sea. The fleet making its way up-Channel from Brest had passed Cherbourg by night on a favourable tidal current. Although too small for its task, it was in many ways the best the French ever had. The ships wrought by Maître Blaise from Naples and his French pupils were the finest in the world. They were manned by merchant seamen and fishermen rostered into the navy from the *Inscription Maritime* introduced by Jean-Baptiste Colbert, who also arranged that their wives and children ashore should be well looked after during the men's national service.

Tourville, victor of the Battle of Beachy Head, was the cleverest admiral in Europe. Unfortunately, in arguing for prudence, his courage had been impugned. His orders, in King Louis's own handwriting, were to fight and do damage to the enemy, whatever the odds. This was the culminating stupidity of a poor plan. Tourville was required to hazard his superb fleet whether or not the invasion had any chance of proceeding.

A misty morning off the Pointe de Barfleur, on May 29, 1692, gradually unveils a sea full of ships of the line. The Anglo-Dutch fleet, strung north and south, makes a wall of guns barring the way around the headland. In the van is the Dutch squadron. Beyond it, the English squadrons stretch to the horizon. The commander is Edward Russell, who served William of Orange during his invasion of England. Altogether there are ninety-nine Protestant ships, with seven thousand guns, moving slowly in a light southwesterly wind, waiting for Tourville's forty-four ships and three thousand guns.

The French arrive from the west, with the ships *Bourbon* and *Monarque* leading the way past the Gatteville reef, where the tidal current is already turning to run westward. In the midst of the second squadron is the huge *Soleil-Royal,* the pride of the French navy. Aboard her, Tourville is planning his battle. He has the advantage of being upwind, and can do what he pleases. He could avoid the fight altogether, but for those orders from the king. He sends his leading ships to attack the Dutch, and takes his second squadron towards the centre of the enemy line where Russell has his flagship.

At 10 A.M. the smoke of guns begins to mingle with the patchy fog that still obscures the scene of battle. Men and boys begin to die as cannon balls sweep the decks, scything limbs and heads and throwing out splinters of wood that stab like swords. The French gunners are deadlier than their opponents, but in the centre, where Tourville is engaging eighteen English ships with eight of his own, *Soleil-Royal* suffers heavy damage to her masts and rigging. The wind dies away, halting the ships but not silencing their guns. At noon the fog closes in for a time, and the fleets drift in confusion in the Barfleur Race, which is shifting the whole tableau north-westward at several knots.

Manoeuvring begins again when the wind revives from the northwest. The ships in the rear of the English line work their way to the west, to sandwich Tourville's centre, only to find themselves sandwiched by other French ships. Again the wind drops, but the mêlée continues, as the tide turns off Barfleur in the afternoon and sweeps the ships southeastward. With more wind, and shrewder tactics on the Anglo-Dutch side, the French would by this time have been massacred.

When the Sun sets through the mist, Tourville resorts to a trick that he learnt from the English. He signals to his ships to drop anchor. This stops their drift, while the main force of English and Dutch ships are carried eastward out of range by the current. The English ships out to the west that tried to sandwich Tourville find themselves drifting through the French fleet and being se-verely pounded as they go, by the light of a Full Moon. The sea blazes as Admiral Russell orders fireships to be set drifting down towards the anchored French ships, but they do no harm. At 10 P.M. after twelve hours' fighting, the guns fall silent.

Tourville has won again. He has sunk one Dutch and one English ship, and damaged many more. Despite the overwhelming odds, not a single French ship has been sunk or captured, although *Admiral, Triomphant,* and especially the flagship *Soleil-Royal* are in bad shape. All he needs to do is get his fleet away, repair it, and wait for the twenty ships of the line he left behind in Brest. But he has nowhere to go. Cherbourg is just fifteen sea miles away, but the French are about to pay for their failure to develop that port. Tourville weighs anchor as soon as the tide turns westward in the morning, resolved to take his fleet through the Alderney Race to Saint-Malo, although it is a difficult route for the large ships of the line.

The days that follow the Barfleur fight are a bad dream for Tourville and his brave men. The wind is still very light, and everything depends on working the tides, taking the current when it serves and anchoring when it is going the wrong way. The Anglo-Dutch fleet follows in a slow-motion chase. By the evening of the day after the battle Tourville has not even passed Cherbourg, so he orders the disabled *Soleil-Royal,* together with *Admiral* and *Triomphant,* to beach themselves there. He tells most of the rest of the fleet to run for it. Twenty-two ships, guided by a Breton pilot, will arrive safely at Saint-Malo. Seven others will reach Brest or Le Havre by various routes, including two going right around Scotland to Brest.

Tourville transfers from *Soleil-Royal* to *Ambitieux,* his second largest ship, and takes the eastgoing tide, leading a force of ten ships back around Barfleur to Saint-Vaast. Two other ships from the general dispersal drift in to join him there. Admiral Russell and part of his fleet are still in the offing, ready to strike. Three days after the Battle of Barfleur, English fireships are loosed against the three ships beached at Cherbourg, and they destroy them. Three centuries later wooden fragments of the mighty *Soleil-Royal* will be discovered at the scene.

The events come to a climax at Saint-Vaast on June 2. With English ships swarming offshore, Tourville wants to run his own twelve ships aground, taking advantage of the high spring tide to get them as far up the beach as possible. There they could lie under the protection of the shore guns and troops, and out of reach of fireships. While King James and the rest of the triumvirate dither about whether to allow it, the tide is falling. Eventually the twelve French ships of the line take the ground farther offshore than Tourville intended.

At night, when the tide has risen enough to float a longboat, the English begin making a bonfire of Louis XIV's navy. A junior admiral called George Rooke leads a raiding force of two hundred boats, and they set six of Tourville's ships ablaze. French caval-rymen gallop into the water, and English seamen fight them with boathooks. On the hillside King James, former Lord High Admiral of England, mutters ruefully: "None but my brave English could do so brave an action!" Next morning the longboats go in again, and finish off the remaining six French warships.

The pall of smoke over the anchorage of Saint-Vaast-la-Hougue marked the combustion of Bourbon as well as Stuart ambitions. Louis had to choke back his belief in the divine right of kings and acknowledge the Protestant usurper William as the lawful monarch across the water. *Ambitieux, Merveilleux, Magni-fique, Terrible* . . . the ships were easily replaceable. What would never be recovered in Versailles and Paris, after Rooke's bonfire, was the confidence to send out large fleets to master the English Channel. King Louis resolved on a naval policy of mere commerce raiding. The privateers Jean Bart and René Duguay-Trouin were the heroes he wanted, not fleet admirals like Tourville. It was a decision that cost France an empire. In all the circumstances, the names of the waterfront streets in Saint-Vaast-la-Hougue are somewhat ironic: Quai Tourville and Quai Vauban.

The coast ahead consists of younger and softer rocks. We have reached the edge of an ancient island, and the granite disappears under the sea bed, sagging beneath a large basin that stretches far to the east. The region of Seine Bay has been flooded for most of the past 250 million years, accumulating thick sediments. The hills behind the village are built of sediments laid down some 50 million years after the Barfleur granite froze. As we follow the shore of the bay, south and then west towards the Seine River itself, the rocks of the coast will become progressively younger. In World War II, when American and British forces embarked on the lib-eration of Europe, they chose land built of Jurassic rocks 170 to 200 million years old for their disembarkation.

The Beaches of Normandy

On the grey, blustery morning of June 6, 1944, American assault troops came ashore on Utah Beach. It lies just ahead of us, at the southeastern corner of the Cherbourg Peninsula. Off Saint-Vaast-la-Hougue, the British cruiser *Black Prince* was dodging shells from German guns on the hills, which she was supposed to be knocking out. A little to the south, the American cruisers *Tuscaloosa* and *Quincy* were having the same experience.

The Germans ashore had more reason to worry. They manned their guns and pillboxes along the coast, and had set up beach obstacles across the shallow water now occupied by vast beds of cultivated shellfish. But they could see the biggest military operation ever mounted in the English Channel unfolding under the cloudy sky that covered Seine Bay. Four thousand landing ships and landing craft were delivering 133,000 troops to five beaches on the Normandy coast. Twelve hundred warships accompanied them.

The first ships to come near the enemy-held shore were the minesweepers that cleared ten approach channels into Seine Bay and a maze of passages approaching to within three to six miles of the beaches. Immediately behind them, six civilian buoy tenders laid eighty buoys to mark out the safe routes. Only then did the warships and landing ships approach the shore. The problems of navigation and seamanship are not often mentioned in accounts of the Normandy landings, but in the congested waters between England and France collisions between friendly ships occurred at a rate of three a day during the first few months, and were more of a menace than the U-boats, which sank only nine ships.

On the morning of D-Day the landing craft pitched into a head wind towards the dunes code-named Utah. The troops they carried had embarked from Devon, on the English shore. Navigation relied on a newly invented radio aid, Decca, but the guiding vessel, *PC 1261,* hit a mine. Deprived of their leader, the landing craft allowed the tidal current to nudge them southward, and finally lowered their ramps on the wrong stretch of beach. It was a stroke of good fortune, because the defences were much weaker there. The troops quickly seized the causeway roads leading across the swamp beyond the dunes. Compared with what was going on farther east that morning, Utah Beach was a walkover. But young Americans died in sunken ships, and on the beach, and inland where the 82nd and 101st Airborne Divisions had been scattered incoherently in a night drop.

The first monument on the shore, in the gap in the dunes at

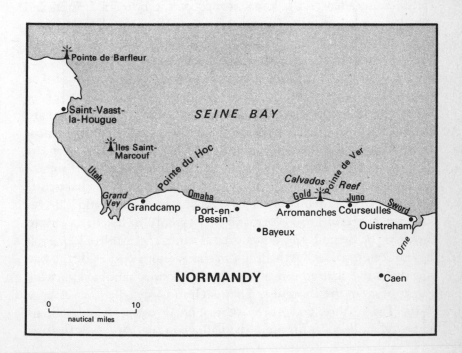

Varreville, does not commemorate the U.S. 4th Infantry Division that hit the beach under fire. It celebrates the landing of the Deuxième Blindée, the French 2nd Armored Division commanded by the general with the pseudonym Leclerc. That force disembarked here eight weeks after D-Day, when the Germans had retreated far from the shore. The ship's prow in pink granite, adorned with the double cross of Lorraine, makes sense only if you understand the French myth that Charles de Gaulle and his Free French liberated France in 1944, and graciously allowed the Americans to help.

The facts are too shaming for a proud nation to remember. The French army collapsed in disorder under the blitzkrieg in 1940. The wartime government at Vichy, and many individuals, collaborated with the Nazis during the occupation. Nearly all of the French troops who were evacuated to England when France fell elected to go home rather than fight for de Gaulle. Political divisions between left-wing and right-wing groups in the Resistance within France reduced its effectiveness. The core of the Free French forces were alien and colonial troops of the Foreign Legion and the African regiments. To conceal this before the division went to Normandy, the stalwart blacks were weeded out. So although some Frenchmen fought the Nazis with exceptional bravery, in the Resistance and the Free French forces, theirs was only a token part of the military effort that set France free. Yet almost every French town has its Place du Général de Gaulle and its Boulevard Maréchal Leclerc, in honour of the "liberators." The fact most firmly censored in French memories is that, on D-Day, even the Americans were outnumbered by British and Canadian troops.

Between the granite of Pointe de Barfleur and the chalk cliffs of Cap d'Antifer, Seine Bay is fifty-six sea miles wide, and it drives back the shore of Low Normandy by twenty miles. Far away to the east, the Seine River flows grandly into the English Channel. As our ketch passes Utah Beach in the western corner of the bay and skirts the charted wrecks on the Cardonnet sandbank, a wide gap appears in the shoreline. That is Grand Vey, the joint estuary of the Taute, Vire, and Aure rivers. The Vire gives vaudeville its name. *Vaux de Vire,* meaning the valleys of the Vire, was the title of a collection of ribald songs of the fifteenth century. The Aure leads up to Bayeux, the last town in France where Viking invaders continued to speak their Norse language. Grand Vey is shallow, and William the Conqueror, as a young Duke of Normandy beset by enemies, fled for his life by riding across the estuary at low tide.

The small fishing port of Grandcamp, which lies to the east of Grand Vey, is midway between the two American invasion beaches, Utah and Omaha. It is shielded by a rocky reef extending a mile offshore. Walk along the sandstone cliffs to the east of the village and you come to the Pointe du Hoc. It dominates Utah and Omaha Beach, and the Nazis had guns there, in the immensely strong reinforced concrete emplacements typical of their Channel defences. The battleship *Texas* pounded the position with hundreds of giant shells, but when the U.S. Rangers set about scaling the cliffs with grapnels and ropes, they found the Germans still holding out in some relatively undamaged bunkers and machine gun posts. The heroic storming of the Pointe du Hoc was made almost futile by the fact that the Germans had moved the guns farther inland. The clifftop remains a wilderness of shell craters and torn concrete. A pinnacle of rock erected in honour of the Rangers mimics the sandstone stack that rises from the sea in front of the Pointe du Hoc.

The most surprising thing about Normandy in 1944 is that the Germans were surprised by the choice of the invasion beaches. They did not really expect the main blow to fall here. They were easily conned by false radar, radio, and visual cues into holding troops at the Dover Strait, in expectation of a second attack in the narrowest part of the Channel. To a sailor, Seine Bay is the obvious coast. It has been used repeatedly to launch and receive invasions. One advantage of Seine Bay is the shelter given by the Cherbourg Peninsula from the prevailing westerly winds and the worst of the Channel tidal currents. For an embarking invasion force, like William the Conqueror's and Henry Tudor's, the rivers provide useful assembly points. For a disembarking force, the long sandy beaches of Seine Bay are preferable to the untidy rocks of Brittany or the sheer cliffs east of the Seine estuary, where Canadians stumbled and died on the flinty beaches of Dieppe in a disastrous raid in 1942.

Nevertheless, in 1944 the entire Channel coast was well defended, as the Americans discovered at Omaha Beach. Four sea miles beyond the Pointe du Hoc,'the cliffs come to an end and a sandy beach fronts the shore. Shingle at the top of the beach makes a natural obstacle for tanks, and the Germans backed it with a concrete barrier. The intertidal beach was strewn with obstacles. The hills still rise steeply, in clifflike fashion, for about thirty metres and then slant back to more than twice that height. A few defiles lead up from the beach towards the villages on the scarp.

This topography, combined with bad luck, made Omaha the most bloodstained beach that morning in 1944, when men who had embarked from Dorset found it hard to step ashore in Normandy. Vierville church marks the western end of the beach, and Colleville church the eastern end, where the hills end their compromise with the shore and return to the sea as cliffs. In the middle, at Les Moulins, forty newly built holiday villas stand beside the beach. Among the pine trees of Saint-Laurent, at the American military cemetrey, only birdsong and the whisper of the waves break the silence now. Nearly two thousand men of the U.S. 1st Infantry Division were killed or wounded in the first few hours of the assault.

The bad luck took the form of the German 352nd Division, which happened to be on an exercise just inland, and was able to reinforce the static companies of second-rate troops manning the fixed defences. The air and naval bombardment fully alerted the Germans, who held their own fire until the first wave arrived at the water's edge. As demolition teams emerged from their landing craft to clear gaps in the beach obstacles, the beach was scythed with shells, mortar bombs, and bullets. Mines on the obstacles exploded to add to the massacre. While those who escaped death or injury crawled for cover beside the shingle slope, the landing craft of the following waves came in like a conveyor belt, delivering more young men to the killing ground.

Ingenious schemes for dealing with obstacles and strongpoints and clearing the beach exits were brought to nothing by the heavy fire and the loss of special equipment in the surf. With a fresh northwesterly breeze, the water was much rougher at north-facing Omaha than at Utah, facing east. While twenty-eight swimming tanks landed to support the infantry at Utah, only five made it to the shore at Omaha. Confusion reigned, as officers and sergeants were killed wading ashore, and regiments became scattered as landing craft disgorged the troops at the wrong spots.

Omar Bradley, in the cruiser *Augusta,* sent a signal to supreme headquarters asking for permission to abandon Omaha if need be. His later verdict was that only the experience of the 1st Infantry Divison saved the day; less battle-hardened troops might well have been thrown back into the sea. By midnight the Americans were far short of their D-Day objectives, but Vierville and Colleville were in their hands, German reinforcements were slow to arrive, and a toehold was secure.

Next day the first of a procession of sixty old merchant ships arrived to be sunk sacrificially to make breakwaters. Used alone, lines of blockships known as Gooseberries gave shelter for landing craft on the open beaches. The sunken ships also provided the first protection for the artificial harbours called Mulberries, which could accommodate large ships. They were built in the manner of a child's construction toy, from floating boxes towed across the English Channel, and sunk in position. A million tons of concrete went into them. The piers and roadways floated up and down, allowing the harbours to be used at all states of the tide. One Mulberry harbour came to the Colleville beach, the other to the British beach at Arromanches, farther east. Two weeks after the landing a gale destroyed the Omaha Mulberry by uprooting the protective caissons and ravaging the floating piers. The Arromanches Mulberry survived, although it was damaged.

From Arromanches onward, broad beaches front the shore all the way to the Orne River, sixteen miles off. They were designated Gold, Juno, and Sword, and British and Canadian troops took them on D-Day. The ground rises farther back from the sea than at Omaha but offshore rocks, many of which emerge at low water, obstruct the beaches. The rocks form the long Calvados reef, which supposedly takes its name from a Spanish ship *Salvador* wrecked off Arromanches in the sixteenth century. This region of Normandy is now called Calvados, and so is its apple liqueur. The innocent coastal resorts of Asnelles, Ver, Courseulles, Saint-Aubin, and Lion, together with the port of Ouistreham at the mouth of the Orne, all experienced the violence of June 6. But the first British soldiers in Normandy in 1944 were here surreptitiously, on January 1.

Two men swam ashore in darkness, late on New Year's Eve, to the Pointe de Ver, where a lighthouse stands among the trees, east of Arromanches. The soldiers were collecting geological samples from the beach, to make sure that the invaders' vehicles would not get bogged down. The alarm about possible "soft going" on the Normandy beaches was sounded by Desmond Bernal, who was chief scientific adviser to the British Combined Operations Headquarters. He was a physicist and philanderer of great distinction, and it was on a seaside vacation with a girl friend that Bernal had visited the Normandy beaches before World War II. Bathing off the beach at Arromanches, he noticed that he was swimming through peat.

When Bernal learnt where the landings were to be, the memory of peat troubled him because tanks and other heavy vehicles might get trapped in it. The peat was formed when the rising sea destroyed coastal forests. Bernal saw the Calvados reef as a drowned headland that marked a former outlet of the Orne river. When the Calvados reef was high and dry, sheltering the present shore, it made, in Bernal's words, "a pleasant wooded valley, rocky only at the edges and marshy in the middle." Off Bernières, on Juno Beach where the 3rd Canadian Infantry Division from Portsmouth eventually went ashore, Bernal predicted that buried peat might hamper operations. He found the diary of a local naturalist, who had recorded that a storm stripped sand away from the beach in front of his house and revealed a layer of peat. The *Proceedings* of the Linnaean Society of Caen, going far back into the nineteenth century, also helped Bernal's investigations. Naturalists' notes on snails and plants unwittingly helped to guide the battle tanks of the twentieth century clear of marshy ground. There were other clues in place names. The Hable de Heurtot, for instance, is nowadays a low-lying promontory, but it turned out to be an old port silted up by a storm in the sixteenth century, and therefore treacherous to tanks.

Chartmakers do not worry unduly about details of rocky shores: they just put in enough rocks to scare off the mariner. When Channel charts came under scrutiny for the Normandy landings, Bernal found that the Iles de Bernières in the Calvados reef appeared as a skimped version of a French hydrographic survey done in 1776. Again the records of local naturalists came to the aid of the invaders. One of them was interested in the Iles de Bernières as erratics—rocks transplanted from their natural setting by the ice—and the fishermen helped him to chart the rocks and told him all their names: the Ass's Back, the Old Woman, and so on. Such information, combined with aerial photography, produced charts that helped to set the first assault ashore without shipwreck.

The anxieties about peat came to a head when air photographs showed peculiar dark streaks on other beaches, and it was to check out such patches near the Pointe de Ver that the first secret landing party was dispatched on New Year's Eve. It was an operation in the James Bond style. Besides the personal danger to the soldiers who landed, there was awesome risk to the Anglo-American plans. If Logan Scott-Bowden and Bruce Ogden Smith were found with their geological equipment, German intelligence officers would quickly deduce that a landing was planned on this stretch of coast.

The heroes arrived desperately seasick. They had crossed from Portsmouth in a motor gunboat and then transferred to a small launch for the last three hours of the run in, with a freshening westerly wind and chilly midwinter rain. The crew of the launch were novices, and lost their anchor and bottom-sounding pole overboard in the rough water. The echo sounder also failed. When the Ver lighthouse unexpectedly burst into light, it cleared up any navigational uncertainties, but it meant there was an enemy convoy somewhere nearby. The flashes illuminated the launch brightly and spoiled the night vision of the swimmers as they plunged into the surf. The launch withdrew five hundred metres from the beach and put down a reel of wire as an improvised anchor.

Once ashore, the swimmers crawled on their bellies along the beach, westward from the village of Ver, probing for land mines as they went. They started by pegging lines to the beach and then unreeling them as they went; every forty-six metres (fifty yards) a bead on the line told them it was time to take samples. They drove augers into the sand and transferred the product to rubber condoms. Two German sentries strolling on the sea wall scanned the beach with their torches. The swimmers crawled across the coast road to check the beach defences. But the sentries stopped for a chat, just at their crossing point, and by the time the swimmers got back to the water's edge they were late for their first possible rendezvous with the launch.

They shivered on the beach until it was time to venture into the surf. They were weakened by seasickness, hypothermia, their night's exertions, and the weight of their gear and samples. The waves knocked them down repeatedly. A further delay ensued, because the launch's makeshift anchor was reluctant to come up, but eventually the half-dead swimmers were pulled aboard. Still sounding with a boathook, the launch went out across the Calvados reef on a falling tide. Infra-red signals found the standby launch far out of position; her crew, also novices, had lost their anchor by letting the cable be snatched from their hands as they were dropping it. But it was a night on which much stouter craft, motor torpedo boats of the Royal Navy, abandoned a mission in the Channel because the weather was too bad.

Less than three weeks later the swimmers were back on the Normandy coast, at Omaha Beach. This time, they came in a midget submarine. Again two sentries appeared, and one of them tripped over the line that Ogden Smith was using to measure out his beach-sampling positions. The sentry did not realize what had made him fall; he brushed off the sand and went on his way with his companion. Next night, at Colleville, the swimmers found themselves illuminated by a bombing raid, and the beach was too shingly for them to move on quietly. They grabbed rock samples and retreated. On the third day, at Vierville, German soldiers used the submarine's periscope for casual target practice with their rifles, without identifying it for what it was.

Geologists as well as servicemen landed before D-Day. A Free French party slipped secretly across to Paris to spirit back to England some detailed geological maps. The middle-aged Sam Bassett, head of the Inter-Services Topographical Unit at Oxford, came ashore at night in a dinghy to explore the beach for himself. He repeatedly pushed his arm into it and declared it firm.

A geophysicist, Tom Gaskell, was Bernal's deputy at Combined Operations Headquarters in 1944. As secretary of the Beach Reconnaissance Committee, which brought together photographic experts, geographers, hydrographers, and other specialists, Gaskell's job was to learn as much as possible about invasion beaches. Beach intelligence had to establish how close inshore the landing craft would run aground, and how wide a zone of surf and dry beach the troops would have to cross under fire. Miniature valleys in the beach, where vehicles could be swamped or men drowned, had also to be identified. Air photos at different states of the tide could be converted into contour maps of the beaches. They were best taken when the tide was rising, because the beach was drier and the contrast with the sea more obvious. Repeated photographic sorties over the Normandy beaches (and in many other places, too, to confuse the Germans) revealed the natural profiles of the beaches to an accuracy of about thirty centimetres.

The air photos also showed obstacles set out on the beach by the defenders. Crossed steel girders were scattered along the beaches like man-made rocks, ready to tear out the bottoms of landing craft, or to blow them out with mines attached to the girders. Other improvised obstacles included stakes with shells and anti-tank mines attached to them intended to damage landing craft by exploding on contact. In addition to these visible defences there were presumed to be land mines sown all over the beaches. No open shores in the world can ever have been scrutinized more thoroughly, or under more difficult conditions, than these beaches of Seine Bay before the D-Day landings.

"Bigot," a rating higher than Top Secret, was the word spattered on documents in advance of the Normandy landings, and Bigots were individuals who knew where the landings were going to take place. The beach maps labelled "Bigot" must have terrified every officer in the assault battalions who was handed them, when the camps were sealed and briefing and embarkation began. Beach obstacles, barbed wire all along the seafront, machine gun nests at intervals of a hundred metres, frequent flamethrowers, fortified houses—all these were in addition to the heavy guns in concrete emplacements guarding the shore, and nonmilitary barriers including civilian sea walls, and sand dunes that might be three metres high and one hundred metres wide. So formidable and continuous did the defences look, even on very large scale maps, that Gaskell's last task before the invasion was to prepare maps on a super-large scale, so that the gaps could be seen to be wider than the obstacles. These were intended to improve the morale of the assault troops.

Two weeks after the landings, Gaskell went with a party of experts to assess the effects of the bombardment from sea and air on the beach defences and gun emplacements in the British sector, which were supposed to be neutralized before the troops went ashore. Their studies confirmed what the first wave learnt to its cost during the assault: that the bombardment was virtually useless at destroying reinforced concrete defences, although it was a great crumpler of German morale. The emplacements and shelters for German troops were not structurally damaged to any marked degree, having withstood direct hits by shells and rockets. Only a lucky shot through the open embrasure of a gun emplacement would put it out of action.

The cruiser *Ajax* put a shell through the embrasure of each of two guns in the most important battery on this stretch of coast, at Longues, west of Arromanches. The scientists calculated the odds against such a double occurrence at fifty to one. That figure was not offered in praise of *Ajax*'s gunnery, but rather the reverse. Fifty cruisers, firing no less accurately than *Ajax* did that morning, should by rights have been necessary to put two guns out of action. Local inhabitants reported that the double direct hits caused the surviving German gunners to run, thinking that the Allies had a super-accurate secret weapon. The general sound and fury of the bombardment gave many an ordinary German soldier an excuse to surrender to overwhelming fire power, rather than fight and die.

One reason why the bombardment was often physically in-effectual was fear of hitting one's own troops. On D-Day the tendency was to overshoot, and to bomb and shell the empty marshes behind the German beach defences. Troops spearheading the British 50th Infantry Division, which came to Gold Beach from Hampshire, complained that heavy bombers assigned to de-molish a fortified hospital east of Arromanches dropped their loads "some distance inland."

Many French people died as civilian real estate was ploughed by the air and sea bombardments that only scratched the Germans' reinforced concrete. Dead and injured cows became a characteristic sight in the Normandy battlefields. British battleship shells cut down the famous spire of Saint-Pierre at Caen, eight kilometres inland, and ravaged a hospital crowded with demented women. The Norman city of Caen was supposed to be liberated on the first day, but its ordeal lasted a month, and fear of hitting the British and Canadian troops drove the bombline southward into the heart of the medieval city, where there were no military targets.

South of Omaha Beach and west of Caen, the granite of the old island of Brittany protrudes deep into Normandy, in the bocage country. Woods and fields are crisscrossed by narrow sunken lanes passing between old hedgerows and linking stoutly built farms. The bocage is ideally suited to defenders. During his literary re-searches before D-Day, Desmond Bernal found in the *Archives* of the Linnaean Society of Cherbourg a proposal for the defence of Normandy written in 1685 by the military engineer Vauban. His idea was to treat the hedges as the first obstacles to an invading English army, and simply issue muskets to the peasants. The mil-itary historian John Keegan describes the German use of the bocage in 1944:

Bocage, for all the soldiers of the liberation armies . . . came to mean the sudden, unheralded burst of machine-pistol fire at close quarters, the crash and flame of a *panzerfaust* strike on the hull of a blind and pinioned tank.

While the British inched forward, the Americans broke out and threatened to encircle the Germans. At Hitler's insistence, his troops made a big effort on August 7 to strike westward. They aimed to slice through the American forces to reach the Gulf of Saint-Malo and cut off the Cherbourg Peninsula. The reading of German orders by the Ultra codebreakers enabled the Americans to redeploy their artillery to meet the thrust. The climax to the Battle of Normandy came eleven weeks after the landing. At Chambois, near Argentan, seventy kilometres inland, Polish Dragoons serving with the British army met American infantrymen. Twenty German divisions were thereby trapped. Altogether the Germans lost a quarter of a million men killed or captured in Normandy, in a disaster worse than Stalingrad, which made the Battle of Normandy one of the decisive events of World War II. The German commander, who had provoked Hitler's wrath by arguing for a strategic retreat, committed suicide.

As our ketch approaches the port of Ouistreham, at the extremity of the invasion beaches, the foggy dusk obscures the lights of Lion and Hermanville, where the British 2nd Infantry Divison landed on Sword Beach after embarking from Sussex. A legend among the troops told of the Angel of Hermanville, seen riding a bike towards the sea amid the shot and shell. She was a young nurse, Marie Bernard, although she was not identified until 1983 after persistent inquiries by the veterans. Then she explained that she had been bathing on the beach on the previous day, June 5, and had forgotten her swimsuit. War or no war, she went back to find it. Coming upon a medical unit at work on the beach, Nurse Bernard interrupted her mission to spend twenty-four hours helping with the wounded. She recovered her swimsuit, but found her bike had been liberated.

Heirs of the Vikings

Satellite pictures show a full-blown Atlantic storm moving towards the English Channel, so the ketch leaves Ouistreham in some haste, to reach the Seine River before the weather breaks. The Chinese and Polish freighters waiting to enter the canal that leads to Caen will be well inland by the time the storm arrives. The sea looks unthreatening. There is a gentle breeze from the southwest, and if you thought of sailing to Hastings, some twenty hours away, there is no warning sign in the sky to stop you. William the Conqueror, without benefit of weather satellites, was lured to sea on such a day as this.

At the British military cemetrey at Bayeux, inland from Arromanches, an inscription reads: *Nos, Gulielmo victi, victoris patriam liberavimus*. It translates as "We whom William conquered freed the Conqueror's land." The Bayeux Tapestry, which is actually linen embroidered by the English, tells the story of the Norman Conquest of England in 1066 in a strip cartoon seventy metres long. No other medieval records of the Channel match its vividness. Among many details, it depicts Halley's Comet at its apparition in April 1066, which was taken as a portent of great events. And Bayeux itself is offered as the place where Harold Godwinson, the chief earl of England, swore a solemn oath that Duke William of Normandy should become king of England when the childless incumbent died.

Harold had been yachting with hawks and hunting dogs off the Isle of Wight in 1064 when he was caught in a storm and cast ashore on the French side of the Channel, near the Somme estuary. The local count imprisoned him, but Duke William demanded his release. Harold then fought alongside William in Brittany, and went home laden with honours and gifts. Whether his oath to William was made under duress, and what its terms were, have been debated ever since. Any flat promise of the crown would have been unconstitutional because only a committee of *witan,* or wise men, could choose the English king.

Who were the Normans, and who the English? Who, for that matter, were the French, whose lands the Normans occupied and whose language they spoke? The short answer is that they were all descended from various Germans of a piratical disposition, who displaced or conquered the Celts living on both sides of the English Channel at the time of the Roman empire. The Roman interlude left no Italian population on the Channel shores, because the Romans liked the oysters and the taxes but hated the climate. They employed local people as troops and administrators, and left them with a language, Vulgar Latin.

The Germans wanted territory for their families. Like the Celts and the Romans, they were Indo-Europeans. From their core area in southern Scandinavia, the Germans spread in pre-Roman times into Germany, Poland, and the Netherlands. They kept the Romans off their lands, and Julius Caesar noted their austere habits and love of plunder. Their raids became devastating in the fourth century A.D., as they were pushed from behind by the Huns bursting in from Asia, and pulled by the alluring riches of the decaying Roman empire. Some German tribes, complete with their cattle, made extraordinary wanderings through the empire, and reached Rome itself via Africa. The conquests of Gaul and southern Britain, beginning in earnest in the fifth century A.D., were more straightforward.

Gaul was invaded by the Franks from the Netherlands and by Burgundians and Alemanni from Germany. Southern Britain was attacked by people from northern Germany and Denmark: Frisians, Jutes, Angles, and Saxons. The name of France comes from the Franks, and that of England from the Angles, while the Saxons are commemorated in the names of English counties, as well as in Saxony in Germany. English remains a Germanic language, but the Franks adopted Gaulish Latin, which evolved into French.

In the ninth century A.D. other Germans living in Scandinavia irrupted as the Vikings. Their conquests included large areas of the British Isles, with the Danes prospering in England. Norwegians took Normandy, which is named for the Northmen. Peasants living far from the sea would look up to find their quiet river filled with a column of longships, as menacing as the battle tanks of later blitzkriegs. But the fierce Scandinavians were only doing to the Franks and Anglo-Saxons what they had done to the Celts four centuries earlier, as they evolved from pirates to invaders to settlers. Vikings assailed Normandy from the Loire River in the south, as well as from the Channel shore. In 857 raiders in the Seine River fought their way up to the Frankish stronghold in Paris, and completely destroyed it. By 911 the king of the Franks had to recognize their possession of Normandy in a treaty made

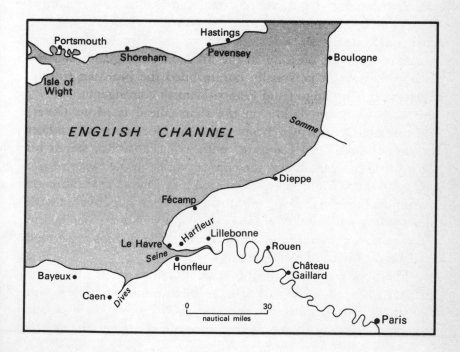

with the chieftain Rolf. The intruding Normans adopted the French language and ways and William the Conqueror was Rolf's great-great-great-grandson.

After becoming Duke of Normandy at the age of seven, William had a dangerous childhood until he defeated rebellious barons at a battle near Caen. The management of his mafia remained tricky. When the news came that the *witan* had made Harold Godwinson himself king of England, William declared that he would cross the English Channel and claim the crown. The only way the duke could get his barons and knights to join him in such a venture was by promises of loot. This altered the character of the expedition. Instead of taking over prosperous England as a going concern, William was committed to tearing the country apart and handing out land to any crony willing to supply ships and soldiers to face the English navy and army.

The Norman castles that tourists are invited to admire, in Normandy and England, are deliberately overpowering symbols of feudal repression. The word *donjon,* which meant the innermost tower within a castle, acquired a more sinister meaning as dungeon. Much the same is true of the Norman churches, because the priests sided with the dukes and barons. The pope was persuaded to give his blessing to the invasion of England, and the Bishop of Bayeux personally commanded the Norman troops. There were also Breton and Franco-Flemish contingents.

The hill rising darkly on the shore ahead is Mont Dives, marking the Dives River, from which the Norman invasion fleet started. The resort of Cabourg, with its large casino, stands on the near side of the estuary; the copper works on the eastern bank belong to the town of Dives. The sand that serves the vacationers has almost blocked the river mouth with a large spit covered with dunes. Only a handful of fishing boats and yachts are perched in the mud, and it is hard to picture several hundred ships assembled here for the invasion of England.

In his book *1066,* the historian David Howarth estimates that William gathered ten thousand men, three thousand horses, and two or three prefabricated wooden forts. They went into about 350 ships, typically fifteen metres long and relying more on sail power than oarsmen. William's flagship *Mora,* with the leopard of Normandy on her prow, was a present from his wife. Across the water, Harold had a fleet of similar size waiting at the Isle of Wight. There was a defending army ready, too, but no sign of William. Although the invasion force was ready by early August, a persistent north wind, unusual for the time of year, kept William and his army in Dives. In September the English decided that the autumnal weather would take care of their defences, and dispersed. Homegoing ships were caught in a gale on September 13, which destroyed many of them.

Unknown to the English, William had sailed the day before, and suffered the same gale. With the first favourable wind for many weeks, the fleet hurried out of the Dives estuary. When the gale hit them, it drove them willy-nilly up the Channel, in which direction there were few large harbours and many dangerous shoals and cliffs. It says a lot for the pilots' skill that most of the ships survived the gale and reassembled in the Somme estuary. William's reputation was on the line. He sent out parties to gather up the corpses from the beaches and bury them secretly. Even so, many of the living were unwilling to face the crossing again so late in the year, and slipped off home. Despite everything, William kept his force more or less intact in the Somme, while it waited two weeks for another favourable wind. He was not to know that the unseasonable north winds were incredibly lucky for him. They had kept him at Dives until the powerful English fleet had dispersed. Now they pinned him in the Somme until Harold's army was drawn far away from the Channel shore.

England had been struck by another invasion, by the most bloodthirsty Viking of them all. Harald Hardrada of Norway arrived on the east coast and proceeded upriver to subdue the city of York. While William was parading the relics of a saint to provoke a change in the wind, King Harold was rushing northward with his army to fight off that other would-be conqueror. The English won an overwhelming victory at Stamford Bridge and Harald Hardrada was killed. But Harold was still in northern England when William's prayers were answered by a southerly wind on September 27.

This time there was no storm. William was making for Hastings on the English shore, because the land there belonged to the monks of Fécamp in Normandy, as a gift from the former English king. In those days there was a good harbour near Hastings, called Bulverhythe. But William's fleet finished up next morning some five miles west of its objective, and entered Pevensey on the last of the flood tide. This harbour, like Bulverhythe, has now disappeared under reclaimed land. After a couple of days there, the Norman force decamped to Hastings. William stayed near the Channel shore for two weeks, waiting for Harold to come and fight him. His army pillaged nearly every village within twelve kilometres of Hastings, and in several cases destroyed them.

On the morning of October 14, King Harold's army was drawn up on a sandstone ridge astride the road from Hastings to London, between the marshy head of Bulverhythe harbour and the thick forest of the Sussex Weald. It was an excellent position. When William's army came marching out to fight, it had to attack uphill. There was a mismatch in weaponry, with Norman cavalry and archers set against English battleaxes and spears, but not decisively to anyone's advantage. From their commanding position, the English should have won.

First the Breton wing of William's army attacked and fell back; then the Franco-Fleming wing did the same. Each time some of the English chased them down the hill, only to be slaughtered by the Norman cavalry. With a concerted downhill charge, Harold might have had the Normans running for their ships, like the Norwegians three weeks earlier. But it was not to be. Howarth suggests that Harold was demoralized by the pope's banner carried in William's army. In the evening the Norman cavalry climbed the ridge around the flanks of the shrunken English line. King Harold was hacked to pieces, perhaps after being wounded by an arrow in his eye. By William's order, the fragments were gathered up and buried in the pagan Viking fashion under a pile of stones on the clifftop at Hastings.

William then sent troops to eradicate the nearby port of Romney, because the occupants of two straying ships of his invasion fleet had been killed there. Dover surrendered without a fight, but even so the Normans looted and burned it. The Norman Conquest took five years of struggle to complete, by which time England was a land of prisons. Finding himself loathed by his English subjects, William left as soon as possible for Normandy, and visited the conquered and partly depopulated country only when he had to. When he died at Rouen in 1087, he had not set foot in England for five years. He was buried at Caen, and his grave was excavated in 1983. From his bones we learn that William the Conqueror was 1.7 metres tall (5 feet 7 inches) and very stocky.

Normandy changes its character abruptly at Dives. Along the Calvados shore from Omaha Beach the landscape has sagged, and for the last few miles we have been passing a low alluvial plain. This entire region, east of the old island of Brittany, has been awash for more than 200 million years because a subsiding depression in the Earth's crust, called the Paris Basin, reached across the Channel into southern England. It accumulated piles of sediments in a shallow sea. The sediments turned to rock. Characteristic of Low Normandy's coastal zone is creamy Caen stone, the color of ripe Camembert. The old Normans built with it, and even shipped it to England for castles and churches. Other Normans in 1944 took cover in the stone quarries by the Orne River while their city was being destroyed. Caen stone is limestone laid down about 170 million years ago, when the largest of all dinosaurs, the long-necked brachiosaurs, were lumbering around the supercontinent of Pangaea. Beyond Dives the ground rises sharply by 130 metres. As the ketch hurries eastward, the aim is to put a high wall of rock between her and the impending storm.

The chalk starts here, as a white crown on the land. It is roughly half as old as Caen stone, and was formed when tyrannosaurs were the top predators ashore and giant seagoing lizards terrorized the fishes. The chalk was plastered over most of western Europe during a great flood, 67 to 93 million years ago. The sea level was at an all-time high and Europe, like other continents, was largely under water. The world was very warm and the whole English Channel lay farther south, roughly at the present latitude of northern Spain. In the surface waters, microscopic plants with chalky hoops bloomed prodigiously, and whole and broken hoops covered the sea bed with a fine-grained ooze. It stayed clean and white because the nearest land was far away, and there was little sand or mud to discolour it.

Over millions of years, the product of successive blooms piled up in thicknesses of chalk that amounted to five hundred metres near Paris, and somewhat less around the eastern English Channel. Seine Bay, where we are sailing, was full of chalk, and you can find it on the sea bed at the entrance to the bay. Most of the local chalk disappeared when the bay was hollowed out. But from Dives onward, a slab of chalk sprawls across Normandy.

It starts in a tentative way, in the scarp at Dives. Deep valleys cut through the chalk of the Auge region beyond, exposing the underlying clay, where forests grow. The time to be here is in the spring, when the land glows white, not with chalk but apple blossom. A mass of chalkland looms like an island away to the northeast, in the white cliffs of Cap d'Antifer. They lead south to Cap de la Hève, which marks the northern side of the Seine estuary and has just a smear of chalk on top of older sandstone and clay. Big radio dishes surmount Cap de la Hève.

The majestic estuary, beloved of Impressionist painters, opens like a funnel ahead, promising shelter. As the ketch enters its narrow dredged channel, chalky clifftops up the river gleam resolutely white in the cloudy sunshine.

Two tall chimneys at Le Havre dominate the scene. The modern docks and oil refineries of the great port monopolize the northern shore of the estuary, along twenty kilometres of reclaimed land. Two dikes that govern the dredged channel run towards the high, wooded southern shoreline called the Côte de Grâce. The hill terminates in Falaise des Fonds, the "cliff of the deeps." Its name suggests that sailors always found deep water here, even before the dredgers came. An abrupt turn to starboard, beside a modernistic control tower, puts the ketch into a short canal that leads across reclaimed land to Honfleur. The dock gates slam behind her and she lies amid tall, slate-roofed houses, under the lee of the Côte de Grâce, safe from any storm.

In the Middle Ages, two ports faced each other across the five-mile-wide mouth of the Seine, like Tweedledum and Tweedledee. They were Harfleur on the northern side and Honfleur on the south. The silt was always troublesome at Honfleur, but at Harfleur it was fatal. By the end of the fifteenth century it was unusable, and the French king ordered that the sandbanks and marshes towards Cap de la Hève be developed into a new port, Le Havre. Now Harfleur is buried among the industrial suburbs of the city, five kilometres from the river that it once served, but Honfleur still functions as a small port.

Honfleur was spared the destruction visited on almost every other port on the Channel coast of France during World War II. Here you can wallow in a medieval maritime atmosphere. The wooden church of Sainte-Catherine, built by shipwrights in the fifteenth century, is constructed like a capsized catamaran. You could say the shipwrights took literally the word nave for the main body of a church, which comes from the Latin *navis,* a ship.

Large ships converge on the ports of the Seine, the Channel's greatest river. The tankers stop at Le Havre, or at the new terminal under the cliffs of Antifer. About ten cargo ships a day make the journey of 123 kilometres (73 sea miles) up the Seine to Rouen. You can go up in a yacht, too, borne on the current of a single flood tide, provided you make at least four knots through the water. The dikes and dredgers have tamed the notorious tidal bore of the Seine, the *mascaret,* caused by the flood tide forcing itself into a constriction at Tancarville, thirty kilometres upstream. Only at quite exceptional tides does a vertical wall of water as tall as a man charge up the river at twelve knots and wreck small boats.

A few kilometres beyond Tancarville, and hidden behind an oil refinery, is the site of another vanished port, Lillebonne, which was *Juliobonna* in Roman times. The river snakes along a picturesque route beside forests and steep cliffs, and the Celts called it *Squan,* meaning "bend." It is a classic case of incised meanders, where a pre-existing river has cut winding gorges as the land has risen. At Villequier, some forty kilometres upstream from Honfleur, the estuary pilots hand over to the river pilots. Oceangoing ships make an odd sight passing under Norman abbeys and castles with legendary names. About one hundred kilometres upstream, the Château du Corsage Rouge is said to commemorate the grand lady who beckoned her lover from across the river by hanging a corset from her window; when the garment next appeared it was stained with the blood of the lover, slain by the lady's husband. A little farther on, the castle of Robert the Devil is named for William the Conqueror's father. Then Rouen comes into view.

The name of Rouen makes many people think of medieval belfries, and Joan of Arc dying in the flames in the market place. The literary-minded recall that Corneille and Flaubert were Rouennais. But if you climb the scarp behind the suburb of Canteleu-Croisset, where Gustave Flaubert wrote *Madame Bovary,* and look back towards the city, you will see mainly a wide expanse of quays, docks, container terminals, and shipyards bordering the Seine. The city bridges block the passage of all but the most bargelike ships, but the Seine leads deep into France and links up with the busy canal networks that range across the country and into neighbouring lands. So Rouen has a second, inland port for barges.

Follow the river beyond Rouen, and you will come eventually to the island that has always been the sacred heart of Paris. The cathedral of Notre-Dame stands there now, with the French capital radiating around it. Some fifty thousand tons of fresh water passes Paris every minute on its way to Normandy, and the Seine has been the main boulevard and highway for Paris for many centuries.

A quick way to untangle the history of France is to ask who controlled the Seine between Paris and the sea. For example, Charlemagne visited Rouen as emperor without anyone barring the gates or bumping him off, which was the acid test of political power in the late eighth century A.D. He was a Frank who fought the Saxons and acquired an empire that included most of the territory of modern France, as well as large areas of Germany and Italy.

The collision between the German-tongued Franks and the Latin-speaking Celts amid the ruins of the Roman empire produced the French language. Being keen to imitate the Romans, the Franks adopted the Vulgar Latin of the time. A few Germanic words have survived into modern French as *bateau* (boat), *guerre* (war), *baron* (baron), and so on. The French name for the English Channel, la Manche, also means "sleeve" in French. The Channel looks vaguely like a sleeve in a satellite picture, but the Franks had no spacecraft and Manche is probably akin to the German *Meer-enge,* meaning strait. Much more typical was the evolution of Latin words into French. *Rota* (wheel), for example, became *ruede* in medieval French and then *roue* in modern French.

The story of Frankish France, based in Paris, starts with the breakup of Charlemagne's empire in the ninth century A.D. The Vikings were on the Seine, pillaging Paris, and from 876 onward they were firmly settled at Rouen. The era of Norman independ-ence was a meagre time for the Franks and their kings, and the embryo of France looked even more pitiful during the short-lived Angevin empire. The kingdom occupied an area less than one tenth the size of present France, hemmed between Angevin pos-sessions and regions of doubtful allegiance to the east.

Expansion began in 1204, when King Philip II advanced into Normandy. To ward off just such an attack, Queen Eleanor's son Richard had built a fortress, Château Gaillard, on a bend of the Seine. Philip's army stormed it, and came on down the river to take Rouen. Other territories fell to him, including Anjou itself. Philip's predecessors had been kings of the Franks; he was the first to call himself the king of France.

Although the Channel appears to be a natural boundary of France today, it did not seem so at the time. Europe was fluid. The pope in Rome had territorial ambitions, the Muslims were in Spain, and the Mongols were about to fall on eastern Europe. In Germany an empire was breaking up. Amid this confusion, the French and English were the first peoples in western Europe to consolidate their nations within their modern boundaries. To find out who they were, they fought each other.

By 1213 England was threatened with a French invasion, and ships of war from Kent entered the Seine to destroy shipping during a series of cross-Channel strikes. A few years later rebel barons in England, at odds with Eleanor's son John, invited a French army to England to assist them. It crossed from Calais and captured London, while French ships led by Eustace the Monk raided England's Channel ports. After King John's death, the English had the problem of getting rid of the French. The first of many sea battles between the English and the French took place off Dover on August 24, 1217, when the English won in Roman fashion by cutting the rigging of the French ships.

Checked in the Channel, the French kings did better in France. By reducing the territory under English control to splinters on the Channel at the Somme estuary, and on the Biscay shore around Bordeaux, France became the most powerful country in Europe. But in 1337 a long and deadly quarrel began, in which the English kings laid claim to the crown of France. The Hundred Years War started with cross-Channel raiding in both directions. The French attacked the Channel Islands and the Isle of Wight; the English went for Sluys in Flanders; the French retaliated against Southampton and Portsmouth; and so on. Then the English landed in force at Saint-Vaast-la-Hougue on the Cherbourg peninsula on July 12, 1346, and hacked and pillaged their way through Normandy. They crossed the Seine near Paris, defeated the French army on the road to Calais, and laid siege to that Channel port; it surrendered in the following year.

An epidemic then overwhelmed the combatants, when bubonic plague from Asia brought death and despair to the whole continent. It reached Normandy by July 1348. Farmers collapsed in their fields and ships with dying crews wrecked themselves on the shore. Although gambling and drinking were banned in Rouen to deflect the wrath of God, the population of Normandy was roughly halved in less than a century. The most learned doctors of Paris agreed that the pestilence was due to an unfavourable conjunction of the planets, but bacteriological reality made rat-infested ships ideal vehicles for the disease, and it vaulted the Channel almost instantly. An English campaign in southwestern France captured King Jean of France in 1356, and shipped him to Plymouth. He was ransomed four years later in exchange for four million gold pieces and the surrender of southwestern France to England.

When the English next invaded France, their first objective

was Harfleur on the Seine. When dawn broke on August 18, 1415, there were many hundreds of English ships off Cap de la Hève, and ten thousand men began going ashore on a beach where Le Havre now stands. Harfleur held out for more than a month, despite the breach in the town's western wall where the English King Henry V urged on his troops, according to Shakespeare:

> Once more unto the breach, dear friends, once more;
> Or close the wall up with our English dead.

A more ironical account of the siege of Harfleur, written in the year it happened, is the earliest known description of a tennis match. Tennis was invented by monks of northern France in the twelfth century, and the events at Harfleur are scored, at fifteen–thirty and so on. The peculiar numbers used in tennis trace back to a coin worth fifteen French pennies; the monks evidently played for money. And the name of tennis comes from the French cry *Tenez!* meaning "Catch!" Eventually Henry won the match at Harfleur, but dysentery depleted his army, and the delay put him so far behind schedule that he could no longer think of attacking Paris. He decided to march his troops up the coast to Calais, which was still in English hands. When the French tried to stop him his archers massacred them.

Henry V was soon back on the Seine for a more systematic conquest. He cut off Rouen's supplies by land and river, and the starving city surrendered in January 1419. Henry died of a fever beside the Seine near Paris three years later, believing that he had won the Hundred Years War, thanks to Isabella of Bavaria. She was the wife of the French King Charles VI, and she often had to rule for him because he was given to bouts of madness. Isabella parleyed with the English king and in 1420 concluded the Treaty of Troyes, which named Henry as heir to the French throne. She signed away the rights of her own son, the dauphin, and her daughter married the English king. Charles VI died in the same year as Henry, and Isabella's infant English grandson was legally king of both France and England.

A union greater than the Angevin empire might have come

of this, but the French answer to Isabella of Bavaria was Joan of Arc. The peasant girl gave lectures on kingship to the dispossessed dauphin, and rallied his army to a series of victories over the English. Even after her cruel death at Rouen in 1431, the French continued to win. They recovered Paris in 1436, by which time Isabella had been dumped unceremoniously in her grave. In 1449 they recaptured Rouen. The English still held much of Normandy, and sent reinforcements via Cherbourg to stiffen the defences of Caen. These were waylaid by French cannons on April 15, 1450, at Formigny, near Omaha Beach. Caen fell in June, and by August all of Normandy was restored to France.

The English monarchs would go on calling themselves "King of France" until 1801, but it was a legal fiction. Among peoples with similar emulsions of German and Celtic blood, two separate and very different nations were in the making. An edict of 1539 made Francien, Frankish French, the official language of all France.

The new port of Le Havre had been opened in 1518, and it was from here that King Francis dispatched a fleet of 225 ships for an invasion of England in July 1545. Seeking revenge for the English capture of Boulogne the year before, he staked everything on a frontal attack on the English naval base of Portsmouth, where King Henry VIII had eighty ships. The English fleet held off the French for a month, in encounters at Portsmouth and Shoreham, while disease took a terrible toll on both fleets. The French ships returned to Le Havre full of dying men. In the end, Francis bought back Boulogne from Henry VIII for two million crowns.

Commercially, the early sixteenth century was a grand era on the Seine. The merchants of Rouen joined with the shipbuilders and privateers from Dieppe, farther up the Normandy coast, to trade "to the ends of the Earth" in the wake of Portuguese and Spanish discoverers. In an early attempt at colonization, a party left Le Havre in 1555 and tried to settle near Rio de Janeiro, only to be driven off by the Portuguese. Another group eight years later was wiped out by the Spanish in Florida. More successfully, Samuel de Champlain, a Dieppe man, sailed from Honfleur in 1608 to establish a permanent French colony in Canada.

·   ·   ·

On July 14, 1789, Parisians raided the armory on the left bank of the Seine and crossed to the right bank to storm the Bastille. So began the French Revolution and, down the river, Normandy was seized by the *grande peur,* the "great fear." Peasants took up arms to protect themselves against marauding bands of unemployed youths, but were soon using them to destroy the feudal records that kept them in bondage to their lords. Three years later France became a republic, and revolutionary committees ran the country. The deposed king was beheaded in 1793. Normans rebelled against Parisian rule in an unsuccessful bid for a federal regime, and the Seine River was one of the escape routes for aristocrats and dissidents fleeing the guillotine.

The revolution was obviously democratic in inspiration, and many liberal-minded people in Britain regretted the outbreak of war with revolutionary France as a reactionary effort to defend an outmoded form of government. But the war acquired legitimacy, in British eyes at least, as French democratic fervour evolved into militaristic nationalism. The armies mobilized to defend the revolution conquered France's neighbours. The struggle gave Napoleon his chance to seize power, and by 1800 the naval administrator at Le Havre was his appointee. Although Napoleon was an enlightened despot who modernized France, his enemies thought him a dangerous monster, and were at pains to deny him the mastery of the world.

Invaders came again to the Seine in September 1870, when the newly united Germans occupied Rouen during the Franco-Prussian War. They cut off Paris from the sea, besieged and took the capital, and held on to northern France until the French had paid for the war. The second German assault, in 1914, was stopped before it reached the Seine, but the third, in 1940, was overwhelming. The panzers broke through to the English Channel at the Somme estuary, and Rouen fell on June 9. Erwin Rommel's 7th Panzer Division trapped and captured forty thousand French and British troops on the coast between Dieppe and Le Havre. He took Le Havre on June 14, the day when other German troops entered Paris unopposed. Rommel then raced across Normandy to Cherbourg.

The French government had retreated to southwestern France, and on June 16, 1940, Winston Churchill made an astounding offer. He proposed an indissoluble union of France and Britain. Paul Reynaud, the French prime minister, wanted to accept the offer and stay in the war. His cabinet did not care for the proposal, nor did his mistress, the Comtesse de Portes. She wrote Reynaud a note: "I hope that you are not going to play at being Isabella of Bavaria."

Next day, the French government asked the Germans for an armistice. British raiders set fire to the oil tanks of Le Havre to deny them to the Germans. For similar reasons, the British navy attacked and destroyed French warships at their North African bases in French North Africa on July 3. The Germans told the French that the English were the real enemies, who had deserted them and then slaughtered Norman and Breton sailors. But when British troops cleared the Germans from the mouth of the Seine in September 1944 the French seemed glad enough to have *les boches* ejected.

At Le Havre in 1984, British refrigerated trucks rolling off the cross-Channel ferries were hijacked by militant Norman farmers who attacked the meat they were carrying. They sprayed it with dye or simply let it defrost. Breton farmers ceremonially set fire to English pork and smashed English eggs. Bickering over budgets and quotas for agricultural products within the European Economic Community stirred atavistic feelings.

Uranium River

The white chalk cliffs of High Normandy stretch relentlessly ahead, precipitating into the English Channel for sixty sea miles, from the tanker port of Antifer as far as the seaside town of Ault, just beyond the boundary of Normandy. All the way, the cliffs run monotonously ninety metres high, which makes navigation awkward. It is easier at night, when the clifftop lighthouses of Antifer, Ailly, and Ault show you where you are.

To American eyes accustomed to geology on the grand scale, the white wall of High Normandy is nothing much, but to the English it is alien. The famous cliffs of Dover are much more compact than all this. The English coast of the Channel is less crooked than the French, yet far fussier as to detail, giving different scenery around every corner. By contrast, the French coast is a succession of monolithic blocks: granite in Brittany and the Cherbourg peninsula; Jurassic hills in Seine Bay; chalk cliffs in High Normandy; then sand dunes fronting the chalk in Picardy. After a brief burst of geological variety in the Dover Strait between Boulogne and Calais we shall reach the broad marshlands of Flanders. The monotony continues far inland. The chalk of High Normandy makes a plateau for most of the way towards Paris, as flat farmland without trees, except for a few planted as wind breaks.

The cliffs have a Gallic grandeur, and a sailor is respectful. Strong onshore winds make it a dangerous lee shore with very few refuges where a boat can look for shelter. Only Dieppe, far to the east, is reasonably safe to enter in all conditions. Smaller ports and villages nestle in notches in the cliffs, called dry valleys or *valleuses*. Chalk is soft and water normally percolates into it, dissolving it away rather than carving valleys. But during the Ice Ages the moisture froze in the surface layers of chalk. The swelling ice shattered the chalk and also made it impermeable to rain and meltwater. Small streams carried the chalk fragments away, creating the valleys that have since dried out. Several of them are now cut short. They used to come down to sea level, but erosion of the cliffs has left the valleys hanging in midair.

The sea has carved a tall arch in the cliff at Etretat. The narrow dark layers that decorate the chalk like lines of print on white paper are made of flint nodules, which the French call *silex*. The glassy silica was excellent material for Stone Age toolmakers, and for much more recent builders of cottages on the chalkland. Flints are supposed to be fossilized burrows of marine animals that lived in the chalky sea bed while dinosaurs were trotting around ashore. The neat alternations of flint and chalk form fairly regular patterns, corresponding with fluctuations in the Earth's climate long ago. When the chalk erodes and disperses, the heavy flints pile up like nobbly potatoes on the beach.

The wet valley of the Valmont River interrupts the cliffs at Fécamp, a friendly port that you can enter if the tide is high enough and the wind not too strong from the west. It lies at an ancient joint in the Earth's crust, and by tradition it is France's main cod fishing port. Fécamp is a workmanlike town, devoted to its fishing fleet and the manufacture of Benedictine, invented by a sixteenth-century monk who collected clifftop plants and distilled an aromatic brew from them. Earlier monks of Fécamp owned Hastings across the Channel when William the Conqueror headed that way. Although the forbidding cliffs have left this chalk coast with only footnotes to history, it has suddenly become important, and very much a part of the modern world.

Beyond the valley at Vaulettes, in a terraced amphitheatre four hundred metres wide, excavated in the white cliff, stands a row of four domed cylinders in white concrete. Four metallic halls, half the height of the domes, glint even on this cloudy day. The scene looks like the set for a science fiction movie to be called *The Alabaster Planet*.

The open side of the amphitheatre has what you might mistake for a miniature harbour, complete with protective breakwaters. It is not a desirable place to enter, because a pumping station there is gulping in sea water at ten thousand tons a minute. From a man-made spring in the sea bed, half a mile offshore, the same water gushes out, warmer by more than ten degrees Celsius, to mix with the tidal currents. This is *la centrale nucléaire,* the large nuclear power station of Paluel. The domes house the four reactors, and the halls contain the turbogenerators. The Channel supplies the cooling water for condensing the steam that drives the turbines.

The westernmost reactor at Paluel started operating here at the end of 1984. It was the first of a new generation of pressurized water reactors of a French design, each delivering 1300 megawatts of electricity. The last of the four reactors, coming into service in 1986, brings the total output from Paluel to 5200 megawatts, equivalent to twenty Rance tidal power stations working flat out. It is also three times the combined capacity of two separate British

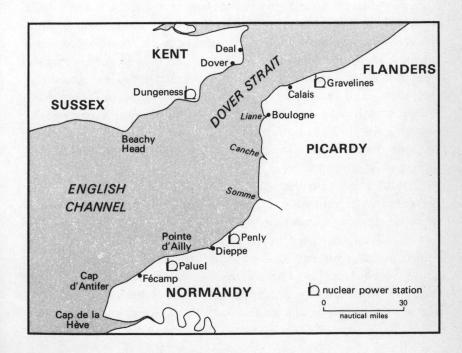

nuclear power stations on Dungeness, seventy sea miles across the water. And powerful as it is, Paluel is only one of a string of French nuclear power stations that are turning the English Channel into Uranium River.

The French are single-minded in their pursuit of civil nuclear energy, and obtain more of their electricity this way than any other country. For them there has been no agonizing over the accident at Three Mile Island that hobbled the U.S. nuclear industry, nor the interminable public inquiries that take place in Britain whenever nuclear installations are proposed. The long-term problem of disposing of highly radioactive waste does not deter them, because they have a system for turning it into glass.

France does not have Britain's access to North Sea oil, nor comparable reserves of coal, so the French do not think they have the luxury of choice and controversy. In any case, it is cheaper to generate electricity from uranium than from coal or oil. While other nations go on investing in big coal-burning and oil-burning power stations, this country aims to obtain seventy per cent of its electricity from nuclear energy by 1990.

Four giant nuclear power stations along the Channel shore will provide between them a quarter of the country's nuclear capacity. One *centrale nucléaire* is "down the river" on the west coast of the Cherbourg peninsula at Flamanville, near Cap de la Hague. Another is "upstream" beside the Dover Strait, at Gravelines near Dunkirk. And two of them are in the chalk of High Normandy. Paluel's twin is under construction at Penly, some twenty miles ahead. This nuclear programme is the most ambitious engineering venture on the French shore of the Channel since the building of Cherbourg harbour.

Remember also the tall chimney at Cap de la Hague, over-looking the Alderney Race. That was our landmark for the nuclear reprocessing plant, which is one of only two factories in Europe that handle spent fuel from any country on a commercial basis. Other people's nuclear washing comes to these laundries. Hot fuel from Sweden or Japan arrives by sea at Cherbourg, packed in massive steel containers, and goes overland to La Hague. The factory extracts plutonium and gathers the noisome radioactive byproducts for disposal. The plutonium goes into strong rooms to wait for the plutonium-burning fast reactors of the future. The plant at La Hague is smaller than the British plant beside the Irish Sea, but it is rapidly expanding to keep pace with the French power programme.

There is little opposition to civil nuclear power in France, outside Brittany. In England local objectors seem to want nuclear power stations to be sited anywhere but on their own patch. In France it is quite the opposite. Other communities are jealous of those blessed with nuclear stations, and the jobs and cash that they bring. In the chosen districts, any delay in starting work provokes an outcry. Prudent communes invest the money in new industries that will keep full employment going when the building phase is over.

From the French point of view, the worst environmental risk on the Channel and its shores comes from the river of oil that flows past their coast in supertankers to meet other peoples' energy needs. Despite a fire and two radiation leaks at La Hague in 1980, they have a far cleaner record than the British in respect of nuclear contamination of Europe's coastal waters. After thirty years spent pulling up a large nuclear industry by its bootstraps, the French want the payoff.

The nuclear programme is very much a product of what Breton nationalists call Superfrance. Since the time of Louis XIV, the country has been run like a single ranch, and its fortunes have depended on the quality of its managers. The elitist *écoles* of Paris turn out men groomed for service in government and industry, where they collaborate in a technocratic fashion to get things done. Their self-confident unity of purpose is almost Japanese. By French standards *les anglo-saxons*, British and American, hamstring their engineers by diffuse and contradictory decisionmaking, and seem to keep losing their nerve. The French have found the British to be unreliable partners in technological ventures, including the Concorde supersonic airliner, which the British wanted to cancel, and the Blue Streak space launcher and a Channel Tunnel project, both of which were abandoned by the British after work had already started.

Thirteen sea miles beyond Paluel, past the dainty *valleuse* port of Saint-Valéry-en-Caux, is Pointe d'Ailly, a tumbledown headland. Chalk erodes cleanly, producing sheer white cliffs, but at Ailly the chalk is thickly overlaid with younger and darker deposits. The undermining of the chalk at the water's edge has allowed the upper layers to collapse in a disorder of sand, clay, and soil, down to the beach. Among the debris are the stones of an old lighthouse, which fell over the edge at Ailly in 1965. The engineers who built it, in 1775, were well aware that the headland was fragile, so they put it 175 metres inland from the clifftop. That gives a measure of the rate of erosion: France is shrinking here at ninety centimetres a year. The new lighthouse, with its smart green dome on a dumpy square tower, should be good for another few centuries. The engineers at Paluel shrug off the effects of cliff erosion, because the economic life of their nuclear power station is only forty years.

After Ailly, the breakwaters of Dieppe protrude from the mouth of the Arques River. The estuary demolished the cliffs to the west of the town but left a fine chalky headland immediately to the east, called the Pointe de Femme Grosse—the Fat Woman. This little Rome of the chalk empire keeps its charm because it was always a footnote. Although Dieppe is big enough to prosper as a fishing and ferry port, the embracing chalk has saved it from any grander commercial or strategic role. Its maritime heyday was in the early sixteenth century, when Verrazano sailed from here to discover New York, and privateers led by Jean Ango ranged to Brazil, Africa, and the East Indies, preying on Portuguese shipping.

The river that gives Dieppe its opening to the sea follows the Bray fault, which launches itself into the sea at Dieppe and runs northwestward across the floor of the English Channel. It seems to be virtually inactive. Only very weak earthquakes have been detected in this region . . . one reason for siting the nuclear power stations here. The dry valley containing the Penly nuclear station is five miles beyond the Dieppe breakwaters. Work began on its reactors six years later than at Paluel, and they will not be operational until 1991. Located on either side of Dieppe, Paluel and

Penly give the old port a new role in life, at the heart of the Channel's nuclear industry.

The industry has to ship its uranium, spent fuel, and plutonium via the Channel. The full extent of the nuclear trade came to light in August 1984, when a French uranium-carrying ship, *Mont-Louis,* collided with a cross-Channel ferry in the Dover Strait, and sank off the Belgian coast. Salvage experts laboured in bad weather for six weeks to recover the canisters of uranium hexafluoride from the sunken ship. Meanwhile, the Belgian government and Europe's maritime pilots joined the environmental groups in the chorus of protests. The French had registered the cargo as "medical supplies" and warned no one of its true nature.

The French uranium, orginating from Canada, was on its way to the Soviet Union to be enriched for sale to West Germany. By the time the nuclear industry had completed its usual slow striptease, Channel voyagers learnt that uranium travelled routinely in passenger ferries between England and France. Spent fuel on its way to the reprocessing plant at La Hague is the most worrisome cargo from the point of view of radioactive hazards, but some of the plutonium extracted from the spent fuel is suitable for making weapons, and so has to be protected against nuclear pirates. When the ship *Seishin Maru* left Cherbourg late in 1984, carrying French plutonium to Japan, she had soldiers aboard, and French, American, and Japanese warships had to take turns escorting her to the other side of the world—a foretaste of new naval duties if the world adopts a plutonium economy.

The ninety-metre cliff is coming to an end, and brown silt in the sea announces the presence of the Somme River. The last broad gap in the cliffs is at Le Tréport, a miniature Dieppe. What seems to be a headland, complete with a lighthouse, appears ahead at the small seaside resort of Ault. It looks like a corner, where you might turn sharply to the right, following the edge of the chalk into the estuary of the Somme. On the contrary, the Picardy coast is swinging left across our bows, and this is no place for the unwary. Beyond Ault, the very low coast becomes difficult to make out on a grey day. The Somme estuary is a sea of mud when the tide is down, and the shallows are fronted with banks made of such fine sand that they are forever on the move. You can't chart them, and they won't hold an anchor. Masters of ships bound for the Somme ports are told that the pilot boat may be unable to come out in rough weather, in which case they should put into Le Tréport or Dieppe and wait for the fisherman-pilot to come to them by road. The *Dover Strait Pilot* warns that ships running aground will break their backs or capsize in the mobile sand. The wrecks of those that have already done so add to the hazards.

Out at sea there are other obstacles. The water has been getting shallower ever since Dieppe, and off Somme Bay there are large sandbanks made of broken shells. They do not rise very near to the surface, but the waves feel them, and break violently in bad weather. Even if you go ten sea miles out, you may hesitate to anchor because there is a minefield left over from World War II. One way and another, the Somme makes a perilous concavity in the Channel shoreline.

Astern of us, to the west, the sea is gaining on the land and undermining the lighthouses on the chalk cliffs. In Picardy the land is gaining on the sea, by means of the vast deposits of sand and mud. Nine hundred years ago, when William the Conqueror's fleet was driven into the Somme during his delayed invasion of England, the estuary was much broader and deeper. The lighthouses of Cayeux and Le Hourdel now rise like chimneys from a spit of new land thirty square kilometres in extent.

The older towns rest on firmer ground, here in Picardy, just as they do in Holland. Saint Valery came this way at the end of the sixth century, and settled on a bleak pimple marked by a chapel. Another hillock, eastward from the river mouth, supports the town of Saint-Valéry-sur-Somme and its medieval ramparts. Porte Guillaume, William Gate, faces the sea just as William the Conqueror did, while waiting for a fair wind for England. Poor Valery's were the bones he disinterred for his windmaking magic.

Here it is the dismal silt, rather than bright chalk, that relegates the coast to the footnotes of history. But inland, where the hills resume north of the Somme, is the forest of Crécy where, in 1346,

English arrows wiped out the noblemen of France. The French king fled, and the English went on to capture Calais. The French nobility took far too long to learn respect for the English long-bows. During the Hundred Years' War, there were replays of the Crécy battle at Poitiers (1356) in western France, and again at Agincourt (1415), just thirty kilometres beyond Crécy, where another English army making for Calais inflicted another crushing defeat.

That left a lot of work for young Joan of Arc to do, in her dazzling two-year campaign that broke the English grip on France. In 1430 she finished as a prisoner at Le Crotoy, a former island just across the Somme estuary from Saint-Valéry—a forlorn spot, then as now. Joan's captors were Burgundians. The English could not afford to let anyone say that Joan's victories were inspired by God, and they wanted her tried as a heretic. They bought the girl from the Burgundians for ten thousand francs. The eighteen-year-old generalissima's last journey was across the brown water of the Somme to Saint-Valéry, and thence to Rouen, where they burned her alive.

During World War I small ships brought supplies up the Somme River to the British troops holding the line alongside their former enemies, against the German invaders. The machine gun was an innovation deadlier than the longbow, and this time it was the British generals who were slow to learn. They carefully planned their greatest military disaster at the Battle of the Somme, a hundred kilometres upstream. On the morning of July 1, 1916, sixty thousand young men in good health climbed out of their trenches to walk towards the German lines. The machine guns mowed them down like grass. When the battle ended four months later, the combined Allied and German casualties had passed the million mark. That was a long time ago, and it is only imagination that the water pouring through the sluice at the bridge at Saint-Valéry is the colour of blood.

The sandy coast of Picardy runs northward from the Somme in an undeviating fashion for thirty-five sea miles, as if it were trying to reach England. At Le Touquet, a resort town standing on new ground at the mouth of the Canche River, the sea boils when the tide is ebbing into a strong wind. The estuary dries out, but on a rising tide you can follow the fishing boats into Etaples, which was a port in Roman times. If you continued up the Canche you would come to the ramparts of Montreuil, embellishing a hill where the river bends. It was first fortified 1100 years ago and rose to become a great city and port. Still called Montreuil-sur-Mer, it is now an inhabited ghost town, deserted by its *mer*. This coast has lost its ports, and gained pine forests instead.

The sandland comes to an end at Cap d'Alprech, where the high ground that has shadowed us inland returns to the sea, but not as chalk. The brown cliffs are built of older rock. Beyond the headland the ground of northern France has been hollowed into a clayey, wooded cavity dotted with hills made of remnants of the chalk. This is the Boulonnais, and just beyond Alprech the port of Boulogne launches its large breakwaters onto a sea bed of Jurassic rock, 150 million years old, which extends in a broad band almost as far as the English coast.

The first sign of England is just a slight mismatch between sea and sky on the northern horizon, but the Hovercraft ferry from Dover, roaring towards Boulogne, has travelled only twenty-five miles. The French coast continues northward towards Cap Gris-Nez, at the narrowest part of the sea. A square white tower far from the shore is the bridge of a supertanker heading northeastward through the Dover Strait.

The odour of Boulogne tells you that it is France's busiest fishing port. The old fortified city, the *ville haute,* rises behind the harbour, and it is crowned by the nineteenth-century cupola of the cathedral. A tall column on a hill north of Boulogne marks the camp of the Grand Army, assembled at Boulogne for Napoleon's bid to capture England. As recently as 1940, this port at the mouth of the Liane River was a major base for Hitler's Operation Sea Lion, another projected invasion of Britain.

Julius Caesar founded Boulogne for that very purpose. The harbour was a catapult aimed at Kent, well placed to loose armies across the Dover Strait. The breakwaters of modern Boulogne enclose three kilometres of coast in a man-made anchorage, but they were unnecessary in Roman times. Two thousand years ago the cliffs to the north and south of the Liane River mouth extended farther into the sea, creating narrows at the entrance. The southern headland, stretching north from Cap d'Alprech, was known to classical geographers as *Ition,* and it gave Boulogne its first Roman name: *Portus Itius*.

The headland sheltered the estuary, which was much broader and deeper than it is today. When the Romans occupied the area in 57 B.C. the inhabitants were living on the peninsula on the left bank, under the lee of Ition. The right bank where Boulogne now stands was unoccupied; at any rate, no pre-Roman remains have been found there. Nevertheless, the low hill supporting the medieval city, the *ville haute,* had a Celtic name rendered by the Romans as *Bononia*.

Caesar raided Britain twice, which meant four crossings of the Dover Strait, out or back. Sean McGrail of Britain's National Maritime Museum has analysed them, and rates Roman seamanship as generally sound. All of the crossings were made at night. Caesar's pilots took advantage of favourable tidal currents, and avoided the chief hazard of the Dover Strait, the Goodwin Sands on the English side. Except on one occasion when the wind failed him, Caesar made his landfall soon after sunrise—the best possible time. He also arrived at his landing place, on three out of four occasions, at the time of high water. Even so, Caesar's first raid, in 55 B.C., was a military failure, and one reason was the lack of an adequate port of embarkation.

A warship was sent to scout the possible landing beaches for this first raid, while Caesar assembled his troops near Cap Gris-Nez and brought his main fleet up-Channel from Brittany. Two legions of infantry were to cross the Dover Strait in eighty ships from east of Gris-Nez, and cavalry in a further eighteen ships from another embarkation point south of Gris-Nez. The cavalry missed the tide. By the time the horses were embarked the current was flowing strongly away from Britain, and subsequent high winds prevented the cavalry landing to support the infantry.

Caesar and his foot soldiers pressed on without them. He

arrived off Dover at about 9 A.M., at low water. The Celts lined the white cliffs, which carried a large hill fort. The Roman fleet anchored off Dover for six hours, waiting for tidal currents to change direction and carry them eastward and northward to Deal, where the cliffs came to an end.

When they moved off, with a favourable wind as well as a fair stream, the Celtic chariots shadowed them. Arriving at Deal in the evening, at high tide, the Roman warships could row high onto the beach, like makeshift tanks, to provide firepower to cover the landing. The ships carrying the infantry then moved in, but the troops hesitated, and Caesar could see why.

> The size of the ships made it impossible to run them aground except in fairly deep water; and the soldiers, unfamiliar with the ground, with their hands full, and weighed down by the heavy burden of their arms, had at the same time to jump down from the ships, get a footing in the waves, and fight the enemy, who, standing on dry land or advancing only a short way into the water, fought with all their limbs unencumbered and on perfectly familiar ground, boldly hurling javelins and galloping their horses, which were trained to this kind of work.
> [Trans. S. A. Handford.]

The blue warpaint of the Celtic-British tribesmen added to their ferocious appearance. After an embarrassing pause, the eagle-bearer of the 10th Legion jumped into the water, and the other Roman troops followed. Caesar reported nothing about his casualties, but they may have been heavy. As is often the way in seaborne invasions, the troops of different outfits were mixed up in a confusion of boats. The Roman legions secured a beachhead, but they could not advance inland without cavalry support. The islanders' chariots were startling, and especially the acrobatics of the charioteers, who thought nothing of running out along the pole between the horses to strike a blow, and then nipping back into the car. The chariot was a deadly anachronism, a prehistoric battle tank perfected in western Asia some eighteen centuries earlier, but out of fashion for warfare long before the rise of Rome.

The Celtic charioteers were as surprising as armoured knights would be, if they turned up on a twentieth-century battlefield.

Even by the fifth day, attempts to land Caesar's horses were being thwarted by bad weather, and that night the high spring tide took the Romans by surprise. According to McGrail, this was their only major error of seamanship. The tide combined with strong winds to play havoc with Caesar's ships. Towards midnight, by the light of a Full Moon, the Celtic warriors laughed to see the rising tide swamping the Roman warships drawn up on the beach, and the anchor warps of the transports offshore snapping one by one. But when the Celts tried to exploit the disaster in an attack, the legions stood their ground, and the whole raid ended in a standoff. When Caesar withdrew to France after less than three weeks, the British tribes promised to send him some hostages. Few of them did.

Caesar then selected Boulogne's Liane River as a base from which the whole army could sail together for the second raid. He ordered the building of wider landing craft, with lower sides, which could be propelled by both sail and oars. Six hundred of them were built. Although some of these failed to turn up at the Liane in time for the embarkation, the Roman warships brought the total fleet assembled in Boulogne's river to eight hundred. The army consisted of about 17,000 men and 2000 horses.

The invasion fleet sailed at sunset, probably on July 6, 54 B.C., in a light southwesterly wind. At midnight the wind died, and impartially the tidal currents of the Dover Strait carried the Roman ships off course, far to the east. The soldiers had to row hard across the currents to reach the shore of Kent by noon the following day. This time the defending tribesmen did not line the cliffs and hills, and Caesar claimed that they were frightened by the sight of so many ships. More probably they had rethought their tactics, although it did them no good. The Celts were concentrated in an inland hill fort. The troops of the Roman 7th Legion locked their shields together over their heads, piled up earth against the ramparts, and stormed the place.

Rough weather at the beachhead again overtaxed the anchor cables, and forty ships were destroyed. By the time Caesar had organized their replacement, and the repair of the others, the Celtic tribesmen had regrouped under the leadership of Cassivellaunus. In the campaign that followed, the ferocity and dash of the Celts was no match for the stolid Roman army, which forced a crossing of the Thames River into Cassivellaunus's own territory. When a last attack on the beachhead failed, Cassivellaunus surrendered. Caesar sailed back to France with prisoners, tribute, and promises of good behaviour. He reported favourably on Britannia, noting its high density of homesteads and its cattle, timber, and tin. The base at Boulogne was further developed, with a view to conquering the island.

According to Claude Seillier, director of the Musée de Boulogne-sur-Mer, the Roman port was south of the *ville haute,* where sea water occupied much of the present land. On low ground between the *ville haute* and a stream flowing into the ancient harbour, a strip of land three hundred metres wide carried the headquarters of the *Classis Britannica,* the Fleet of Britain. The railway and a highway run across it now, and shops and cafés cover Roman graveyards. Seillier's museum lies athwart the Roman seafront road. Other busy boulevards, together with the railway station and the stadium, rest on land reclaimed from the estuary, and so does the district of Capecure, with the modern docks below the bridges that cross the present narrow river. In these places you walk over the anchorage where landing craft took on Roman infantry and cavalry bound for Britannia.

Julius Caesar's imperial successors built military roads to Boulogne. One coming from Amiens was on the direct route from Rome itself. Another went via Arras to Cologne on the Rhine, and this road helped to define the frontier between Roman Gaul and untamed Germany. A major linguistic boundary still runs due east from Boulogne, across northern France and Belgium, to Maastricht in the Netherlands. It separates French speakers in the south from Germanic-tongued Flemish speakers in the coastal strip of Flanders, which was never thoroughly Romanized.

Endless fighting with the Germans was one reason why the conquest of Britain was postponed for a century, and a further delay was due to the lanky psychopath, Little Boot. The young

Emperor Caligula came to Boulogne in A.D. 39 to lead an invasion in Britain. Like other sadists, he had no taste for honest warfare. The Roman historian Suetonius reported that Caligula made the legions line up in battle order along the shore of the Channel, complete with their siege engines. He then ordered them to gather seashells. Instead of embarking for Britain the soldiers found themselves filling their helmets and tunics with what Caligula was pleased to call plunder. Caligula declared that he had won a great victory over the sea, and promised the men four gold pieces each. He sent some of his warships to Rome for his expected triumph, and made tall Gauls dye their hair red to look like alien prisoners. To crown this madness, and mitigate it, Caligula called for the erection near Bononia of a large lighthouse that would rival the famous Pharos of Alexandria. The lighthouse duly arose on the northern headland at the mouth of the Liane River, and it came to be known in medieval times as the Tour d'Ordre. It fell in a landslide in 1644.

No tears were shed when two officers of the Imperial Guard assassinated Caligula. His lighthouse must have helped to guide warships when, under the stammering Emperor Claudius, the Romans at last accomplished their conquest of Britain. Suetonius was characteristically cool about the Claudian victory, calling it a campaign of no great importance. For an observer in Rome, that was a fair comment, but the event was notable in the history of the English Channel because it gave the Romans possession of both shores.

Sparse accounts of the landings in Britain in A.D. 43 leave the role of Boulogne obscure. Four legions took part, three of them originally stationed on the Rhine River, and the fourth brought from the Danube. The Romans themselves may have come to realize that the shortest crossing of the narrow seas was not necessarily the best. To insist on using the military roads to Boulogne just because they were there would have been wasteful of leg muscles and boot leather. The sensible way of launching the attack would have been to embark the troops on the Rhine, float them down the river, and then conduct them across the southern North Sea to the beaches of Kent, at England's southeastern tip. Even if that was what the invasion commander Aulus Plautius elected to do, Boulogne was probably the home port for the escorting warships. It was also well placed to become the main supply base for supporting the army in Britain, once it had safely landed.

From Boulogne the Emperor Claudius embarked to join his troops in Britain, taking with him a force of elephants that dismayed the British Celts. No trace has been found of a triumphal arch erected in Boulogne at Claudius's point of embarkation, but archaeologists have recovered large numbers of Roman bricks and tiles stamped "CLBR," for *Classis Britannica*. The Fleet of Britain set up subsidiary bases in Kent, first at the beachhead of Richborough, and, in A.D. 117, at Dover, which they called *Dubris*. The fleet also took charge of iron mines in Sussex, west of Kent. Boulogne remained its chief base. But in Seillier's opinion the *Classis Britannica* became less of a battle fleet and more of a ferry service for the Roman garrison in Britain.

German pirates began raiding the Channel coasts before A.D. 200, and by A.D. 230 they had forced the Fleet of Britain to abandon its British installations. Within half a century the Saxons had burned down Boulogne itself. The *Classis Britannica* had to be replaced by more mobile naval detachments operating in the Channel from well-defended bases, and the Romans fortified the *ville haute* at Boulogne. A Celtic general, Marcus Aurelius Carausius, was told to suppress the Frankish and Saxon pirates, but he was then accused of collusion with the pirates and with embezzling the booty from his battles. To save his neck, Carausius revolted and made himself emperor of Britain and the Boulonnais. That was in A.D. 286, and not until seven years later were the Romans able to recover Boulogne, after a siege in which they blocked the entrance to the port with stakes and stones.

The German tribesmen broke into northern France by land at the end of A.D. 406. Boulogne escaped destruction in the first wave of the assault, and friendly troops were able to land there from Britain two years later. But soon afterward the Germans burned it again, and put an end to Roman Boulogne.

Petroleum River

The view of the sea from Boulogne is misleading. It looks spacious enough, between here and England, but our ketch has been avoiding sandbanks all the way from the mouth of the Somme. Ridges built of sand and broken seashells stand on the sea bed like long ramparts. Their crests come to within a few metres of the sea surface. A small boat can pass over them without difficulty in settled conditions, but in rough weather the waves break on the banks, creating lines of white and violent water. Provided you know where they are, you can not only avoid them but find calmer water between the banks and the shore. A great crescent of sand, thirty sea miles long, blocked our passage northward off the Picardy coast, and forced us close to Cap d'Alprech. Another coastal bank runs north from Boulogne. More serious for the shipping are the great sand ridges scattered in the middle of the Dover Strait.

The sand ridges vary in length from six to thirty sea miles, and rise some twenty metres above the surrounding floor of the Dover Strait, running roughly in the direction in which the tidal currents ebb and flow. They are created and maintained by eddies in the tidal currents. It is a conspiracy of sand and water; the banks encourage the eddies. Between the ridges much of the sea bed is covered with sand waves, resembling the dunes in a windy desert. They vary in size, the largest of them being walls twenty metres high and hundreds of metres wide. On the chart they look like amoebas, and they are troublesome in the deep-water shipping lanes.

The Varne light vessel is the gatekeeper of the Dover Strait. Between Boulogne and Dover, somewhat nearer the English than the French shore, she rides to her anchors right in the middle of the lane allocated to westbound shipping. She warns of the sand ridge called the Varne Bank, which runs for six miles southwestward from the light vessel. At night a bright red flash every twenty seconds is the signature of the Varne light vessel. Halfway along the sandbank, on the English side, the green Mid Varne buoy, with a quick flashing green light, marks the summit where the sand lurks within four metres of the surface, as a menace to any sizeable ship. Under an older system of buoyage, the Mid Varne buoy was painted black, with a quick flashing white light. A maritime pileup beside the Mid Varne buoy provoked the change of paint, not only in the Dover Strait, but worldwide.

One Monday morning, January 11, 1971, the tanker *Texaco Caribbean* was rammed by the Peruvian cargo ship *Paracas,* which was proceeding up-Channel on the wrong side of the Varne Bank, against the recommended flow of traffic. An explosion tore the tanker in two parts, which then sank onto the gravel twenty-three metres beneath the surface, taking nine men with her. The twin wrecks of *Texaco Caribbean* created an alarming hazard in the main shipping lane, beside the Mid Varne buoy. Radio broadcasts to ships kept repeating the news of the event. The ship *Siren,* belonging to the English lighthouse authority, Trinity House, raced to the Varne, and before the winter night set in, she anchored as a temporary lightship. Putting the wrecks between her and the Varne Bank, she exhibited shapes and lights that in theory warned shipping to keep clear. The visibility that night was less than a mile.

Before dawn broke next morning, the German cargo liner *Brandenburg,* outward bound, passed the red flashing light of the Varne light vessel, travelling at high speed. She then passed on the wrong side of the Trinity House ship, and ran over one part of *Texaco Caribbean,* which tore her bottom like a can opener. The German ship sank at once, and although some fishing boats grabbed survivors who were swept towards them by the tide, more than half her thirty-one crew and passengers lost their lives.

Confusion and danger reigned at the Varne that Tuesday. There were now three wrecks close together, counting *Texaco Caribbean* as two. Trinity House ships brought supplies of green wreck buoys and a frigate arrived with antisubmarine sonar to pinpoint the wrecks. Despite the frantic activity off the Varne and increasingly strident warnings by radio, some ships persisted in crossing the danger area. By the Wednesday afternoon it was marked by six green buoys in a diamond pattern. At its sharp end, where the down-Channel shipping approached the area, a green-painted light vessel flashed a bright green light. All this had so little effect that the light vessel men lived in constant fear of being run down.

During the succeeding weeks of January and February 1971, the nightly scene was the Fourth of July, Varne version. While the Varne lightship and the Mid Varne buoy winked their usual red and white messages, the wreck area was ablaze with flashing green lights. As ships came rushing towards the area, in a nonstop

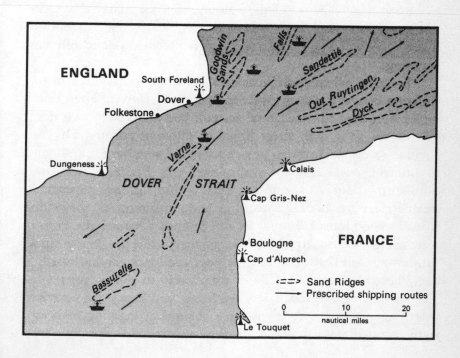

procession, the light vessel flashed warnings at them individually and loosed pyrotechnics. Many ships got the message, but others did not. After dark on February 27 the Greek cargo ship *Niki* struck the wrecks. She, too, sank quickly, with the loss of ten lives. There were then four wrecks off the Varne.

Trinity House doubled the number of green wreck buoys, and added a second green light vessel, so that the diamond area, two sea miles long, was virtually fenced off. The lifeboat service provided a fast inflatable launch that could sprint to meet oncoming vessels and address them by loud hailer. No further ships added themselves to the *Texaco Caribbean–Brandenburg–Niki* pileup, and the wrecks were hastily dispersed. But the events off the Varne caused a scandal among seafarers and especially in the International Association of Lighthouse Authorities.

Regardless of any lack of vigilance in some of the ships that violated the vividly marked danger zone, there were still many experienced and alert seamen who failed to understand what all those navigational marks meant, and which way they were supposed to steer. The use of the colour green for marking wrecks had been traditional in British waters for nearly two centuries. The trouble was that, in other seas, green often had a quite different meaning.

In 1971, when these accidents occurred, more than thirty different buoyage systems were in operation. Two different principles were applied. In a lateral system, you marked the two sides of a route, as if with street lights of different colours. Or you could use a cardinal system, which indicated whether a ship should pass north, south, east, or west of the buoy. Endless local variations from country to country, even within Europe, meant that mariners needed books displaying and explaining all the oddly shaped and coloured buoys. In the English Channel the French were using a mixed lateral-cardinal system, while the British stuck firmly to a lateral system, red for port and black for starboard.

There was ambiguity about which way to read a lateral system. In Europe if you passed a red buoy, you kept it on your left (port) hand if you were going up a channel or entering harbour. In the United States it was the other way around. Entering harbour, you left a red buoy on your right (starboard) hand—in accordance with the rule "right red returning." Applying that mnemonic in Europe is still one of the simpler ways in which Americans can drown themselves. A more subtle uncertainty concerned which direction was deemed to be "up the channel"—not an obvious matter in open waters like the English Channel or the North Sea. Worst of all, many mariners were accustomed to green paint and green lights meaning "Leave me on your right (or left) hand." It is little wonder that Americans, Russians, Germans, and Greeks were bewildered by the green lights at the Mid Varne, or that their near-instinctive reactions to warning signals failed to work correctly.

Reform of the buoyage had been on the international agenda since 1936. An agreement was drawn up under the League of Nations, but World War II put an end to that. In 1956 the International Association of Lighthouse Authorities started again, but matters of money and tradition were involved, and the political will was lacking until the Varne disaster. Then agreement followed with what (by diplomatic standards) was breakneck speed. Within five years, IALA's System A had been approved by the International Maritime Consultative Organization. It combines the best features of both the lateral and cardinal systems, and from 1977 it began coming into use in Europe, Africa, the Middle East, and Australasia. By 1980 IALA's System B, which retains the "right red returning" rule, had been approved for use in the Americas and the Far East. In both systems, green is a lateral mark (right hand in A and left hand in B). Green is emphatically not to be used for marking wrecks.

The first buoy of the new system was the Sandgate buoy, inshore from the Varne and close to the scene of the disaster. Tenders from France, Belgium, and the Netherlands, and the Trinity House flagship *Patricia* stood by, while the tender *Ready* lifted out the previous black buoy and replaced it with a black-and-yellow cardinal buoy. The international flotilla then adjourned to Dover harbour for a party. The years of conversion that followed were expensive for yachtsmen as well as for the lighthouse authorities, because everyone's books and charts had to be updated. But now one can sail anywhere and know to keep to the east of a black buoy with a yellow stripe, as our ketch is now doing, leaving Boulogne.

Low, ruddy cliffs, with hills behind, lead to Cap Gris-Nez. It rises fifty metres above the sea, and here the northward-running French coast turns sharp right. It is also the headland closest to England, being just 17.3 sea miles from the breakwaters of Dover harbour. Between 1940 and 1944 the Nazi invaders had long-range guns there, to terrorize British convoys sailing through the Dover Strait. When there were no ships to shoot at, they lobbed shells into the docks and town of Dover. Now Gris-Nez provides a vantage point for radar surveillance of the shipping passing the choke point that the headland itself creates.

The chief cargo flowing up the English Channel today is crude oil. Europe's industry and transport could not function without the daily transfusion of about a million tons of liquid fuel from the Middle East and other faraway parts of the world. Iron ore passes on its way from Brazil to the steel mills of Germany, Britain, and Belgium in specially strengthened ore carriers, while tramp ships bring grain for Europe's bakeries from the Great Plains of North America. But no commodity compares in volume with the cargoes of the VLCCs, the very large crude-oil carriers, or supertankers.

A centuries-old pattern persists, with food and raw materials coming eastward up the English Channel to nourish the stomachs and industries of northern Europe, while manufactured exports go the other way, down-Channel. When it comes to navigational rules and pollution control, these countercurrents of trade create an asymmetry in the Channel, to the disadvantage of the French. The worldwide maritime rule of driving on the right means that clean cargoes and empty tankers pass westward on the English side of the Channel, while inbound tankers, heading east with their dirty cargoes, travel on the French side. From Ushant to the Dover Strait, a combination of charted traffic lanes, shortest courses, and navigational prudence keeps the laden tankers well offshore. But as the Channel comes to its narrow funnel at the Dover Strait, the giant ships must pass within seven miles of the French shore. They also have to wriggle between the sandbanks.

Imagine that you are the master of a laden supertanker, bound from the Persian-Arabian Gulf to the refineries of Rotterdam in the Netherlands. You don't have to take on a deep-sea pilot to guide you through the sandbanks and the separation schemes of the Dover Strait, but pilots are available at Cherbourg on the French coast and Brixham on the English coast. The pilot may remain aboard for a week, taking the ship up to Rotterdam and then back again to his base. Collecting him from Cherbourg on the way in from Ushant is easy enough, but on the way out you will have to cross the inbound shipping to take him home to Cherbourg. If you use a Brixham pilot, the problem is the other way around. Critics are amazed that large ships have to dodge across the main shipping routes of the English Channel, either to pick up or to set down the pilot. The Dutch deep-sea pilots have set a better example to their French and English colleagues by using helicopters to board and leave their ships.

The deadweight of crude oil presses the bottom of a super-tanker twenty metres below the surface of the English Channel. That is a six-storey building searching out the bottom. At low tide the crests of some of the sand ridges lurk within a couple of metres of the surface, and in a storm they can be seen in the troughs of the broken waves. Careful zigzagging leads you comfortably between the western sand ridges and past Cap Gris-Nez, but when the Sandettié light vessel appears ahead, the trickiest part of the passage begins.

Most eastbound shipping swerves to the south of the Sandettié bank, through a wide but rather shallow lane. The deep-water route passes north of the Sandettié bank, and nerve-rackingly close to the westbound traffic lane. Here, in the throttle of the Dover Strait, a gap only four sea miles wide separates the Sandettié bank from the South Falls bank lying to the north. This opening has to accommodate all of the westbound traffic as well as the deep-draft eastbound ships. The separation zone between the traffic lanes is abolished because there is no room for it. Great ships lumbering in opposite directions pass each other at a combined speed that can reach thirty knots, with only a solitary yellow buoy to separate them, and a slanting line printed on the chart. The eastbound deep-water lane becomes just one mile wide. Having swung to port to get north of the Sandettié bank, you must promptly alter course to starboard to thread your supertanker through this needle's eye.

A mile may sound like plenty of room, but a large oil tanker is a sixth of a mile long. In the shallow water, an interaction with the bottom causes your ship to slew sideways as she turns. The modest course alterations of some twenty degrees, to port and then starboard, in the Sandettié slalom will each take five minutes to execute, during which time you will have travelled more than a mile through the water. If you wanted to stop to avert a danger, it would take you three miles and twenty minutes to come to a halt. Then you would be out of control. At low speed your rudder becomes ineffective and you are at the mercy of the wind, and tidal currents flowing at up to four knots. A few degrees of error in steering will put her on the sandbanks and break her open like an egg. A few minutes' mistiming of your turn can lead you into a head-on collision with the westbound traffic on your left.

Your crew have Channel Fever, a notorious cause of accidents. After the long voyage around the tip of Africa, they are already thinking more about the Dutch girls than the radar echoes. Apart from the westbound shipping passing close on your left hand, there may be other vessels travelling eastward with you in the deep-water lane, at different speeds. You all have your schedules to keep so, contrary to official advice, you may be overtaking, or being overtaken. The fact that ships are altering course around the Sandettié bank makes them tricky to plot. There are no stop-lights or flyovers on this watery highway, but the radar shows yachts, fishing boats, and ferries scurrying *across* the shipping lanes.

The high-speed ferries that ply between England and France make no obvious procession. There are several ferry ports on each side of the Channel, and permutations of routes: Calais to Dover, Boulogne to Dover, Boulogne to Folkestone, and so on. These ferries are skippered by men who know these waters and their dangers better than anyone else, and they cross the shipping lanes as the rules prescribe, at right angles. The glowing spots on the radar screen nevertheless represent vessels crowded with up to 1600 passengers. Some ships following the main traffic lanes imagine that they need not give way to ferries crossing the lanes. This is quite wrong—only fishing boats and small craft under twenty metres, like our ketch, are excluded from the normal rule that gives priority to ships coming from starboard. Ships coming up on a ferry's left side, which are supposed to keep out of her way but don't, are known to the ferry captains as "Port-hand Charlies." When one of these comes resolutely on, the only safe option for the ferry may be to turn a complete circle to starboard. This may confuse not only the passengers but all other ships in sight.

According to Captain John Arthur, the former commodore of the Sealink line, the worst difficulties on the bridge of a cross-Channel ferry arise from a contradiction in the rules. Those intended to prevent collision are at odds with the rules governing proper behaviour in the traffic lanes. A ferry approaching a lane that is carrying through traffic ought to alter course, to cross it at right angles, but she cannot do so if another ship is approaching from the port hand, which is supposed to give way to her. The anticollision rules require that the ferry, as the "stand-on" vessel, should "keep her course and speed." This may mean that the ferry slants into the shipping lane on whatever course she was following when the "give-way" ship came into view, in violation of the traffic rules. "The ferry master," Arthur says, "is conscious that the whole area is under surveillance."

Arthur and his fellow captains have been grumbling about this contradiction for years. It is like a flaw in a theorem of geometry. It creates uncertainty, confusion, and indecision, and seems certain to drown people. Problems can be resolved on a fine day by common sense and good seamanship, when all concerned can see what the various ships are trying to do. They become perplexing in fog, when the ships are reduced to echoes on a radar screen, moving in all directions. The worst accident in the Dover Strait that experts can visualize, by the way, would be a collision between a cross-Channel ferry crowded with passengers and one of those floating bombs that carry liquefied natural gas.

Given that the Dover Strait is fraught with shipping of every kind, shape, size, speed, and purpose, and vulnerable to bad weather and fog, collisions are surprisingly rare. Up to five hundred vessels a day use the Dover Strait. The air is full of voices, of ships' radios announcing their intentions or reporting snags, and of the French and English traffic surveillance staffs trying to keep some sort of order, warn of dangers, and identify rulebreakers who go the wrong way in a shipping lane, or slant across it to reach their destinations by the shortest route.

Radar surveillance of the Dover Strait dates from 1972, and traffic separation, which began on a voluntary basis in 1967, became compulsory in 1977. The number of collisions between ships going in opposite directions fell from ten a year in the period 1961–66 to fewer than one a year after 1976, and those that still occurred were in the inshore traffic zones where ships can go both ways. There was little effect on the number of collisions (about one a year) between ships heading in the same direction.

"We are the policemen of the maritime highway," says the young uniformed *administrateur-adjoint* at CROSS Gris-Nez, Philippe Marchand. The station's clifftop windows give a grandstand view over the Pas de Calais, the French name for the Dover Strait. CROSS stands for Centre Régional Opérationnel de Surveillance et de Sauvetage, and CROSS Gris-Nez is the most northerly of five centres for surveillance and rescue around the shores of France. The Gris-Nez centre co-operates continuously with the British Coastguard at Langdon Battery, across the water on the Dover cliffs. Gris-Nez and Langdon take it in turns to broadcast the information bulletins for all vessels in the Strait, which go out four times an hour. These report the weather, movements of supertankers, and other "large vessels constrained by their draft," peculiar operations such as cable laying or hydrographic surveys going on in the Dover Strait, defects in the buoyage system, and any violators of the traffic rules who pose a threat to other ships.

The big ships proceeding up and down the shipping lanes stand out clearly on the radar screens, and a memory trace shows their recent movements. The Thomson-CSF computerized system tags each vessel and deduces its position, course, and speed;

it also predicts where a ship will be in fifteen minutes' time if she continues on her present course and speed. The next development will be to teach the computer the rules of navigation, so that it will automatically pick out any ships infringing them. About four do so every day.

The delinquent vessels—rogues in British terminology, *contrevenants* in French—are usually easy enough to spot. But the "policemen of the maritime highway" lack the means to identify every offender, still less to compel her to alter course. And even given the name of the fishing boat, there would be no certainty that she would respond to radio instructions, or that any subsequent action would be taken against her. All that CROSS Gris-Nez can do is put in a report to the relevant Quartier des Affaires Maritimes. As one of the main tasks of Affaires Maritimes is to look after the interests of the fishermen, who have a lot of influence in the smaller ports, the skipper might get nothing worse than a quiet reprimand. If the offending vessel is foreign, any complaint has to go through the Foreign Ministry in Paris. In such a case, the ship's master is unlikely to suffer for violating the traffic rules in the Dover Strait. But watch out for the cross-Channel ferries if you are a rogue, because they have a strong interest in suppressing lawlessness in the Dover Strait, and will gladly broadcast your ship's name if they can read it.

Oil tankers and liquefied-gas carriers remain under special surveillance all the way up the English Channel. Under French law, when you bring a supertanker into French waters in the English Channel you must report into the CROSS system, and supply full information about your cargo, course, speed, and destination. You must also confess to any defects in your ship's equipment and maintain a continuous listening watch. Coming around the western tip of Brittany, you report first to CROSS Corsen-Ouessant. Then you are handed over to CROSS Jobourg, on the Cherbourg Peninsula. By the time you reach the Dover Strait, CROSS Gris-Nez is expecting you. If the radar on the clifftop is working at its maximum range, it will show echoes from your huge bridge sixty sea miles off. Tankers on the French side are therefore under much the same observation as passenger aircraft flying over a crowded continent. Unlike air traffic controllers, CROSS cannot tell them where to go.

Although surveillance of navigation represents ninety-five per cent of the work, another section of CROSS Gris-Nez monitors reports of pollution, due, for example, to tankers cleaning their tanks, but such offenders are even harder to identify than the traffic violators. And this section, with its own radar displays and radio facilities, maintains a listening watch on all distress frequencies. CROSS Gris-Nez is ready to help save your crew, should your ship come to grief in the Dover Strait. When a rescue operation is required on the French side of the Dover Strait, the centre co-ordinates it. In 1983 a hundred lives were saved in rescues supervised by CROSS Gris-Nez, twenty were lost, and twenty sick or injured seafarers received medical help at sea. But Marchand was modest about this aspect of his centre's work: "In matters of rescue, compared with CROSS Corsen-Ouessant we are little boys."

In an unexpected twist in relations between the French and the Anglo-Saxons, French maritime experts have been to the fore in pressing for the international recognition of English as the *de facto* language of the sea. Although the CROSS stations naturally talk with French vessels in French, and put out their information bulletins in French as well as English, nearly all of their dealings with foreign ships are in English. When the experts abandon their nation's policy of asserting the French language at every opportunity, they must have a good reason. It is to make sure that maritime English acquires some of the exactitude of French.

A native speaker of English may imagine that a conversation in broken English between a Frenchman and a Japanese tanker captain must be at best comical, at worst a generator of dangerous misunderstandings. But the French experts say that nonnative speakers get on quite well, because their vocabulary is limited and their questions and answers have to be simple and direct. The worst difficulties at sea arise with conversational English spoken by native speakers.

British and American seafarers regard the jargon of nautical English as a badge of their skill. But some elementary terms, including "hold," "bridge," "cable," and "warp," have alternative

meanings even in a nautical context. "Port" is one of the ambiguous words least obvious to a native speaker and most glaring to
foreigners; another is "channel," which may refer to a fairway for
shipping or a VHF radio channel. And how is a Brazilian ship's
officer who has studied his English in a book supposed to know
that we smart alecks pronounce "leeward" as "loo'ard" and "fore-
castle" as "fokesull?" As for "make fast," which means to make
secure, who would wonder if a Saudi captain thought he was being
told to speed up?

With changes in communications at sea, conversational English has become a menace that rivals storms and rocks. VHF radio
brought a massive switchover from Morse Code transmissions to
radio telephones. Spoken language replaced written messages, and
the words came at a hundred per minute instead of ten, allowing
less time for understanding. The native speakers were very chatty
and informal, just when stricter management of shipping needed
briskness and precision. The first move to bring linguistic discipline was the Standard Marine Navigational Vocabulary approved
by the Intergovernmental Maritime Consultative Organization
(IMCO) in 1977. Six years later Seaspeak emerged as a more radical
effort to clean up the English language.

Seaspeak is a joint effort of experienced seafarers and linguists.
Maritime experts at Plymouth Polytechnic transcribed many recordings of radio conversations at sea, and the Literary and Linguistic Computing Centre at Cambridge University analysed the
forms and vocabulary of the transmissions. On that basis, Seaspeak
was devised. It was sponsored mainly by a British publisher, Pergamon Press, but there was plenty of moral support and help from
official agencies. The practices of air traffic control had valuable
lessons. In Seaspeak, VHF procedures and repetitions are crucial
for understanding, and for checking that a message has been understood. For example, the phrase "Nothing more," when uttered
first by one party to the conversation, means "I have nothing more
to say, have you?" If the other party then says "Nothing more,"
that means "No, I have not."

Seaspeak goes much further in modifying the forms of ordinary English to construct spoken messages with the greatest

possible clarity. The speaker announces the character and status of a message at the outset: "Question. What is your cargo?" Instead of "Question," it might be "Information," or "Advice," or "Warning." To the inventors of Seaspeak, polite redundancies are abhorrent: "I wonder if you would mind giving me please a rough idea of when your E.T.A. might be?" We are told to stick to "Question. What is your E.T.A.?" By 1985 Seaspeak was under test at ports in several European countries, including Le Havre and Southampton in the English Channel. Several hundred ships took part in the trials. The aim is to have English in this tamed form adopted as the international language of the sea, first by the member nations of the European Economic Community, and eventually by all seafaring countries.

The Dam and the Tunnel

A reptile living in this part of Europe 300 million years ago would have seen a tall range of mountains filling the region of the English Channel. The northern edge of the mountains ran from just south of Cap Gris-Nez across to the English shore, and the ferry on her way from Boulogne to Folkestone is unknowingly tracing that ancient boundary in the Earth's crust. It is called by geologists the Hercynian front, a name that derives from the Harz mountains in Germany. The range extended grandly from the Channel region eastward into Poland and westward via Ireland as far as Kentucky. North America was at that time welded to Europe, and the mountains were the product of the collision with the huge southern continent of Gondwanaland. This was one of the chief events in the history of the Earth's land masses, when they were gathering to make a supercontinent. In those days a reptile could have walked from France to Australia.

Few visible traces of the Hercynian mountains remain in the vicinity of the Dover Strait. They have long since worn away and subsided, and younger sediments have been plastered over them. A memory of the old joint nevertheless persists in deep-lying rocks, as a line of weakness running beneath the Dover Strait. Blocks in the Earth's crust shifting in relation to their neighbours (upward, downward, or sideways) show a tendency to split and move parallel to the line of the old front. The crust is not entirely at rest, and earthquakes can still occur in the Dover Strait.

The northern face of Cap Gris-Nez, where the French coast

makes a sharp turn to the right, marks a fault line where the Boulogne block has risen up, bringing to the light of day the old, grey rocks that give Grey Nose its name. When the ketch rounds this corner, the last headland in France looms over her bows: Cap Blanc-Nez. White Nose, needless to say, is made of the faithful chalk. The Gris-Nez fault runs inland, behind Blanc-Nez, and the colours of the headlands are diagrammatic. Six sea miles separate them, and 60 million years of geological time. Blanc-Nez, too, has been uplifted, and the coastline beyond it contains much younger rocks.

Across the sea are the white cliffs of Dover. The chalk headlands facing each other across the Dover Strait are the stumps of a ruined chalk dam, which formerly joined Britain to France. Nature built the chalk dam between 50 and 20 million years ago, when Europe was being squeezed between Africa in the south and the widening Atlantic Ocean in the north. A zone of emphatic uplift followed the old Hercynian front, from this corner of France into southern England. It made a broad ridge faced with chalk and filled with clay and sandstone.

While the land rose, the sea level fell. Faraway Antarctica was running as a planetary refrigerator, and the present series of Ice Ages began some 3 million years ago. The main bed of the English Channel, away to the west, repeatedly dried out when ice sheets in northern Europe and North America stole the ocean's water. This happened perhaps thirty-five times at intervals of about ninety thousand years. For a long time the chalk dam remained intact, so that when the sea rose during warm interludes between the Ice Ages, it separated the English Channel from the North Sea. Land animals could walk freely between France and Britain, including the first human beings to show up in this part of the world.

Early traces of human beings in England are so few and so concentrated in time that archaeologists speak of "an afternoon in the Hoxnian" as the occasion when archaic members of the species *Homo sapiens* wandered into Britain around 230,000 years ago. A broken skull of a young woman found at Swanscombe, beside the Thames estuary, resembles other skulls of "archaic" *Homo sapiens* found in Germany dating from the same warm interval. Some of the pioneers who crossed the dried-out Dover Strait brought an Asian technology that used pebbles to make choppers and sharp flakes. Other people of a rival African tradition made hand axes, sharply pointed stones of the size and shape of the human hand, which they used as hunting weapons and tools. The two technologies overlapped in Europe, and both showed up in Britain. Archaeologists first discovered hand axes in France, at Saint-Acheul beside the Somme River, and as a result the worldwide name for the hand-axe technology is Acheulian.

The Neanderthalers who came here 128,000 years ago were not our ancestors, although they were successful hunters who left signs of their presence in Kent in the form of much improved stone tools. That warm interval brought subtropical conditions to the region of the English Channel, and hippopotamuses wallowed in the Seine and the Thames. Lions wandered northward, too, following the same game as the Neanderthalers. The newly evolved polar bears replaced them at the onset of the last Ice Age.

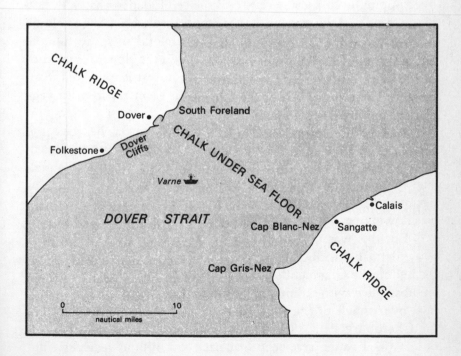

The chalk dam was put to the test at the end of each Ice Age. Before the rising sea flooded the bed of the English Channel, the North Sea was filled with fresh water, from melted ice and heavy rainfall. The remains of an ice sheet straddling the North Sea prevented the water from flowing away into the ocean. Instead, it rose perhaps sixty metres above the present sea level, flooding northern Europe as far as Russia, and pressing against the chalk dam, until the North Sea ice sheets melted and released the water.

Picture the stresses on the dam. Time and again, after successive Ice Ages, the glacial lake of the southern North Sea fills and empties. During the warm interludes, sea waves attack both faces of the dam, while fresh water seeks out underground weaknesses. During the Ice Ages, swelling ice magnifies any cracks near the surface.

The chalk dam fails suddenly. The glacial lake overtops it, and waterfalls attack the crest and the downstream slope of the dam with catastrophic effect. The greater the damage, the greater the rush of the water, and worse damage quickly follows. The overtopping occurs at the centre of the chalk dam—that is to say, in the middle of the present Dover Strait. It releases a huge volume of pent-up water. The ground shakes, a cloud of spray fills the air, and a jet of chalky water cascades down the slope. At the foot of the dam, birds screech and scatter as a forest is uprooted in an instant. The old dry bed of the Channel is soon aswirl with vegetation and drowned animals.

East of the Varne sandbank, a hollow in the bedrock 170 metres deep may mark the very spot where the Anglo-French Niagara carved its way from the North Sea to the English Channel. The main torrent rushed as a wall of water along the dried-out Channel, to link up with the Seine River, which until that moment was flowing peacefully past Cherbourg towards the Atlantic Ocean.

But this was no orderly event. According to Alec Smith, a geologist at Bedford College, London, a ragged network of valleys formed in the Channel floor when the dam burst. Many of them are now filled with sediments, but they show up in sea-bed soundings over much of the floor of the Channel, from Boulogne to the Cherbourg Peninsula. The date of the Channel dam burst is uncertain. It could have been a quarter of a million years ago, but sixty thousand years, corresponding with a mild spell during the most recent Ice Age, seems more likely. The first breach produced a gorge, and ice, rain, and waves have widened it to the present gap of almost twenty miles between England and France.

By the time of the last thaw, modern humans like ourselves had taken charge of the world, and you can imagine them living on the floor of the English Channel ten thousand years ago. They were not consciously occupying the future island of Britain, but were roaming across continuous terrain that happened to include it. As the rising sea slowly drove its tongues between the mainland and Britain, it may have seemed to the inhabitants of the Channel like a greedy monster that kept nudging them uphill and making sudden storm-driven incursions that killed large areas of their forests with salt. The Channel floor slopes so gradually upward from west to east that the beaches washed by the tides must have been very wide.

The average rate of advance of the sea was about 150 metres a year, and there was time to adapt. As people found themselves wading where they formerly paddled, and swimming where they had waded, they rode on logs and invented rafts and boats. The Dover Strait became a water barrier about 6500 B.C., and the sea was roughly at its present level by 3000 B.C.

Anyone who would like to terminate the English Channel at Blanc-Nez has geology on his side. As the port of Calais comes into view, with the low coastline of Flanders beyond it, we are slithering over the rim of one of the world's great basins. The North Sea is an ancient hollow created by a stretching and thinning of the continental crust, when Britain edged westward away from Europe. In the central rift valley of the North Sea the crust has dropped four thousand metres. Another rift valley, the Ruhr Graben, runs from Germany to the North Sea through the Netherlands, where the bedrock has subsided about one thousand metres. The hollow has been barely filled by the sediments from the Rhine, Maas, and Schelde rivers. The Low Countries of Belgium and the Netherlands are low because they are on a downgoing elevator, and it is at Blanc-Nez that the sinking feeling starts.

Between the upthrusts of Gris-Nez and Blanc-Nez and the downwarp of Flanders, something has to give, and the Dover

Strait is an earthquake zone. At 6 P.M. on April 6, 1580, the watchtower of Calais split, and half of it fell to the ground. Across the water, a piece of Dover Castle's wall fell into the sea. The earthquake's epicentre lay under the floor of the Dover Strait, nearer to France than England. By modern reckoning, it reached about 5.6 on the Richter scale of earthquake magnitudes; for comparison, the earthquakes at San Francisco in 1906 and Tokyo in 1923 were both about 8.2.

A tsunami flooded the Channel shores, but a contemporary report that the great wave overwhelmed thirty ships at sea may have been exaggerated. Towers and chimneys suffered along both shores of the Dover Strait, and minor damage occurred far inland, near Paris and in central England. In London, where church bells rang of their own accord, two teenagers were killed by falling masonry. ". . . 'Tis since the earthquake now eleven years"; Shakespeare's London audience would remember the panic of the 1580 earthquake, and that would set the first performance of *Romeo and Juliet* in 1591.

Two hundred years earlier, an earthquake had destroyed the bell tower of Canterbury Cathedral, in Kent. Others happened in southeastern England in 1750, and in Belgium in 1938 and 1983. These historical data have been gathered by Robert Muir Wood and Charles Melville. They have been trying for some years to have earthquakes taken seriously by the English, who think them as alien as belly dancing. The theory of plate tectonics at first reinforced the prejudice that England was an earthquake-free zone, because England was far removed from any active plate boundary. By the late 1970s the new geology had adapted to the idea that active faults could occur within continental regions, making earthquakes not only possible but inevitable. Nobody suggests that this region around the Dover Strait is as active as California or Japan, but the rarity of the events means that the inhabitants are unprepared for them.

Just beyond Cap Blanc-Nez is Sangatte, a seaside village distinguished by the tall, square belfry of its church. Calais is a few miles farther on. A green whistling buoy marks the start of a zone west and north of Sangatte where anchoring is forbidden on account of the submarine cables that come ashore here.

If you could drain the sea you would find that a broad ribbon of chalk begins on the sea bed just where the chalk comes to an end in the cliffs. It runs northwestward towards England and extends eastward beyond Calais. Chalk is ideal for tunnelling, and this is the sea-bed chalk nearest to England. As a result, Sangatte enjoys dubious fame among engineers as the French terminus of the long-discussed Channel Tunnel.

In August 1983 a bright yellow machine crawled out of the sea and up the Sangatte beach, flying the British flag. It was a 176-ton remote-controlled trenching machine that had cut its way across the Channel floor from Folkestone on the English shore, preparing the route for an electric power link between their two countries. It also caused complications in the busy shipping lanes. The barge controlling the trenching machine was protected by six buoys and two guard ships, but even so one ship missed it by only fifty metres. Although not quite in the same class as a Channel Tunnel, this venture of Electricité de France and the Central Electricity Generating Board was an expensive engineering feat, using new underwater technology. It was a culmination of more than a century of cable laying.

The first submarine cable for electric telegraphy was strung along the sea bed from Dover harbour to Cap Gris-Nez on August 28, 1850. A French fisherman destroyed it instantly. The engineers had exchanged the first cross-Channel messages and gone contentedly to bed when the fisherman found he had great difficulty in hauling up his anchor. It was fouled on what he took to be an unfamiliar form of seaweed. Not realizing it was copper wire coated in latex, he cut off a length of it as proof of his botanical discovery, and when the engineers woke up next morning they could not communicate. In the following year another cable was laid, and the public began using the submarine telegraph service on November 13, 1851. One of the first customers was Baron Reuter, founder of the famous news agency, who cabled stock market prices between Paris and London. By 1891 his successors could use the telephone.

Similar mishaps plagued the first attempt to connect the electricity supply networks of France and England. The Swedes had set the example by laying a direct-current power cable to an off-shore island, and a cross-Channel power link was established between Boulogne and Dungeness in 1961. Protocol required French and British ships to run a pair of cables from their own shores to a point in mid-Channel, where they were joined. But the cables lay exposed on the hard limestone and sandstone that paves the western part of the Dover Strait. The charts showed mariners where they lay, with a wiggly pink line, and warned them not to anchor or trawl nearby. On no account were they to cut the cable should they foul it. As the whole enterprise depended on a willingness of sailors to read small print, it was doomed.

The electric currents flowed well at first, but then the trawls and anchors began to damage the cables and the down times became progressively longer. After twenty years the link was declared dead. But it had proved the potential value of a reliable link, and ways were already being worked out for burying cables in trenches cut 1.5 metres deep into the sea bed. The first idea was to parallel the Boulogne–Dungeness route, but the rocks were too hard and uneven for the trenching machinery. The geology drove the Anglo-French engineers to the chalk and clay of the Sangatte–Folkestone route.

The niceties of international cooperation were met, in this project, by each country laying a pair of cables all the way across the Dover Strait. The French were first to lay their cables. Their sea-bed vehicle started from Sangatte in June 1984, and after hair-raising encounters with mines and bombs on the sea bed, the work was completed at Folkestone 120 days later. It had taken much longer than intended, and a fault was soon discovered in one of the cables off Cap Blanc-Nez. Meanwhile, the British had cut their trenches, but a mishap during trials delayed their cable laying until 1985. Schemes for repairing the cables include the use of an underwater "habitat" where divers can work at an ordinary air pressure on the sea bed.

Each of the two pairs of cross-Channel cables carries one thousand megawatts of power. Although this represents only a small part of the generating capacity of either country, the link is useful because it reduces the need on both sides of the Channel for spare electrical generating capacity to deal with emergencies and daily peak demands. The one-hour clock difference between France and England and varying domestic habits mean that the peaks occur at different times. In principle the power can flow in either direction to meet them. This, at any rate, is the use emphasized by the British engineers, but their associates see it rather differently.

For the French the cable link is the start of an export drive for selling the cheap electricity from the French nuclear power stations. While the British nuclear programme faltered amid public controversy and interminable inquiries, French electricity became thirty per cent cheaper than British electricity. The prospects seemed bright for sending power solely in one direction under the Channel, through this and any later power links. It is a droll outcome, seeing that the British are supposed to have the energy riches in their North Sea oil and vast reserves of cheap coal. Critics of nuclear energy in Britain will find themselves unavoidably using it when they switch on their lights, courtesy of Electricité de France and the link that runs under Uranium River.

If electricity can travel beneath the sea bed, why not people? To many foreigners, it seems odd that the French and the British have not managed to dig a Channel Tunnel long before now. After all, it has been discussed for nearly two hundred years. To regular users of the Channel, the need for it seems less compelling than it does to distant observers. The sea crossing from Dover to Calais takes only about an hour by modern car ferries. An umbilical cord would have symbolic meaning, linking England more firmly to Europe, but for symbolic reasons, too, the idea creates doubts among the English. The most compelling argument in favour of the Channel Tunnel is that it will cure seasickness.

The Dover Strait is Lake Vomitorium. More people travel across it than over any comparable stretch of agitated water. It is more often uncomfortable than dangerous. The height of the worst waves is only half what you can encounter off northern Brittany, and the violence of its tidal currents does not compare with the Alderney Race, which voyagers from England to the Channel Islands have to face. But the waves can be rough enough here, and also irregular, which many people find disagreeable.

The cliffs on either side of the Dover Strait intensify the wind by funnelling it, especially when it blows from the northeast. The waves bounce off the cliffs, and they are also deflected by head-lands, breakwaters, and shallows. As a result, one train of waves often crisscrosses another, producing humps and hollows in the water that cause boats to corkscrew. Long-distance waves, coming up-Channel or in from the North Sea, feel the relatively shallow bottom here and become steeper. Big waves break savagely on the sandbanks. And strong tidal currents flowing into the wind ("wind over tide") produce shorter and steeper seas.

London newspapers still publish forecasts of the state of the sea in the Dover Strait, but the schedules and reservations of the ferry companies make no allowance for it. Indeed, ferry captains pride themselves on maintaining their services in bad weather. The wind has to get up to storm force 10 before there are can-cellations.

Seasickness is a terrible private agony. Victims used to pray to Saint Elmo, who was martyred sixteen centuries ago by having his intestines taken out on a windlass. In medieval law, contracts made at sea had no validity because a victim of seasickness might agree to anything that would shorten the voyage. Everyone is different, because evolution has failed to prepare our species for its eccentric methods of travel, and each person's body and brain are left to make their own compromises with an unstable world. A great deal of medical research has gone into motion sickness on behalf of the fighting services, the airlines, and the manned space programmes, but they have not cracked it. More than half the astronauts in the first half dozen flights of the U.S. Space Shuttle suffered from what is politely called "space adaptation syndrome."

Seasickness starts in the brain rather than the stomach—that much is clear. Sensors deployed inside the ears send in data about motion and orientation, which the central nervous system matches with information from the eyes. The senses, brain, and body work together very efficiently on land. But start rolling, pitching, yaw-ing, bouncing, and corkscrewing in the Dover Strait on a windy day, and your brain is overtaxed, trying to make sense of unfa-miliar data. If the eyes show walls and tables like a house on land, the feelings of motion are a blatant contradiction of ordinary experience. That is why closing your eyes or getting on deck and looking at the horizon are standard precautions.

The motion continues—interminably, as it seems to the victim—and the strain begins to take on physical forms. Stress hormones pour into the blood, and the resulting pallor and sweating are very like the reactions of extreme fear. Then a short circuit occurs in the stem of the brain and stimulates the absurdly irrelevant vomiting reflex. Brain researchers have found all sorts of natural chemical agents that set our moods and stimulate or repress large networks of brain cells. If these neurotransmitters, as they are called, play a role in seasickness, that could explain the delay between the onset of the motion and the feelings of sickness. The chemicals may take time to accumulate.

The most practical remedy is to find your sea legs, which really means training your brain. How else did pressed men in the old sailing navies become competent seamen? The brain eventually copes with the bewildering sensory signals, and the extent of this adaptation becomes obvious when the sailor steps ashore. He feels the ground rolling under his feet, and sees solid walls moving. The brain learns much more quickly if you move about actively at sea than if you just sit. This is one reason why sailors seem immune to seasickness while the passengers are retching, and why women often think they are more vulnerable than men. But sailors are not a race apart in any physiological sense. On every ferry in the Dover Strait you will hear the words intended to restore the victims' self-esteem: "Admiral Nelson was seasick too."

So was Queen Victoria, and she gave her blessing to the idea of a tunnel under the Channel, "in the name of all the ladies of England." That was in 1858, when the French engineer Aimé Thomé de Gamond had already been working on the project for twenty-five years.

Thomé, a balding, middle-aged man of grave mien, carried out the first geological survey of the sea bed by repeatedly plunging naked to the bottom to collect samples. A rowing-boat, manned by a French pilot, Thomé's daughter, and a young assistant, bobbed about in the Dover Strait, while sailing ships and steamers scurried past. Thomé wore a turban to hold the lint, saturated with butter, to protect his ears. Ten inflated pigs' bladders girdled his waist for buoyancy, and four bags of flints served as ballast to drag him to the sea bed. Plunging twenty or thirty metres, like a graceless pearl diver, he would grope in the darkness for a geological sample, drop his ballast, and shoot spluttering back to the surface, all in less than a minute. On one dive a conger eel bit his chin.

In this rough and ready way, Thomé satisfied himself that no peculiarity in the geology would prevent the driving of a tunnel under the sea bed. He visualized a large-bore tunnel running from Cap Gris-Nez to East Wear Bay, between Dover and Folkestone. It would carry steam trains on two tracks and the smoke would escape from ventilating shafts rising above sea level in islands built of stone, each with its own lighthouse. The crowning glory of the scheme was to be the Etoile de Varne, a station at the Varne sandbank. Created for the work of driving the tunnel, the Etoile de Varne would later allow the travellers to break their journey, ascend to the surface, and admire the sea. It would also be a port for shipping.

Ventilating islands were unnecessary, according to engineers on the English side of the Channel. They favoured a pair of tunnels, each narrow enough for the passing trains to act like pistons, pushing stale, smoky air out ahead of them and drawing fresh air in behind. More systematic work by British geologists indicated that tunnellers could follow the grey Lower Chalk, free of the machine-blunting flints present in the white Upper Chalk. Geologically, there seemed to be no serious obstacle to boring through the sea bed. The only stumbling blocks were the cost, and English anxieties about invasion via the tunnel. Whenever one was circumvented, the other would crop up, and that has been the pattern for a hundred years.

The schemes of Victorian times almost bore fruit under the leadership of a British railroad magnate, Edward Watkin. He intended his tunnel to follow the chalk from Dover to Sangatte. In 1880–82 pilot tunnels were driven out from the English coast. The first, at Abbots Cliff, between Dover and Folkestone, penetrated under the sea for about a kilometre offshore. A second tunnel was started from a mineshaft at the Shakespeare Cliff near Dover, where a tunnelling machine of advanced design, with revolving cutters driven by compressed air, progressed through the chalk at a rate of about a centimetre per minute. French engineers started to tunnel outward from Sangatte, to link up with the English under the sea.

Queen Victoria changed her mind, and she was only one of a growing number of people in Britain who became agitated about the risk of invasion. British generals dreamed up worst-case contingencies in which French troops disguised as tourists would take possession of the tunnel outlet at Dover, with the assistance of Irish Republicans. Watkin and his engineers countered these fears with drastic methods of halting an invasion by that route. More imagination went into ways of sealing or destroying the tunnel than into its construction. The main proposal was to let the sea pour in, so that the French should suffer the fate of Pharaoh's army pursuing the Children of Israel. This was supported by schemes for ranging Dover's guns on the tunnel exit, installing explosive charges in the tunnel, and injecting shingle, smoke, carbon dioxide gas, or burning oil into it.

In 1882, when the British and French were at odds over who should control Egypt, the British government banned further work on the tunnel. It asserted its jurisdiction over the sea bed beside the English coast, and withdrew the concession to the Channel Tunnel Company. Watkin's men went on boring, under the pretext of maintaining ventilation in the tunnel. By the time an infuriated government had managed to put a stop to it, the Shakespeare Cliff pilot tunnel was two kilometres long, and the French had made similar progress on their side. Battles continued in Parliament, of which Watkin was a member. Again and again he introduced a Tunnel Bill, and every time his parliamentary colleagues, hating the idea of a fixed link to the continental mainland, threw it out.

During World War II aerial pictures of earth-moving at Sangatte suggested to British photo interpreters that the Germans might be preparing to invade England by tunnelling under the Channel. Geophysicists duly carried out tests in the English stump of the nineteenth-century tunnel, and set up seismic detectors. These, they promised, would detect any German digging operations before they reached the English coast, allowing plenty of time to take action. Peculiar structures at Sangatte turned out to be launching pads for V-2 rockets for bombarding London, and not an attempt to complete Watkin's tunnel. When British engineers were consulted about the possibility of supporting the Allied invasion of France by way of a Channel Tunnel, they said the work would take eight years.

A new generation of opponents of the Channel Tunnel pointed to the bridge over the Rhine River at Remagen, captured by U.S. troops in March 1945 against all the best intentions of the German defenders. Bernard Montgomery, commander of the Allied armies during the Normandy landings, was one of those who sustained the old military objections. "Why give up one of our greatest assets—our island home?" he demanded. "Why make things easier for our enemies?" But enthusiasm for the project was never farther below the surface than the sea-bed chalk. By 1960 the Channel Tunnel Study Group, a private Anglo-French-American consortium, had prompted the British and French governments to assess the modern possibilities on offer: a bored tunnel, a submerged tube, a bridge, or some combination of these.

Three years later, having chosen a rail tunnel, the governments commissioned the first thorough geotechnical investigations of the Dover Strait, and more than seventy exploratory boreholes were drilled in the sea bed. In 1973, under a solemn agreement between the two governments, work began on the new Channel Tunnel. It was to be a pair of bored rail tunnels between Fréthun behind Sangatte and Cheriton near Folkestone. Electric passenger trains and special trains adapted to carry road vehicles would run through the tunnels. Work began on the approaches through the cliffs on the two shores, but again the British government stopped the project. Because of the economic recession and alarm about the cost of a high-speed link between Dover and London, it tore up the treaty.

Talks resumed between the vacillating British and the patient French in 1979, and the two governments invited fresh proposals. In 1982 an Anglo-French Study Group reported on a variety of schemes. One proposal was for a bridge thirty-six kilometres long, divided into spans of two or three kilometres, mounted on sea-bed piers that would have to be protected from impacts by free-range supertankers. The most ambitious scheme was a hybrid, with road traffic crossing on bridges from the shore to artificial islands, and then spiralling down to pass under the main shipping lanes in a tube buried in the sea bed, nineteen kilometres long. For neither kind of bridge were the objections of seafarers properly answered.

Bored tunnels carrying rail traffic promised to be far cheaper—half the price even of the simpler bridge. The French and British railway authorities backed a scheme in which the total length of a tunnel would be fifty-six kilometres—fourteen kilometres would be in the landward approaches on the two coasts, and thirty-six kilometres under the sea. The idea of a drive-through road tunnel was greeted more coolly. The old problem of ventilation and the inevitability of road traffic accidents were two of the difficulties.

The bankers found only one option that seemed right from a financial as well as a technical viewpoint. It was very similar to the 1973 project, with a pair of seven-metre rail tunnels carrying conventional trains and also ferrying road vehicles on rail trucks. The capital cost was reckoned by the promoters at £1.9 billion sterling, at 1982 prices, with completion in 1992. Allowing for overruns, inflation, and interest charges, the bankers in 1984 visualized completion in 1993 and a net cost of £7.5 billion (say, $9 billion) by the end of the century. This compares with £25 billion ($30 billion) predicted for the composite bridge-tunnel.

Even the lesser figure seemed beyond the ordinary workings of the banking system, and the two governments were asked to support part of the loan finance. The British government was at first briskly unhelpful. An administration busy divesting itself of nationalized industries was not going to underwrite a project that should, so it thought, stand or fall by the sternest tests of profitability and the attraction of private capital. After a meeting with President Mitterrand late in 1984, Prime Minister Thatcher became warmer about a Channel link, and let it be known that she personally favoured the expensive bridge-tunnel hybrid.

The traffic of people and goods across the Channel is expected to double by the early twenty-first century. But improvements in ships and ports, containerization of cargoes, competition from air travel, the decline of the railways, and rising labour costs, all help to make the Channel Tunnel less necessary and less attractive commercially. Had it been completed in the nineteenth century it would have counted as an engineering wonder. Now, by Japanese norms, it is a straightforward task.

It may be third time lucky for the Channel Tunnel. In January 1986, on the basis of advice from expert scrutineers, Mitterrand and Thatcher agreed in principle that work should proceed in 1987 on the Channel Tunnel Group's low-risk, low-price scheme for twin rail tunnels, with drive-on provision for cars. The socialist president of France, like the British conservative prime minister, would have preferred EuroRoute's grander bridge–tunnel hybrid, but he had to strike a political balance, involving Boulogne and Calais, where his communist opponents had the majority, versus his own socialist stronghold in the hinterland. The rail tunnel seemed less likely to sink the ferry fleets.

While disappointed commercial rivals licked their wounds, the people of the Dover Strait once again prepared for the on-slaught of the engineers. Although sceptics wondered what would go wrong this time (strikes, perhaps, or snags associated with the newly discovered earthquake risks), the general belief on both sides of the water was that the idea of the Channel Tunnel would finally escape its jinxes. By early in the 1990s people would be travelling between England and France without getting seasick. The London scientific journal *Nature,* though, regretted that the chance had been missed to build a dam across the Dover Strait, to make good the recent loss (geologically speaking) of the old chalk walkway.

Whatever the outcome, the village of Sangatte already has its place in history, from four centuries ago, when anchoring off its beach was not prohibited. The Spanish Armada halted at Sangatte after sailing up the Channel. It abandoned its best anchors on the sea bed fourteen metres under our keel, in a seamanlike but unre-warded manoeuvre that had a decisive effect on the history of the world. The key to the events surrounding that fateful episode lies farther ahead in Flanders. The weather, though, is thwarting our eastward progress. The forecasters promise fog, the shore is fading from view, and we must hurry to Calais while we can still see the way in.

Different Kinds of Madness

Radio reports from the Varne light vessel give the visibility as less than fifty metres. In a clamorous duet at the entrance to Calais harbour, the western pier's bell is interrupted by a double roar from the eastern pier's diaphone. The ferries attack the air with their single blasts, but all the noise does nothing to disperse the fog that covers the Dover Strait. The best course in this kind of weather is to head for a good restaurant. The nearest is just across the dock gates, at the corner of the Boulevard de la Résistance and Rue Royale. Its Franglais name is Le Channel. Where better to swill the claret in memory of François-Marie Arouet?

He came to Calais as a result of a quarrel with a French aristocrat who made fun of his *nom de plume,* Voltaire. The aristocrat set thugs on him to beat him up, and the judges punished Voltaire for this crime by sending him to prison in the Bastille. Then they banished him from Paris, where his witticisms had made him the darling of the salons. This was in May 1726 when Voltaire was thirty-one years old. He left Paris under police escort in the coach of a female admirer. He headed north to Calais because he was already half in love with England, although he had never been there. He seems to have hesitated here for two weeks before setting off across the Channel. Perhaps it was foggy.

Voltaire is the French writer most admired in England, and not just because he explained the English to the French in fairly flattering terms. He was mentally anchored in mid-Channel, like a literary light vessel. Growing up in Paris, he took aboard the dry, critical literacy of French theatre and high society, and made himself a master of its forms. But as to content, he became increasingly a sceptic and a dissident, and began taking his intellectual bearings on England. He wrote to a friend:

> It is a country where they think freely and loftily, without being held back by any servile fear. If I followed my inclination, it would be there that I settled down, simply with the idea of learning to think.

As Voltaire left no account of his voyage from Calais, it was presumably painless. He spent more than two years in England. Afterward he put together his *Lettres Philosophiques,* which purported to be written from England, but were, in fact, composed with care after his readmission to Paris in 1729. The book first appeared in London in 1733, in an English translation. In Paris the public hangman burnt the French volumes outside the Palais de Justice. Voltaire never again felt safe in his home city, and spent most of the rest of his life near France's border, ready to run.

Voltaire's book on England created an intellectual rift that has lasted ever since. In matters of the mind, the English Channel is far wider than the Atlantic. Voltaire riled his compatriots by telling them that English success in science, commerce, and the wars against France flowed from their tradition of personal freedom. And he put his finger on the philosophical nub by comparing René Descartes and Isaac Newton, who to this day remain sharply opposed models of excellence for the French and the English.

The choice was between the rationalist philosophy of Descartes and the empiricism evolving in England. Descartes believed that you could deduce how nature worked just by thinking about it. The English stressed the need for open-minded experiment. Voltaire acknowledged that Descartes was a great mathematician, that he destroyed "the absurd fancies with which youth had been beguiled for two thousand years," and that his persecution came about because he tried to use reason to pursue the truth. But Voltaire put the knife in, up to the hilt, when he wrote of Descartes:

His philosophy was nothing more than an ingenious novel, at the best only plausible to ignoramuses. He was wrong about the nature of the soul, proofs of the existence of God, matter, the laws of dynamics, the nature of light; he accepted innate ideas, invented new elements, created a world and made man to his own specification. . . . I don't think we really dare compare in any way his philosophy with that of Newton: the first is a sketch, the second a masterpiece. [Trans. L. Tancock.]

When Voltaire was in London, he met a young naval officer called John Byng. Thirty years later Admiral Byng let an equal French squadron stop him relieving the island of Minorca in the Mediterranean. After an inconclusive fight, he gave up, and Minorca fell to the French. Byng was court-martialled and sentenced to death. Voltaire remembered meeting him and personally begged the British government to spare his life, but Byng was shot by a

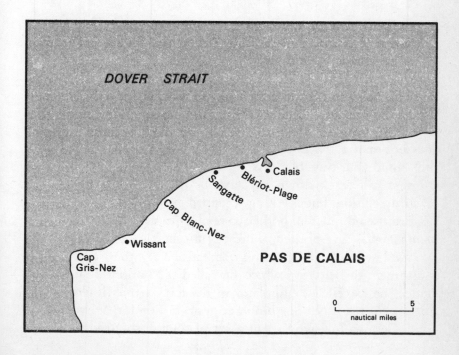

firing squad on the quarterdeck of a warship in Portsmouth harbour on March 14, 1757.

A year later Voltaire incorporated the scene in his best-known book, *Candide,* together with his best-known phrase, *pour encourager les autres:* "In this country we find it pays to shoot an admiral from time to time to encourage the others." Voltaire and most of his readers imagined he was being bitingly satirical, but he was only expressing what the British public actually thought.

Half a lifetime after his own visit, Voltaire was less approving about the English than he had been in *Lettres Philosophiques,* and called them "serious and gloomy." In the story Candide is put off by the grim event at Portsmouth, and he refuses even to set foot in England. He asks a friend if the English are as mad as the French; the reply is "Yes, but theirs is a different kind of madness."

The English refusal to trust pure reason makes them seem anti-intellectual on the French side of the Channel. Their attitude is nearly a denial of the philosophical enterprise. George Orwell noted, two centuries after Voltaire:

> As Europeans go, the English are not intellectual. They have a horror of abstract thought, they feel no need for any philosophy or systematic "world-view."

This helps to explain why Voltaire was not the only intellectual on the run who came this way, seeking sanctuary across the water. The English don't care what you think because thought does not matter. As long as you "keep your fingers out the till" and "mind your own business," you will be tolerated. Their government can crack down fiercely enough on people preaching practical sedition, but anything wrapped in wordy theory is harmless because no one will bother to read it anyway. The *Communist Manifesto* was first printed, quite openly, in London in 1848.

And when Karl Marx was threatened by the French with banishment to Brittany, which he called the Pontine Marshes of France, he travelled to England in the ferry from Boulogne on August 26, 1849. No one hindered him. In London he was just a polite German Jew who spent a lot of time in the reading room at the British Museum, writing long-winded stuff about the bourgeoisie and the proletariat. Marx's grave in London sums up the English attitude to overarching theories and their authors. Neither adulated nor desecrated, it is simply neglected.

Americans are not English. Although they speak the language, and share certain attitudes to personal freedom and experimental science, they have too much input from continental Europe to be carefree about grand theories. They twitch far more about communism than the English do, and take religion more solemnly. Americans also spend much more money on doubtful theoretical constructs such as astrology and psychoanalysis. There, by the way, goes another cross-Channel fugitive to England: Sigmund Freud in 1938.

Enmity between the French and English, the frogs and *rosbifs*, persists close to the surface. They are publicly rude to each other and about each other. They rely on quasi-racist stereotyping, antiquated in style but endlessly refreshed by complaints about violent football fans, careless drivers, greedy farmers, or yachtsmen who don't pay their harbour dues. Americans, Dutchmen, and other mutual friends are startled and embarrassed by this behaviour. President Mitterrand of France likened it to the bickering of a married couple, but that was too bland a view of the relationship. *Us* married to *them?* Never!

In Joan of Arc's time the English were *les goddons,* because of their habit of saying "God damn." Whether *les rosbifs* comes from the Englishmen's liking for prime ribs or from the colour of their faces, it seems too jolly for epithetic warfare, and *les anglais* uttered with emphasis is more abusive. By an English tradition, the incomprehensible appetite of the French for amphibian limbs makes them forever the frogs. Or does it? The use traces back to Frogland as a name for marshy Holland, and the Dutch were the original frogs. The name that alliteration as well as diet made apt for the French was only recently transferred to them. On the other hand, in prerevolutionary France, the aristocrats referred to their own people in Paris as *les grenouilles,* the frogs.

In 1984 the weekly *Le Nouvel Observateur* published the results of a poll which asked French people what they thought of other countries. Their British neighbours ranked very low. The *Sunday Times* of London promptly commissioned a similar poll of British people, which showed that the dislike was reciprocated. In each case, the cross-Channel neighbours lagged behind the Chinese in popularity. As for national leaders, the British prime minister, Margaret Thatcher, was in a small rogues' gallery of people especially disliked by the French, along with Fidel Castro, Colonel Qaddafi, and the Ayatollah Khomeini. The British took a kindlier view of President Mitterrand.

Since the days of Queen Eleanor's Channel-straddling empire, there have been plenty of military reasons for mutual bitterness, but both the French and the English like and admire the Germans, much grosser enemies of the recent past. The French are correct when they call the British reluctant Europeans, yet the Swiss spurn integration more firmly than the British and come top of the French list of good neighbours. As for legal, religious, and philosophical divisions that trace back to the Romanization of the Franks and the Reformation of the English, and the great intellectual rift that Voltaire observed at the dawn of modern science, these contrasts do not stop the English liking Italians, or the French getting on with Americans. Differences between Joan of Arc's people and Francis Drake's people remain as plentiful as the squalls of the Channel, and part of the ethnic richness of Europe. But why should every difference become a matter for sneering, and every minor incident a nurtured grievance?

Consider this: the French and English dislike each other because they want to. Whether a person is a monk or pirate chief, he will act the part in which life has cast him. In the same way, a person born in France will play the role of being French, and a good Frenchman detests the English. If you are English, you scorn the French. The inhabitants of the two sides of the English Channel are foils for each other's national self-image. History, world views, and current politics merely colour a monochromatic decision about social identity.

Like a latter-day Voltaire, a French émigré in England illuminated behavior of this kind. In experiments at Bristol University, Henri Tajfel showed that people automatically support any team or group to which they are assigned, at the expense of other groups. An arbitrary label alters a person's behaviour in predictable ways. "Gratuitous discrimination," Tajfel called it, and it cut across theories that blamed human conflict on hormones or demagogues. He defined instead a "generic norm" in human behaviour, favouring in-group collaboration. While Tajfel was doing this work, in the 1970s, tape recordings by William Labov of the University of Pennsylvania were showing how people alter their language to make it harder for competing groups to understand.

Once those miscellaneous German pirates and their Celtic victims had sorted themselves out into the French and the English, the role of the Channel, as a geological explanation for enmity, was paradoxical. It was too easy to cross. The distances were not great, and sea travel was five times faster than overland travel in the era before steam trains. Traders and fishermen had far more in common with the inhabitants of the opposite coast than with kings and magnates in their own capital cities. If the peoples of the shores were not to be muddled about their social identity, it became all the more important for them to emphasize their own peculiarities, to notice every irritating little difference in the foreigners' hairstyles or eating habits.

At least there was no doubt about who was who in this in-group–out-group distinction. Although it was never a barrier, the English Channel was a highly visible dividing line, scratched in the Earth's surface by millions of years of rifting and erosion. "We are the folk who belong on our side of the water, and on no account are we to be confused with that other disagreeable lot."

The narrowest part of the Channel, between Calais and Dover, where the opposing cliffs of the two countries lend grandeur to the scene, has a special magic that makes it the proving ground for many kinds of new technology. The danger from wind and waves is real enough, and the distance between the shores, roughly thirty-three kilometres, is far enough to be taken seriously, without being entirely foolhardy for inventors working with prototype systems. For instance, the name of Blériot-Plage, just east of Calais, commemorates Louis Blériot, who took off from there in 1909 in the first powered aircraft to cross the English Channel.

Pioneer aeronauts had flown across by balloon more than a century earlier: the French balloonist Jean-Pierre-François Blanchard and his companion, an American physician called John Jeffries. The first manned flight of all had been made at Paris by two men in a hot-air balloon, devised by the Montgolfier brothers, little more than a year before; that was followed soon after by Jacques Charles and his assistant flying over Paris in a hydrogen-filled balloon. It was in a hydrogen-filled "Charlière" that Blanchard and Jeffries set off from Dover on January 7, 1785. After a few miles the balloon began to sink towards the waves, and Blanchard dumped all his water ballast. The balloon rose a little, but as the aeronauts approached Calais it was again threatening to dunk them in the sea. Everything movable and removable was jettisoned from the basket, and the balloon passed low over the shore and continued for some distance inland. A few months later two Frenchmen fell to their deaths at Boulogne, trying to cross the Channel the other way, in a hot-air balloon suspended under a hydrogen balloon—a combination that burst into flames.

Blériot's Channel flight put powered aviation in the headlines. When the Wright brothers began flying in North Carolina in 1903, the public paid little attention, either in the United States or in Europe. In 1906, Alberto Santos-Dumont made the first European powered flight, in a short skip at Bagatelle, near Le Touquet on the Channel shore. By the summer of 1909 flying fever was raging among inventors on both sides of the Atlantic. Blériot and two rivals were on the French shore with their flying machines, waiting for the weather and their machinery to be right at the same time. The *Daily Mail* of London had put up a prize of a thousand pounds sterling for a flight across the Channel.

On July 19 Hubert Latham became the first aviator to be rescued from the Channel. His Antoinette machine launched itself from Cap Blanc-Nez, but he ditched with engine failure in the middle of the Dover Strait. A French warship picked Latham up. At dawn on July 25 Louis Blériot revved up the 25-horsepower engine in his Blériot XI monoplane, at the strip just east of Calais, and clambered into the air over the waves. He landed thirty-six minutes later near Dover Castle. After that the public took flying seriously. The French were the greatest enthusiasts in those early years, with by far the greatest number of pilots. Even Belgium had more pilots than the United States at the end of 1910. But military chiefs were losing their scepticism about aviation, in time for World War I.

A pedal-powered aircraft made its first crossing on June 12, 1979. Bryan Allen, an American, left Folkestone Warren in *Gossamer Albatross* from a runway of hardboard sheets. At the first attempt at a takeoff, he crashed in a hole in the runway and his glasses fell off. During the flight Allen was bathed in sweat and troubled by cramp. He came down repeatedly to within a foot of the water, and two thirds of the way across he signalled to the accompanying team in inflatable boats that he wanted to scrub the flight and take a tow. But even while a boat was manoeuvring under him to grab the tow ring, Allen changed his mind and climbed away. After 169 minutes he touched down on the beach below Cap Gris-Nez. Four years later John van der Starre, from the Netherlands, crossed from Dover to Calais on a sailboard in 61 minutes.

In the summer of 1984 BBC Television collaborated with the people who produce the *Guinness Book of Records* to see how many sensible, frivolous, and record-breaking Channel crossings they could pack into one live show. They had two commercial Hovercraft, an army helicopter, two microlite aircraft, a power boat, and biplanes flying upside down. Aboard a conventional ferry people were jogging, roller-skating, hulahooping, dancing, and cooking their way across the English Channel. The "policemen" of the Dover Strait, at CROSS Gris-Nez and Dover's Langdon Battery, were not pleased, but a subtle difference in official attitudes appeared on the two sides of the water. The British Coastguards strongly advised the BBC team not to go ahead, but admitted they had no power to prevent it and ended up helping unofficially to see it done safely. The French CROSS station, on the other hand, declared that they could prohibit the stunts, and would do so unless the BBC satisfied them as to the safety arrangements— which it did.

Folk come from all over the world for the chilly privilege of swimming the English Channel. French prisoners of war may have escaped from England by that means, but the first cross-Channel swim in the sporting records is credited to Matthew Webb, a young captain in the merchant service. Webb took nearly twenty-four hours to swim from England to France on August 24–25, 1875. No one else can be first, but he or she can be the fastest, the slowest, the oldest, the youngest, or the most persistent. August is the favourite time to try, when the water of the Dover Strait is at its warmest (16° Celsius, or 61° Fahrenheit) and relatively calm.

No one will blame you if you run over a Channel swimmer in a supertanker, least of all the experts. The Anglo-French Safety of Navigation Group takes the view that all "unorthodox" crossings of the Dover Strait are highly irresponsible. "Potential participants," it declares, "should be persuaded to look for a challenge elsewhere, in areas where they do not constitute a hazard to other people going about their lawful activities." But the sea is a big place, and the odds against being hit by a ship if you swim across the Dover Strait are roughly 4000 to 1. The odds are much the same for a yacht in thick fog. Although she is a bigger target, she passes through the danger zone more quickly and has close shaves with fewer ships. Knowing the probabilities is little comfort, out there in a small boat with the foghorns sounding all around. So the ketch stays put in Calais until the visibility improves.

Who Won the Armada Fight?

We have entered a flattened, sandy world, like a gigantic version of Somme Bay. The banks offshore are matched by the dunes of the shoreline, and the seascapes scarcely alter from Calais to Germany, even though the names change: Flanders, Zeeland, Holland, Friesland. The off-lying shoals give shelter to ports that would otherwise be open to the northwesterly gales, but they make a maze for mariners. The ketch is passing cautiously around the curtain of sand that guards Calais. The factory buildings and chimneys crowded to the east of the town announce our arrival on the most heavily industrialized section of the French coast. The modern activity need not overpower one's sense of history. On the contrary, it confirms the role of Flanders as an ancient centre of European industry, with Calais at its western gateway.

The main through traffic in the Dover Strait passes beyond the Out Ruytingen shoal, away to the north, but ships bound for Dunkirk, twelve sea miles farther along the coast, thread their way inside the Dyck and Gravelines banks. Pairs of red and green buoys, at intervals of about a mile, show the stupidest sailor where to go. After Calais, the next forest of chimneys is at Gravelines, where modest breakwaters guard the mouth of the Aa River. Amid the factories there are church spires and a windmill. A Vauban fortress, moated by the river, stands at the core of old Gravelines. In contrast, the six concrete reactor domes of the Gravelines nuclear power station occupy the shoreline east of the Aa.

At the time of the Armada fight, when weaving was the great

industry of Flanders, France ended at Gravelines. Dunkirk, away to the east, belonged to the Spanish Netherlands. Gravelines is now virtually a suburb of Dunkirk. Beside the nuclear power station, the first large breakwater of Dunkirk's modern Port Ouest launches itself into the sea. This is where the tankers and cross-Channel ferries come. The traditional harbour, now called Port Est, is eight miles farther on, but the intervening shoreline is packed and odorized with oil refineries, blast furnaces, shipyards, grain silos, refrigeration towers, cement works, and other factories.

The eastern end of Dunkirk is less industrialized, and the wide beach of Malo-les-Bains is full of sunbathers and swimmers. Just five miles on, among the sandbanks, an arbitrary line on the chart says it is time to take down the French courtesy flag that the ketch has carried since Ushant and haul up the flag of Belgium instead. Belgian Flanders begins in the prospering resort of De Panne. Five miles farther on is Nieuwpoort, a modest harbour at the mouth of the Yzer River. Nieuwpoort and Dunkirk were the main bases for the invasion of England at the time of the Spanish Armada.

At that time much of Europe was theoretically united in the person of the Habsburg emperor. In practice this meant that the Low Countries belonged to Spain and were subject to a hard-line Catholic rule, which injured the mercantile empire of Flanders, as seafarers, merchants, and artisans fled from repression. The Protestant religion was a rallying point for people with grievances about foreign domination, high taxes, and poor wages. It also sanctified piracy against the shipping of the "Inquisition dogs." Dutch unrest against their Spanish masters had become open warfare twenty years before the Armada fight.

Dutch independence began at Dover, when it was a base for the Sea Beggars, Dutch Protestant guerrillas living as pirates with English connivance and support. At the end of March 1572 they sailed in force from Dover and established beachheads in their homeland. Other towns in Holland rose in revolt. The liberated Dutch offered their country to Queen Elizabeth of England, but she politely refused it. But it is easy to see why King Philip of Spain regarded Protestant England as the root of all evil, and sent his Armada to the Dover Strait to extirpate it.

On a Saturday afternoon, August 6, 1588, 120 Spanish ships anchored just short of Calais at Sangatte. The English fleet, which had dogged them all the way from Plymouth, followed suit, dropping anchor off Cap Blanc-Nez. Reinforcements brought the number of English vessels to 150. The French governor and townsfolk of Calais went out along the shore expecting to be entertained by a battle; instead, they found the Spanish rowing to the beach, offering to buy fresh food. As the tidal current of the Dover Strait gathered strength that evening, the Spanish thought it prudent for each ship to put out two anchors. Next day their commander, the Duke of Medina Sidonia, found out that the plan for the invasion of England had gone wrong.

The Armada's mission was to escort a Spanish army from Dunkirk and Nieuwpoort to the Thames estuary, where it was to land and advance on London. But letters sent ahead of the Armada by fast boats to the Duke of Parma, who commanded the army in Flanders, had elicited no reply. As soon as he had anchored,

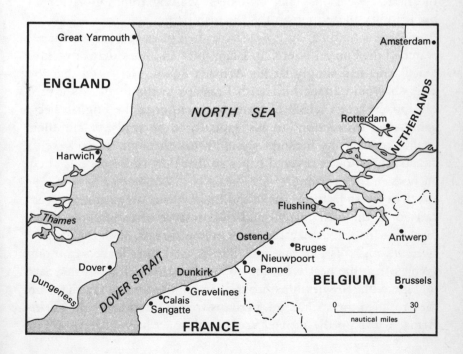

Medina Sidonia sent his secretary ashore to ask Parma to bring his fleet out of Dunkirk. But during that Sunday one of the earlier messengers turned up with bad news. Parma was still at his headquarters in Bruges, his army was far from ready, and the landing craft were not fit for the voyage to England. The fleet of small, armed flyboats that Medina Sidonia believed Parma possessed at Dunkirk was non-existent.

The weak link in King Philip's plan was that he overlooked the sandbanks, and the Dutch. The Armada could not shield the Spanish army's barges during the first crucial miles of shallow water, leading out to sea from the Flemish coast. Philip did not understand about deep-draft and shoal-draft shipping, or what life was like in the Flemish tideways. Parma did, although he preferred to lie to the king and declare that his army was ready to sail. Even if it had been, and had put to sea from the Flemish ports as intended, the off-lying shoals would have kept the deep-draft ships of the Armada well offshore, while presenting little obstacle to the shallow flyboats of the Dutch. There was no doubt whose side the Dutch were on. They had been waiting for months for an opportunity to pounce on the Spanish barges.

Medina Sidonia, an honourable man plagued by seasickness, watched the Sun set over Cap Blanc-Nez and nursed a conviction that Parma had simply let his Armada down. He feared that the English would attack him with fireships in the night. As a precaution, he sent a screen of boats to lie closer to the English fleet, and issued instructions to his captains to be ready to cut their anchor ropes if any fireships should break through. They were to attach buoys to the severed ropes so that they could pick up their anchors in the morning.

The fireships came out of the English anchorage at midnight, carried by the tidal current and the pressure of an offshore wind on their sails. Eight sizeable ships in line abreast, with their hulls, rigging, and sails bursting into flames, and their loaded cannons going off in the heat were too many for the small Spanish boats to cope with. Six fireships broke through the screen. By the time they reached the anchorage, perhaps five minutes later, the entire Armada was on the move. Seamanship of a high order got 120 ships under way in darkness. They suffered no collisions with the fireships and few with one another. One galleasse, *San Lorenzo,* lost her rudder on a neighbour's anchor cable.

The Spanish commander's orders were to re-anchor when the danger from the fireships had passed. Morning found the Spanish flagship, *San Martín,* and three or four Portuguese ships duly lying a sea mile north of Sangatte, and the rudderless *San Lorenzo* rowing towards Calais. But all the other ships of the Armada, some of them lacking suitable spare anchors, were scattered along the Flemish coast. Many of them were off Gravelines, and Medina Sidonia headed off to join them. The English commander was personally distracted by *San Lorenzo* and tried unsuccessfully to seize her before she went aground. As a result, it was Francis Drake, in *Revenge,* who led a general charge of the English fleet against the disorganized Armada.

Gravelines gives its name to the last and fiercest battle between the Spanish Armada and the English fleet, although the fighting probably took place far out at sea, beyond the Out Ruytingen shoal. The action shifted rapidly to the east, past the coast of Flanders, and both fleets had to be careful not to be blown on to the sandbanks. On that Monday morning, August 8, 1588, Medina Sidonia took the first assault of the English fleet himself, while about thirty of his ships were rallying to his support.

The English did not repeat an error they made in earlier skirmishes, coming up the Channel, of shooting from too far off. They now swept much closer to the Spanish ships before loosing their broadsides—although they remained too distant and too mobile for the Spanish soldiers to have any hope of boarding them. The English had the nimbler ships and better guns. They also had plenty of ammunition, replenished since the Channel fights, while the Spanish were running short of powder and shot. The result was murder. At the right range, the English cannon balls smashed through the oak hulls of the Spanish and Portuguese galleons.

By 4 P.M., when a squall put an end to the battle, the English had done more harm than they knew. One damaged warship sank outright in the squall; two others drifted helplessly towards the shore and fell into the hands of the Dutch. An armed merchantman

See "Drake" Ernle Bradford where it States the opposite., in a full account of the battle.

sank next morning. Most of the surviving ships had been ravaged by the gunfire. The flagship *San Martín,* for instance, had suffered more than a hundred hits and was leaking badly. There was a lot of blood, too, on the gun decks; the Spanish counted six hundred dead and eight hundred badly wounded in the fight. The English had suffered far fewer casualties, and their ships remained essentially undamaged. The Spanish iron shot was too brittle to harm the English hulls.

By the Tuesday both fleets were out of ammunition, but the English kept up what their commander called "a brag countenance." They watched contentedly as the wind continued to blow from the northwest. It was driving the unweatherly Spanish ships towards certain doom on the sandbanks off Zeeland, which sprawl far out to sea. As the signs of the shoaling gathered around the Armada, in the colour of the water and the shortness of the waves, the Flemish pilot in the Spanish flagship declared that only God could save them. The flagship and other big vessels drew six fathoms (eleven metres), so when the leadsman reported seven fathoms (thirteen metres) everyone was tensed for the impact.

Reconstructions of the weather maps for the peculiar summer of 1588 show a ridge of high pressure moving east across the North Sea that Tuesday. As a result, when the Armada was within a few minutes of disaster, the wind suddenly backed to west-southwest, and the ships were able to turn sharply to port, into deeper water. The Spanish soldiers, sailors, and priests all agreed that God had worked a miracle. But salvation off Zeeland only started a much longer ordeal for the Spanish ships. While the seamen rummaged them, looking for spare anchors, various ideas were debated about finding a harbour in northern Europe, or turning back towards Dunkirk. The decision was to sail home to Spain by way of the north of Scotland and the west of Ireland. The English still feared that the Spanish army in Flanders might invade, even without the Armada to escort it. But Parma heard the news of the Battle of Gravelines at Dunkirk, where he was going through the motions of loading his army into the barges. He ordered the embarkation to stop.

The English fleet saw the Armada off, as far as the latitude of Edinburgh, and then left it to its fate, which was terrible enough. According to David Howarth's recent estimate, more than ten times as many soldiers and sailors succumbed to shipwreck, starvation, or disease on the long voyage home as died in battle. Only about half of the ships that left Spain ever returned there, and only a third of the men. Most of the lost ships were wrecked in gales on the Scottish and Irish coasts, often because they had left their best anchors at Sangatte.

Santa María de la Rosa was one. Six weeks after the Battle of Gravelines, Captain Marcos de Aramburu of *San Juan* was sheltering from a gale in Blasket Sound, on the westernmost tip of Ireland, when *Santa María de la Rosa* came in with her sails in tatters. Aramburu's log tells what happened to her:

> She managed to come to a stop with one anchor which was all she had and with the tide entering from the southeast she was held steady for a while. At two o'clock in the afternoon the tide turned and she began to swing on her anchor and dragged down the Sound. We also dragged not two cables length from her. She struck a submerged rock in the south entrance and went down right away with everyone on board, not a soul was saved.
> [Trans. K. S. Douglas.]

Survivors of the Armada wrecks, struggling ashore, were often killed by the local inhabitants, either on their own initiative or by order of the English. Each ship's company had its peculiar agony, but one of the grimmest sequels occurred here on the coast of Flanders, a year after the battle. Parma had sent a ship to Scotland to collect destitute Spanish survivors. As they approached Dunkirk the Dutch attacked them, and they were shipwrecked again: only three men out of 270 survived.

The outcome of the Armada fight and the gales that followed it damaged Spanish pride and boosted English morale, but the commercial pay-off went to the Dutch. Their ships already carried grain and fish from northern Europe to the Mediterranean, and they developed cheap, easily handled bulk carriers called *fluyts*. They went on to monopolize the spices of Indonesia. For almost two centuries, Amsterdam ruled the world's commerce and Dutch shipping was everywhere.

The English did not like it, and waged bitter naval wars against the Dutch. In the Channel, at the Battle of Dungeness in 1652, the Dutch trounced the English. Following a later battle, in the North Sea, the Dutch fleet sailed up the Thames, burned the English ships, and towed away the flagship as a prize. The English could not subdue the Dutch, but they could easily harass Dutch ships in the English Channel, especially those seeking refuge in English ports in bad weather. It became a case of live and let live. England developed its own trading empire, under the shadow of the Dutch fleet, while Dutch ships and merchants thronged London's river.

Meanwhile the French, with English help, had conquered western Flanders. The Battle of the Dunes, fought near Dunkirk on June 14, 1658, was a strange replay of the English Civil War. Oliver Cromwell's republican army was ranged alongside the French, while an English royalist force supporting the Spanish was led by James, Duke of York—he of New York, Saint-Vaast-la-Hougue, etc. When the Anglo-French force beat the Anglo-Spanish force, and Dunkirk fell, it was given to Cromwell as a reward for his services. English proprietorship of Dunkirk was brief, because four years later King Charles II sold the port to France for ready cash—five million livres. Exactly a hundred years after the Armada fight, in 1688, the Dutch invaded England and put a Dutchman on its throne.

What about Belgian nationhood? The ketch acknowledges it with the black, yellow, and red flag at her crosstrees, as she cruises off the beach of De Panne. The French conquests left Belgium as a morsel of Spanish territory, which afterward came under Austrian rule. The French revolutionary army annexed it in 1795. Twenty years later, after Napoleon's defeat at Waterloo, the victors gave Belgium to the Dutch. But the Belgians revolted in 1830, and next year they appointed a king: Prince Leopold of Saxe-Coburg, an uncle of Britain's Queen Victoria. It was here at De Panne that

Leopold arrived by sea from England and stepped ashore to claim his crown.

The nation was born of an uneasy union of Dutch-speaking Flemings in the coastal strip and French-speaking Walloons, who lived south of the old Boulogne–Maastricht linguistic boundary. Each group had its own reasons for wanting independence. The Flemings were estranged from their Dutch cousins by more than two centuries of separation. The Walloons were enjoying great success as ironmasters; in the Industrial Revolution they were running second only to Britain, and well ahead of their French cousins. Independent Belgium prospered and acquired an overseas empire when its ships groped their way up the Congo.

Belgium itself, being an ex-colony, resembles some nations of mismatched tribes left over from the colonial era in Africa. With no love lost between Fleming and Walloon, the country runs like two nations under one flag. They can't even agree on the names of their towns. De Panne is La Panne to the Walloons, and Antwerpen in Flemish becomes Anvers in French. The capital, the only part of Belgium where the linguistic groups coexist in large numbers, is Brussel for the Flemings, and Bruxelles for the Walloons. At present the Walloons are worried because the Flemings are outbreeding them. It looks hopelessly unstable, but you can turn that around to say there may be hope for those new African nations, seeing that Belgium has lasted with its tribalism for a century and a half.

Escape of an Army

A bird hits one of the stainless steel wires holding up the ketch's mainmast and falls with a plop onto a cockpit cushion. It creaks to its feet and staggers about. It is a pipit, an early migrant heading south for the winter. After a few minutes the bird cautiously tries spreading its wings, and hops onto the cockpit coaming. It looks gravely around the sea and sky, like Captain Cook on his quarterdeck. Then it glares fixedly at Belgium, and is suddenly away, flying strongly towards De Panne. An English sailor friend used to shout at the wild birds migrating south across the Channel: "Don't go there, they'll eat you!" But he was not as good a navigator as the birds, and he drowned himself on a sandbank.

The buoys advertising the Flemish banks lie scattered inshore and out to sea. The tidal current is changing direction, making this a suitable time for turning westward, at the end of *Charmed*'s passage from Ushant to the Belgian frontier. It is a moment, too, to eye an historic beach, as the ketch swings through the wind.

To the east is Nieuwpoort, marked by breakwaters and a tall building near the mouth of the Yzer River. In World War I, when the Germans invaded and the Belgian government retreated down-Channel to Le Havre, the Yzer was the seaward anchor for the lines of trenches that stretched across Belgium and France to the Swiss border. Upstream along the Yzer is Ypres, or Wipers as the British troops called it, who lie buried in large numbers thereabouts. The sons of the Wipers generation were on the Yzer in

1940, when it formed the eastern end of the Dunkirk perimeter. There they had to check the all-conquering Nazi panzers, which had pinned French and British armies against the Channel shore and threatened to extinguish them.

During those desperate days, the British army had its head-quarters at De Panne, where the submarine telephone cable from Dover came ashore. The French headquarters was in a bunker near the harbour of Dunkirk. The breakwaters of Dunkirk's Port Est, seven sea miles away, look very much as they did in 1940, except that a pall of smoke hung over the city then. Along the intervening beaches, the sunbathers and swimmers were replaced by a beaten army, and the sea was full of ships and boats of all kinds.

In nine days between May 27 and June 4, 1940, two armies escaped by sea: 225,000 British troops and 123,000 French. The rescue prevented an abject defeat in France and Belgium becoming a total disaster that would make Adolf Hitler's triumph certain. And it was a masterpiece of improvisation. Operation Dynamo

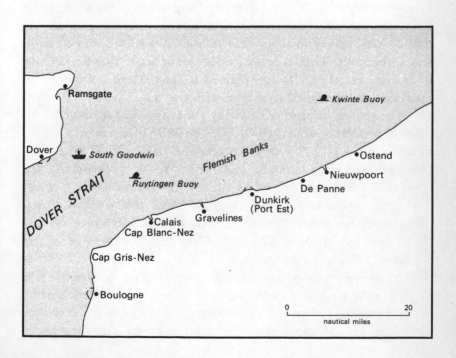

was launched after only a week's warning to the British navy at Dover that a large-scale evacuation might become necessary.

For soldiers ashore, the concern was to hold off the German tanks. Their blitzkrieg had bypassed France's Maginot Line and reduced the opposing armies to chaff in the wind. When the British Expeditionary Force and the French First Army found themselves encircled with their backs to the sea, plans for a breakout faded as communications and control disintegrated. While some French planners hoped to reinforce Dunkirk from the sea, the British began to think of evacuation across the Dover Strait. But first the troops had to be moved to the coast and a long perimeter defended at a line of canals paralleling the coast, several kilometres inland.

The German army was already attacking Dunkirk from the west, close to Gravelines, when Hitler ordered the tanks to halt for a couple of days at the Aa River. With hindsight this decision seems ludicrous, but neither Hitler nor the defenders had any idea that so many of the trapped soldiers would get away. The British knew that only a miracle could save their army, and they did not believe in miracles. Neither did they have much time for the futile "honour," which the French kept talking about, being under orders to die bravely. The attitude of the French to the evacuation was ambiguous. They accused the British of neglecting the defence of France, but they also complained bitterly when a minority of their own troops failed to escape with the rest.

The sailors charged with saving the armies had to solve tricky nautical problems, starting with the barricade of sandbanks off the Flemish coast. How to get from England to Dunkirk? Peacetime ferries from Dover take the most direct route, approaching the coast near Calais and following the shore, inside the Dyck bank. The first ships sent for the evacuation went that way, but they came under fire from German guns on the shore between Gravelines and Cap Gris-Nez. The ferry *Mona's Isle* lost her rudder and the coaster *Sequacity* was sunk.

An alternative was to use the Zuydcoote pass, well to the east of the port. It is a roundabout way from Dunkirk to Dover, because you start by travelling twenty-three sea miles in the wrong direction, around the end of the Kwinte bank. The time spent following this route more than halved the number of troops each ship could rescue. And small units of the German navy lay in wait at the Kwinte buoy. In the early hours of May 28 the British destroyer *Wakeful* was sunk there by a German torpedo boat. She went down so quickly that nearly all the troops she was carrying were drowned, together with most of her own crew. When the destroyer *Grafton* stopped to look for survivors from *Wakeful,* she was torpedoed by a U-boat also lurking at the Kwinte buoy. The ferry *Malines* took most of the troops and crew off *Grafton* before she joined *Wakeful* on the sea bed. Two nights later, torpedo boats sank the French destroyer *Siroco* at the same turning point.

By May 29 minesweepers had cleared a third passage, which approached Dunkirk from the north, between the Out Ruytingen and Inner Ruytingen banks. It was an unconventional route that could be used only in daylight, but it cut the crossing time by a third, compared with the Zuydcoote route. The German dive-bomber pilots still found it easy to track down the ships forced to follow the narrow gaps between the Flemish banks.

The next problem was getting the troops aboard. The original idea was to send the ships into Dunkirk harbour, but the fierce German attacks brought too great a risk of sunken ships blocking it. Large ships, banished from the port, had to lie a mile offshore and gather troops from the open beaches. At first the ships' own boats had fetched the soldiers in small parties. If the boats simply beached and filled up with troops, the added weight pushed them into the sand and made them immovable until the tide rose. It was all painfully slow and, at a rate of a few thousand men a day, there was no hope of saving the trapped armies before the Germans took Dunkirk.

The solution, the key to the great escape, lay in the *jetée est,* the eastern breakwater of Dunkirk harbour. Two straight structures slanted towards a fairly broad entrance, just as they do today. The western breakwater was a solid affair built on rocks, which made it unapproachable by ships and boats. On the other side of the entrance was a more modest line of upright piles driven into the sand, with a wooden catwalk on top, three metres wide. It was not designed to have ships lying alongside it, but the water was just deep enough. Captain William Tennant of the British navy decided to experiment. The ferry *Queen of the Channel* was told to tie up to the breakwater, and a thousand troops were able to walk aboard her. *Queen* was bombed and sunk on her way home, but she had proved the point.

Ship after ship—ferries, destroyers, fishing boats—came to the breakwater. The soldiers filed down its kilometre length to climb aboard, while the sailors fretted about the rise and fall of the tide, and the dive-bombers screamed. Most of the troops evacuated from Dunkirk embarked that way. The *jetée est,* engineered to break the waves of a North Sea storm, withstood the unexpected punishment from crowds of ships leaning against it in the tideway.

Troops were scattered along this coast, far to the east of Dunkirk, and almost a hundred thousand of them, more than a quarter of the total, embarked from the open beach. Luckily, the sea remained calm. Lines of trucks driven into the water made makeshift piers. But the desperate need was for shallow craft that could go to the beach and ferry the soldiers out to the big ships. By chance, small wooden boats were already being requisitioned by the British navy to cope with German magnetic mines, and these provided the nucleus of an armada of small craft that set off for Dunkirk from Ramsgate on the coast of Kent on May 30. This is the image of Dunkirk that is most vivid in British folklore today: little ships crossing the sea to rescue the troops. Lifeboats, inshore fishing boats, dredgers, sailing barges, private motor cruisers, yachts, many of them manned by their civilian owners and crews, who suddenly found themselves in the midst of ferocious war.

The toll of ships was frightening, and the courage needed by the sailors who kept coming back to face the dive-bombers and pick up more troops can be gauged by the quality of the few who refused. Some ferry captains walked off their ships, and one sailed down-Channel to get away from it all. A British destroyer was immobilized in Dover harbour when her crew cracked. Even some lifeboat coxswains in Kent would not set off for Dunkirk.

Did the British concentrate on rescuing their own troops, as the French were to claim? At first they did, saying that the French should organize their own evacuation. But French ships were clearing troops at less than a tenth of the rate managed by the British, and late on May 30 Winston Churchill ordered the British ships to take off equal numbers of French and British troops. The surge in the numbers of Frenchmen rescued during the last five days showed that the order was obeyed. It was a wasted effort, because nearly all of them chose to go home after France surrendered to Hitler two weeks later.

The European canal network soon began delivering barges to Dunkirk and nearby ports, so that the German army could follow the British across the Dover Strait. By mid-July 1940 the Nazi plan for the invasion of England, code-named *Seelöwe,* or Sea Lion, was meant to be ready for execution within a month or two. The German army wanted a very wide front extending more than halfway down the English Channel. The navy pressed for a much narrower attack. The compromise was that the assault force should consist of about 100,000 troops, concentrated mainly in a Dover Strait crossing. Setting out from Boulogne, Calais, Dunkirk, and Ostend, in Belgium, infantry divisions with tank support would land on a number of English beaches between Folkestone and Beachy Head. A diversionary landing force was to leave Le Havre for Brighton on the Sussex coast, while airborne troops descended on Kent.

The landing craft were adapted from the river barges. Occupied Europe had plenty of them, but many were unpowered. These were to be towed across the sea by tugboats, and then mated to powered barges for the run into the beaches. The British navy was to be kept at bay by minefields and U-boats, but everyone knew that control of the air was essential. While Hitler remained prudently cool about the entire enterprise, Hermann Göring asserted that his Luftwaffe would smash the Royal Air Force. Joseph Kennedy, the U.S. Ambassador to the Court of St. James's, promised journalists that Hitler would be in London by August 15.

The German air force tried to destroy Britain's fighter defences on the ground and in the air, and RAF Fighter Command struggled to remain in being until the autumn gales of the English Channel made invasion improbable. The Battle of Britain began with bomber attacks on the convoys of ships passing through the

Dover Strait, carrying coal to the ports on England's south coast. When the sea bed was sufficiently littered with coal and corpses, the British Admiralty decided to use the Dover Strait only at night. It disregarded a German radar near Cap Gris-Nez, and the threat posed by bombers based in Normandy as a convoy went farther down-Channel. When dawn broke on August 8, 1940, a coal convoy on its way from the Thames estuary to Dorset found German torpedo boats waiting for them. Three ships were sunk. Dive-bombers attacking the convoy off Brighton were driven off, but further assaults near the Isle of Wight sank seven more ships. Others were badly damaged, and only four out of twenty merchant ships arrived at their destinations. In the air fighting that day, the Germans lost thirty-one aircraft, the RAF nineteen.

The British navy suffered such heavy losses at Dunkirk and during the Channel convoy fiascos that it virtually withdrew from the scene. The destroyers, backed by battleships, meant to return when Sea Lion took to the water, but they would need strong fighter protection if they were to survive long enough to sink the barges. The defence of the narrow seas therefore depended on the British fighters, Spitfires and Hurricanes, and they in turn relied on radar. The mysterious Eiffel Towers of a primitive radar chain stood at intervals along the English coast, and allowed the scarce fighters to be deployed with maximum effect. The German air crews were dismayed to find the enemy always airborne and waiting for them.

They tried to knock out the radar in time for the main air offensive. On August 12, precision bombers from Calais attacked coastal radar stations at Dover, Rye, and Pevensey, and another one inland in Kent. On the same day, a long-range radar on the Isle of Wight was hit by bombers from Normandy. A vital station at Littlehampton on the Sussex coast was overlooked. Although some damage was done to the others, their backup systems put them quickly back on the air. The Germans were slow to think of jamming the radars.

From his forward headquarters at Cap Blanc-Nez, Albert Kesselring controlled the Luftwaffe's Air Fleet 2, which took the lead in the assault on England. His fighters, mainly Messerschmitt

109s, used airfields near the coast between Dunkirk and Boulogne, so as to remain within the range of London. The bomber bases were scattered more widely. Kesselring's direct opponent was Keith Park, commanding the fighter group in southeastern England, under guidance from Hugh Dowding, the chief of Fighter Command. The German strategy was to send bombers with fighter cover to attack airfields and civilian targets, and force the RAF to fight. They expected to win by attrition, and they were nearly right. By early September 1940 the British seemed to be losing the Battle of Britain. Aircraft were in short supply, and so were experienced fighter pilots. But Dowding and Park husbanded them with great skill, as they fought a new kind of war, in which high-speed aircraft were plotted by radar and deployed by radio.

The climax came on September 15, the last target date for Operation Sea Lion. Four hundred German fighters roared away across the Dover Strait in support of a hundred bombers heading for London. Three hundred British fighters climbed to meet them. There were fierce battles all the way to London and back. The British claimed 185 German aircraft shot down. The true figure was nearer 50, but the show of strength by the defending fighters persuaded the Germans that they could not count on controlling the air over the English Channel.

The equinox was drawing near, and on September 17, 1940, the Germans began dispersing the forces assembled for the invasion of England. There were sighs of relief from the French, Belgian, and Dutch barge owners, who had been press-ganged to steer their craft across the Dover Strait on behalf of the invaders. The escape from Dunkirk and the standoff in the air enabled the British to survive as Hitler's only remaining opponents at that stage of World War II. The radar pulses sweeping across the sea from the towers at Dover kept Britain an island in the age of flight.

The ketch heads for England, in the same general direction as the Dunkirk soldiers and Kesselring's fighters, making for the coast of Kent. The modern traffic lanes of the Dover Strait must be crossed at right angles, and they force us to take an indirect route that first slants away from the French coast, almost as far as Cap Blanc-Nez. Then, like children crossing a street, we turn sharply to starboard towards the South Goodwin light vessel, which lies eleven sea miles away, across the shipping lanes. Because of the strong currents, we have to steer crabwise to maintain a rectangular course over the sea bed. When a ship comes into view, the game consists of taking repeated bearings to see whether any risk of collision exists. Our small vessel is required to keep out of their way, and the visibility is not good.

A few miles away to starboard lies the Out Ruytingen sand ridge, the last of the Flemish banks. A light vessel that used to mark the Out Ruytingen has been replaced by a buoy. These waters have no more poignant tale of nationhood than a covert operation carried out by Irish nationalists, which began at the Out Ruytingen light vessel on a misty day like this. It took place just before the outbreak of World War I. The leader was Erskine Childers, an Anglo-Irish yachtsman and writer, torn between loyalty to England and his enthusiasm for Irish freedom.

Yachtsmen know Childers best for his novel, *The Riddle of the Sands* (1903). We still chuckle at his description of the guest joining a scruffy boat in a Baltic fjord, dressed in the uniform of a fashionable yachtsman at Cowes. "Aren't your men here?" is his inept question when the skipper meets him off the train, and his portmanteau is too large to pass through the hatch of the small cutter. *Dulcibella* of the novel was based on Childers's own little *Vixen*. In 1897 he had her in Boulogne, intending to sail to the Mediterranean, but an unrelenting west wind defeated him. *Vixen*'s log has him running "two-reefed in bumpy sea to Calais." From there he took his boat to Germany, and the setting of his novel. It is a story of espionage mixed with hazardous sailing inside the German Frisian Islands, whence the Germans are preparing to launch a fleet of barges to invade England. Childers made it up, yet the German navy was toying with just such a plan.

In 1914 Childers was in the Dover Strait again, exchanging fiction for madcap reality. Two yachts were to smuggle German rifles down the Channel and around Land's End to Ireland, for delivery to a nationalist fighting force, at a time when all Ireland was still under British rule. A tugboat, *Gladiator,* brought guns from Hamburg to the Out Ruytingen light vessel. At one P.M. on a foggy Sunday, July 12, the Irish yachtsman Conor O'Brien (who spelt his name, eccentrically, as O Brien) arrived in his sailing cutter *Kelpie*. He was Childers's fellow conspirator, and he wrote an account of the operation.

O'Brien hove to within sight of the tugboat, and rowed a boat over to her. He was an hour late for the rendezvous. "A pale bearded figure of romantic and conspiratorial aspect," by the name of Darrel Figgis, stood on the tugboat's deck, "suffering from an awful toothache." O'Brien addressed him in the Celtic tongue, but was rebuked for it. *Gladiator*'s German crew were supposed to think them Mexicans, and customs officers at Hamburg had been given to understand that fifteen hundred Mauser rifles in bales of straw and the forty thousand rounds of ammunition in boxes were machine parts.

O'Brien was grateful for the poor visibility, otherwise "it would have been rather a public place for the job." He had already stripped the cabin, ripped up the floorboards, and unshipped the skylight, and he had his ballast in the form of bags of gravel, ready to pour overboard. *Kelpie* hauled alongside the tugboat and the transhipment began. The arms filled the cabin until there was room only to crawl over them, and to recline "in the Roman manner" around a makeshift table under the skylight. At dusk, as the work ended, another yacht hove in sight.

This was *Asgard,* a Norwegian-built two-master skippered by Childers. The boat had been a wedding present from his father-in-law. Cruising yachtsmen already had a reputation for going idiotically hither and yon, and it provided excellent cover for the operation. The women in the boats added to the illusion. Childers's wife, Molly, was with him in *Asgard*. The rest of his crew consisted of another yachtsman, Gordon Shephard, two Donegal fishermen who had thought they had embarked for an ordinary cruise, and Mary Spring Rice, who was no sailor but had started the idea of running the guns.

Looking back, after more than seven decades of bloodshed in Ireland, between Republicans who wish to be rid of the British and the Unionists who still command a majority in the north, people on both sides may be baffled by Childers's split loyalty. Why was the fierce patriot, who had warned the British about the Germans in *The Riddle of the Sands,* taking guns to the Irish Volunteers who were preparing to fight the British? There is no deep mystery. Childers had grown up in Ireland and he understood why the British were regarded as oppressors. As clerk of the British House of Commons he had seen the repeated successes of the Home Rule movement frustrated by the House of Lords. By April 1914 a constitutional change had removed that obstacle. But the British army in the north of Ireland was conniving in the illegal shipment of rifles to the Ulster Volunteers, who were preparing to oppose by force the lawful devolution of power to Dublin. Civil war was brewing, and the Irish Volunteers were crying out for weapons to defend themselves.

Childers, O'Brien, and their shipmates saw themselves as redressing the balance, with natural justice on their side. It was also an adventure suitable for incorrigible romantics. As O'Brien put it:

> In those good old days all the best people were engaged on one side or the other, in the contraband trade; so I, to be in the fashion, had put my yacht and my services at the disposal of the other side . . . I think that as early as that very few of us contemplated a war with England.

O'Brien's *Kelpie* cast off from *Gladiator* and set sail for Ireland. As she disappeared in the mist, the tug came alongside Childers's *Asgard,* and the German crew passed aboard the rest of the guns and ammunition—the greater part of the consignment, in fact. Molly Childers grumbled about the grease of the rifles, which smeared over everything, and the gun runners nearly blew themselves up when an oil lamp fell through the hatch and bounced off Molly onto a heap of packing straw. At 2:30 A.M. the transfer was complete, and the tug towed the thoroughly untidy yacht in the darkness as far as Dover, so that when dawn broke *Asgard* was ahead of *Kelpie.* Although they did not sight each other again, both skippers were fretting about the stability of their heavily laden "cargo yachts," and the manoeuvres of British warships that unwittingly harassed them. Our ketch will follow in their wake, as far as Land's End.

First we have to find England. Fog circles around us, and we join the Dover Strait Band with our puny aerosol trumpet. A menacing tuba shifts past our stem. A less strident but more persistent horn transforms itself into a German coaster that breaks out of the fog and passes close enough to leave us sweating. A herd of ferries is lowing in the direction of Dover—a place to avoid in these conditions. Then the sound we want to hear becomes audible from dead ahead: the distinctive double blast of a light vessel. The diaphone warns off the shipping; us, it leads towards safety.

When the light vessel suddenly breaks into our circle of visibility, she is towering only fifty metres off. Another yacht is hanging from her on a long warp, and we shall follow that example. At close quarters, the din of the diaphone is stupefying. The crewmen kindly take our rope, but they are wearing earmuffs, which make conversation difficult. In the quiet intervals, they speak English, so we have come to the correct country. Huge white letters on the red hull declare: SOUTH GOODWIN.

Echoes in the Sand

Beside the white cliffs of Dover, toylike ferries come and go between the breakwaters, five sea miles away. Because of the heavy traffic, and rough water in Dover harbour, it is not a good place for yachts. The nearer cliffs of South Foreland make a rounded corner where the English coast turns northward. They are very like the chalk cliffs of High Normandy, complete with the dark horizontal lines of flints. The cliffs are ragged because of rapid erosion, and the white lighthouse looks as if it will soon be due to fall into the sea. Still beyond the prevailing visibility, almost fifteen miles to the north, is North Foreland, where the coast takes another emphatic turn into the estuary of London's river. A broad bay between the Forelands accommodates the towns of Deal, Sandwich, and Ramsgate. With night coming on, our ketch proceeds to a traditional anchorage near Deal.

Off the coast between the South and North Forelands is the maritime black hole called the Goodwin Sands, long known as the "ship swallower." It devoured a previous South Goodwin light vessel. On the night of November 26–27, 1954, she broke her anchor chain in a severe storm from the south, and finished up six miles away, on her side on the sands. Next morning an American helicopter lifted off a fisheries official who had been visiting the light vessel. He reported that some of the seven-man crew were still alive, trapped inside the wreck. But the bad weather prevented naval divers from boarding her until twenty-four hours later, by which time the light vessel was filled with sand.

Five miles from South Goodwin, the town of Deal presides over the sands like Pluto over the underworld. At low tide, the crests of the sandbanks rise a metre or two above the water, and you could celebrate your arrival in England by playing a short game of cricket on them. Hovercraft from Ramsgate used to skim impertinently over the Goodwins, bound for Calais. A deep channel slants through them, called the Kellett Gut. Flotsam—seaweed, plastic bags, beer cans, sticks—is caught in the tidal eddies that encircle the banks.

The Goodwin Sands extend roughly twelve miles north–south and are more than two miles wide at their broadest part. Legend has it that they were once an island, Lomea, belonging to Earl Godwin, father of King Harold Godwinson. Although Godwin sailed rebellious fleets in these waters, the names seem to be a coincidence. Godwin or Goodwin means "good joy"—think of *win* in the word "winsome." Applied to the sands it is heavy sarcasm in Old English style. Archaeologists and geologists doubt

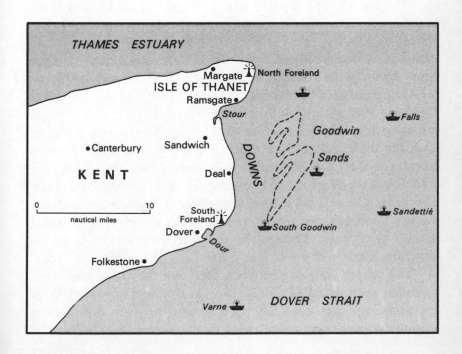

that they were ever habitable. The sands have probably culled boats and ships in the funnel of the Dover Strait for thousands of years. Many ships were lost when they chose to go near the Goodwin Sands on purpose, because they act as breakwaters shielding the shore.

Protection of a different sort came from the three castles in as many miles that stand on the shore near Deal. This was always the chief corner of Britain for watching out for seaborne invaders. The mesolithic hunters were the last to walk across before the sea rose to flood the Dover Strait after the last Ice Age. All later immigrants had to come by boat: horticulturalists, plough farmers, Beaker folk, Celts, Romans, Anglo-Saxons, Vikings, Normans, and refugees that included Flemish Protestants and German Jews. As Daniel Defoe put it:

> From this amphibious ill-born mob began
> That vain, ill-natured thing, an Englishman.

The Dover cliffs showed many of them the way, and if the Goodwin Sands did not catch them, they could find good landing places nearby. The chalk of South Foreland slopes down a more approachable beach at Deal. A sheltered channel used to cut through Kent. Away to the north of us, Ramsgate harbour and the North Foreland stand on a former island of chalk, which the Celts called *Tanat,* or "fire island." It is still the Isle of Thanet, even though you can go there by bus nowadays. The channel separating Thanet from the mainland of Kent offered access to Canterbury and a shortcut to the Thames estuary. In Roman times, the present site of Deal was therefore at a strategic corner, and that helps to explain why Julius Caesar landed here. He reported that not a single ship was lost while carrying troops, on any of his army's four crossings of the Dover Strait. Perhaps the archaeologists investigating the Goodwin Sands will prove him a liar.

The stretch of water between Deal and the Goodwins, four sea miles wide, is called the Downs. In the days of sailing ships this anchorage was crowded with vessels of every description, waiting for a fair wind or sheltering from gales or fog. Deal served

Smugglers are usually camera-shy, but a snapshot taken in July 1914 shows Erskine Childers at the wheel of his yacht *Asgard* while sailing down the English Channel with an illegal consignment of German rifles for the supporters of Irish Home Rule. His shipmate was another pioneering cruising yachtsman, Gordon Shephard.

(From A Thirst for the Sea *by Hugh and Robin Popham, Stanford Maritime, London)*

The notorious Goodwin Sands claimed one of the light vessels that warn other ships to keep clear when she was torn from her moorings by a storm in 1954. Her crew perished and the sands swallowed her. *(Skyfotos)*

For more than two centuries the Dutch ship *Amsterdam* has lain in a Sussex beach, showing her timbers at times of very low tides. In 1984, diving archaeologists began exploring the wreck in earnest, using a platform erected nearby. *(Peter Marsden)*

The lighthouse of Beachy Head, 32 metres tall, is dwarfed by the chalk cliffs of the English Channel's grandest headland. Erosion that cuts back the cliffs at an average rate of a metre a year keeps them sheer and white. *(Skyfotos)*

"H. R. H. The Prince Royal awakening the Spirit of Brighton" is the title of a painting by Paul Nash (1944) commemorating the part played by King George III's playboy son in making Brighton a fashionable resort. The nymph's waist is inscribed with the old name of the fishing village: Brighthelmstone. *(Royal Pavilion, Brighton)*

"The Chain Pier at Brighton" was painted by J. M. W. Turner about five years after it was opened in 1823. It survived the weather of the English Channel until 1896, and gave the seaside visitors a focus of interest on an otherwise featureless shore. *(Tate Gallery, London)*

When Queen Elizabeth II inspected her navy from the Royal Yacht *Britannia* at the Spithead Review of 1977, there were already misgivings about the survival of conventional warships in the era of homing missiles. These doubts were confirmed by losses in the Falklands War five years later.
(John Hillelson/Georg Gerster)

Members of the Royal Yacht
Squadron at Cowes, in 1895,
included Edward Prince of Wales
and Kaiser Wilhelm II of
Germany (foreground, right).
The Squadron survives as the
most exclusive of yacht clubs,
but its notions of sail power have
been left behind by the French
multihulled yachts that sprint
across the Atlantic. One of these,
Elf Aquitaine (below), is seen
leaving Plymouth at the start of
the 1984 *Observer* Singlehanded
Transatlantic Race. *(Photographic
Records/Royal Yacht Squadron* and
Patrick Roach)

The author at the wheel of the ketch *Charmed. (John Dollar)*

A brand-new ship, *Union Star*, was smashed on the granite of Cornwall after her engine failed in a violent storm in 1981. This shipwreck cost the lives of eight people aboard the ship, as well as the entire eight-man crew of the Penlee lifeboat. *(Royal Naval Air Station, Culdrose, Photographic Section)*

as the port of the Downs. But when the wind blew strongly from the south into the gap between the Goodwins and the shore, the anchorage became uncomfortable, to put it mildly. And a westerly storm, whistling over the flat shoreline between Deal and Ramsgate, could cast the anchored ships onto the sands.

The worst event of that kind occurred in the early hours of a Saturday morning, November 27, 1703. On the previous evening Daniel Defoe, living in London, thought that his children had been fooling about with his barometer. The mercury had sunk lower than he had ever seen it go. A fierce storm then hit southern England. As a good journalist, Defoe quickly produced a book, *The Storm,* which he described as "a collection of the most re-markable casualties and disasters which happened in the late dreadful tempest, both by sea and land."

As Defoe explained, all the ports and anchorages were crowded with ships. Strong winds had raged for nearly two weeks before the culminating storm, "so that the sea was as it were swept clean of all shipping." Inbound ships arrived home ahead of schedule, and outward-bound ships were driven back into port, "for the wind had blown so very hard, directly into the Channel, that there was no possibility of their keeping the sea whose course was not right afore the wind."

On the night of November 26–27, 160 merchant ships and eighteen warships lay at anchor in the Downs. Almost all of them were ripped from their moorings. The fortunate ones were driven out to sea, but others were lost on the Goodwin Sands. These included four ships of the line, *Northumberland, Restoration, Stirling Castle,* and *Mary,* of which the last was the flagship of Rear Admiral Edward Beaumont. An eyewitness described the scene in a letter written while his own ship was still riding out the last of the storm.

> These ships fired their guns all night and day long, poor souls, for help, but the storm being too fierce and raging, could have none to save them. The ship called the *Shrewsberry* that we are in, broke two anchors, and did run mighty fierce backwards, within sixty or eighty yards of the sands, and as God Almighty

would have it, we flung our sheet anchor down, which is the biggest, and so stopped. . . . To see Admiral Beaumont that was next to us, and all the rest of his men, how they climbed up the main mast, hundreds at a time crying out for help, and thinking to save their lives, and in a twinkling of an eye were drowned. . . . I have not had my clothes off, nor a wink of sleep these four nights, and have got my death with cold almost.

Another ship at anchor in the Downs was narrowly missed by *Stirling Castle,* and her captain, J. Adams, reported "a sight full of terrible particulars":

She had cut away all her masts, the men were all in the confusions of death and despair; she had neither anchor, nor cable, nor boat to help her; the sea breaking over her in a terrible manner, that sometimes she seemed all under water; and they knew, as well as we that saw her, that they drove by the tempest directly for the Goodwin, where they could expect nothing but destruction. The cries of the men, and the firing their guns, one by one, every half minute for help, terrified us in such a manner, that I think we were half dead with the horror of it.

Captain Adams's own ship then began dragging her anchor, so she put out to sea under an improvised sail, narrowly skirting the Goodwins. She ran before the wind for three days, her captain and crew not knowing where they were. When they sighted land ahead and made distress signals, the pilots who came out to meet them and take them to a safe anchorage turned out to be Norwegian.

From Deal, on the morning after the great storm, some survivors of wrecked ships could be seen by telescope walking to and fro on the Goodwin Sands at low tide, and signalling for help. In Defoe's words, "they were sure to be all washed into another world at the reflux of the tide." Some boats from the town were already nearby, but they were searching for booty from the wrecks, not for survivors. Thomas Powell, mayor of Deal, urged the customs officers to go out in their boats to save the lives of the

men on the sands, but they "rudely refused." Mayor Powell offered his townsfolk five shillings for every man whose life they
could save. Rescuers then came forward. They put out in commandeered boats, and lifted more than two hundred men to safety.

The entire ships' companies of *Northumberland* and *Restoration*
had been drowned. There was one survivor from *Mary* and seventy
from *Stirling Castle*. The lives lost in the four warships amounted
to 1188, but there is no reckoning of the merchant seamen who
perished. Defoe scorned as an "extravagancy" a French report that
altogether three hundred ships and thirty thousand seamen had
been lost in the Channel in the great storm.

The Goodwins change shape as the sands shift, especially
during rough weather. Buried ships can then reappear on the sea
bed. In 1979 amateur divers from Ramsgate found the wreck of
a wooden man of war partly disinterred in a slope of the Goodwins.
She was identified as *Stirling Castle,* with her hull largely intact
after 276 years. Small items were recovered from her, including
bottles of wine. Then the sands moved again and reburied her.

This glimpse of *Stirling Castle* made marine archaeologists
eager for the next time a ship appeared on the sea bed. They wanted
to be ready to discover her secrets, before waves and currents
destroyed a possibly frail craft, or before the sands swallowed her
again. But that meant knowing where the wrecks were, and which
ones might be ready to emerge from the shifting sands.

The fishermen of Ramsgate knew of many obstacles on the
Goodwin Sands, where their nets were liable to snag. An amateur
archaeologist interviewed the fishermen and compiled a list of
more than two hundred "net fastenings." Each of these may be
an exposed wreck or a piece of a wreck, and many more boats
and ships may lie buried more deeply. Ships of every era, back to
neolithic times, were in peril at the Goodwins. Even if only one
a year were swallowed in the sands, the tally would run into
thousands. X-ray the sands and you would expect to find fifty
centuries of maritime history and prehistory.

The Goodwins Archaeological Survey is "X-raying" the sands
with the most advanced geophysical and underwater technologies.
Industrial firms have lent gear and technical experts to the project.

In its first season, in the summer of 1983, the surveyors sailed in a small vessel packed with equipment, towing their detectors to and fro across an area representing about ten per cent of the Goodwin Sands. The team identified about a hundred geophysical "targets."

In this high-tech wreck-hunting, sidescan sonar, as its name implies, surveys the sea bed with acoustic pulses directed sideways. It yielded forty-four of the first batch of targets. A pinger, sending acoustic signals to penetrate the topmost ten metres of sand, picked up three of the same targets, and another ten apparently buried too deeply to show up at the sand surface. Some of these lay on the bedrock under the sand. A proton magnetometer detected forty-six objects containing iron, only one of which showed up also on the sidescan sonar. All the while, radio beacons on the shore fixed the positions of the vessel and its detectors to within a few metres.

The searchers also used a Type II Seapup, a mechanical fish under remote control. It inspected some of the wrecks poking through the sea bed, with a video camera and a photographic camera. The Goodwins are difficult for divers because of the strong tidal currents and the poor visibility underwater, which ranges from nil to five metres.

If the blips are to translate themselves into major finds, one of the chief tasks is to understand better how the sands move, and in particular to know when deep channels are liable to change their positions and uncover the buried wrecks. Most of the archaeological digging will have to be done by the sea itself, when the ship swallower regurgitates its undigested meals.

From a shallow anchorage a little north of Deal, the streetlights of Sandwich are visible two kilometres inland. The name, meaning "sandy market," traces back to the ninth century. Sandwich became for a while a major port and naval base, but it was almost cut off from the sea by the time the eating habits of an earl of Sandwich gave the town's name to the most famous of fast foods, around 1762. He was an insatiable gambler who sent for slices of cold beef between two pieces of toast so that he could eat without interrupting the game.

Sandwich is embalmed in its sand, and you can reach it by the Stour River only in a shallow-draft yacht, when the tide is high. A cluster of houses beside Sandwich has a resounding name: Great Stonar. It used to be a port too. Beyond it lie the remains of a fort that stood by the shore in Roman times and is now four kilometres from the sea. Golfers of the snooty Royal St. George's club exploit the sand dunes that straddle the former gap five sea miles wide, from Deal to Ramsgate ("links" is the Old English word for dunes). Marshy ground fills the lost sea bed across a swath of Kent.

Ports as well as ships have been wrecked all along the coast of southeastern England. The Cinque Ports, of which Sandwich is one, sum up the coastal changes most briskly. They were an association of five great English ports with special privileges and naval duties connected with the defence of the Channel shore. They failed to prevent the Norman Conquest because King Harold dispersed his fleet when the summer ended. After the Conquest, two other "head" ports joined the original five, and the list of seven Cinque Ports reads, from east to west: Sandwich, Dover, Hythe, Romney, Rye, Winchelsea, and Hastings. Every one of them has lost its natural harbour, and Winchelsea was washed away in a storm.

There is no decent harbour left anywhere along the southeastern coast of England between Dover and Newhaven, a distance of fifty-six sea miles. Both Dover and Newhaven rely on manmade breakwaters. The destruction of the Cinque Ports made southeastern England less important from a maritime point of view than its location close to France would suggest, and it drove ship owners and admirals either northward to the Thames or downChannel, nearer to the Atlantic. Nature's damage nudged the English into concentrating their wealth in London and redeploying their seamen towards the western ocean.

These local changes are part of the endless contest of sea and land, conducted by nature on all the beaches of the world. If the Earth's crust stopped moving up and down, and the sea stayed at a constant level, erosion would reduce the land to a swamp like Florida. In practice what you see are upstart cliffs and headlands being hacked back by the sea, and bays and estuaries filling with sediments. The best time to be a sailor was when the sea first rose after the Ice Age. Rivers cut deep valleys when the sea was low, and their flooding by salt water provided fine harbours.

As the sea came close to its present level five thousand years ago, worldwide marshmaking began. The present warm interglacial period has lasted too long. Many of the world's important ports survive only with expensive sea works and endless dredging. Others have been bequeathed to fishermen and yachtsmen, who find them increasingly difficult to use. Pull out the plug and let the sea level fall again in a new Ice Age, and the marshes and sandbars would be cleaned away, in readiness for a fresh start.

The present sea bed is a large beach temporarily covered by the interglacial supertide. As the rising sea came up-Channel, it carried before it a generous supply of sand and broken stones from the outlying continental shelf. Sandy shores and dunes were grander five thousand years ago because much of the available sand and shingle has since been incorporated into new land. Ground-up seashells and dismembered cliffs have partly made up for the losses, but the English Channel is running out of the stuff that seaside dreams are made of.

The waves are responsible for what beaches there are. Without their peculiar action, the sand and shingle would settle on the sea bed and leave only rocky or muddy shores. The waves push the sediments up the beach, and when you wade at the water's edge your ankles feel the uphill pressure that comes with each new wave. The contrary pull is weaker on shingle beaches because the water drains away between the stones, and shingle beaches are steeper than sandy beaches.

A change in the weather can alter the slope and width of a beach in a matter of hours, when different kinds of waves hit it. Storm waves of long wavelength are destructive, and beaches are often less spacious in winter than in summer. And when fine sand dries, the wind blows it away. Dunes at the back of the beach are piles of windblown sand stolen from the sea. Exceptionally stormy weather in the thirteenth century left sand piled high and dry on the beaches, and many dunes of the Channel shore are seven hundred years old.

Near headlands like South Foreland, strong currents and waves tend to sweep the beaches away. Without their protection, the headlands are open to attack by the sea. On the other hand, sediments gather in bays, where the sea is weaker, creating the familiar sandy beaches of coves. River estuaries fill up with mud and sand. The overall effect is to streamline the coast. The lightest silt and sand travel most easily, whether up the beach or along the sea bed. Heavy shingle accumulates at the beach level where the wave action is strongest. Large pieces of shingle might not move at all, but for the fact that seaweed grows on them and can eventually lift them.

The most damaging outcome of beach mobility is the longshore drift. When a wave hits a shingle beach at an angle, it pushes the pebbles slantwise up the beach. Then they roll straight back towards the water's edge. The next wave gives another slanting push, and you can watch the pebbles zigzagging downwind. Sand travels in the same direction, but much of its movement takes place when it is churned up in the water of the waves. Because the prevailing winds of the Channel are from the west, the drift is towards the east. The beaches are on the move all the way from Land's End to the Dover Strait, and the eastward longshore drift has been a continual theme in the history of the coast.

So has the choking of rivers. To approach a river from the sea, ships and boats must negotiate the submerged dam of sand across the estuary, where the waves break. River bars often drive seafarers away from promised shelter, or drown them if they try too hard to reach it. Bars grow when offshore currents find room to spread themselves after rounding the headland at the mouth of an estuary. The currents become weaker, and drop some of the load of sediment they are carrying. This process also creates spits of sand that project from the headlands and are nourished by the longshore drift. A sand spit running northward from Deal forced Sandwich's Stour River into a hairpin bend and made it prone to silting.

The inflowing tide carries its finest sediments right into a river mouth and leaves them there as silt. When silt and mud pile up in the estuary to reach the level of high tides, salt-resistant vegetation begins to grow on it, and human beings are tempted to hasten the process by actively reclaiming the land. Towards the end of the fifteenth century, the archbishop of Canterbury, who owned land beside the water, extended his property by walling in the tidal mud flats. The last straw for Sandwich was the wrecking of a large ship belonging to the pope in the entrance to the Stour in the mid-sixteenth century. She trapped the sand and created a dangerous man-made bar.

After a nocturnal glimpse of Sandwich, the ketch now turns firmly down-Channel, heading westward at dawn past Dover, the second of the Cinque Ports. Its eastern breakwater marks the site of the Bronze Age shipwreck of more than three thousand years ago, mentioned earlier. The eight-hundred-year-old keep of Dover Castle, on a high hill behind the cliffs to the east of the town, is the obvious landmark, but the ramparts of the two-thousand-year-old Celtic hill fort that surround it are more impressive. The outer walls of the castle end abruptly at the cliff's edge because part of the structure has fallen into the sea. At the western end of the castle church is a Roman lighthouse, the counterpart to Caligula's pharos at Boulogne. It was erected soon after the Roman conquest in A.D. 43. The creek that made Dover a harbour in those days has vanished under the streets and buildings of the modern town.

The name of Shakespeare Cliff, one hundred metres tall on the western side of the port, acknowledges the playwright's *King Lear*. Edgar guides to Dover his blinded father, Gloucester, who wants to throw himself off the cliff. At what he pretends is the very edge of the cliff, Edgar declares:

> The fishermen that walk upon the beach
> Appear like mice, and yond tall anchoring bark
> Diminish'd to her cock, her cock a buoy
> Almost too small for sight. The murmuring surge,
> That on the unnumber'd idle pebbles chafes,
> Cannot be heard so high.

The cliffs are the best clue to the old port's history. They stay white and sheer because they are always eroding, revealing fresh surfaces of chalk. In Roman times they extended several hundred metres nearer to France. They sheltered a neat harbour between them in the valley of the Dour River, which gives Dover its Celtic name and occupies a fault in the shoreline. Now the coast is sawn back, to put the town on the seafront and the castle close to the cliff's edge.

The travel writer Tobias Smollett related how he was set down on the open beach at Dover in 1758, when the ship that brought him from Calais could not enter the harbour at low water. Smollett, who was literally jaundiced, suspected deception:

> Every parcel and bundle, as it was landed, was snatched up by a separate porter: one ran away with a hat-box, another with a wig-box, a third with a couple of shirts tied up in a handkerchief, and two were employed in carrying a small portmanteau that did not weigh forty pounds.

Each porter demanded half a crown, a lot of money in those days. Smollett regarded Dover as a den of thieves given to "fraud, imposition, and brutality," but even a rogue likes to seem plausible, and the port was plainly unsatisfactory.

A century later Matthew Arnold, writing his poem *Dover Beach,* was struck by how exposed the shoreline was, and used it as a joyless image of the decline of faith:

> . . . Retreating to the breath
> Of the night-wind, down the vast edges drear
> And naked shingles of the world.

The shingles here are naked no more. Dover owes its monopoly of the ferry services to human reconstruction of the shore. Arnold was in his grave when work started on the artificial breakwaters in 1897. They enclose more than a mile of Dover beach and jut far out into the strait. Fourteen million travellers now pass through Dover every year, more than seventy per cent of the cross-Channel passenger traffic.

Wreck of
a Dutchman

The chalk comes to an end before Folkestone. Vertical movements have brought clay and sandstone older than the chalk up to sea level, and the shoreline slants through the strata like a knife through multicoloured ice cream. Alternating ribbons of sandstone and clay stretch inland from Folkestone, across Kent and the neighbouring county of Sussex, making the forest district called the Weald. The first colour change is from white to blue-grey, and the cliffs east of Folkestone seem badly in need of a facelift. The chalk has given way to an older mudstone called gault, which has fallen towards the sea in landslides. The beach and the sea bed are cluttered with the large stones that gave so much trouble to the men laying the cross-Channel power cable. Copt Point, at the western side of Folkestone's modest ferry port, has a slightly firmer look because its foundations are yellow-green sandstone. As the ketch continues westward past Sandgate, where the sea has carried away a sixteenth-century castle, the sandstone changes colour to a grey-green, and then to grey.

This is dinosaur territory. The sands and clays composing this shore were laid down about 115 million years ago, when the whole region was a subtropical lake evolving into an arm of the sea, on the edge of the Paris Basin. Whenever the water level was relatively low, sand accumulated; when it rose a little, clay formed. These conditions alternated many times, leaving clay layered with sand, and sand shot through with clay. Dinosaurs lived beside the lake, and the very first dinosaur fossils were identified in 1822 in the Weald of Sussex by a doctor and his wife, just thirty kilometres from the present Channel shore.

Who would guess that Hythe, the third of the Cinque Ports, ever possessed a harbour? The beach sweeps past it without even a kink, and the town is now a seaside resort. While Sandwich succumbed to sand, and Dover's harbour was sawn off, Hythe borrowed an estuary that turned out to be terminally sick. That was in the course of the oddest changes to occur on this coast. Defying the general trend towards straighter shorelines, a salient of swamp and shingle has invaded the sea beyond Hythe. It is called Romney Marsh, and it covers a hundred square kilometres that formerly belonged to the English Channel.

In Roman times it would not have been necessary to make a ten-mile dogleg around Romney Marsh and its headland at Dungeness. After sailing for two or three miles across what is now sheep pasture, trading ships reached the harbour of *Portus Lemanis,* sheltered by a spit of land opposite a cliff on which a fort stood guard.

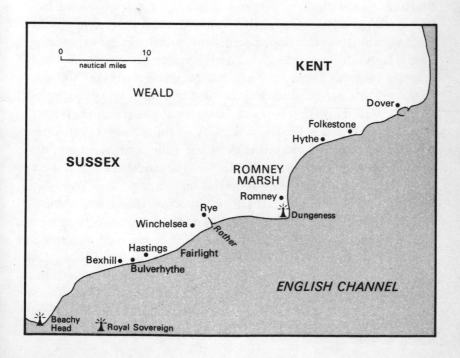

The Romans cannot have liked this part of the coast, with its dense forests inland and its swamps beside the sea. Even in the twentieth century Romney Marsh is a no-man's-land between Kent and Sussex, and the most thinly populated corner of southeastern England. *Anopheles atroparvus* lives here, a mosquito capable of transmitting malaria, which was indeed prevalent as "marsh fever" until early in this century. So what were the Romans doing here?

The prize was iron. Even before the Roman invasion, the Weald was England's prime source of iron ore. By modern standards, when steelmakers have access to far-flung mountains of high-grade ore, the clay ironstone of Kent and Sussex seems poor stuff, but it is widely scattered in beds laid down 120 to 130 million years ago and now exposed at the surface. The forests of the Weald provided charcoal to smelt the metal used in Iron Age swords, and later in the cannon balls that hit the Spanish Armada. So, in Roman times, ships left *Portus Lemanis* with cargoes of Wealden iron.

The clay of the Weald is not robust, and the story of Romney Marsh begins with the sea gnawing the clay to create a wide bay. It is outlined by the fossil cliffs running inland, west of Hythe. Sand spits and bars developed across the mouth of the bay, creating a silty lagoon up to fifteen kilometres wide. Because it was shallow, the bay was greatly affected by the small changes in the level of the sea that occurred during the past five thousand years, as the world's glaciers melted or grew like climatic thermometers.

Noah's Flood is the most famous of those sea-level changes. Around 2900 B.C. it swamped the river valleys of Mesopotamia, and here in Kent the water poured over the sand-bars and marshes of the big lagoon, restoring it to the sea. A deposit of blue clay, found under Romney Marsh, seems to correspond with Noah's Flood. About eight hundred years later the opposite happened: The sea level dropped, and the bay dried out well enough to support oak and beech trees. Bronze Age seafarers passing this way would have seen a forest behind the sand dunes.

A warmer climate and a rising sea destroyed the forest in the tenth century B.C. The sea returned to the ancient cliff line, killed the trees with salt, and buried the resulting peat under the sand

and mud of a new lagoon. A fall in the sea level around 120 B.C. left the ground dry enough for the Romans to occupy parts of Romney Marsh after their conquest of Britain. After A.D. 150 the sea rose yet again, setting the stage for the German pirates who went far up the rivers on their raids.

During the centuries that followed, the rivers began taking more direct routes to the sea. One of them, the Rother, broke through the spit that straddled the old bay, to emerge at Romney, which gives the marsh its name. That outlet lay eight miles southeast of *Portus Lemanis*. In A.D. 893 a large Viking fleet was able to follow the new river right across the marsh to the ancient shoreline, and into the forest beyond.

The shifting of the Rother River left *Portus Lemanis* with only a small stream. What remained of the entrance channel still made an adequate harbour, well sheltered from the west. The Cinque Port of Hythe was established there around A.D. 1000. The name simply means "landing place" in Old English. As the harbour silted up, the landing place gradually moved eastward. A grand church, completed in the thirteenth century, dates the zenith of Hythe's port. Within three hundred years the beach drifting along the shore of the marsh extinguished it. The waves and tides massaged the beach until the last hint of a harbour was erased.

When the Rother River adopted it, Romney flourished as a port for about four centuries. The Rother eventually jilted Romney as well. The people of Romney had seen trouble brewing ten kilometres upstream, where subsidence of the land was threatening to divert the river. Sometime before the middle of the thirteenth century they built a canal right across the marsh, in an effort to force the Rother to keep flowing towards Romney. Called the Rhee Wall, it has often been mistaken for a Roman dike, but it was a medieval canal that was still being extended in 1257, before the English Channel summarily overruled these efforts to save Romney's port.

The further removal of the Rother was a minor consequence of a succession of storms and floods that savaged northwestern Europe during the thirteenth century. They were made worse by the high sea level prevailing after a period of warm centuries. A great storm of 1287 outflanked the Rhee Wall, captured the Rother River at its trouble spot, and drew it westward onto a new course near Rye. With no river to keep the sand and shingle at bay, Romney rapidly became another of the Channel's waterless ports. The tower of its church is visible two kilometres behind the dunes.

At the sharp end of the salient beyond Romney Marsh, Dungeness is a barren expanse of shingle. The scattered man-made structures, including the tall black-and-white lighthouse and the lifeboat shed, have the air of a space station erected haphazardly on a lunar plain. The marsh was friendly by comparison. At night Dungeness can look weirdly beautiful, but daylight reveals a forlorn scene, better known to seafarers than the population ashore— although some people seem to journey here especially to dump their garbage. If "grotty" did not exist in English slang, you would have to invent it for Dungeness: ugly, grotesque, useless.

Not quite useless. A few working people come here to quarry the shingle, fish from the beach, or build reactors. Britain's contribution to Uranium River takes the form of two nuclear stations that stand side by side on Dungeness, and overpower the flat landscape. One pair of large buildings houses the Magnox reactors of the first power station. When, in 1965, Dungeness A began dispatching 410 megawatts of electricity along the transmission lines strung over the shingle, the nuclear industry based on gas-cooled reactors seemed to be in good shape. In those days everyone remembered that, in 1956, the British had completed the world's first nuclear power station. In 1966 work began on the Advanced Gas-cooled Reactor (AGR) of Dungeness B. But nearly twenty years were to pass before it began supplying its 1200 megawatts in 1985. An unbelievable succession of difficulties and delays with Dungeness B epitomized an industry that literally ran out of steam.

The shingle at the water's edge is white and orange in colour, and with every wave it hisses like a soda syphon. It marches eastward with the prevailing wind. If the shore in front of the nuclear power stations is not to be allowed to erode, the beach has to be fed. Shingle dug from the eastern side of Dungeness travels in a fleet of six trucks to the other shore, where it is dumped into the sea, west of the power stations. About 30,000 tons of the stuff makes this journey every year to appease the god of the longshore drift. Other stones are carried farther west, to feed the beach at Hastings. Of greater concern than the longshore drift may be the fact, unappreciated when the nuclear stations were sited here, that the sea bed of the Dover Strait, close to Dungeness, has earthquake-prone faults.

Migrating birds use Dungeness as a point of arrival or departure, and a disused lighthouse is an observatory for birdwatchers. Aircraft, too, find the pointed headland an excellent landmark, and it is from the air that you can best see how Dungeness is built. It looks raked, with its curved shingle beaches stacked in front of one another in nearly parallel ridges. The youngest are nearest the shore. The headland is advancing in a southeasterly direction towards France at an average rate of two metres a year.

The main shingle ridges were thrown up by violent storms. The highest ridge of shingle, ten metres above the high-water mark, has been identified with the storm of 1287 that altered the river courses. If you trace it, you find that Dungeness was a different shape seven hundred years ago. That old beach is set two kilometres back from the existing shoreline on the eastern side. On the southern shore, near the nuclear power stations, the 1287 ridge slants towards the present beach and has been cut short.

Rye is the prettiest of the Cinque Ports. It belongs to Sussex, because Kent peters out somewhere among the shingle of the southern shore of the Dungeness salient. Standing on a promontory of the ancient cliff line, beside the vagrant Rother River, the town overlooks Rye Bay. This indentation in the coast extends for twelve miles from Dungeness to the headland of Fairlight, or Fairlee, where the cliff line escapes from the marsh and shingle to return to the present shore. The 1287 shingle ridge on Dungeness, lopped off by the sea, points in the direction of Fairlight. That was where the shingle banks rooted themselves thousands of years ago, and from which they fanned out to occupy much of what is now Rye Bay, west of Romney Marsh.

Rivers broke through the shingle fan and began creating estuaries and harbours about fifteen hundred years ago. The Tillingham and Brede rivers met near the site of Rye and flowed together into the sea. Even when most of the water still went eastward to Romney with the Rother River, the western estuary accommodated fishing and trading ports. Promehill and Winchelsea stood on the shingle at opposite sides of the estuary, and Rye on its small cliff upstream. By 1191 Winchelsea and Rye had become important enough to join the confederation of Cinque Ports.

Winchelsea did not last long on its shingle foundations. A storm in 1250 combined with high tides to wreck ships, breach the sea defences, and demolish many houses. Little more than a year later another storm washed some of Winchelsea's citizens into the sea, and people began to wonder if they had built their port in the right place. Later a church fell into the sea, and in 1283 work began on a new port of Winchelsea, five kilometres away, on the firmer ground of the ancient cliff line. Both the king and the warden of the Cinque Ports helped to plan it. They were just in time. The great storm of 1287 destroyed Old Winchelsea, and its rubble rolled away to join the rest of the shingle on Dungeness. Promehill village, across the river, disappeared in the same event.

New Winchelsea was meant to be a showcase of medieval town planning, but the concept was too ambitious. The town had three centuries of modest success, but the Brede River silted up and left it high and dry. The town remains unfinished seven centuries after it was planned, standing above a quiet stream three kilometres from the sea.

When Rye won the Rother River in the storm of 1287, the enlarged estuary made it a greater port than before, with easy access to the open water of the Channel. Rye reached its peak in the fifteenth and early sixteenth centuries. But the shingle banks began again to fan out across Rye Bay. A castle built in 1539 beside the approaches to Rye is now more than a kilometre inland. As the shingle squeezed the mouth of the Rother, the approaches became longer, narrower, and shallower, until only fishermen and smugglers had much use for the port.

Engineers tried in vain to overcome the shingle and silt. Although Rye's battle to keep open is still going on, it is really a matter of not quite admitting defeat. To reach the town now, you have to go two miles up the Rother on the flood tide, and be ready to settle on the mud when the tide goes out. Rye remains very handsome, crowded with old houses and inns and topped by St. Mary's church; it is more like a film set than a real town. It attracted strangers, including the American writer Henry James, who chose Rye for his retirement. On a meadow that used to carry salt water, the townsfolk of Rye burn a boat each year, in a ceremony that traces back to the pagan pirates.

The loose shingle bank called Winchelsea Beach is just a few centuries old, but the Fairlight cliff, a few miles farther on, includes the oldest rocks of England's southeastern shore. Only a few wind-swept bushes cover the cliff. At its base, obscured by mud, shales called the Fairlight Clays are 138 million years old. The upper part of the cliff is made of gleaming yellow sandstone. These strata have yielded fossil bones of iguanodon dinosaurs.

The most westerly of the Cinque Ports, Hastings, lies beyond Fairlight, and it is backed by the same towering sandstone. Except that its cliffs are buff-coloured instead of white, Hastings gives a good impersonation of Dover. It has a ruined castle on the high ground above the town, and houses near sea level cover a river mouth that formerly sheltered shipping. In its heyday, Hastings contributed twenty-one ships to the king's navy to fulfil its duties as a Cinque Port. Like Dover's cliffs, those at Hastings have been cut back by the sea. It stopped being an effective harbour in the fourteenth century. Fishermen still launch their boats from the shingle beach, and their tall wooden net lofts stand beside the shore on the eastern side of Castle Hill. The ruined stump of a breakwater, built in 1893, marks the last attempt to save a once-famous port.

East of Hastings, a railway runs along a low shore to Bulverhythe. It continues to Bexhill by crossing the vanished estuary where William the Conqueror eventually berthed his invasion fleet in 1066. The Battle of Hastings took place eight kilometres inland, where the ground rises. In the sea close to Bulverhythe is a plat-form used by diving archaeologists.

Below the half-tide mark the beach is almost flat. At times of strong spring tides, when the water falls low, you can visit the sea bed. Tacky clay is interspersed with quicksand. If you stand still, you may start sinking in; if you hurry over the clay, as slithery as the wet stuff on a potter's wheel, you may spend the rest of the day removing the Cretaceous ooze from the seat of your pants. But the clay has a remarkable quality. The roots of trees, splayed out immediately on top of the clay, have been preserved after a lapse of five thousand years. They look and smell like salt beef. Plainly this shore has been ideal for the survival of wood, and that helps to explain why, just a few metres away, lies the best preserved of all the historic wrecks of the English Channel.

The treasure ship *Amsterdam* from Amsterdam ran aground on purpose in 1749, and the beach ingested her and kept her sound. For two hundred years the whole plan of the ship, more than forty metres long and ten metres wide, remained outlined by blackened frames protruding through the sand. She lay tilted up at the bows, at the shoreward end, and canted gently to port.

At three o'clock on a windy Sunday afternoon, January 26, 1749, the dignitaries of Hastings were in church when they heard gunfire—the signal of a ship in distress. The mayor, the customs officer, and other members of the congregation quit the service and hurried off along the shore to see what was happening. They found the ship cast far up the beach by a combination of high tide and strong winds. By good luck *Amsterdam* had passed between two rocks, either of which could have destroyed her, and come to rest safely on the sandy clay.

As the waves roared around her, the astonished townsfolk could make out the sound of drunken singing coming from the doomed ship. The tide gradually left her that night, and men in varying degrees of intoxication emerged to wade to the land. Three women passengers were carried ashore. Next morning, forty sick crewmen were lowered onto the beach. Everyone aboard who was alive when *Amsterdam* grounded came off safely, although some of the sick men died later. But their rescue was not the only thought in the local people's minds.

Smugglers and wreckers knew a plump East Indiaman when

they saw her. They slipped aboard on the first night and made off with a hundred kilos of silver ingots from a chest in the captain's cabin. By dawn hundreds of Sussex folk were gathered like vultures around the ship, and the mayor sent for a party of soldiers to disperse them. A few days later a would-be robber was shot dead as he tried to board *Amsterdam*. This enraged the local men, who regarded gifts from the sea as natural perquisites, but it discouraged further looting.

Amsterdam's cargo included 2.5 tons of silver. It was a portion of a much larger consignment shared among thirteen East Indiamen outward bound from the Netherlands that winter to meet an urgent demand from Java for silver needed for trade. The Spanish mined the silver in Mexico and Peru, and shipped it to Europe. Dutch traders sold goods to obtain the Spanish silver, and then sent it on to the Orient, to buy Asian products for the European market. By the global reach of the maritime empires, American metal could finish up in China.

Amsterdam's treasure was worth far more than the ship herself. Her captain's first concern was to see the silver, minus the stolen chest, taken into safekeeping in Hastings. Then he tried to have the rest of his cargo offloaded and his ship refloated. But as the days went by *Amsterdam* settled into the unstable beach. By the time the salvors started work, the weather was bad again, the tides were wrong, and the ship had gone down a metre and a half into the clay. Too much wetting had made the hatches swell and jam, so to get at the cargo the workmen resorted to axes, fire, and eventually gunpowder. With the explosion they managed to destroy the upper works of the ship and also the engineer in charge, who lies buried at Hastings. When the salvage attempt was given up, two months after the wreck, the ship had gone down almost nine metres and was awash at low tide. That's how it came about that the ribs of *Amsterdam* were left showing on the sea bed.

In 1969 engineers who were laying a sewage pipe on the beach became curious about the wreck. They attacked it with their mechanical shovel and made some remarkable finds. These finds rekindled interest in *Amsterdam,* especially for Peter Marsden, who laboured for the next fifteen years to launch his project to inves-

234 · THE ENGLISH CHANNEL

234 · *THE ENGLISH CHANNEL*

tigate the wreck properly, and if possible to raise her. Marsden works for the Museum of London and had made his reputation with his work on several ancient boats found in London. To whip up interest in those gnarled ribs on the Sussex beach, Marsden published *The Wreck of the Amsterdam* (1974). This book gave the results of a preliminary archaeological investigation, and an account of the multiplying horrors that led a shipload of drunken Dutchmen to run themselves ashore at Bulverhythe.

Amsterdam was the newest ship in the Dutch East India Company's fleet. The durability of the wreck shows that the shipbuilders in the port of Amsterdam did their work well. Getting her to sea was quite a performance, because the Zuider Zee was so shallow that she had to be lifted by pontoons across the sandbanks. From the gilded lion of her figurehead, along her double gun decks carrying fifty-four guns, past her three tall masts, to the brightly coloured carvings at her stern, *Amsterdam* must have been a fine sight.

Her captain's name was William Klump, and he was thirty-three years old when he was given command of *Amsterdam* for her maiden voyage to Java. Klump had a crew of 203, together with 125 soldiers and 5 passengers—two company officials, their wives, a sister-in-law, and a cargo of cloth and wine as well as silver. The manning of such a vessel for a two-year round-trip to the Far East and back was another matter. By the usual practice, down-and-outs were recruited from the waterside slums of Amsterdam, and they brought disease with them.

After two false starts in shifting winds, *Amsterdam* set sail from the Netherlands in company with seven other East Indiamen, on January 8, 1749. With an easterly wind behind them, the fleet came to anchor in the Downs, near Deal. When they set off again on the night of January 12, the wind went to the southwest, virtually putting a cork in the English Channel. As the ships beat to and fro, inching into the wind, they became scattered. On the fourth day after leaving the Downs, *Amsterdam* was alone, and she had barely cleared Dungeness.

A gale sprang up, still from the southwest, which developed into a violent storm that raged for ten days and caused flooding in England's coastal towns. Away to the west, *Amsterdam*'s sister *Overschie* was driven ashore near Portsmouth. But *Amsterdam* herself was still off the Cinque Port coast, and in the eighteenth century it had no safe harbour to offer. As she floundered in mountainous seas, men began to die.

Some were washed overboard. More died of disease, made worse by the unsanitary life in a crowded sailing ship in bad weather. Others wrestled manfully with the few sails that *Amsterdam* could safely set, and then retired below to die of hypothermia. Less than three hundred miles from home, a fine ship had become a floating hell pinioned in the stretch of water between Dungeness and Beachy Head. Fifty men died during the ten days of the storm, and forty more lay sick or exhausted below deck, unable to help save the ship.

After a week in the storm, Klump nosed *Amsterdam* cautiously towards the shore in the lee of Beachy Head, looking for a little shelter. But a wave dropped the ship heavily on the sea bed, tearing off her rudder. Out of control, she drifted northeastward along the Sussex shore, until Klump gave the order to anchor. For three days *Amsterdam* clung to her anchor off Bexhill, and men went on dying. When a boat from Hastings braved the weather to enquire if he needed help, Klump said that he meant to take the ship to Portsmouth for repair as soon as the weather improved.

Despair ran deeper among the crew. On the day of the wreck, January 26, some of them broke into the store of gin and wine. Then, with "Dutch courage," they mutinied, and said that the ship must be beached. Klump had no option but to agree. He did it in a seamanlike manner, precisely at high tide, and with *Amsterdam* firing her guns to signal her plight. Yet Marsden scents a cover-up about the events of that day.

Klump made light of the mutiny. He offered no explanation to the British officials about why there was so much drunken singing. And although the survivors left many personal valuables behind them in the ship, they were curiously reluctant to go back to retrieve them. Marsden speculates that they felt guilty or frightened about some dreadful climax aboard the ship. A possible explanation emerged in 1983, when a pathologist said that bones found in the wreck belonged to a boy less than sixteen years old.

Dutch researchers found *Amsterdam*'s payroll in the company's records, and worked out that this dead lad was Adrian Welgevaren, the captain's cabin boy. He came from Leerdam, south of Utrecht. Unless he died on the very day that the ship was run ashore, he would have been buried at sea with the rest of the dead. Two suspicious musket balls were retrieved from the same section of the wreck. Did one of the mutineers shoot the cabin boy?

With some restraint, Marsden described the "indiscriminate energy of the excavator" that plunged into the wreck in 1969. It smashed old timbers and broke most of the items it recovered. Crowds of local people and visitors, like wreckers of old, grabbed what they could. The enthusiastic engineers dug into the bow section, ferreted amidships, and played lucky dip in the stern. Dozens of bottles of wine came up from the midship section, together with five bronze cannons. The bites into the stern section brought to light many small objects—spoons, candlesticks, cooking pots, and the bones of young Adrian Welgevaren. A random dig beside the ship found, and broke, *Amsterdam*'s mainmast.

Even so, the engineers handed the objects that they saved to the Receiver of Wreck, and notified the marine archaeologists. As a result, Marsden was launched on a new career. He surveyed the wreck with sonar, a proton magnetometer, and long steel probes. When a pump emptied water from the ship to afford him a glimpse of the interior, Marsden was convinced that this wreck was quite exceptional. *Amsterdam*'s hull was two thirds intact, containing most of the cargo and stores of a classic Dutch East Indiaman.

Quite apart from the nautical interest in the ship and her fate, and all she can reveal about the shipbuilding of her era, *Amsterdam* is a time capsule of eighteenth-century life and crafts. In 1983 an *Amsterdam* Foundation was set up in the Netherlands to raise her and take her back to the port of Amsterdam where she was built. No one was sure how that might be done or paid for when the archaeology began in earnest in the summer of 1984, with an Anglo-Dutch team of divers working under Marsden's direction.

The wreck is covered by the sea except for a few hours each month, so the exploration and clearing of the inside of the hull is being done by underwater techniques developed on the sunken wreck of *Mary Rose,* which was raised off Portsmouth in 1982. Waves breaking in the shallow water at Bulverhythe create peculiar difficulties, and at low tide the divers' range of vision is only about thirty centimetres. At high water there is two or three metres' visibility. Great quantities of sand have to be removed. New finds include a carved fish tail and other fine woodwork from the ship's stern, and a lead-clad barrel containing what is probably butter. Clearly, *Amsterdam*'s latest adventure is only just beginning.

The East Indiaman is above all a symbol of trade in the days when the Dutch ruled the waves. In the terminology of the historian Fernand Braudel, Amsterdam was the world's dominant city when its namesake set off on her first and last voyage. The Netherlands then had a population of only 2 million, compared with 6 million in England and 24 million in France, but the Dutch were more single-minded about the sea than either of their rivals. In addition to Indonesia, where *Amsterdam* was bound, the Dutch empire included present-day Malaya, Sri Lanka, South Africa, Surinam, and various islands in the Caribbean.

After more than a hundred years at the top of the commercial tree, the Dutch were near to tumbling. If Rembrandt had lived in the eighteenth century instead of the seventeenth, he would have found far less fire in the eyes of his Dutchmen. The Netherlands had become complacent and conservative, and much of its capital was being invested in property and foreign bonds, instead of ships and colonies. Braudel prefers economic rather than military explanations for the transfer of mercantile supremacy, and he sees London replacing Amsterdam as the dominant city when spectacular bankruptcies began crippling the Dutch economy in 1763.

The fourth Anglo-Dutch naval war, 1780–84, confirmed the switch of power. The British were infuriated by Dutch trading with the American rebels, and although the British navy was sorely stretched, the Dutch fleet had been neglected to the point where it was unable to protect its merchant ships. A Dutch convoy attempting to go down the English Channel was intercepted by a small British force off Portland and promptly surrendered. Half a century after Captain Klump waded ashore at Bulverhythe, the

Dutch East India Company itself was bankrupt. Then British shipping rather than Dutch became the common sight in the English Channel and all around the world.

The Channel's global importance appears in this: for four centuries, from the rise of Antwerp in 1501, through the long reigns of Amsterdam and London, this waterway provided access to the oceans for the dominant trading cities. The Bulverhythe beach has preserved, in tangible form, a sailing ship of the type that created the modern world.

The Seaside Age

From Hastings westward, the rocks of the coast grow younger again. The resorts of Bexhill, on the high sandstone, and Eastbourne, beside the high chalk of Beachy Head, oppose each other like bookends across a low shelf of land fronted with shingle. Pevensey Levels show you where a second ribbon of the Weald Clay meets the English Channel. Here is another lost harbour, which the Romans fortified and into which William the Conqueror sailed before reconvening his army at Hastings. Now it is a small-scale version of Romney Marsh.

Pevensey harbour was blocked by the shingle of the longshore drift. During the centuries that followed the Norman Conquest, a miniature Dungeness grew here. By the sixteenth century a knob of shingle projected three kilometres into the waters where our ketch is sailing. But what the sea gives it can take away, and all that remains is a slight pimple called Langney Point, with shingle ridges like those at Dungeness. Along the beach are four defensive towers built during the Napoleonic Wars. There used to be another eight towers, but they disappeared with the shingle they stood on. These reversible changes of the coastline (now you see it, now you don't) are a bit disturbing. What if Dungeness itself decided to decay and dump its shingle and its power stations somewhere up the coast?

Five miles out from Langney Point, the modern Royal Sovereign lighthouse stands near a bank of shingle on the sea bed. A warship of that name "discovered" the shoals by running aground.

The coasters now passing outside the lighthouse are on the direct route from Dungeness to Beachy Head. The contrast between the two headlands could not be greater. The one is the lowest of the English Channel's major capes; the other is the tallest. Beachy's name comes from the French *beau chef,* meaning "beautiful head." It has nothing to do with beaches, and the "Head" is redundant.

From the low shoreline at Eastbourne a great white whale of chalk heads purposefully out to sea, and its nose of sheer cliffs stands 160 metres high. Being so big and white, Beachy Head is like a canvas waiting to be coloured in, and to have details added or subtracted. It can appear like frail cumulus on the horizon, or as a towering killer in an angry dawn, dripping with blood and foaming at its chops. Moonlight can make Beachy look like a pearl, or a sheet of steel, or a grey wig. Today, the dainty clouds of summer are painting irregular shadows on the cliffs.

A pile of chalky rubble reaches halfway up the cliff behind the grey and red lighthouse. Five thousand years ago Beachy Head stretched several kilometres farther towards France. It is still crumbling at an average rate of a metre a year, but to put it like that is misleading, because the chalk comes away in chunks. The sea attacks from the bottom, and the ice from the top. Water swells when it freezes in cracks in the chalk. It loosens a section of the cliff, perhaps ten metres wide, and drops it into the sea. The rubble then protects that part of the cliff for a few years, until the sea breaks it up and carries it away, so that undercutting can begin again. At low tide you can see a flat chalk beach extending from the base of the cliff. This also erodes, and again freezing does the main damage. After a severe frost the sea beside the Sussex coast turns white, not with ice but with grains of chalk let loose by the ice.

From a point two miles due south of Beachy lighthouse, the distance to Brighton is fifteen sea miles on a straight run. As to scenery, it is chalk all the way. Beachy Head is an amputation of the South Downs, a chalk ridge that runs roughly east–west across Sussex. Immediately west of the headland, dry valleys hanging high above the sea make a famous succession of humps in the cliffs: the Seven Sisters. The Cuckmere River then breaks out of

a rather private valley that was much appreciated by smugglers,
Virginia Woolf, and other crowd-shunners. The entrance to Cuckmere Haven is sheltered by Seaford Head, which can easily be
mistaken for Beachy Head by sailors coming from the west. A
second river penetrating the chalk, the Ouse, harbours Newhaven.
Cross-Channel ferries leaving the port for Dieppe show their passengers white cliffs handsomer than Dover's.

Ashore, the downs wear a covering of turf. It is so widespread
that you might think that chalk is naturally treeless. But those
grassy slopes were formerly well wooded with oak, hazel, elm,
and lime, according to the botanists who study the pollen that the
trees left behind them. Climatic changes may have helped to denude the chalk hills, but human beings bear the main responsibility. Stone Age farmers, who arrived about 4300 B.C., found the
chalk ridges much easier to deal with than the thick forest of the
Weald, and they cleared trees to grow their crops and graze their
animals. Except around large settlements, trees kept coming back—

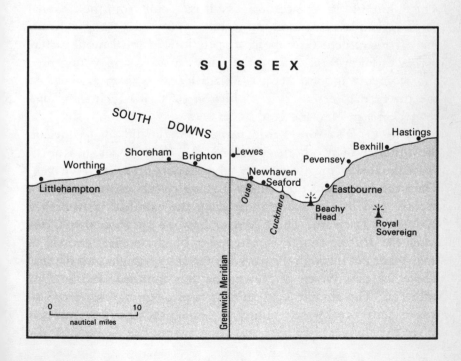

especially beech. But Bronze Age and Iron Age farmers cultivated the hills intensively, and by the time the Romans came, three quarters of the forest had gone for good. The turf was produced by grazing sheep. Bare white patches on the hills are the work of farmers in the 1980s, who invite severe erosion by planting winter cereals on the high downs.

The Ouse River leads up from Newhaven to Lewes, another famous old port, but big ships cannot sail there as they did in the Middle Ages. Tom Paine, the anarchist who championed the common man in the American and French revolutions, was an exciseman at Lewes from 1768 until 1773, when he was sacked after pamphleteering and lobbying lawmakers in an effort to obtain better pay for excisemen. But perhaps he was not very diligent at his work. Although tobacco was subject to excise, he married a tobacconist's daughter and retailed tobacco himself. At Lewes you can still see the Bull House where Paine lived and ran his store; also the White Hart pub where he first tried out his ideas of freedom in debates in a "social and intelligent circle" of Lewes townsfolk. The failure of his tobacco business drove Paine from the Channel shore to Pennsylvania and immortality. Nowadays, the environmental movement Greenpeace has its international headquarters in Lewes High Street. From the quiet Sussex town, young men and women wage war against Canadian sealers, Russian whalers, and the French secret service, which in 1985 sank their ship *Rainbow Warrior* in New Zealand waters.

The Ouse's losing battle against shingle and silt resulted in the downfall of two ports—Seaford, as well as Lewes. In Roman times the river came out roughly where it does now, at Newhaven. Then the longshore drift threw a shingle spit across the river's mouth, and by the sixteenth century the exit had moved four kilometres eastward. The haven of Seaford grew up there. But when the drifting shingle threatened to block the river entirely, a man-made cut through the bank led the river straight into the sea. There the new haven of Newhaven was founded, and Seaford withered. The shingle kept shifting and clogging the river entrance, until breakwaters tamed it. Geologists take their students to see the shingle piled high and wide against the western breakwater of Newhaven harbour, where the longshore drift has been arrested. Denuded Seaford could be ravaged by the sea.

Among the houses of Peacehaven, east of Newhaven, a white pillar on the clifftop announces that the ketch is just entering the Western Hemisphere. It marks the Greenwich Meridian, the imaginary line that runs from North Pole to South Pole, through the Old Royal Observatory at Greenwich on the Thames. This is the zero of longitude for navigators, and the reference line for timekeepers all around the world. It was not always so. National pride was involved, and chartmakers used more than a dozen different zeroes of longitude. For the French, Paris was the reference, and their clocks ran 9 minutes and 21 seconds ahead of those in England. Americans favoured Greenwich, and set their time zones so many hours behind Greenwich Mean Time. Most of the world's shipping came to use charts based on the Greenwich Meridian. At a decisive conference in Washington, D.C., in 1884 the French had the good grace to abstain when it came to the vote. Now they accept that the zero of longitude runs across the Channel from Peacehaven to Villers on the Normandy coast.

At Brighton, the chalk downs slant inland, the tall cliffs give way to the Sussex coastal plain, and the shingle beach becomes much easier to reach from the landward side. Long before it was a resort, Brighton was a major fishing port. It was one of the first places to benefit from the destruction of the harbours of the Cinque Ports, and if you had to keep boats on the open shore, Brighton's beach was better than most.

Early in the seventeenth century, when it sent its fishing fleet to the North Sea to catch the herring, Brighton was the largest town in Sussex. By 1700 it had gone into a decline, and local shipowners were switching to the coal trade from Newcastle, which was less labour intensive. The sea then carried away much of Brighton's beach, and a hundred houses with it. When Daniel Defoe visited the diminished town in 1724, he commented sourly that the cost of a proposed sea wall seemed to be more than all the remaining houses were worth.

But Brighton still had its fishermen, and around 1750 you would have found six dozen boats hauled up on the beach. They were distinctive craft called hoggies, as ungraceful as their name, but very practical, with their bluff bows, flat sterns, and piggish lines. They used leeboards instead of keels to stop them drifting to windward under the pressure of their spritsails. The fishermen tending their nets on Brighton beach had an excellent view of one of the oddest changes in human behaviour ever recorded. People from far away poured over the Sussex downs like lemmings and flung themselves naked into the sea.

The seaside vacation is now so well established, from Cannes to Hawaii, that the idea of someone inventing it is hard to grasp. When it happened, the inhabitants of the shoreline, who previously rated their environment simply by its havens and its yield of fish and shellfish, were amazed and delighted to find that the beach itself was a marketable resource. Brighton was the unlikely workshop that marinized our species, and converted coastlines into cash.

Unlikely because Brighton's pebbly beach is quite disagreeable for human bottoms or bare feet. The scenery is dull, with no headlands, rocks, offshore islands, or big ships to vary the view of a grey sea. Worst of all, the water of the Channel is chilly, and it was even colder during the Little Ice Age when the business began. But Brighton is the place on the south coast nearest to London, and geological faults had created passes through the chalk hills behind it, making the journey easier.

The seaside "holiday" originated as a medical alternative to "taking the waters" at spas in an age when consulting a doctor was likely to do you more harm than good. Those who could afford it went to drink and plunge into highly mineralized spring water, at Bath or Aix-les-Bains, and they supposed it was good for them. The spas also became pleasuredromes for the ruling classes, where the waters were just an excuse for the young and fit to gather, gamble, and flirt. The spa at Scarborough in Yorkshire happened to be beside the sea, and as a gimmick it offered a choice of spring water and sea water to drink. By 1735 men and women were bathing naked in the sea at Scarborough for the sake of their health. The modest or ungainly could strip and dress in bathing machines—covered wagons parked at the water's edge.

The crucial step was a matter of making the seaside independent of any spa. Faddists who had heard of sea bathing tried it elsewhere, and a family called Clarke are enshrined in local history as the first such visitors to Brighton, in 1736. But the individual with the best claim to the invention of the seaside vacation was Richard Russell, a physician working at a spa in Kent. He published a colourful *Dissertation on the Use of Sea-Water in Diseases of the Glands* in 1750, and two years later he built a clinic at Brighton.

Russell's fashionable patients knew he was to be found at his house on the seafront. Some of them built homes of their own nearby. Russell urged them to drink a pint of sea water every day, and to plunge in the sea. To those who complained that the water was dreadfully cold, Russell had a smart answer: the colder, the better. Indeed, he said, to enter the sea without the pores of the skin well closed could be injurious to health. The best time to bathe was at dawn in midwinter. For every high-class nymph the local men might behold as they prepared for their day's fishing, a dozen quivering senior citizens, obese or skeletal, with cardio-vascular disease or cancer, were quietly killing themselves in obedience to Dr. Russell's theories. But soon the healthy rich followed the invalids to Brighton, and made adultery its heavy industry.

It took about twenty years. While the British navy and army were snatching India and Canada away from the French in the late 1750s, the emphasis was still on the curative qualities of Brighton's sea water. By 1780 the English gentry were finding Brighton a grand place for gambling, drinking, and jousting with the *corps d'amour* at the Castle or the Ship Inn. King George III then had two preoccupations: to keep George Washington out of New York and George, Prince of Wales, out of Brighton. In 1783 both his hopes were dashed.

Although Brighton pretended to be ravished by the handsome young prince, it seduced him. When he defied his father's wishes and set off down the Brighton road, the town already possessed the elegance, gaiety, and morals of a high-class whore, and was the largest resort on the English coast. The prince's infatuation redoubled Brighton's success. He leased a farmhouse to be near his illicit wife, Mrs. Fitzherbert, who inhabited what is now the YMCA.

In 1787 the Prince of Wales began adapting the farmhouse into a Royal Pavilion. Its interior was decorated in Chinese style, and the prince entertained his guests in the manner of Nero, by singing to them in his music room. The Pavilion was built and rebuilt, with no expense spared, until it was finished in 1822 as a Moghul palace complete with domes and minarets. Large stables and a covered riding school stood in the grounds. Of all England's buildings, the Royal Pavilion remains the most fantastic, in the truest sense of the word. Queen Victoria continued the royal patronage until 1845, by which time the railway from London was open and Brighton's prosperity was secure.

Other coastal villages were soon competing feverishly to exploit the new craze for the sea. George III favoured Weymouth, far along the Channel coast in Dorset, with a less rambunctious royal presence than his son's. Victoria built an Italian-style palace in greater seclusion on the Isle of Wight. For the promoters, every accessible beach was a potential new Brighton. Whatever its characteristics, some medical hack could be found to extol them.

Brighton itself lacked trees and a river, so its doctors claimed that trees gave off noxious steam, while rivers weakened the brine of the sea. Physicians on forested shores praised the health-giving exhalations from the trees. Estuarine mud, seaweed, rocks, or surf were healthy or harmful according to whether or not your resort possessed them. The medical publicists commended Dover's "astringent" air and advised patients to take a sailing packet to Calais, "in hopes of being made seasick."

Seaford, the extinct port towards Beachy Head, was the model for Jane Austen's *Sanditon* in the novel that she started in the year of her death, 1817. She was planning to lampoon the resort proprietors. Sanditon was an aspiring village on the Sussex coast, where the old cottages were made smarter with white curtains and the sign "lodgings to let" went up. The detested rival was "Brinshore," and Sanditon's promoter condemned Brinshore's stagnant marsh and putrefying seaweed. His own beach was unimpressive, so he proclaimed Sanditon as a place to go for its healing sea breezes. To the promoter's wife these seemed more like abominable storms, and if you ever saw the waves breaking over the front at Seaford in a southwesterly gale, you would know what she meant. Charles Lamb, the essayist, began the tourist's habit of complaining about the tourists, and on a visit to Hastings he wrote, "Nature, where she does not mean us for mariners and vagabonds, bids us stay at home."

Rising prosperity and steam trains eventually spread the benefits of the Seaside Age all along the shore of the English Channel. Even failed resorts found merit in the eyes of visitors who wanted peace and quiet. Lewis Carroll in *Alice in Wonderland* (1865) summed up the coastal scene:

> Alice had been to the seaside once in her life, and had come to general conclusion, that wherever you go to on the English coast you find a number of bathing machines in the sea, some children digging in the sand with wooden spades, then a row of lodging houses, and behind them a railway station.

Seaside fever vaulted to France like a contagion. Dieppe claims to be the oldest of the French coastal resorts, and it is certainly the nearest to Paris. The gambling casino was the emblem of an aspiring resort, and the proprietor of a famous Paris restaurant, Maxim's, set one up at Trouville in Normandy in the 1850s. A promenade of wooden duckboards, *les planches,* enabled grand visitors from Paris and England to promenade along the beach without getting their shoes sandy. After a contretemps about the rent, the entrepreneur moved across the mouth of the Touques River to Deauville, and took his clientele with him. *Les planches* were again arranged on the sand, and Deauville became the most international and snobbish of Channel resorts. Aristocrats in the nineteenth century and film stars in the twentieth flocked to the planks, bars, and gaming tables. They called it the 21st Arrondissement of Paris.

Cabourg, on the Dives estuary, was laid out in the 1860s as a miniature Paris, with streets converging on the casino like the avenues of the capital on the Arc de Triomphe. Marcel Proust spent his summer vacations there, and immortalized Cabourg as "Balbec" in *A la recherche du temps perdu*. The strongest challenge to Deauville came from the Canche estuary, south of Boulogne, where Le Touquet advertised itself as Paris-Plage. Impressionist painters haunted the Seine estuary, and post-Impressionists flocked to Brittany. But it was in England, staying in a hotel at Eastbourne in 1905, that Claude Debussy composed *La Mer*—the musical culmination of artistic enthusiasm for the seaside.

The seaside towns offered the visitor bridges to nowhere— piers on stilts jutting out into the sea. They might occasionally receive passengers from a visiting ship, but served mainly to let people walk over the water and catch fish with rods.

An old chain pier at Brighton, memorialized in a Turner painting, was destroyed in a storm in 1896. The present Palace Pier, complete with a theatre, marks the heart of Brighton's water- front, although connoisseurs say that the West Pier is a finer struc- ture. The most daring piece of engineering was a pier on wheels, which ran on underwater rails under the cliffs to the east of Brigh- ton. At low tide you can sometimes see the remains of the track.

The sea never submitted meekly to its exploitation for local profit. Resorts had to fortify themselves with sea walls if the hotels were not to be flooded or even destroyed in storms. Often, as at Brighton, it was convenient to combine a coast road and prom- enade with a sea wall. But anything that blocked the river of sand and shingle flowing eastward in the longshore drift could denude the beaches of resorts farther along the coast. Hence the battle of the groynes. In 1818 the port of Shoreham, west of Brighton, built breakwaters to protect its river mouth and tamed the shingle with wooden fences, or groynes, running down the beach to the water's edge. These choked off the supply of shingle to Brighton's fashionable beach. Brighton built groynes of its own, to hoard what it had. That left the cliffs east of Brighton starved of shingle, and the erosion of the chalk accelerated. The large breakwaters of Brighton Marina, built in the mid-1970s, created a supergroyne. For some of the cliffs away to the east, new sea defences became necessary in the 1980s, at a cost of £2 million per kilometre.

Flint-built houses of Brighton's old fishing port have become shops selling antiques in the narrow Lanes, and the Royal Albion Hotel occupies the site of Dr. Russell's clinic. At the nearby Grand Hotel, the Irish successors of Childers and O'Brien tried to blow up the British prime minister and her cabinet in 1984. Only on a very hot day will you see many people swimming in the sea at Brighton, and nowadays it is the Sun that people worship on the beach.

In just thirty kilometres of shoreline west of Brighton there are four major resorts (Hove, Worthing, Littlehampton, and Bognor Regis) and about ten lesser places where visitors flock. People like to retire to the seaside, and an immigration of the elderly became a major invasion in the twentieth century. In Bexhill, Eastbourne, Hove, and Worthing one third of the population is over retirement age. The unkind name for this stretch of coast is the Costa Geriatrica.

All the resorts of the English Channel have lost business to sunnier places accessible by air or fast roads. Plenty of them are visibly decaying, but not Brighton, which remains one of the world's liveliest resorts. The large marina has lured in the yachtsmen. The University of Sussex and a plethora of language schools have also brought new blood to the town. An aura of naughtiness reminiscent of Paris still hangs in the sea air, and a Londoner who admits he is going to Brighton for the weekend must expect a few nudges and winks. The test for the leisure industry is fun, and I doubt if anyone ever comes to Brighton without enjoying it. In two hundred years the town has learnt how to cater to every taste, and the elegant Georgian terraces look out tolerantly on modern entertainments. A cataract of houses and apartment blocks tumbles down the chalk slopes and presses towards the sea, where the lemmings decided to stay.

Green and Pleasant Land

The coastal plain of Sussex, leading west from Brighton to Selsey, is at first glance as uninspiring a stretch as you might find on this side of the English Channel. With only short interruptions at the marshy remnants of estuaries and harbours, most of the low shore is fronted with resort towns and ranks of caravans and chalets. The recommended landmarks are in keeping with the ephemera of the Seaside Age: the chimneys of the Shoreham power station, the chapel of Lancing School, the pier at Worthing, the fairground helter-skelter at Littlehampton. At Bognor Regis the Queensway apartment block warns the wary of the Bognor rocks offshore. In poor visibility the coastal navigator can be reduced to trying to distinguish one hotel from another. But in clear weather the best landmarks are Celtic hill forts.

The chalk hills, still marching westward, remain conspicuous beyond the widening plain. A narrow ribbon of younger clay, thick with fossil shells, reaches into the sea at Lancing and reappears near Bognor. The remains of old chalk cliffs and sandy beaches, lying inland, belong to interglacial periods earlier and warmer than our own. During the intervening Ice Ages, wind-blown dust smothered the region with thick deposits of loess, known locally as loam or brick earth. It makes the Sussex coastal plain one of the most fertile parts of England.

Celtic farmers favoured it, and so did the wealthy men of the Roman era, who had plenty of villas hereabouts. It became a major grain-producing district. The tall spire of Chichester Cathedral guides your eyes to the site of *Noviomagus,* a Roman port and iron-working town. A sumptuous palace at Fishbourne near Chichester probably belonged to the king of the Regni, who was on good terms with the Roman conquerors. German pirates burned down the palace, around A.D. 280. If pirates came again, they would find plenty of glass to break, because this is now greenhouse country.

There are lost villages under the ketch's keel. The coast east of Bognor Regis was cut back half a kilometre in the nineteenth century, until sea defences checked the fierce erosion. Selsey, the low, rocky headland on our bow, marks the western end of the bay that began at Beachy Head. It was formerly an island. The gap has been closed by a natural dam, leaving only the vanishing harbour of Pagham on the eastern side. Selsey was a major Roman port, and for the Saxons who gave it its name, "seal island," it was one of the first places where they settled in England after the Roman empire collapsed. Eventually the Saxon city of

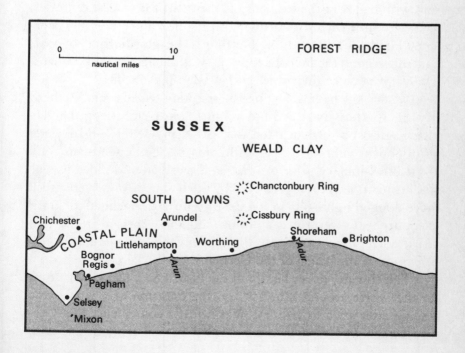

Selsey, complete with its cathedral, was washed away by the sea, and the bishop retreated to Chichester in 1075.

Sussex means "South Saxons." In their language, if not always in their genes, the English are the descendants of the German pirates, among whom the Saxons were prominent. Compared with the Romanized Celts, who lived in villas with glazed windows, mosaic floors, and hot baths, the seafarers who harassed and eventually dispossessed them were a rough lot. At a time when thieving, massacre, and enslavement were routine, the only moral difference between the warlike German tribes and the Roman armies was a matter of scale. Steal a cargo or loot a town and you are a pirate; steal a country or a continent and your historians will hail you as a civilizing benefactor.

People of English stock should have a little sympathy for their ancestors, the Angles, Saxons, and others who lived on the sand dunes in the German Bight of the North Sea, surrounded by hostile tribes who would cheerfully take their land and sell them off as slaves. But shed no tears. These were extremely tough-minded folk who had kept the Romans off their turf for several centuries, and were in the habit of drowning prisoners in ceremonies worshipping the Earth goddess Nerthus. The glorification of war, endemic among the Indo-Europeans, was plainest in the Germans. The very name of their chief god Woden meant "fury."

Woden still haunts the English-speaking world every Wednesday. He was heavily armed and mounted on an eight-legged horse. His magical powers included that of "army-fetter"—paralysing an opponent's forces by panic. In this myth the Germans took aboard the military principle that battles are often decided by one side losing its nerve. As perceived by the Romans, they were much more dogged fighters than the Celts, who were inclined to attack in a surge of overheated emotion and then despair at the first setback. Deprived of Roman discipline, the Celts were to have a hard time at the hands of the Germans.

The climate, never kindly in the North Sea, had taken a turn for the worse around A.D. 270, on the occasion of a worldwide cooling after a warm century. Was it just a coincidence that German pirates swarmed in the English Channel around A.D. 280, when the palace at Fishbourne was destroyed? To check their raids, the Romans fortified the coast. Around A.D. 300 five forts sprang up at naval bases on the Channel: Richborough, near Sandwich; Dover; *Portus Lemanis* near Hythe; Pevensey; and Portchester in Portsmouth harbour. In a letter to a friend, a Roman official described the German pirates:

> To these men a shipwreck is a lesson in seamanship, not a matter of dread. They know the dangers of the deep as men who fight them daily. For since a storm puts their victims off guard, and conceals their approach, they gladly take their chance among wrecks and wave-lashed rocks in the hope of profiting from them. [Quoted by J. A. Williamson.]

In A.D. 410, when the Visigoths were at the gates of Rome, the emperor announced that the British Celts could no longer expect his support. About thirty years later new armies appeared in Britain. One of them was led by Hengist, who may have been an Angle; his troops were possibly Frisian Islanders. These German warriors came at the urgent request of the British Celts to assist them against invaders in the north. This was neither the first time nor the last that a country has been lost by invitation. Hengist first demanded the Isle of Thanet from the Celts, as a reward for helping them, and then he attacked them. He took Kent, and some of his warriors headed down-Channel. They leapfrogged past their Saxon cousins, who were concentrating on the fertile villa land between Brighton and Selsey. The arrival of Celtic refugees in Normandy, around A.D. 460, may date the Saxon conquest of western Sussex. East of Beachy Head, the marsh and fortress of Pevensey remained a centre of Celtic resistance until about thirty years later.

Other groups of Germans were settling on Britain's eastern coast, in Essex (named for Saxons) and East Anglia (named for Angles). Down-Channel in Hampshire, the "West Saxons" founded Wessex, and Hengist's ill-defined people from Kent took over the Isle of Wight. The various invading tribes embattled with the Celts soon had a sense of identity as the new inhabitants of an island kingdom. The Sussex king Aelle was recognized as the first overlord of the Anglo-Saxons in England as early as A.D. 490. At some stage during the centuries that followed their common language came to be called *Englisc*.

The invaders created a land of villages. They dispersed across the countryside into thousands of small communities—neither lonely peasant farms nor grand estates of the Roman style, but compact villages that shared out the available land among their inhabitants. Technology helped because the Anglo-Saxon conquest roughly coincided with the invention of the mouldboard plough, which enabled the Anglo-Saxons to farm the rich but heavy soil of England's forests. As a result, the invaders were not confined to the silts of the river valleys or the dry, high ground of the chalk, but were able to scatter almost at will.

Some ten or twelve kilometres inland is the conspicuous Celtic hill fort of Chanctonbury Ring. Under its shadow you will find a typical swarm of Saxon villages: Washington, Ashington, Sullington, Storrington, West Chiltington, and so on. Compare these with some of the coastal names in this strip: Lancing, Worthing, Goring, Ferring. The *ing* means a plural, like *s* in modern English, so Worthing is the place of the Wurths, the people who had Wurth as their leader; it is still pronounced Wurthing. The *ton* in the other names means a fence or enclosure, and by extension a village. Washington is the village of Wassa's people. (Another Wassa and his folk settled in northern England, whence came the family of George Washington.)

Those villages beyond Chanctonbury stand in the clay of the old Wealden forest, in soil quite different from either the chalk of Chanctonbury or the loess of the coastal plain. The fussiness of English geology played at least as important a part as the mouldboard plough in shaping Old English society. The geological grain roughly parallels the Channel shore, creating a roller coaster, with a rapid succession of ups and downs.

The great contrasts in the landscape, within the distance of a day's march, enabled the South Saxons to create a shire rich in natural resources. There was good grazing on the chalk downs, and arable land on the plains north and south of them. The forest on the high sandstone, away to the north, offered immense supplies of timber. Sussex already had its own iron industry, and plenty of building materials. The subunits of early Sussex, called rapes, were roughly twenty kilometres wide and reached up to twice that distance inland. Each of them cut across the geological grain to incorporate the various kinds of terrain, from the coast to the forest ridge. They included the Lewes rape, focused on the Ouse River, the Bramber rape on the Adur, the Arundel rape on the Arun, and the Chichester rape behind Selsey. Bundle these self-sufficient rapes together and you had a robustly self-sufficient county—virtually a Little England.

No obvious topographic barrier separates Sussex from Kent, or from its other neighbour, Hampshire. To a military eye the county boundaries make no sense at first sight. But if you think of the county not as a fortress but as a warlike economy, it becomes much more formidable. Each of these coastal counties could put an army into the field, and a fleet of warships to sea, entirely equipped, armed, clothed, and victualled from its own resources.

While the French were to some extent forced by their geology to centralize in order to pool the resources of their very different *pays,* in the English villages and shires nature backed devolution. All the centralizing efforts of national leaders, lawyers, and bureaucrats have failed to eradicate the independence of the shires. Education is an example. Napoleon's dream—more or less fulfilled—was that the same lesson should be taught at the same hour in every school in France. In England every county draws up its own syllabuses, and resents guidance from London. For fifteen hundred years the wish to unite England for action on the world stage has had to contend with strong decentralizing pressures, and with local committees and individual Englishmen sticking up for their rights.

Christ ousted Woden. England was converted by Celtic Christians based in Scotland, and by the Roman missionary Saint Augustine, who crossed the Dover Strait in A.D. 597. The South Saxons were among the last of the English on the Channel shore to give up their old religion, even after a bishop set up shop at Selsey in A.D. 681. On the other hand, English missionaries set off to try to convert their kin in northern Germany.

Woden came back with a vengeance with the Vikings from

Scandinavia, who called him Odin. Their arrival, beginning a little before A.D. 800, enriched the ethnic mix in northern Europe. While Norwegian Vikings were settling in Scotland, Ireland, and Southern Brittany, the power of Danish Vikings was growing in the North Sea and the English Channel. The Danish Vikings took possession of large areas of eastern England and began to farm them, but they would have been insulted if you tried to suggest they were peaceable agriculturalists. They made repeated attacks down-Channel by land and sea, between A.D. 870 and 884. Alfred, king of Wessex, succeeded in holding them off. The crucial campaigns in the defence of Wessex were fought on land and culminated in the recovery of London from the Danes. But the mobile Vikings had to be countered at sea as well. Alfred founded a navy, and recruited seamen from those old homelands, the Frisian Islands, to man it. This force could not prevent all piratical raids, but it helped to deter major invasions.

The self-destruction of the navy, more than a century later, opened the way to the Danish conquest of the Channel shore. The fleet based at Sandwich in Kent in 1009 was said to have been the greatest ever mustered by the English. During a deadly quarrel between two English leaders, one appropriated eighty ships to try to capture the other, but a storm drove many of the ships ashore. His rival promptly came along the beaches and burned all the wrecks. What was left of the fleet retreated up the Thames. Almost at once the Danes appeared with their own fleet at Sandwich and began to overrun Kent, Sussex, and Hampshire. The leaders of Wessex decided to accept defeat, and at Southampton they hailed the violent young Danish leader as King Canute.

Within two years Canute was king of all England, and by 1019 ruler of a Scandinavian empire as well. His drunken Vikings had killed the archbishop of Canterbury, but Canute himself found it politic to respect the Christian Church in England. The Anglo-Danish empire did not last long, but underwent spontaneous fission when a nephew of Canute became king of Denmark. By 1042 an Englishman was once more on the English throne. In that same year, across the English Channel, the teenager William became Duke of Normandy. But when William inflicted his conquest, his followers and successors had to compromise with long-established English ways. The linguistic outcome was curious. The heirs of German-tongued Norwegians tried to impose Latin-based French on the Anglo-Saxons. They failed, and finished up speaking a different Germanic language, English.

The influence of the Celtic languages on Old English had been slight, except in providing a model for the English continuous tenses, as in the form "I am sailing." The second Germanic wave, the Vikings, implanted many Norse words into English. The consequent creole shed many of the formal grammatical inflexions of Indo-European languages in general and German in particular, and set English on the road to becoming one of the most casual and flexible of languages. Although French was the official and literary language in England for three centuries after the Norman Conquest, the truculence of the English ensured their language's survival. Pretending that you cannot understand what the foreigner is saying has always been an effective form of passive resistance, even if it does invite thumps. And English nannies taught infant Norman princes to speak English.

When English reasserted itself in the thirteenth century, first in literature and then in official usage, the German inflexions had gone, the continuous tenses were becoming rampant, and the vocabulary had recruited many words from France, complete with variants from different dialects on the other side of the English Channel. *Channel* itself, for instance, comes from mainstream medieval French; the Norman word was *canal*. Complexities of English spelling reflect old ways of speaking. House, for example, was pronounced *hoos* a thousand years ago. In the event known to linguists as the Great English Vowel Shift, the city slickers of London circa 1400 affected new ways of saying many words, which gradually imposed themselves on much of the country as the "right" way to speak.

After the Norman Conquest, England was the offshore island of the Norman and Angevin empires. Only when Joan of Arc and her companions expelled the Anglo-Normans from France did the limits of the nation become plain. Then there were the civil Wars of the Roses to get out of the way, before England (plus Wales) became coherent under Henry Tudor, the Welsh conqueror, in 1485. A revolution was needed to modernize the country, and this occurred in the civil war between parliamentarians and royalists that began in 1643. The English beheaded their king in 1649, nearly a century and a half ahead of the French, but before long they adopted a constitutional monarchy as a congenial and stable form of government. The British like to think of the United States as a young country, but Great Britain itself was not completed until the union of England and Scotland, less than seventy years before the Americans revolted.

The chief advantage to the English in living on an island was not that they were safe from invasion but that the navy was the chief instrument for preventing it. The Greek cities that cradled democracy also relied primarily on their navies. Sailors are not good for crowd control, and the English refusal to support a large army deprived would-be autocrats of what, in many other countries, was the chief instrument of repression. But ever-widening democracy had the paradoxical effect of strengthening central government, so that now the prime minister has greater authority than any sovereign ever had, including personal mastery over the country's nuclear weapons.

This centralizing trend is at odds with the long tradition of local and personal freedom that keeps re-emerging like a ghost at the feast:

> I shall not sleep from mental fight
> Nor shall my sword sleep in my hand
> Till we have built Jerusalem
> In England's green and pleasant land.

I don't know how many English men and women who sing that rousing hymn in church or at public gatherings understand that William Blake, the artist and poet who wrote it here on the Sussex shore, near Bognor, was preaching revolutionary anarchism.

Blake's dissenting voice still mutters in the Channel wind. It says that the honoured British engineers of the Industrial Revolution made their fellow citizens slaves to machinery. It says that the war against the French Revolution, waged by the British admirals with sailors snatched by the press gangs, set back the cause of democracy for a lifetime. Behind the pomp of Britain's rise to world domination, Blake tells us, ordinary men and women were in tears.

Since his time the industrial cities have waxed and waned, far from the Channel shore. London has passed its peak of power and population. The empire has dissolved. The villages and towns of Sussex and the other Anglo-Saxon shires are the only units of England that have really stood the test of time. To say so is not sentimentality, but harsh realism.

Ruined Selsey is encumbered by dangerous shoals, where once its cathedral stood. A big rock, the Mixon, is marked by a black mast protruding from the sea. The ketch is feeling her way between Selsey Bill and rocks that stretch far out to sea.

If William Blake had lived to see the offshore drilling platform that planted itself like an interplanetary invader on the sea bed in June 1984, he would have regarded it as another satanic piece of machinery, but the Selsey fishermen did not mind it. Stationed three miles south of the Mixon rock, the rig made a temporary lighthouse. Esso and Premier Consolidated, who had the exploration rights, declared it a "tight" hole, meaning that they were not going to reveal what they had discovered because the results would be useful to competitors. But the rumour in the pubs of the Selsey peninsula was that Esso had found the English Channel's first offshore oil.

For the shoreline and its people it seemed like a promise of rejuvenation. The reason why the geologists expected to find petroleum off Selsey Bill will become clear as we sail westward along the coasts of Hampshire and Dorset. It ties up with the landforms that helped to make Portsmouth and Southampton two of the Channel's major ports. And the present decline of both those places is a good reason for hoping that geology will come to their rescue with an abundance of oil.

Pomp of Yesterday

When the Isle of Wight first comes into view, beyond Selsey Bill, it looks impressive but not particularly odd. Projecting towards us is the steep, white Culver Cliff, which would not be out of place at Dover, Beachy Head, or across the English Channel in High Normandy. It is the stump of a line of chalk that runs across the island from east to west. A loftier set of hills runs away south-westward towards the island's outermost tip, but the northern half of Wight, facing the mainland of Hampshire, is lower ground. The lozenge-shaped island, forty kilometres long, straddles a great step in the Earth's crust, such that the high land to the south shelters the coastal waters to the north. In particular it protects Portsmouth's anchorage at Spithead, and the approaches to Southampton.

Wight used to be part of the mainland. Running in front of Hampshire and the next county, Dorset, the block of uplifted land barred the way to rivers trying to reach the sea. The rivers turned east and escaped through the gap between Selsey and the eastern tip of Wight. The Solent, the water between Wight and the mainland, began as an estuary, and it still looks like a river mouth as we sail towards it.

The Solent and the Spithead anchorage constitute one large harbour, but the tributary rivers have created other havens, of which the grandest is Southampton Water. In addition, three very large puddles occupy the low shore between Selsey and Southampton Water, each with a narrow exit to the sea. The first is Chichester harbour, which divides Sussex from Hampshire and is packed with yachts. Langstone harbour is for the birds—dunlins especially. The third puddle is Portsmouth harbour, England's premier naval base for nearly five centuries.

Fighters are flying in very low from Selsey, as if bent on annihilating our unarmed ketch. It is the destroyer up ahead they are after, and we just happen to be in the way. The battle computers in *Exeter* are plotting the attackers and training her guns and missiles on them, just as they did in the Falklands fight of 1982. Even before the noise of jet engines stuns us, bright flashes and smoke from the destroyer simulate her defence.

Even without the mock warfare, the scene at Spithead would be the busiest since we entered the English Channel at Ushant. Ferries and a noisy Hovercraft are shuttling to and fro between Wight and the mainland, and a cross-Channel car ferry is coming out, bound for Cherbourg. About twenty yachts are darting in all directions. Other warships are following the dredged channel

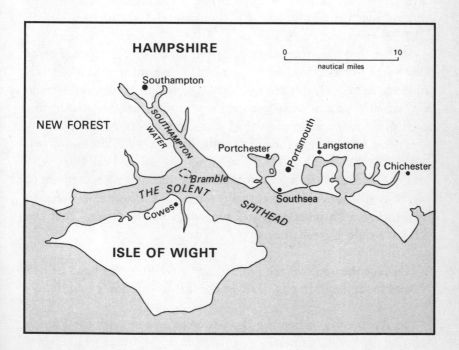

to Portsmouth, between the Spit Sand and the castle on the shore at Southsea.

From Southsea King Henry VIII watched a naval battle on July 19, 1545. The French force, consisting of 225 ships and 30,000 troops, had sailed from their new base at Le Havre to invade England. An English fleet of only 60 ships was drawn up outside Portsmouth to meet them, keeping within the protection of the shore guns and using the shoals to guard its flanks. There was very little wind, which gave the advantage to the oar-driven galleys. The French galleys kept shooting at the English, trying unsuccessfully to taunt them out to sea, until the English galleys drove them back. It was a standoff, and the French had to content themselves with burning villages on the Isle of Wight.

They believed they had sunk one of the finest English ships by gunfire, but in fact *Mary Rose* capsized spontaneously in a brief gust of wind during an awkward manoeuvre. The water rushed in through open gun ports. Netting that covered her decks to keep out French boarders became a trap for her crew, many of whom were already ill with dysentery. *Mary Rose* sank in full view of the king just a mile away on the Southsea shore. She took nearly all of her men with her.

More than four centuries later, on October 11, 1982, a giant crane lifted *Mary Rose* from the sea bed, at the culmination of years of intensive underwater archaeology. Quite apart from the broken hull, which you can see ashore at Portsmouth, artifacts from cannons to wooden plates give a vivid picture of life in Tudor England. Most evocative are the personal effects: jackets, shoes, purses, razors, combs, and so on. Of the 660 sailors and soldiers who drowned in *Mary Rose*, 78 complete skeletons were recovered. One of them was laid to rest in Portsmouth Cathedral in 1984, in a ceremony with plainsong and incense, like the funeral that the victims would have had in 1545:

Deliver the souls of the faithful departed from the hand of hell and from the deep pits. Deliver them from the lion's mouth . . .

In April 1797, when the British were at war with the French and Dutch, the Channel Fleet mutinied at Spithead. The crews

politely refused to work the ships, but undertook to sail if the
French fleet entered the Channel. When a German prince visited
Portsmouth, the mutineers voluntarily dressed their ships with
flags in his honour. Meanwhile, they asked for better pay, better
sick pay, and less repellent food. After a few weeks the government
agreed to the demands. But when the fleet in the Thames estuary
joined in the mutiny, it took on a more revolutionary colour and
the ringleader, Richard Parker in *Sandwich,* wanted to sail the ships
to join forces with the Dutch enemy. As a precaution, Trinity
House removed the buoys that marked the sandbanks and left the
Goodwin light vessel unlit. In the end Parker and twenty-eight
others were hanged.

Fom Portsmouth's doorway, between the Blockhouse Fort
and the Round Tower, you can see the masts and spars of Nelson's
last flagship, *Victory,* soaring among the cranes of the dockyard.
She is more than two hundred years old, and in the 1920s she was
put into a dry dock and restored as she was when Nelson was
killed aboard her at Trafalgar in 1805. If you look at the massive
yards and anchors, and the ranks of guns, you will understand
why it took 850 hardworking men to sail and fight a ship less than
sixty metres long at her main deck.

Victory is an imploded forest in which the most visible decks
and hull planking account for only ten per cent of the wood. Seven
hundred large oak trees, each about a hundred years old and individually chosen, went into the construction of this one ship—
the equivalent of more than thirty hectares of forest. The qualities
of oak that make it especially suitable for building the framework
of a ship include its habit of throwing out branches at right angles
to the trunk—ready-made for the knees that secure the deck beams
to the frames. *Victory*'s keel was built of seven great pieces of elm;
the masts and yards of tall, straight conifers amounting in all to
more than six hundred metres.

The timescales for growing a wooden ship were formidable.
The oak trees had to be about a hundred years old when they were
felled, and then the timber had to be seasoned, if possible, for ten
or twenty years before the completion of the ship. The defores-
tation of southern Britain was part of the price of a maritime
empire. The royal forests reserved oak for warships. Nearest to

Portsmouth is the New Forest, which in 1608 was deemed to possess more than 10,000 tons of wood fit for the navy. By 1783 the New Forest stock had dwindled to one third of that amount. Replanting did not begin on any great scale until the end of the eighteenth century. By the time those trees matured, ships were being built of steel.

The Roman fort at Portchester survives on the harbour's inland edge. England's first naval dry dock was built at Portsmouth in 1495. In 1800 one of the world's first fully mechanized production lines was running at Portsmouth dockyard, making blocks (or pulleys) for warships like *Victory*. During the Spithead Review at Queen Victoria's Diamond Jubilee in 1897, a cheeky, turbine-powered boat *Turbinia* demonstrated the superiority of steam turbines over the piston-driven warships that chased her away. Fort Blockhouse at Gosport, on the other side of the harbour entrance, became the base for the submarines of the twentieth century. In 1944 Southwick House, in the northern outskirts of Portsmouth, was the headquarters for the Normandy invasion. Even in 1977, during the Spithead Review at Queen Elizabeth's Silver Jubilee, one could sail past the long ranks of anchored warships and imagine that nothing much had changed since Queen Victoria's time. At any rate, Portsmouth, or Pompey as sailors call it, seemed to have security of tenure.

The Falklands operation was Portsmouth's last fling; its days of military glory are over. The navy is concentrating its shore facilities down-Channel, at Plymouth. The dockyard in the Thames estuary has closed, and Portsmouth has been reduced to a secondary base. It is now literally a museum port: apart from *Victory* and *Mary Rose*, the restorers have acquired the sailing frigate *Foudroyant*, the first British ironclad warship *Warrior*, built in 1860, and the old submarine *Holland I*. In the D-Day museum at Southsea Castle, the Overlord embroidery is longer than the Bayeux Tapestry. Despite a continuing bustle of ships and boats, words that Rudyard Kipling wrote in 1897 have come true at Spithead:

> Far call'd our navies melt away—
> On dune and headland sinks the fire—

Lo, all our pomp of yesterday
Is one with Nineveh and Tyre!

West of Fort Gilkicker, the Hampshire shore turns to point towards Southampton, twelve miles to the northwest. A sunken heap of clay, peat, and gravel called the Bramble bank obstructs the entrance to Southampton Water. On a Wednesday afternoon, August 5, 1620, the small ship *Speedwell* arrived from Delfthaven in the Netherlands, and anchored in Southampton Water. Aboard her were Pilgrim Fathers and Mothers—sixty-six members of the Leyden congregation. Next morning she went up on the tide to Southampton, where another ship was waiting to accompany her across the Atlantic. Her name was *Mayflower*. The voyage was to be the climax of the wanderings of the Puritans, who judged first England and then the Netherlands to be unwholesome.

The Puritans were a pain in the neck to their neighbours and were lampooned on the London stage. There was no real persecution, but they feared that their children were being corrupted by the pleasures of life in seventeenth-century Europe. The idea of going to America took hold of the bolder spirits among the Puritans of Leyden. They turned down a Dutch offer of free transport, homes, and cattle in Nieuw Amsterdam in favour of creating an English-speaking colony in the northern part of Virginia. When their leaders crossed to London, they found that the Merchant Adventurers were ready to supply two ships in return for eventual profits from the Puritans' efforts in America.

Speedwell came to rest on her anchor near *Mayflower,* off Southampton's West Quay. *Mayflower* had docked in London two months earlier, bringing wine from Biscay. With a charter for a voyage to North America, "to the neighbourhood of the mouth of Hudsons River," her fifty-year-old captain, Christopher Jones, brought her around to Southampton for the rendezvous. It was here that the whole group of voyagers came together. The Puritans from Leyden met with other Puritans from London, and a few additional emigrants were added to the party by the Merchant Adventurers.

Mayflower was probably thirty metres long, and *Speedwell* was

266 · *THE ENGLISH CHANNEL*

smaller. Both ships were packed with stores for the colony. There would be no shops where they were bound, so they had to take everything they needed, from seeds and nails to guns and chests of drawers. The livestock consisted of pigs, goats, sheep, rabbits, and poultry, together with cats and dogs. Spices, gin, wine, and beer were among the comforts the Pilgrims permitted themselves.

Captain Reynolds of *Speedwell* thought his vessel was over-laden, and he fussed about trimming her before the two ships weighed anchor on Saturday, August 15. A favourable north wind drove *Mayflower* and *Speedwell* down Southampton Water and out past the Isle of Wight, and the Pilgrims expected that the next ground they trod on would be in North America. They were going to be frustrated, and we shall cross their path again, down-Channel.

When *Mayflower* was here, there were orchards in Southampton, then a small fortified town. A railway station replaced the mill pond of a tidal water mill in 1840, and Southampton's transformation began. Former oyster beds and mud flats at the junction of the Test and Itchen rivers were dug out to make enclosed docks. In a fierce competition with Liverpool for the transatlantic passenger traffic, the docks grew southward into Southampton Water: Empress Dock 1890, and then Ocean Dock 1911, specially built to lure the Cunard and White Star liners to Southampton. The New Docks—river quays, really—along the dredged bank of the Test were opened in 1934, but Ocean Dock remained the traditional berth for the largest ocean liners.

Southampton advertised its "double high water"—a prolonged period of high tide, allowing plenty of time for deep-draft liners to manoeuvre around the sandbanks. It occurs because Southampton is roughly halfway along the Channel. The tides slosh to and fro like water in a bath, and the rise and fall are greater at the two ends of the Channel than in the middle. In a simpler world, the level of the water in this central region might not change at all. In practice, the rise and fall of the tide along the coast south and west of Wight is unusually small, and this allows another tidal cycle to make itself felt. Like a musical instrument, the Channel carries an overtone that, if left to itself, would produce high and low tides four times a day. In most places the main twice-daily tide smothers it, but here it shows up, and gives Southampton its "double high water."

At midday on September 20, 1911, a four-stack ship races down Southampton Water at nineteen knots, lapping the wooded shores with her bow wave. She is the White Star liner *Olympic,* the largest and most lavishly appointed ship in the world. She has just left the brand-new Ocean Dock, bound for New York. She slows down to wind her way around the Bramble bank, and hoots twice to say she is turning to port, to go east of the Isle of Wight. The cruiser *Hawke* is coming up the Solent from the west heading for Portsmouth. Just off Cowes on the Isle of Wight, she rams the liner on the starboard quarter, and rips a twelve-metre hole in her. No lives are lost, and the American multimillionaires go back to Southampton in a tender. The navy claims that *Olympic*'s great bulk sucked *Hawke* into the collision, while the cruiser was trying to turn away from the liner.

Olympic's master at the time of the collision is the famous "E.J.," Captain E. J. Smith. The owners think him blameless, and seven months later E.J. is in command of *Olympic*'s sister ship on her maiden voyage to New York. After a gala sendoff from Ocean Dock, all eyes are on the new luxury liner as she rounds the Bramble and heads out to sea, unharassed by cruisers. It is April 10, 1912. If you count the lifeboats and say there are only enough for half the 2200 souls aboard her, bystanders will retort that these ships are unsinkable. But this is the last the Solent will see of the new White Star liner. E.J. and 1500 of his people will meet their deaths among the icebergs of the Grand Banks, aboard the hasty *Titanic*.

Southampton's days of splendour as a liner port seem with hindsight like a flash in the pan: seven successful decades between the dispatch of troops to the South African War in 1899 and the maiden voyage of *Queen Elizabeth* 2 in 1969. After World War II the numbers of oceangoing passengers continued to grow because a rapid increase in travel of all kinds hid the impending crash. The passenger traffic in the oceangoing liners at Southampton peaked at about a thousand a day in the early 1960s. That would be the equivalent of a couple of wide-bodied jets coming and going at Heathrow Airport.

Jet aircraft crippled the oceangoing passenger services. Why spend five days crossing the Atlantic when you could do it in a few hours by air? The liner *United States,* holder of the once coveted Blue Riband for the fastest Atlantic crossing, was laid up in 1968. The 70,000-ton *France,* the grandest of the last grand ships making the transatlantic run from the English Channel, dropped out of service in 1974, when the French government withdrew the subsidy that had kept her going for a dozen prestigious years. *France*'s crew refused to take her into Le Havre for the last time. The liner lay anchored at the mouth of the Seine for two weeks while the mutinous seamen pleaded with their government. Then she rusted in Le Havre for five years, until the Norwegian Caribbean Lines bought her and renamed her *Norway.* They refitted her to serve hamburger-eaters rather than gastronomes, halved her engine power to save fuel, and sent her to Miami.

By 1984, QE2's owners were stressing her "glittering confection of glass and aluminium which effectively opens up the Club Lido to the stars," and her gymnasium, "the perfect antidote to the seductive cuisine." *Royal Princess,* a new 45,000-ton liner for the P & O company, was named at Southampton in 1984 by the Princess of Wales, but the logic of modern tourism means that you fly to the sunshine before you join your cruise. While the terminals at Southampton and Le Havre were emptying, Miami and St. Thomas in the Virgin Islands were enlarging theirs. There are plans for a cruise liner as large as a supertanker, 250,000 tons, with a citylike skyline of high-rise blocks of cabins rising above the deck, and an Olympic pool. Such a ship won't have much time for the grey skies of the English Channel.

The Hamble River, issuing into Southampton Water on its eastern shore, is one of a dozen havens around the Solent that have been commandeered by yachtsmen. Its narrow estuary is a pincushion of aluminium masts. The spit that half blocks it carries a living memento of the transatlantic liners in a colony of American clams that flourish there. Some that escaped chowderization during a crossing from New York must have been tipped out with the rubbish as a liner neared Southampton. These tough Yankee quahogs resisted the attentions of the local gulls, until the birds learnt how to break them open by dropping them on the gleaming roofs of yachtsmen's cars parked at the nearby marina.

Ahead of us, the Solent looks like a *pointilliste* painting where the artist has gone crazy with his white dots. This is Cowes Week, the main event of the English yacht-racing calendar. Cowes occupies the northern corner of the Isle of Wight, facing Southampton Water. Twin towns, East and West Cowes, nest under wooded promontories on the two sides of the Medina River. Near the western headland is the round turret of the Royal Yacht Squadron, Britain's most senior yacht club. Don't think of joining it without extraordinary social and yachting connections. Don't even try to enter the place without an invitation, unless you happen to belong to the New York Yacht Club. That club sent the schooner *America* to Cowes in 1851, and she beat fifteen British contenders in a race around Wight, so winning the Squadron's brand-new "hundred-guinea cup." Spirited away to New York, it became the America's Cup. British yachtsmen expended much effort and treasure in repeated attempts to recover it, until the Australians in *Australia* at last forced the New York Yacht Club to unscrew the trophy from its base.

The Royal Yacht Squadron's boats have the privilege of carrying the white ensign of the Royal Navy, which puts on them an obligation to sail with punctiliousness and courtesy. The Squadron is a thriving relic of grander times, when sailing yachts much bigger than any around us competed for the advantage of the Solent wind. In the halcyon days before World War I they had paid crews to handle more than a thousand square metres of sail. The German emperor's *Meteor II* was bigger than the British king's *Britannia. Shamrock,* belonging to the Irish tea magnate Sir Thomas Lipton, was away across the Atlantic to try and win back the America's Cup. All were rigged like the nineteenth-century revenue cutters that chased smugglers off the English shores.

All were gaff rigged. That is to say, the mainsail had four

edges, unlike almost every racing yacht that you see today, which has a triangular mainsail called bermudian because it traces back to boats of Bermuda three centuries ago. To be successful, the bermudian rig needs a tall, strong mast, and that is something twentieth-century technology provides rather well. The bottom edge of the triangle is attached to a swinging boom.

Off the western headland of Cowes, one boat stands out among dozens of others because she is gaff rigged. The gaff is another swinging spar, pivoted two thirds of the way up the mast, which supports the top edge of the four-sided sail. Although she is much more beautiful, the gaffer looks old-fashioned and unfit to compete with all these racing machines and their highly efficient triangles.

When King George V died in 1936, his beloved *Britannia* was taken out to sea and sunk in a Viking sacrifice, and that seemed to be the end of the gaff-rigged racers. A visitor from Mars, observing today's scene off Cowes, would think that centuries of evolution in the design of small sailing vessels had settled at last on the bermudian rig as the fastest available. Why else should all these keen racing yachtsmen be sailing such boats? The astonishing fact is that the gaff rig is better. If windpower and maximum speed are what the racing crews really want, they have the wrong sails. Many old-timers said so when the triangles were driving out the gaff rigs in the 1930s. Not until half a century later did controlled trials, here in the Solent, put the issue to the test. They were done not for the benefit of yachtsmen, but for the sake of the world's fishermen.

"The commercial sailor has to make every square metre pay," says Colin Palmer, who carried out the rig tests for Gifford Technology of Southampton in July and August 1983. The boats were manned by experienced yachtsmen, but the races were unusual because there was no jockeying for position and the boats interfered with each other as little as possible. A bermudian six-metre catamaran served as the yardstick, while a variety of rigs were tried on an exactly similar catamaran pitted against her. One traditional rig proved inferior. That was the lateen or "latin" rig, of Middle Eastern or Indian origin, in which a single triangular sail hangs loose-footed from a long yard. It kept up with the bermudian rig in a light breeze, but when the wind increased the lateen lagged behind on the windward leg of the course.

The gaff-rigged boat and her bermudian rival both had a triangular headsail, like *Charmed*'s jib. It helps to control the boat, and also funnels the wind onto the leading edge of the mainsail, where the rushing air creates a suction that helps to move the boat forward. When the gaffer and the bermudian boat were running downwind there was nothing to choose between them, but as soon as they turned to tack into a head wind, the gaffer showed herself about fifteen per cent faster. *BUT NOT SO CLOSE WINDED?*

The spritsail was quicker still. This has a rectangular mainsail supported by a spar running diagonally from near the bottom of the mast to the top outer corner of the sail. The spritsail proved to be thirty per cent faster to windward than the bermudian, and around seven per cent faster with the wind on the beam. The spritsail was a traditional rig in south-coast fishing boats, and also in sailing barges on the Thames River. It was probably the first kind of fore-and-aft sail to challenge the ancient square sail, when the Dutch introduced it early in the fifteenth century. They evolved the gaff sail from the spritsail about a century later, perhaps because it was safer to handle in bad weather.

Research aimed at improving fishing boats in the tropics prompted the comparisons of rigs. Many Third World fishermen have modernized their craft by getting rid of their sails and relying on outboard motors or diesel engines. But the price of fuel is driving the fishermen back to greater reliance on windpower, which costs nothing. The effect of sails in steadying a boat in rough water is another virtue that was forgotten in the rush to mechanize. For every yachtsman who sails for fun, there is still a fisherman somewhere doing it for a living. Speed and efficiency under sail matter far more to him than to someone competing for a trophy. That may be why bermudian mainsails are rare on working boats.

Don't expect any quick transformation in the Solent yacht-racing scene as a result of scientific sail testing. The boatbuilding industry is geared to turning out nice bermudian yachts, with rigging and gear highly refined for the racing crews, or childishly easy for cruising yachtsmen to handle. For serious innovations, look to the small fishing boats being tried out on the Solent. Edwin Gifford of Gifford Technology also runs Catfish Limited, a non-profitmaking company that develops small sailing boats for peasant fishermen in the tropics. His wife, Joyce Gifford, is an expert on beaches and tropical weather. Two recent Gifford designs use a sail called the tunny rig, invented by the yachtsmen Wayland and Aruna Combewright, who built a canvas boat for £2000 and sailed it across the Atlantic.

The tunny sail looks, at first glance, like a rectangular Chinese junk sail, but it is really a flexible aircraft wing standing on end. The sail is doubled around the front of the mast on a number of fish-shaped battens that give the sail the cross sectional shape of a wing. To refine the shape to suit the wind, depending on which side of the boat it is blowing from, there are ropes leading inside the batten framework. These enable the crew to bend its trailing section one way or the other. Gifford refined the tunny sail, using a cross section developed for light aircraft by NASA in the United States, and tested the resulting design in a wind tunnel at Southampton University. He then incorporated it in an 8.5-metre catamaran designed for the fishermen of Sri Lanka, using two small tunny sails side by side, with masts on both hulls. An extra square sail can be set between the masts, for running downwind. Gifford also designed a larger tunny rig for a 12-metre fishing boat for Scottish waters.

Windpower is making its comeback in ways that suit hardheaded shipowners rather than sentimentalists. Ships fitted with rigid auxiliary sails can save twenty per cent or more of their fuel, and they stay steadier at sea. The Japanese took the lead when they fitted out *Shinitoku Maru* as the first wind-assisted freighter in 1980, but engineers on the Hamble believe they can do better in the design of the sails. If the idea catches on, we may see supertankers sailing among the yachts at Cowes.

The yachtsmen who use windpower to its limits have abandoned Cowes. Some have decamped to Plymouth, where OSTAR starts, the *Observer* Singlehanded Transatlantic Race. OSTAR means as much to ocean-racing men and women as the America's Cup does for round-the-buoys sailors, and at present it is dominated by Breton yachtsmen who sail routinely at twenty knots. Other enthusiasts forgather at Portland, for the Johnnie Walker Speed Week, held in the blustery weather of October. There, sailboards have passed thirty knots and boats propelled by kites have touched twenty-five. So Cowes, too, like Portsmouth and Southampton, begins to feel like a place the world is leaving behind.

The Source
of the Oil

The Solent bends southwestward, at its elbow at Cowes, to run towards the Needles Channel at the far end of the Isle of Wight. Rural scenes open up, quite different from the ports astern. The trees and heaths of the New Forest embrace the Beaulieu River on the Hampshire shore. There my wife's great-great-great-great-great grandfather built *Agamemnon,* the first ship of the line that the young Horatio Nelson commanded. Wide mudflats front the New Forest shoreline, and they are growing southward, narrowing the Solent. This is most obvious near the Lymington River, where grass grows out of the sea. Salt-resistant vegetation has always confirmed the local victories of the land by colonizing the mud, but here the process accelerated in 1870, following a dramatic natural innovation in the kingdom of plants.

A brand-new species of maritime grass appeared in Southampton Water: Townsend's cord grass, or *Spartina townsendii.* It is a tall, vigorous hybrid of the small native *Spartina stricta* and the American *Spartina alternifolia,* and it surpasses all other species as a conqueror of the sea. It takes possession of unstable mud flats when they are still being flooded by high tides. It thrusts its roots deep into the mud, and pokes long stiff leaves through the intruding tides. The grass becomes a trap for silt, which builds upward into the air. Both by natural spread and deliberate transplantation, *Spartina townsendii* now occupies large stretches of shoreline in Britain and across the Channel. In its Solent birthplace it seems to be trying to draw a veil over an obsolescent waterway.

The shallows nudge the deep-draft shipping towards Wight, where low hills make modest headlands along the shore. In the light summer haze they seem like theatre flats set up one behind another to create an illusion of distance. The ground comes to sea level at the Newtown River. A trading port, Francheville, flourished here until the fourteenth century, when a French raiding party destroyed it. The port never recovered, and its estuary now belongs to the blacktailed godwit. Beyond the marshes, the upward step in the Earth's crust makes a line of more pronounced hills, rising 150 metres above the younger rocks of Wight's northern shore. The Hamstead Beds in the foreground have yielded fossils of piglike mammals of about 30 million years ago, together with ancient primates, storks, and crocodiles.

Yarmouth on Wight, not to be confused with Great Yarmouth on England's eastern coast, was the home of Robert Holmes who, with a small squadron, snatched Nieuw Amsterdam from the Dutch in 1664 and renamed it New York. Two years later he

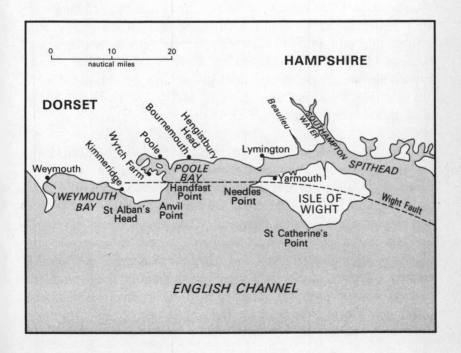

destroyed 170 merchant ships in a raid in Dutch waters. He did not scruple to shoot at English shipping from Yarmouth Castle if they neglected to stop and pay a toll to him for the privilege of passing through the Solent. The church houses an apt monument to the piratical Holmes. A statue of King Louis XIV seized from a French ship was decapitated, and a head of Holmes replaced the Sun King's.

The western exit from the Solent is a scenic stretch of water, rich in geology and history, extending towards an idiosyncratically handsome headland, the Needles. Far ahead, on our ketch's bow, the Needles look like sailing ships lurking off the western tip of the Isle of Wight. The way towards them passes Hurst Castle, built by order of King Henry VIII more than four hundred years ago, at the end of a long spit projecting from the Hampshire shore. A grey landing ship is inward bound past Fort Albert, a brick building on the shore of Wight, less than a mile from Hurst Castle.

The currents funnelled through this narrow opening have scoured a deep channel. The sea surface popples like water in a saucepan just coming to the boil. When a four-knot tide is ebbing through the narrows into a strong southwesterly wind, steep waves build up rapidly. Many a yachtsman retreats at this point. Beyond Hurst Castle, the visible shore of Hampshire swings away to the northwest, but a large bank of sand, gravel, and shingle fills the sea. It forces large ships to follow the trend of Wight towards the Needles, but there a mile-long ledge of chalk protrudes under the sea until it almost meets the shingle.

Morning shadows subdue the multiple colours of Alum Bay, just east of Needles Point, but even so you can see the streaks of upended sandstone in narrow bands of white, black, yellow, green, red, pink, and brown. The strata are aligned vertically up the cliff face, drawing a surprising diagram of the Wight fault. All along the fault line, a great block of the Earth's crust has risen about a kilometre, lifting up the chalk and other old material of the island's southern segment, so that they stand higher than the much younger rocks of the northern part. The sands of Alum Bay, intermediate in age, are draped over the step like a stair carpet.

The Needles look less like sewing implements than broken

teeth. They are stacks of chalk sticking out of the sea and ranging westward in a row from the foot of the tall white cliffs of Needles Point. One of the Needles stacks, called Lot's Wife, fell down in 1764, and an arch of chalk collapsed in 1815. Under the water near the lighthouse, divers have found four wrecks piled on top of each other: a Roman ship of the third century, of which only coins remain, the warships *Assurance* and *Pomone,* wrecked in 1753 and 1811, and the schooner *Dream,* which added herself to the sorrowful man-made stack in 1837.

Between the Needles and the Dorset shore, which gleams in the morning sunshine far to the west, the Channel has robbed England of an expanse of territory as large as Wight. The Needles prolong the island's chalk like a line of dashes that points towards Dorset. There, in a mirror image of Needles Point, the headland of Handfast Point projects this way, complete with chalk stacks. A wall of chalk, like the dam that once straddled the Dover Strait, formerly rooted the Isle of Wight in Dorset. In its shadow, Dorset's Frome River flowed eastward across a fertile plain all the way to Spithead. When the sea broke through and took its bite out of southern England, it made so thorough a job of it that you would never know from the contours of the sea bed that deer once roamed on high hills here, or that a great geological fault runs underneath our keel towards Dorset. The chalk and clay cliffs of Wight's seaward coast fall away behind us towards St. Catherine's Point, and give a good picture of what had to be removed to open this western doorway to the Solent. The sea is gradually abolishing the Isle of Wight too.

The low shoreline of the mainland rises to modest cliffs of sandstone, clay, and gravel, beginning at Barton-on-Sea. This rather nondescript resort has a certain glory among geologists because one of the stages in their global timescale is called the Bartonian. That makes it rather easy to specify the age of the assorted rocks in the cliffs: 41 to 45 million years. They are older towards Hengistbury Head, which separates two indentations in the coast, Christchurch Bay and Poole Bay.

Hengistbury Head protrudes across a river estuary. It was a cross-Channel port when London was an uninhabited swamp, and this was the destination of prehistoric trading vessels crossing from Alet on the Rance estuary. Like Alet, it is a natural fortress, a knob of greyish sandstone thirty-six metres high and a kilometre long, with a skyline sloping gently down from west to east. Spectacular erosion of the cliffs at Hengistbury's eastern tip has left red boulders littering the foreshore. A narrow spit connects Hengistbury to the shore. Unlike Alet, Hengistbury has no medieval town. The summit is covered with gorse and heather, and the most notable residents are skylarks.

If you stood on top of Hengistbury Head you would see at once why prehistoric people counted it a special place. The headland shelters and commands the entrance to two rivers, the Stour and the Avon (not the Stratford Avon, by the way). Their joint estuary is called Christchurch harbour. The Avon was an important waterway leading almost due north for fifty kilometres towards the ceremonial centre of Stonehenge. That was already an ancient monument when the Gaulish-Celtic traders came with their shipments of wine, but the location of Stonehenge is a clue to the likely whereabouts of farming populations before the Anglo-Saxon ploughs widened their horizons. The Stour River gave access to another region, and by transhipping the cargoes to Poole harbour, just eight miles to the east, prehistoric traders could find markets far up the Frome River, in western Dorset. The archaeologist Barry Cunliffe identifies this furzy headland as the main "port-of-trade" in the pre-Roman commerce with Brittany. The arrival of wine and other luxury items disrupted the social systems of the Celts, and their arrival at Danebury, fifty kilometres inland, was quickly followed by the abandonment of that hill–fort citadel. Half a millennium later, the Avon River was the line at which the Celts checked the advance of the Saxons along the Channel shore.

Christchurch harbour is now close to failure. A few motorboats, sailing dinghies, and shallow-draft catamarans lie there, but at low tide it almost dries out. A pair of sandy spits lined with brightly coloured chalets nearly close the narrow entrance, called the Run. The village beside the entrance is Mudeford, and the name means muddy ford. At low tide there is often only half a metre of water in the Run, and you can in principle run across the Run, to save your pennies from the ferryman. Michael Green, the original Coarse Yachtsman, once walked into Mudeford from the sea, towing his yacht behind him.

A habit of striding about on the bottom of the sea is one of the hallmarks of a Coarse Yachtsman, according to Green in *The Art of Coarse Cruising*. "I am proud," he writes, "to have planted my footprints on the beds of some of the most famous rivers and seas in Europe." After a hundred years of books by Posh Yachtsmen telling of passages accomplished with never a hitch, except those due to storm-force winds or negligent paid hands, Green helped to set new norms of candour that crept into the yachting literature in the 1970s. He extended to the high seas his volumes on Coarse Sports, which means standard sports such as golf or rugby football as undertaken by people who are not very fit, or very competent, or very well equipped.

Coarse Cruising is a matter of things going wrong, vital equipment being lost, people treading on the food, or manoeuvres being executed with something less than the panache to which Posh Yachtsmen aspire. There is enough of the Coarse Yachtsman in all of us to respond with a twinge of guilt or sympathy to Green's vignettes. Plenty of good advice is delivered backhandedly in *The Art of Coarse Cruising*. For example, it is no use exhibiting a distress signal calmly.

> Do panic. Shout loudly. Screech. The finest SOS in the world is the human voice booming "Help!" It certainly has as much chance of being effective as hoisting a square flag with a black ball underneath.

Similarly, Green's verdict that small yachts have *no* right of way, but must keep clear of bigger boats, is close to the mark, as is his advice always to carry 144 boxes of matches aboard. Green himself crossed the Dover Strait at night in a sailing dinghy without any lights or lighting, and when his matches were used up he was quite glad to be nearly run down by a tanker because he could read his chart in the glow from the portholes.

Even the prehistoric Coarse Skipper who fetched up at Selsey instead of Hengistbury needed to have an explanation ready on his lips. Green recommends for all contingencies: "We were seized by a Giant Hand." That explanation might have been greeted with less scepticism in the Iron Age than in a yacht club's bar today, and many strange tales of mermaids and sea monsters may have begun as excuses for misadventures.

The Avon River is the traditional dividing line between the counties of Hampshire and Dorset, and although the administrative boundary has wandered to and fro along the shore, the latest ruling puts Hengistbury firmly back in Dorset. The houses that begin to crowd the clifftops of Poole Bay, west of Hengistbury, are outliers of the conurbation of Bournemouth. A dip in the cliffs surrounded by tall buildings shows where its centre is. Bournemouth was vacant heath like Hengistbury until early in the nineteenth century. Then planting of pine forests began, and the building of a few private houses. When the developers moved in, backed by medical commendations of the pines, they set out to create a more snobbish place than Brighton, and in large measure they succeeded. In some ways it is more splendid, with better beaches and plenty of attractions for the modern visitor, but it lacks the high spirits of the Sussex town.

In 1984 an offshore drilling rig settled on the sea bed four miles from Bournemouth. While vacationers splashed in the surf, the men on the rig spent two months during that summer boring almost two thousand metres into the underlying rocks. Like Esso and Premier off Selsey Bill, British Gas and British Petroleum remained mute about what they had found. It was another "tight" hole. But on the evening of August 18, people on the seafront at Bournemouth could see a flare of natural gas lighting up the sea around the rig, and the *Financial Times* of London was quick to report the apparent discovery of a significant gas field.

There was no cause for surprise. The offshore site lies within a few miles of Britain's main onshore oil field, Wytch Farm, beside Poole harbour. The narrow entrance to the harbour opens up beyond Bournemouth, where the Dorset coast begins a decisive sweep to the south. Although the town of Poole now seems like a western suburb of Bournemouth, it has a much longer history. Its large, puddlelike harbour, fed by the Frome River and studded with islands, has served Iron Age traders, medieval pirates, D-Day landing craft, and modern freighters.

In 1973, prospectors working for British Gas drilled in the scrubland and cow pasture on the southern side of Poole harbour. They discovered oil trapped in sandstone nine hundred metres underground. Four years later they found greater quantities lower down. The upper field was exploited first, and nodding donkeys pumped up enough oil to fill five tanker trains a week—about 1.5 million barrels a year, an unspectacular but useful amount. In 1984 British Petroleum bought the Wytch Farm field with a view to developing the deeper strata, and increasing the output tenfold.

Now notice the geological setting of Wytch Farm. The Wight fault runs ashore at chalky Handfast Point, south of the Poole harbour entrance. From the low ground around the harbour the terrain rises steeply towards the high chalk of Ballard Down. This leap matches the step in the Isle of Wight. Poole harbour corresponds with the low northern shore of the island, while the high ground of southern Dorset is part of the same upthrust block as southern Wight.

The fault between the low and high blocks has helped to trap oil in formations deep underground. Similar traps may exist all along the Wight fault: under Poole Bay offshore, under the Isle of Wight itself, and east of the island. There the fault runs under the sea past Selsey Bill, and curves southeastward until it meets the southern edge of the uplifted block midway between Brighton and the Seine estuary. Looking westward, the fault continues across southern Dorset, to re-emerge at the English Channel shore eleven miles west of Handfast Point. Altogether about ninety miles of the fault line, mostly under the sea bed, is awaiting exploration.

If offshore oil eventually helps to restore the fortunes of this coast, some of the credit will be due to the late Edward Bullard of Cambridge University, who pioneered the technique of seismic sounding for probing the rocks under the sea bed. He set off explosions and detected echoes of the shock waves coming back from deep-lying layers, where they found the character of the rocks changing. Bullard did his first seismic shooting at sea in the Channel's Western Approaches.

In the pioneering days, Bullard created the shock wave by

detonating an explosive charge in the sea. Now the bangs come from arrays of powerful airguns, towed on either side of the stern of a survey ship, and fired in a carefully synchronized fashion several times a minute. Hydrophones spaced along a streamer cable pick up the echoes. The cable is a hollow tube filled with oil, and it unwinds from a large drum in the ship's stern. This tube can stretch for several kilometres, to the confusion of other shipping. The recording equipment generates a profile of the strata under the sea bed, which looks like a geological cross section drawn with a soft pencil. An expert eye can trace a particular layer for many kilometres, follow its undulations, and spot the likely traps for oil.

The uplift of the Wight block by a kilometre ranks as a substantial effort in recent mountain building. It is a strange thing to happen in the geologically tranquil Channel, far removed from any of the active plate boundaries where you can expect mountains to form. Geologists used to speak vaguely of an "Alpine storm" affecting England during the past 50 million years, while the Alps were forming far to the southeast. The timing is right, but simply to imagine waves of deformation radiating from Switzerland to England makes no sense, because northern France has remained relatively undisturbed. If the major events in the Mediterranean region, due to Africa colliding with Europe, really made themselves felt two thousand kilometres away in southern England, the puzzle is to explain how the impulse leapfrogged across Normandy and focused itself in southern England.

Robert Muir Wood has suggested a solution to the mystery of Wight. England was caught between the events in the Mediterranean and the opening of the North Atlantic Ocean to the north and west, beyond Ireland and Scotland. The strains required small internal adjustments among the blocks, which were brought about mainly by sideways movements. In this part of the continent, the western region of the Channel had to shift a little to the northwest, relative to the eastern region, and nature opportunistically sought out old faults between blocks where this movement could occur.

One was the fault running northwest across the Channel from

High Normandy to the eastern end of Wight. Others pointing in the same direction lay farther west in Dorset and Devon, and they were linked to the cross-Channel fault by the Wight fault. But this ran in the wrong direction, making a kink in the system, such that the northwest-moving block rammed hard against southern England. Something had to give, and the result 40 million years ago was that the southern part of the Isle of Wight and Dorset reared up, and the ground to the north was pushed down. If Muir Wood's theory is right, it explains the Solent and its ports as a flooded downthrust region, protected from storms by the up-thrust. It also says why the Isle of Wight peters out at its eastern end, where the composite fault line curved to the southeast across the Channel and became more freely moving. And it expresses, more generally, why the geology of southern England has been so much busier than that of northern France.

As the ketch heads southward, across the Wight fault, from near Poole harbour down to Anvil Point, the rocks of the shore increase in age from 40 to 140 million years in a distance of just four miles. Around the corner made by Anvil Point, St. Alban's Head towers more than a hundred metres high in its limestone eminence, but it has a claylike slope at its foot, pointing towards a submerged reef that runs four miles out to sea. The low cliffs just west of St. Alban's Head are built of dark and crumbly Kimmeridge Clay. Kimmeridge itself is a diminutive Dorset village of thatched cottages, and in Old English the name means "comely stream."

Like Barton with its Bartonian, Kimmeridge is famous among Earth scientists for the Kimmeridgian stage. In the geological timescale, it spans the interval 145 to 154 million years ago, late in the Jurassic period. But there is more to it than a date. The Kimmeridgian was a great time for oil formation in many parts of the world, and the rocks of Kimmeridge Bay are dark with petroleum.

Ashore at Kimmeridge you can inspect rusting rails that date from a venture in the nineteenth century to quarry inflammable shale from the cliffs. It is so saturated with oil that you can set fire to it, and it will burn like coal. The project failed because customers objected to the sulphurous smell that Kimmeridge shale gave off when it burned. The Celts had another use for the jetlike shale: they made brightly polished ornaments from it. Just across the hills, on an island in Poole harbour, archaeologists have found a factory where Kimmeridge shale was turned into armlets, more than two thousand years ago.

During the Kimmeridgian stage, northwestern Europe lay closer to the tropics, and it was experiencing great tension. As Peter Ziegler, a Dutch oil geologist, puts it, the British Isles were being wrenched away from Europe like a tooth from a jaw. Rift valleys were widening in the western English Channel and the North Sea, and in this central region of the Channel a flooded basin extended across large areas of England and France. Sediments rich in organic remains settled on the sea bed. Later sediments buried them deeply and the Earth's internal heat matured the organic material to make petroleum.

Although the discovery of large oil fields under the North Sea in 1969–70 distracted attention away from the English Channel and its inflammable cliffs, the first find at Wytch Farm followed only a few years later. Its upper reserves of oil originated in rocks like these, visible on the shore, but buried deep underground on the other side of the Wight fault. The uplift of the Wight block brought the oily strata to sea level at Kimmeridge Bay, where they are easy to reach but offer only a meagre supply. Kimmeridge itself has only a minuscule oil field. Oil moves around and most of it escapes from its source rocks. Under Wytch Farm, the Kimmeridgian oil has migrated into other underground strata, especially to a layer called the Bridport sandstone, and the fault has helped to trap the oil by blocking its sideways movement with impermeable rocks. Out of sight below the sea bed is the much older source of the larger reserves, trapped in deeper sandstones at Wytch Farm.

No one really expects the English Channel to be as rich as the North Sea, but everything points to the existence of important hydrocarbon fields, especially near the Isle of Wight. Across the Channel, the French have struck oil near Paris. The whole region has been awash for most of the past 200 million years, accumulating sediments, some of them oily like Kimmeridge's. The sediments are thickest in the rift valley of the western Channel and the Western Approaches, but traps for the oil may be scarcer there than in the central English Channel. Here the thickest sediments, totalling three to four kilometres, occur in a ring around Wight.

A coastwise course takes the ketch past Warbarrow Bay and Lulworth Cove, where the sea broke through a wall of limestone fronting the shore, and dug out the softer rocks behind. Ahead lies Weymouth, a seaside resort and fishing port that also dispatches ferries to the Channel Islands. The grey cliffs of Ringstead, beside Weymouth Bay, contain more of the Kimmeridge shale. In 1826 the Ringstead cliffs ignited spontaneously and burned for four years. The smell was terrible.

Slingers and Fishermen

A lump of limestone looms across our bow, barring the way westward. It is Portland, a tall island sloping down towards the south, like an arrowhead aimed at Brittany. A shingle beach links Portland with Weymouth and prevents us passing inside.

There are two perils off Portland Bill, the island's southern tip. One is the Shambles sandbank, three sea miles long, which sprawls east of the Bill and causes waves to break with excessive enthusiasm. Its name means "slaughterhouse." More variable in position, the Portland Race is a maelstrom where the tidal currents that flow southward down both sides of Portland collide with the main Channel currents travelling east or west. Their combined effect can set water moving at ten knots in places. A ledge of rock running out from the Bill makes the bottom very uneven and adds to the severity of the tide race. The *Channel Pilot* describes it as "an area of overfalls and steep heavy breaking seas in which the streams are subject to great and sudden changes in both direction and rate."

An inshore passage generally offers a half-mile corridor of orderly water between Bill and Race. It is safest to approach Portland's miniature harbour of Church Ope Cove well to the north of the Bill in order to hug the shore all the way around. The harbour lies underneath a clifftop hotel called Pennsylvania Castle and it was formerly used for shipping the famous Portland Stone, quarried from the island. The novelist Thomas Hardy, son of a Dorset stonemason, described Church Ope Cove as "the single practicable port of exit from or entrance to the isle on this side by a seagoing craft; once an active wharf, whence many a fine public building had sailed—including Saint Paul's Cathedral."

The Portland Stone makes a limestone lid for the island, with sheer edges at the cliffs. It slants down to sea level at the Bill. Farther north it squelches out softer sandstone and clay lying underneath it, so that the cliffs are splayed at sea level. In all this towering mass rising to a height of 150 metres, the best Portland Stone comes from a narrow layer near the top about four metres thick. It is a fine oolitic limestone, made up of vast numbers of grains, like fish roe. Portland Cement, by the way, is a plagiarism: it has nothing to do with the island except its supposed resemblance to Portland Stone. A very steep track leads down the cliff to Church Ope Cove, and you have to visualize teams of horses not hauling but checking the loads of stone on their descent to the harbour. The quarrymen are still busy up there, but the stone

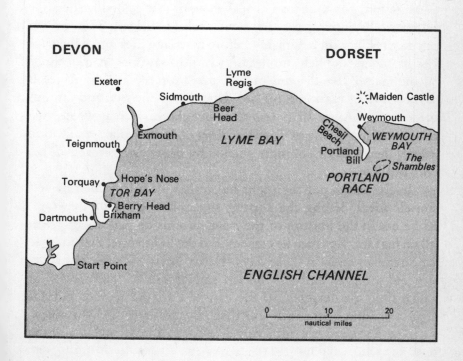

leaves Portland by truck. It is an austere island, which Hardy called the Gibraltar of Wessex.

Hardy made Portland the setting for *The Well-Beloved,* and wrote of "the solid and single block of limestone, unique and white," where the sun flashed on "infinitely stratified walls of oolite." With less exaggeration, he told of doorsteps rising behind chimneys and "gardens hung up by one edge to the sky." Hardy noted the insularity and inbreeding among people for whom even their neighbours in Weymouth were foreigners or, in the dialect, "kimberlins." The sounds of the island run through the book: the "lisping" of the sea beneath the cliffs, the "canine" growl of the pebbles on the beach, and the "whirr-whirr, saw-saw" noises of the quarrymen and stone-sawyers, which Hardy calls the "island's snores."

The Well-Beloved is the fanciful tale of a quarry owner's son who becomes a fashionable sculptor and courts young women of three successive generations. At twenty he promises to marry a girl called Avice, but when he is departing for London she declines to meet him for a nocturnal leavetaking at a ruined castle. She fears that he intends to carry out the old "Island Custom" of proving fertility by pregnancy before marriage. In a letter she begs him to understand her "modern," that is to say Victorian, feelings on the matter. By the end of the story, forty years on, Avice II has the idea of marrying off her daughter to the rich and famous academician. Avice III is less than delighted. Hardy wrote two versions of the ending of *The Well-Beloved.* In its initial serialization (1892), the sculptor attempts suicide by drowning himself in the Portland Race.

In the middle of the night he steals a skiff in which he sets himself adrift, letting the current sweep him towards the Race. As he lies in the bottom of the boat, promising pailfuls of water fall on his face. But then he crashes into the light vessel that marked the Shambles bank in those days. Hardy knew his tides: the lovelorn old sculptor embarks on his suicide bid at "half-flow," at which time the currents off the east of Portland would, indeed, carry a drifting boat south and then east, towards the Shambles.

The Race and the light vessel figure in a different way in the final version of the novel (1897). Avice III runs off at night with a young Frenchman, and they take a boat to row to Weymouth ("Budmouth"). They launch it and jump in, only to find that they have no oars, and are being unwillingly swept towards the Race. They set fire to their handkerchiefs and Avice's umbrella, and the light vessel acknowledges these distress signals with a coloured flame. At daybreak a boat puts off from the light vessel to rescue them.

Robin Pingree, a tidal expert at Plymouth's marine biological lab, once showed me a sample from the Shambles bank. It was a mass of finely chopped shells of mussels and other species, looking as innocent as tea leaves. Pingree then posed a riddle about the Shambles: "Why is there no bank on the other side of Portland Bill?"

By jutting sharply into the main tidal flow of the English Channel, Portland creates large eddies in the currents. One circulates in an anticlockwise loop east of the Bill, and binds the sediments of the Shambles bank. On the ebb tide, a clockwise eddy forms on the west side, so where is the sandbank? In fact, a small bank does exist a mile or so west of the Bill, but it has fourteen metres of water over it, compared with four over the Shambles. As the eddies are very similar on both sides of the Bill, why is the western bank so much smaller?

By way of answering his riddle, Pingree stood a jar of water with tea leaves on a turntable that revolved anticlockwise, to mimic the effect of the Earth's rotation. He then stirred the water to create an eddy, simulating the Portland tides. A sweep of his hand, in the same direction as the jar was rotating, set the tea leaves swirling, but they soon built a neat cone at the centre of the jar. It was a fine model of the Shambles bank. When he stirred the other way, against the rotation, the tea leaves settled in a much more disorderly way, with only a small concentration towards the centre. Pingree then explained that the tidal eddy east of Portland Bill reinforces the effect of the Earth's rotation, and makes the Shambles. On the west side the rotations quarrel and the bank is small.

With the tidal current doing most of the work, and the sails keeping us at the right distance from the shore, our ketch sidles past the tall white-and-red lighthouse at Portland Bill. Here the ground is only a few metres above sea level, and it is littered with cut and abandoned masonry. At a close but safe distance, the race froths with white water. From the far side of the Bill, looking northward, you can now make out the bank of shingle thirteen metres high that links Portland with the mainland. It is called Chesil Beach, and makes a natural wall of shingle that continues for fifteen miles along the Dorset coast. The sea sometimes overtops the bank during storms, and where the natural causeway reaches Portland, a storm destroyed some low-lying houses in 1978. The inhabitants were, though, taken by surprise, when they found the sea throwing huge quantities of pebbles at them in February 1979. The wind was blowing from the east at the time. Oceanographers explained the event as due to an unusually strong swell from an Atlantic storm that was, in effect, focused by the Channel topography on to Chesil Beach.

The tall column of the Thomas Hardy monument on Blackdown Hill, standing in the midst of "South Wessex" five kilometres behind Chesil Beach, has nothing to do with the author of the novels. It marks the birthplace of Admiral Thomas Hardy. He died a year before the novelist was born, and had been captain of *Victory* at the Battle of Trafalgar. To him, the dying Nelson said, "Kiss me, Hardy." It has been a catchphrase in England ever since, but the Victorians thought it indecent, and reasoned that what Nelson must have meant was, "Kismet, Hardy."

If you were lost in the fog off Chesil Beach, you could tell how far along it you were by going ashore and checking the size of the pebbles. The beach is a grading machine, which keeps fist-size pieces of shingle at Portland but sends pea-size pebbles back to the far end, during southerly gales. The rounded and graded pebbles offer an excellent supply of missiles, should you want to fight in the manner of David against Goliath, using slings. Hardy's code name for Portland was the Isle of Slingers. Concealed from view behind Captain Hardy's Blackdown Hill is Maiden Castle, a Celtic fortress where archaeologists found forlorn piles of Chesil Beach pebbles, still waiting for a slinger to hurl them at the Roman assault troops.

Chesil Beach extends into Lyme Bay, an almost semicircular dent in the English coast, which takes its name from the played-out port of Lyme Regis, the last town in Dorset. With every gale, 200-million-year-old ammonites and other fossils fall out of the cliffs near Lyme. As Devon begins, the bay runs on past Beer, Sidmouth, and Budleigh Salterton, to the Exe River, where Exmouth substitutes as a port for silted Exeter. Then the curving coast trends southward.

In its rocks and its peoples, Lyme Bay is a transition zone between eastern and western England. The shore changes from blue and yellow rocks 200 million years old, through a zone of white chalk less than 100 million years old, and then to red sandstone nearly 300 million years old. Human roots become older, too, and London's England begins to lose its grip hereabouts. There is no emphatic boundary, like that between the French and the Bretons, but a gradual human cline extends from the Anglo-Saxon core of southeastern England to the Celtic stronghold of Cornwall in the far southwest. The change begins in Dorset, because here the Celts stood and fought the invaders, starting with the Durotriges against the Romans, at Maiden Castle.

Their neighbours, the Atrebates, living in Sussex and Hampshire, were a treacherous lot who virtually invited the Romans in. The course of the Roman conquest of the Channel shore, in the years A.D. 43 to 47, depended on the attitudes of the various Celtic tribes. An anti-Roman confederacy, led by the Catuvellauni, controlled a broad tract of southern Britain, hemming the pro-Roman Atrebates against the Channel. To the west of the Atrebates were tribes with independent minds: the Durotriges of Dorset and the Dumnonii of Devon and Cornwall.

The Romans first smashed the Catuvellaunian army ranged against it in Kent. To protect their bridgehead, they appointed a puppet king over the Atrobates. The archaeologist Barry Cunliffe, noting how quickly Sussex and Hampshire became thoroughly Romanized, says that a military force may have been sent down-Channel by sea for the takeover. The 2nd Augustan Legion was responsible for the subsequent advance along the Channel coast against the Durotriges. The Celtic hill forts provided their traditional defences. The most dramatic evidence of battle has been unearthed at Maiden Castle. It is a ship-shaped fortress almost a kilometre long, surrounded by multiple ramparts.

The Roman infantry advanced under cover of heavy ballista fire, from rampart to rampart, and then burned huts at the gates to provide a smoke screen for the final assault. Once inside, they put the Durotrigian women and children to the sword, as well as the defending troops. Many skulls and bones bear the marks of sword cuts, and one backbone has a ballista bolt embedded in it. Roman generals are often shadowy figures, but Vespasian, who commanded the 2nd Legion at Maiden Castle, later became emperor.

Vespasian's conquest of Dorset left Devon and Cornwall under the control of the Dumnonii. Cunliffe points out that cross-Channel voyaging gave those people closer cultural, political, and economic ties to the Celts of Brittany than to other British tribes. He suspects that, as traders, they were probably quite friendly with the Romans. They were not a nuisance, like the stubborn Celts of Wales, and to conquer them outright in difficult terrain must have seemed more trouble than it was worth. The Romans garrisoned Exeter in eastern Devon, but a treaty left the Dumnonii as semi-independent allies.

The Celts held out longer against the Anglo-Saxons. On the coast of Lyme Bay, at Sidmouth, they built a brand-new hill fort towards the end of the fifth century A.D. Dorset kept its independence for two centuries after Kent, Sussex, and Hampshire were in the hands of the newcomers. The Celts holding the line at the Avon River, near Hengistbury Head, were then outflanked. By about A.D. 650 the West Saxons had established a durable beachhead on the Exe River in Devon, and shortly afterward they assimilated Dorset into Wessex. Full control of Devon did not come until a further century had elapsed. Still the people of Cornwall held out, although often by agreement, as in Roman times. The English did not fully take charge of Cornwall until shortly before the Norman invasion—five centuries after the capture of Kent.

A light south wind carries the ketch at nightfall into Devon's Tor Bay. It is a gap between two reefs of old-fashioned coral that thrived on a volcanic sea bed 375 million years ago, until a worldwide environmental crisis obliterated them. The coral corpses made the tough limestone that endures against the sea in the headlandsthat shield the bay. Rainwater dissolves limestone more effectively, to make caves. In the genteel suburbs of Torquay, at the root of the northern headland of Hope's Nose, is Kent's Cavern, which was occupied by cavemen 120,000 years ago.

Berry Head, across the bay, is easy to recognize because it is planed flat on the top, and low, wide forts help to give the headland a wholly man-made look. Between Berry Head and Hope's Nose the sea has quarried out the sandstone that formerly filled Tor Bay, cutting it back to the low red cliffs that now surround it. On the flank of Berry Head, four miles from Torquay, is the fishing port of Brixham, where the Dutchman William of Orange landed in 1688, to snatch the crown of England.

Most of the houses along the shoreline are late additions. Subtract them, and you are left with the wooded cliffs of Devon, on which many eyes have gazed longingly. In the Napoleonic Wars, when ships of the Brest blockade came briefly home to Tor Bay, the crews were not allowed ashore, in case they failed to return. And Napoleon himself was eventually held prisoner in a warship anchored in the bay.

After his defeat at the Battle of Waterloo in 1815 Napoleon fled to the Biscay shore, intending to escape across the Atlantic to the United States. Only the year before the British had burned Washington at the culmination of a war provoked by the British navy's high-handed treatment of American shipping. But Napoleon's hopes of a welcome in the gutted American capital were not put to the test. The inevitable British blockading squadron barred his way out of Rochefort. Napoleon's life was in danger from angry Frenchmen, so he went aboard the British warship *Bellerophon* and surrendered himself to the protection of his enemies. They brought him to Tor Bay while the victors decided what to do with him.

Any day, for weeks on end, the former master of Europe was to be seen here, pacing *Bellerophon*'s quarterdeck. Sightseers flocked from all over England and went out by boat to gape at him. They found, if they waved, that the caged tiger might wave back quite amiably, and even make complimentary remarks about the scenery. As this was early in the Seaside Age, when new resorts were competing for visitors, Torquay had a great fillip from Napoleon's sojourn in Tor Bay.

·　　·　　·

The morning's course out of Tor Bay shaves Berry Head, where the houses of Brixham climb up the cliffs from the harbour lying at the headland's root. The water sparkles like aerated ink, and a large fishing boat comes roaring in past Berry Head, heading home to Brixham. Eight hundred years ago the village stood beside a small river mouth, which is now built over. In the centuries that followed, men from Brixham used all sorts of nets and lines to catch a wide variety of fishes until, in the seventeenth century, they took up the trawling that made Brixham famous. They developed specialized boats and learnt how to get the feel of the bottom, from the vibration of the ropes that towed the trawl nets. Later they adopted gaff-rigged cutters, invented in the Netherlands, which offered greater towing power and faster delivery of their catches to market.

At the end of the eighteenth century, fishermen set out from Brixham to look for new grounds suited to their trawling skills. They went up-Channel and began working off Dungeness and the Varne Bank. By 1820 a Devonian colony flourished at Ramsgate in Kent. Then they moved along England's east coast and discovered the great North Sea trawling grounds. The trawler ports of Hull and Grimsby owed their growth to the fishermen of Devon. So did Fleetwood on the Irish Sea.

Back at Brixham, the boats were improving. The fishermen and their builders sharpened the bow and deepened the heel, giving finer lines to the hull under water. A second mast was put up towards the stern, for a small mizzen sail, and the mainmast was stepped back to make room for a large staysail. The result was the perfection—no other word will do—of the classic Brixham trawler. First appearing in the 1870s, it was perhaps the finest sailing boat ever built for work: beautiful to look at, capable of more than twelve knots, and yet suited to fishing in any sort of weather. The Brixham trawler was widely imitated, and the modern sail training vessels of the Swedish Cruising Association are based on its design.

Until fifty years ago the herring was the most sought-after fish in the English Channel. Brixham men were using drift nets to catch it in the twelfth century. The herring played a leading role in European history because it was usually abundant and cheap, and a pair of herrings a day would supply all the protein a person needed, and about half the fat and calories. The German merchants of the Hanseatic League, who dominated northern Europe's commerce in the fourteenth century, founded their fortunes on a great herring fishery off southern Sweden. That fishery collapsed around 1420, perhaps because exceptional tides of that period altered the salinity of the Baltic Sea. Germany's loss was Holland's gain.

The Dutch North Sea fishery boomed in the sixteenth century, and Amsterdam, they say, is built on herring bones. Brine-pickling, invented by the Dutch for preserving the herring, made it a more tradable item. The Dutch fished off England's east coast, and this was one cause of the naval wars between the English and the Dutch in the seventeenth century. The French destroyed the Dutch herring fleet in 1703, and it never recovered its former dominance. In 1750 the English built the first large herring fleet of their own, using busses, ships based on the Dutch design.

The herring appeared at different places at different times of year, and the fishing fleet chased it along the coasts. There was a myth that the fish came from the Arctic because it showed up progressively farther south as the season advanced. In fact, different populations of herring were involved, which bred in different areas; for example, off northeastern England, on the Dogger Bank of the North Sea, and off Normandy in the English Channel. Currents driven by the prevailing winds carried the larvae to nursery grounds off the Dutch and German coasts. When they gathered size and strength, they swam away into deeper water. Adult herrings were abundant in the western English Channel in midwinter.

In summer there were the pilchards. Western Devon, and especially Cornwall beyond, used to be great places for catching these large sardines. Every August men called "huers" would stand on the cliffs to watch for a reddish shadow in the water that told of a pilchard shoal. Then, like hallooing huntsmen, they would alert the fishermen waiting below. "Hevva! Hevva!" they shouted. The team would rush to the spot, and a long seine net, fitted with floats along one edge and sinkers on the other, spilled out of the main boat to encircle the shoal. "Lurkers" in other boats splashed their oars to discourage the pilchards from escaping. The fishermen then towed the net and the trapped shoal onto the beach, where they could keep the fish alive and haul them out at leisure. In the mid-nineteenth century, the West Country fishermen were catching 10 million pilchards in a season. They sold for ten a penny, and were a fine source of protein for workers who earned only a hundred pennies a week. But beach seining stopped in Cornwall around 1905.

Then the herring vanished. In 1936, after ten years' gradual decline, the Channel herring fishery was abruptly exterminated. For the next thirty years the pilchard predominated in the offshore catches. In the late 1960s, for no obvious reason, the mackerel became abundant in the waters of Devon and Cornwall, and the public quickly learnt to enjoy their rather oily flavor. For every mackerel caught in 1960, the fishermen were hauling in a hundred by 1978.

These changes in marine life in the western English Channel have perplexed and often ruined the fishermen. Everyone suspects overfishing as the cause of major changes in fish stocks, and large fleets of visitors using Newlyn in Cornwall as a base for catching pilchards may have undermined the local beach seining industry. The disappearance of the Channel herring certainly followed a fishermen's free-for-all. After World War I ended in 1918, a fleet of two hundred steam drifters from eastern England would make their rounds of the British coast and reach this part of the world at Christmas. They settled like Vikings on the ports of the West Country and pillaged the herring. Very profitable it was, too, until the crash came.

With hindsight, the visiting fishermen were not entirely to blame. Unluckily, they hit the herring hard at a time when it was declining for natural reasons. A recent parallel was the collapse of Peru's anchovy industry, the world's greatest fishery in the 1960s, which was devastated in the 1970s by the natural interruptions called El Niño. What seems like a sustainable catch can become flagrant overfishing when the weather changes.

Frederick Russell, a celebrated marine biologist at the Plymouth Laboratory, chronicled the demise of the local herring in the 1930s. He monitored from year to year the gradual disappearance of an arrowworm, an elegant but diminutive swimmer, from the western English Channel. He saw the food available to fishes declining markedly, together with the plant nutrients available in the surface waters. When the herring went, favourite fishes of the sea bed—cod, plaice, lemon sole, and so on—also became scarce. But half a century later the reasons are still debated.

Alan Southward recalls that the first theory was that the English Channel was being starved of nutrients, perhaps because less water was flowing in from the Atlantic. But the missing phosphate could be accounted for in the bones of thriving young pilchards. Another notion was of a life-or-death competition between pilchard and herring, with the pilchard winning. Southward himself believes that the herring failed in 1936 because of a change in the world's climate. The water of the western English Channel became warmer. The herring and the arrowworm preferred cool water, while the pilchard liked it warm.

The rise of the mackerel supports Southward's belief that climatic change makes the Channel fisheries unstable. It followed a general cooling of the Earth in the 1950s and 1960s. The spell that ended at midcentury had been the warmest for a thousand years, so perhaps the cold-water herring would have disappeared from the western Channel even if the fishermen had left it in peace. But there was no nucleus of survivors to regenerate the shoals when the climate cooled again.

Drastic seesawing between herring and pilchard seems to have happened in the past. The Little Ice Age reached a peak of chilliness around 1700, and that was a good time for the herring, even in West Cornwall, a traditional pilchard area. In warmer spells the pilchard predominated, and during each changeover fishermen would find they had the wrong kinds of nets and boats.

The fact is that the English Channel was never a great fishery at the best of times. The Breton fishermen congregate on their southern shore, preferring Biscay. The Channel catches were good enough to entice men out to sea, and give subsistence to the local people. But ambitious men, hearing word of far bigger hauls, would go to fish somewhere else. The North Sea attracted them long before the Brixham trawlers went there, and in the fourteenth century a successful naval action against the French ended with a fight between the English fishermen from the North Sea and the Channel. Men from Ramsgate and the French Channel ports found their way to Iceland and its cod fishery, and their competition damaged the fishing industry of the West Country. The seafarers of southern Devon seemed more interested in the Biscay wine trade, but the loss of English control of Bordeaux in 1453 left the local economy in a bad way until the Newfoundland cod fishery gave it a new lease of life from about 1500 onward.

Beside the famous transatlantic voyages of Cartier, Drake, and so on, there was always a maritime underworld of nameless, secretive fishermen who never set foot in a palace but knew the way to North America, possibly even before Columbus. Portugal's fishermen had been to the African coast ahead of Henry the Navigator's explorers, and by 1500 they were bringing salted fish home from Newfoundland. Spanish, Breton, Norman, Dutch, Scandinavian, and English fishermen quickly followed their lead. When Humphrey Gilbert arrived at St. John's in 1583 to take formal possession of Newfoundland, he found an English fisherman ruling as "admiral" over a polyglot collection of camps around the harbour. In other words, fishermen were crossing and recrossing the Atlantic freely in small ships, while merchants and mathematicians were still trying to figure how it might be done.

The fishermen of these coasts also provided the cadres of excellent seamen for the fledgling empires. An Elizabethan commentator described the transformation:

> . . . not a slop of a ropehaler they send forth to the Queen's ships, but he is first broken to the sea in the herring-man's skiff or cockboat; once heartened thus, he will needs be a man of war, or a tobacco-taker, and wear a silver whistle—these swaggering captains or huftytufty youthful ruffling comrades, wearing every one three yards of feather in his cap for his mistress' favour, such as we stumble on at each second step at Plymouth, Southampton and Portsmouth. [Thomas Nashe, 1598]

The Drake
Phenomenon

From Berry Head southward, a succession of headlands advertises a variable geology, with white, red, and grey cliffs. For a short while you can look into Dartmouth—a particularly well-sheltered harbour, but difficult to reach overland because of its high, forested hills. Dartmouth rose to medieval prominence as an entrepôt, gathering in dried fish from other West Country fishing villages for export, and importing wine from Bordeaux. But nearby Plymouth outstripped Dartmouth, which now trains naval officers and caters for tourists and yachtsmen. As the ketch moves on, the Dart estuary disappears, leaving just a dip in the skyline to tell you where the entrance might be.

A bell with an unusually fine tone belongs to the Skerries Bank buoy. On the shingle beach to the east, the misnamed Slapton Sands was the scene of an American D-Day rehearsal in 1944, which turned out disastrously when German torpedo boats sank two tank-landing ships and drowned seven hundred men. The people of Devon were ordered to keep silent about the bodies that washed ashore and were buried in unmarked pits. Divers had to check the identity tags of drowned men to make sure that no one who knew the invasion plans had been taken alive by the German navy.

Beneath the cliffs that lead towards Start Point, under the masts of a radio beacon, the village of Hallsands was smashed in a gale in January 1917. It is a weird place to visit. A steep track leads down to a limestone ledge where the broken gable ends and floor plans of houses look like ruins of a prehistoric town. Winding gear at the old slipway has rusted into a red lump. The destruction of Hallsands was predictable, when dredgers collected more than half a million tons of shingle from this shoreline for a building programme in Plymouth harbour, and so took away the natural protection of the beach. It was only a matter of time before an easterly storm hit Hallsands like heavy artillery and drove the villagers up the hillside.

The southern tip of Devon is a mass of ancient shale hardened into schist, which has resisted the sea's attempts to straighten the coastline. The strata slant down on the landward side, and the cliffs slant down to the sea. The Old English names tell you how people saw these coastal features a thousand years ago. The Start just denotes "promontory" but, standing on a corner, it was the most important promontory for coasting sailormen. Off to the west lie Prawle Point and Bolt Head. The Prawle means "pry hill"—in other words, a lookout. The Bolt is the word we use for missiles, and seen from afar the four-mile coast of the Bolt looks like a straight arrow shaft floating on the sea. Bolt Head is the thicker end, with cliffs coming down in stages from 130 metres, like a serrated arrowhead.

On the near side of Bolt Head is Salcombe harbour, an estuary whose name signifies "saltwater creek." Salcombe is the great port that never was, with several miles of navigable water that remain scarcely more developed than they were in Old English times. A sand-bar stretches right across the entrance, with scarcely a metre of water over it at low tide, and it makes Salcombe a dangerous place to visit, especially if the tide is ebbing against an onshore wind. The Bronze Age wreck discovered near the entrance suggests that Salcombe's problems are not new. A hundred generations of seafarers have said to themselves, "Why go into Salcombe, with Dartmouth or Plymouth near at hand?"

The Bolt is a sombre wall of cliffs four miles long, rough like the undressed stone of a megalith builder, but tall and heavy. Literally heavy, because we are sailing over a gravity anomaly, where the high density of the rocks below increases the force of gravity by about forty parts per million, so that here a person weighs a few grams more than usual and the ketch sinks a few hundredths of a millimetre deeper into the water. Two things have happened: the rocks have been squeezed and baked, making them denser than the general run of material in the continental crust, and then they have been pushed northward and upward over the ordinary rocks of southern Devon and the adjacent sea bed. The Start Point Thrust, geologists call it, and its leading edge cuts through the indented shoreline just behind the Bolt Tail.

Ahead, a pointed, well-vegetated rock, the Great Mewstone, is a sailor's landmark for the eastern side of Plymouth Sound. Away to the westward, Rame Head is also tall and pointed, and it lies in Cornwall, well beyond the Plymouth entrance. A break-water more than a kilometre long runs square across Plymouth Sound, leaving entrances at either end. Beyond it, the high ground of Plymouth Hoe lies dead ahead, a fossil coral reef that grew at the same time as the limestone of Tor Bay. Off the Hoe is Drake's Island. If Plymouth Sound resembles a cathedral, the Hoe is its high altar and Drake's Island an untidy pulpit.

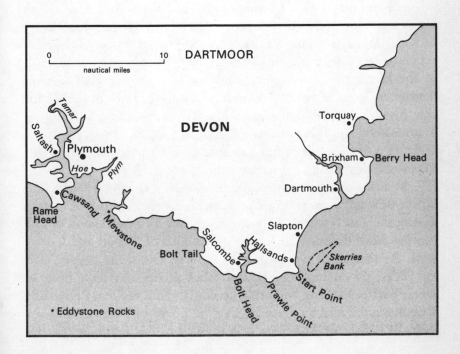

On the cliffs beside the eastern entrance, a wall like a man-made Bolt is a memorial to the Royal Navy's dead. Plymouth without the navy would be like a cathedral without a congregation, and the Royal Dockyard of Devonport is the mainstay of Plymouth's economy. The harbour is deep enough for aircraft carriers, although the big ships have to follow a zigzag channel between Drake's Island and the Hoe, and on through the narrow entrance to the Tamar River.

Devonport Dockyard was founded only three hundred years ago, and that leaves Plymouth's special status four hundred years ago, at the time of the Spanish Armada, requiring an explanation. What forces swept it to the centre of the world stage? For a start, Plymouth has one of the finest harbours on either side of the Channel, because it lies on a wrench in the Earth's crust.

The "Alpine storm" that pushed up the hills of southeastern England and the Wight block, around 40 million years ago, reactivated old cracks in the West Country. Devon and Cornwall are broken along a number of faults running across the present landscapes from the English Channel to the northern coast. One meets the sea at Tor Bay, and another at Plymouth. The Lynher River, flowing towards Plymouth harbour, follows the fault closely for much of its course, and the Tamar River sidles in to join the fault in the Hamoaze, the deep estuary used by the navy. The fault continues across Plymouth Sound, and into the floor of the Channel. Along this line, Cornwall slid northwestward past Devon in a miniature English version of California's San Andreas fault, creating a zone of crumbly ground. River water pours towards Plymouth from high ground on three sides.

In addition to the sideways movements along the faults, the whole of southwestern England has risen by three hundred metres during the past few million years, as shown by a succession of old beaches now stranded high among the hills of Devon and Cornwall. As this uplift went on, pre-existing rivers cut deeper into the rocks, producing gorges. But other agents may have been at work, particularly ice. Victorian geologists believed that Plymouth Sound was created by glaciers, like the fjords of Norway and sea lochs of Scotland. This idea was revived in the 1970s, when the

Ice Age history of the Channel shore was under review. One glacier was supposed to have driven into Plymouth Sound from the English Channel, and pushed boulders from Drake's Island and the western coast onto Plymouth Hoe. Another was said to have come down the Tamar valley, producing a drop in the bedrock, where the river now enters the deep Hamoaze.

All along the Channel shore, from Scilly in the west to Seaford near Beachy Head, geologists have found boulders and pebbles that have come from far away, apparently transported by ice sheets or icebergs from Brittany and even Scotland. The boldest theory is that the English Channel itself was a glacier, fed from an ice sheet south of Ireland. All bets are off until confusions due to up-and-down movements of the land have been sorted out. Even if the Ice Age water was liquid, the low sea level enabled the rivers to carve deep estuaries. When the Victorian engineer Isambard Kingdom Brunel built a high railway bridge across the Tamar north of Plymouth, he had to go twenty-five metres below sea level to find bedrock.

Early seafarers found that Plymouth Sound had no dangerous bar like Salcombe's, so it was much safer to enter. But it was exposed to the sea, and unhindered waves lashed Plymouth Hoe. To escape from southerly gales, ships tucked themselves around a corner. They could turn left into the Tamar, where Saltash stands on the Cornish bank in the best corner of the harbour. Saltash is much older than Plymouth, and its burghers gnashed their teeth about their upstart neighbour when ships turned right and sheltered in the narrower mouth of the Plym.

Sutton Pool is a small natural harbour on the northern shore, around which Plymouth grew under the auspices of the monks of Plympton, up the river. Apart from the fishing and the wine trade with Bordeaux, Dartmoor, looming behind Plymouth, was a source of tin, and Plympton was one of the medieval stannary towns where tin miners brought their products. Dartmoor also produced wool for export in those more fertile days. In the fifteenth century Plymouth won its independence from the monks, but it had greater rivals at Dartmouth to the east and Fowey to the west, while nearby Saltash controlled the modest output of

English silver coming down the Tamar. Plymouth was to outstrip Saltash with foreign silver.

Plymouth was a ready-made lair for pirates, who could pounce on shipping heading up-Channel from the Atlantic and Biscay. In practice, if not in theory, the sea has always been a lawless place. Before radio was invented, who was to know what went on when two ships met ten leagues offshore and there were no survivors to tell the tale? Chaucer's amiable fourteenth-century merchant skipper from Dartmouth, in *The Canterbury Tales,* was not particularly scrupulous.

> The nicer rules of conscience he ignored.
> If, when he fought, the enemy vessel sank,
> He sent his prisoners home; they walked the plank.
>   [Trans. N. Coghill.]

"Enemy" was often a euphemism for "prey." The Hundred Years' War between France and England kept tempers high, and private wars between English, French, and Breton ports brought repeated cross-Channel raiding reminiscent of Viking days. Truces and treaties at a national level meant little in the West Country, from where Morlaix in Brittany was at half the distance of London. By the fifteenth century the Channel's most notorious pirates were the "gallants" of Fowey in Cornwall, some twenty miles west of Plymouth. Their unrelenting attacks on English as well as French and Italian shipping so exasperated the king that he arranged for the men of Dartmouth to steal Fowey's ships.

When, in the sixteenth century, Spain began using the English Channel as its main link with the Habsburg possessions in Flanders, silver from the Indies and other Spanish treasure flowed up the Channel on the flood tide. Plymouth's Elizabethan period of richness began when its sea captains found a religious pretext for predation. A Protestant could serve God by piracy on the world's richest sea routes. This was the seaborne expression of the bitter religious wars in Europe that followed the Reformation.

King Henry VIII of England had broken with Rome in 1534, taking the treasures of the Church. Twenty years later his Catholic daughter, Queen Mary Tudor, tried to force the country back into the papal fold, and earned the name of Bloody Mary for her persecutions. Queen Elizabeth succeeded her in 1558 and put matters right, from the Protestant point of view. In France the struggle eventually went the other way, but not before the Protestant Huguenots had waged open warfare with the Catholics.

In 1568 the Huguenot commander Gaspard de Coligny launched a campaign against Catholic shipping. He dispatched armed ships from La Rochelle on the Biscay coast and handed out letters of marque to English sea captains who were willing to join in. The Dutch Sea Beggars did the same at the eastern end of the Channel, among the professional and amateur pirates of Dunkirk and the English ports. The treasure ships of Spain were the prime targets, and the Channel was about to become too hot for them. From the Catholic point of view, if seamen from countries with which Spain was not at war attacked its merchant ships, the aggressors were simply pirates, whatever commissions they held from heretic rebels.

The Huguenot pirates from La Rochelle, including two English ships, intercepted a Spanish treasure fleet bound for Flanders in the autumn of 1568. Pursued into the English Channel, the Spanish ships took refuge in Fowey, Plymouth, and Southampton. The Spanish captains did not realize how much the political and religious weather of the Channel had deteriorated in the previous few months, and they found that they had only saved the pirates the trouble of getting the cargoes to their bases. The ships were looted and the booty sold off to the merchants of the lucky ports at knockdown prices. The Spanish ambassador was furious, and demanded in particular the return of fifty-nine barrels of silver. Queen Elizabeth's officials rescued the silver, but she decided to borrow it for her own use.

The sea captains of Plymouth had whetted their appetite for the treasure of the Spanish empire. But the Protestants had overstepped the mark by severing the Spanish trade link via the English Channel to Flanders. Goods and treasure went overland from the Mediterranean instead, and the men of Devon had to look for prizes farther afield. Some already knew the way to the heart of Spain's American empire, but two ships sailing home from Mexico past Rame Head early in 1569 reported most of their expedition dead or captured. From then on, the spirit of revenge hung over the hills and harbours of Plymouth like a malignant mist that only blood and silver would dispel.

In your mind's eye, shrink modern Plymouth to a cluster of medieval streets at the eastern side of the Hoe, in the days when England was a quiet, underdeveloped, ignorant country at the fringe of a busy continent. While the Spanish and Portuguese were encircling the world with their oceangoing ships, and the French from Dieppe and Saint-Malo were exploring North America and plundering Portuguese shipping, the English were woolgathering. There were far more sheep than people in sixteenth-century England, and woollen cloth was the main export, sent into the English Channel and the North Sea in small, undistinguished ships. The intrusion of the English into world affairs some four hundred years ago was an astonishing event, as sudden and consequential as the modernization of another backward island, Japan, one hundred years ago.

There was a false start when the English had allowed Giovanni Caboto to make an ocean voyage in their name. Caboto, or Cabot, was a Venetian rival of Columbus, who touted his own ideas about sailing westward to China around various courts of Europe. Absentmindedly, the English king authorized a modest, one-ship expedition from Bristol in 1497, in which Caboto formally discovered and claimed Newfoundland for him. The only Englishmen to follow in his wake were the fishermen, and they found themselves greatly outnumbered by French and Spanish boats.

In half a century after the discovery of America, the only publication in English that even mentioned the New World was a pamphlet printed in Antwerp in 1511. A few merchants had heard enough to wonder about those lands across the ocean. The Spanish and Portuguese discouraged trespassers in their empires, and guarded their navigational secrets. But in the 1530s the Plymouth merchant William Hawkins found Portuguese pilots willing to guide him to West Africa and Brazil. His small ship *Paul,* returning to the Plym with a cargo of brazilwood and coarse

African pepper, planted an idea in the sailors' heads. Hawkins made his small West Country port more mindful than most of the Atlantic Ocean and what lay beyond it.

In the 1540s an upward revaluation of the English currency badly hit the exports of woollen cloth, and made the merchants think harder about new trading possibilities. The chief snag lay in navigation. King Henry VIII, Queen Elizabeth's father, had brought in Italian shipwrights and German gunmakers to develop the navy, as well as French pilots to brush up the seafarers' knowledge of the European waters. But oceangoing navigation, the intellectual problem of tracking mobile objects on a sphere with the help of the wheeling stars, was an utter mystery to the English, who did not possess so much as a geometry textbook. In 1548 they recruited the Pilot Major of Spain to train English navigators and make sure they had the necessary instruments, tables, and charts. He was Sebastian Cabot, Giovanni Caboto's son. In those days skilled navigators could sell their services to the highest bidder. Under Cabot's guidance, trading and exploring ventures began taking English ships to Africa, the Middle East, and Russia.

Even so, the English continued to bribe or kidnap foreign pilots whenever possible, and it was with a Spanish pilot that a trading expedition from Plymouth found its way to the West Indies in 1562. Four years earlier the loss of Calais had cut England's last anchor on the European mainland, and Elizabeth had replaced her sister, Mary, on the throne. John Hawkins, son of the man who had been to Brazil, set sail from Plymouth with four ships and headed first for West Africa, where he collected hundreds of black slaves. Some he kidnapped, some he bought from the Portuguese. Then he headed for Haiti in the Spanish West Indies, where he traded the slaves for pearls, gold, and sugar. This was so profitable that further voyages followed. Queen Elizabeth became one of Hawkins's investors, and when she knighted him he adopted for his coat of arms a black man, bound.

The Spanish cracked down on the Devonians. A Spanish fleet arriving at San Juan on the Mexican coast in 1568 found Hawkins there with six ships, one of them badly in need of repair. The English were manning guns on the shore, and saying they would let the Spanish in only if they promised to leave them in peace. What cheek, from a bunch of heretic smugglers! The Spanish pretended to agree and let a week pass before they pounced. All but two of Hawkins's fleet were lost. *Judith,* commanded by Hawkins's cousin Francis Drake, made off quickly. Hawkins himself, after a hard fight and a dreadful voyage home, reached Plymouth in *Minion*. Both men were obsessed with what they saw as Spanish treachery.

Hawkins had learnt more than hatred at San Juan. Before he was beaten, his English ships managed to destroy two Spanish warships, including the flagship, by long-range gunfire. This contradicted existing ideas about naval warfare, in which battles were settled by boarding. When, a decade later, Hawkins became the chief administrator of Elizabeth's navy, he developed a fleet of low-cut slim-line ships, heavily armed with long-range guns and designed to fight at a distance. These would provide the core of the fleet that eventually met and outmanoeuvred the Spanish Armada. One long-term result of the "hands off" theory of naval warfare was to rid the English navy of soldiers. The sailors manned their own guns and wielded cutlasses if need be, while officers trained in seamanship also looked after strategy and tactics. The Spanish and French continued to divide their crews into seamen and soldiers, which was bad for morale, and this is a possible explanation for why the English later tended to win in straight naval fights and were slower to surrender when beaten.

Francis Drake made Plymouth his base for piracy on a global scale. His prime target was the Spanish silver from Peru, which travelled by sea up the Pacific coast and then overland across narrow Panama to the Caribbean coast. In 1573, with an improvised party of Devonian seamen, French Huguenot pirates, and escaped African slaves, Drake intercepted a mule train carrying silver across Panama. When he returned to Plymouth in the small ship *Pasha,* he had made his fame and fortune. He was then about thirty years old.

Drake was an upstart by the norms of the stratified society in which he lived; his father was a tenant farmer and lay Protestant preacher. But a consummate seaman with a proven lust for treasure was very useful to the English court. Richard Grenville, a gentle-man adventurer who lived at Buckland Abbey, near Plymouth, had proposed a voyage to the Pacific Ocean. Elizabeth and her cronies agreed, but they sent Drake instead of Grenville. Osten-sibly it was a voyage of exploration, but Drake's chief aim was to tap the Peruvian treasure at its source.

On his way around South America he had trouble with the gentlemen aboard his ship, *Pelican,* so he put the most important one on trial and had him beheaded. Soon afterwards Drake made a speech in which he required "the gentleman to haul and draw with the mariner." For the historian Angus Calder in *Revolutionary Empire* (1981)

> It was a remarkable moment, displaying precociously how na-tionalism, imperialism and democracy would, in Britain, ad-vance pretty steadily together until by our own century there had arisen the concept of a democratic, secular state where Brit-ons "hauled" together, defying all foreigners.

As he entered the Pacific, Drake renamed his ship *Golden Hind.* Then he fell upon Peru and its coastal shipping, raiding ashore and attacking two dozen Spanish ships, which were taken com-pletely unawares by an English pirate showing up in the Pacific Ocean. One prize yielded more silver, gold, and precious stones than *Golden Hind* could safely carry. Drake was supposed to look for a new route home around the north of Canada, but after a visit to California and a glimpse of western Canada, he headed west for the Moluccas, where he made room for precious cloves. When he returned to Plymouth on September 26, 1580, he had circumnavigated the world and brought amazing plunder and profit for the queen and his other sponsors.

The news electrified the English with a sense of their own competence. It was as if a Sri Lankan astronaut had orbited the Earth. When Drake sailed *Golden Hind* out of Plymouth again, it was to go up-Channel to London's river. There she went on show to the public, like the space capsules of four centuries later. Queen Elizabeth banqueted aboard the little ship and then knighted her lowly captain. Drake rubbed the salt in by buying Buckland Abbey, home of Richard Grenville, whose idea the voyage had been. He used an intermediary, otherwise Grenville would never have agreed to the sale.

Grenville carved a different niche in history when he sailed from Plymouth on April 9, 1585, with five ships and two pinnaces, to plant an English colony in what was then known generally as Virginia, in honour of England's virgin queen. Humphrey Gilbert, another Devonian, had died two years previously when his ship foundered under him in the Atlantic, after a failed attempt to colonize Newfoundland. Both schemes had been promoted by the chief Devonian at Elizabeth's court, Walter Ralegh, who raised the money for Grenville's venture by sending ships to sea to do a little pirating. Grenville, too, robbed ships, on both his outward and homeward passages. The colonists were left on Roanoke Island, off the present North Carolina.

Ralegh was a rather unsuccessful pirate who had turned soldier and taken part in a genocidal repression of an Irish rebellion in 1580. Soon afterwards, as the favourite of Queen Elizabeth, he became rich and influential. He kept close ties with Devon, and his was the chief voice in London speaking of colonial possibilities. He was a scholar and poet, too, but he retained a pirate's vision of heaven:

> Then the holy paths we'll travel,
> Strewn with rubies thick as gravel,
> Ceilings of diamonds, sapphire floors,
> High walls of coral and pearl bowers.

Outwardly, Spain's power was growing. In 1580, when Portugal's king died, King Philip II had added that country and its maritime empire to his own. But the Spanish economy was growing weaker, and it relied heavily on foreign bankers. In 1585, a few weeks after Ralegh's colonists had departed for America, Philip ordered the arrest of all English ships trading in Spanish waters. This action invited the full wrath of England's pirates. A fleet of more than twenty ships led by Drake first fell on northern Spain, where they rescued some of the English ships and crews, and then set off across the Atlantic to rampage in the West Indies. They burned Santo Domingo in Haiti, Cartagena east of Panama, and St. Augustine in Florida. Drake called at the Roanoke colony and found it out of food and at odds with the Indians, so he carried that first contingent home. His assault had brought Spanish shipping to a standstill. When the bankers of Europe withheld credit, the Bank of Spain collapsed.

In the war that then broke out between Spain and England, the invasion of England was Philip's main aim. Drake became a naval commander, and he delayed the Armada's sailing by a year when he "singed the king of Spain's beard" in a brazen attack on supply ships in the harbour at Cadiz, in 1587. He also captured a large Portuguese ship full of spices from Indonesia—his finest prize. Even more valuable were the charts she was carrying, which opened the road to the East for English merchants.

On Plymouth Hoe, on July 29, 1588, Drake and the other commanders were playing at bowls when word came that the Armada had been sighted off the Lizard, away to the west. If Drake really did say, "There's time to finish the game and beat the Spaniards too," he would have had good reason. The tidal current was setting into Plymouth at the time, and an onshore wind meant there was no hope of moving the fleet until nightfall. Some of the ships were beached, having the summer growth of barnacles and weed scraped from their bottoms under the eye of the mayor, John Hawkins's brother. So while signal fires were carrying the news of the Armada's sighting all across the kingdom, the fleet was a scene of fretting men and immobile ships.

As the Spanish did not mean to attack Plymouth, the delay did not matter; in fact it helped the English fleet to station itself upwind of the Armada. In the long chase up the Channel the average speed was two knots. Although they barked like terriers with their long-range guns, the English ships did little harm to the Armada until the culminating fight off Gravelines.

Even with their country in mortal peril, the admirals could not repress their piratical instincts. Drake was supposed to be leading the fleet as it shadowed the Armada at night off Start Point, but he extinguished his guiding lantern in order to chase after likely prizes for himself. He snapped up the big *Neustra Señora del Rosario,* which had been damaged in collision with other Spanish warships. The fleet commander, Charles Howard in *Ark Royal,* behaved in the same way at the Battle of Gravelines. In his place, Drake led the charge; the name of his ship: *Revenge.*

Revenge for the attack at San Juan had been a motive nursed by Drake for twenty years, along with religion and patriotism, but it was just another excuse for piracy. Like an English Joan of Arc, Drake put the capstone in his country's nationhood. For this reason, English historians later tried to present him and the other Devonian sea dogs as explorers rather than slavers, impudent fellows rather than thieves, daredevils rather than terrorists. They were undoubtedly brave, imaginative men, with a taste for poetry and the sea air; so were the Vikings. Here is Angus Calder's verdict on the leaders of Elizabeth's West Country:

> They moved on from petty piracies in the Channel and blood-spattered projects for colonies in Ireland to immense ventures which brought them all the fame they had wanted, and they hitched their self-seeking so wholly to their religion and to their sense of Englishness that generation upon dazzled generation after them would hardly notice their insatiable pecuniary avidity.

Another fifteen years of war with Spain left plenty of scope for privateering, but Drake's days of glory were over and Plymouth's nearly so. Only a quarter of a century separated John Hawkins's first slaving expedition to Haiti from the invasion of Portugal, led by Drake in 1589, which turned out almost as disastrously for the English as the Armada for the Spanish. Drake was "beached" and became mayor of Plymouth. So Richard Grenville was vice admiral in *Revenge* instead of Drake, when she fought a final solitary battle against impossible odds. *Revenge*'s last stand, in the Azores in 1591, was the outcome of an attempt to ambush a Spanish treasure fleet that went horribly wrong. Grenville was mortally wounded, and when *Revenge* sank she took a Spanish prize crew with her.

In 1595 Francis Drake and John Hawkins set off from Plymouth together for one more raid on the West Indies. The Spanish were ready for them, and the expedition was a total failure. Disease killed first Hawkins and then Drake, far from home. Walter Ralegh took part in a successful attack on Cadiz in 1596, but he was lured into a futile and dangerous quest for the gold of El Dorado. He fell from favour at Queen Elizabeth's death, and her successor eventually cut off his head to appease the Spanish. That malignant act was symbolic: the new regime had no work for pirate chiefs.

In England's transformation from a country of shepherds and weavers to a belligerent maritime power, the pirates of Plymouth supplied the charisma. Shakespeare provided poetry surpassing Ralegh's. But building a trading empire needed a puritanical marriage of venture capital to technical and administrative skills. The initiative passed to the sobersides of eastern England, and the English Channel became London's gateway to the world.

The Virginia Company of Plymouth sent settlers to Sagadahoc, Maine, in 1607, but it was no more successful than Roanoke, and the few survivors gave up in the following year. Meanwhile, the Virginia Company of London had planted at Jamestown the first durable English-speaking colony in what is now the United States. The Channel carried the ships *Susan Constant, Godspeed,* and *Discovery* westward from the Thames at Christmas, 1606. John Smith, whom the Powhatan girl Pocahontas befriended and protected, was an east-coast man, and it was beside the Thames in 1617 that Pocahontas died, as Mrs. John Rolfe, while longing for a ship to take her home. Merchants of London also backed the *Mayflower* voyage.

Plymouth's own ships had ploughed their furrows around the world, linking the green pastures of England to the fever swamps of Central America, the forests of Virginia, the cliffs of California, and the volcanic islands of Indonesia. But the long-term pay-off went to other ports—mainly London, but also Bristol, Plymouth's West Country rival, which followed John Hawkins's example and grew rich on the transatlantic trade in black slaves. Plymouth would be nothing now without the navy.

At a marina near the mouth of the Tamar River, our ketch

lies for the night between the two realms of civilian and naval Plymouth. The Royal Dockyard of Plymouth, founded in 1689, changed its name to Devonport in 1824. For three centuries the navy has developed and redeveloped the eastern side of the Hamoaze, first to handle larger sailing ships of the line, and then steam-powered warships, superdreadnoughts, and aircraft carriers. Engines have by tradition been Devonport's speciality, and it is unsurprising to find it coping nowadays with submarine reactors.

Nuclear submarines are frequent sights in the Hamoaze. These are not Britain's missile-carrying boats, like the French ones across the water in Brest, but hunter-killers. A nuclear boat's advantage in being able to stay submerged for months on end comes at a high price. When it is time for her to be refuelled and refitted, that can take two years, and servicing the hunter-killers amounts to forty per cent of the work at Devonport Dockyard.

At a site where battleships used to take on coal, opposite the fields on the Cornish bank of the river, the pressure hulls of submarines are ripped open like cans to expose the reactors. The ghosts of Hawkins and Drake would be amazed by the operation. Inside a reactor access house lowered onto a submarine's hull, workmen dressed like surgeons extend the reactor upward with a temporary radiation shield filled with water. Then, piece by piece, they hoist the spent fuel out of the reactor core and replace it with fresh fuel. The supervisor worries about criticality and leaks of radioactivity as intently as his ancestors fussed about the caulking and teredo worms.

Free Traders

A wind from the east carries the ketch through Plymouth's western exit, between the breakwater and the red cliffs of Picklecombe Point, now a part of Cornwall. The dainty village of Cawsand, opposite the breakwater, is tucked inside the next headland. Farther on, Rame Head is less wooded, and has a ruined chapel on top of its distinctive cone.

The weather is too misty for seeing the Eddystone lighthouse, but you can hear its horn sounding three warning blasts every sixty seconds. Captain Christopher Jones of *Mayflower* described the Eddystone as "a wicked reef . . . great ragged stones around which the sea constantly eddies, a great danger." In his day there was no lighthouse on the Eddystone. The reef rises steeply out of the sea bed nine sea miles offshore and barely breaks the surface, so that even on a fine day the danger may be hard to see. Lying off Plymouth and close to the coastwise sea routes, it could hardly be worse placed. Captains, shipowners, and merchants kept begging Trinity House to erect a lighthouse, and offered to pay for it, but the Elder Brethren said the task was impossible. They were nearly right, given the technology of the day.

The people of Plymouth decided to do the job for themselves and appointed Henry Winstanley to build the tower. His workmen had to contend with breaking waves that repeatedly swept across the rocks in bad weather. By dogged persistence, and despite being kidnapped by a French *corsaire*, Winstanley completed his first tower in 1698, and strengthened it later. It was a wooden structure, pinned to the rock with iron rods, and the light was a candelabra. Winstanley's work stood for five years, until he was visiting the lighthouse with a party of workmen on the night of Daniel Defoe's great storm of November 26, 1703. By morning the waves had swept the Eddystone clean. The lighthouse had vanished together with its designer and his men.

Within five years another lighthouse had arisen on the Eddystone, simpler and stronger than Winstanley's, but a fire destroyed it in 1755. While a light vessel (then a novelty) kept station off the Eddystone, John Smeaton put up a fine tower of interlocking masonry of Portland Stone. He invented a water-resistant mortar for the purpose. This lighthouse, completed in 1754, might have lasted indefinitely, but the rock it stood on began to split. When the present lighthouse was erected in 1852, the upper part of Smeaton's tower was taken away stone by stone and rebuilt on Plymouth Hoe.

Cawsand's picturesque cottages lead in narrow streets down to a quay and a pleasant beach that faces the morning sun. Even today it is an out-of-the-way spot; anyone approaching by land has to make a grand tour around Plymouth harbour to reach it. Yet Cawsand offers a sheltered bay in a strategic position beside the Channel, concealed by Picklecombe Point from Plymouth town and all the king's men. As a result, this village was a prime centre for smuggling in the early nineteenth century.

In March 1824 a Cawsand smuggling cutter called *Two Brothers* arrived here from France on a moonless night. A revenue cruiser spotted her approaching the shore, and chased her on to the uncompleted Plymouth breakwater. At daylight the smugglers were found clinging to the wreckage of their boat, along with more than a hundred tubs of French brandy. Other tubs had broken open in the wreck. It was one minor incident in the never-ending war between the seafarers of the English Channel and officials who want to tax their cargoes and stop the running of contraband.

When *Two Brothers* came to grief on the breakwater, British revenue agents were busy on the other side of the Channel, spying on boats taking illicit cargoes aboard. From Jersey in the Channel Islands, they sent word of a Cawsand boat loading three hundred barrels of brandy and several bales of tobacco. Later in the same year they reported Cawsand smuggling boats at Roscoff in Brittany. Two of them, bound for the Deadman, were both called *Maria*. The smugglers played games with their boats' names to confuse the opposition. In 1833 a boat called *Dove,* also from Cawsand, had assumed the name *Help* while in Roscoff, but that did not stop her losing three separate cargoes to coastguards on the Cornish shore.

The profits to be made in smuggling were detailed by Henry Shore, a Victorian coastguard officer who quoted an old smuggler reminiscing about the runs around 1830. A cargo of 150 tubs of spirits bought in Roscoff would cost about £120. A "freighter" could hire a boat, skipper, and crew to make the run for about £100. The same brandy, duty paid in England, was worth £1080. A skipper venturing on his own account, in his own boat, might gross as much in a night's work as a farm labourer would earn in two years of honest toil. He could afford to lose cargoes, and even his boat.

More than fifty vessels from this small fishing community

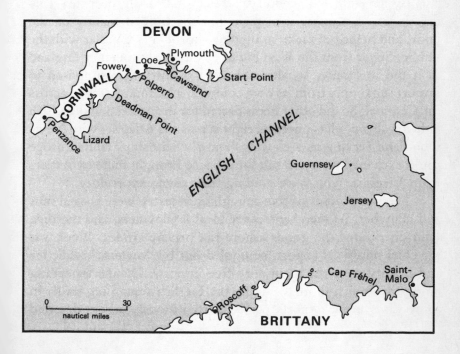

were active in smuggling in the ten years from 1832 to 1842. Shore, who listed them, wrote of the Cawsand villagers:

> Their boats were in demand all along the south coast of Cornwall, while the men who sailed them enjoyed a reputation for skill, daring, and enterprise which was unequalled in any part of the kingdom.

Several of the Cawsand smugglers were former revenue men or coastguards who had lost their jobs for negligence, drunkenness, or collusion with the men they were supposed to be hunting.

Smuggling had boomed in England at the time of Queen Elizabeth I, who was always hard up and notoriously stingy, and used an ill-conceived method of gathering taxes. A customs officer bought his post from the queen and received virtually no salary, so he had every motive to come to an arrangement with traders and smugglers, to take something for himself and nothing for the revenue. Bribery reached to the highest levels of Elizabeth's government.

By the eighteenth century, taxes on salt, malt, beer, tea, coffee, cocoa, chocolate, and spirits put the burden mainly on the poor, and helped to make smuggling thoroughly popular with the public. Sugar from the West Indies cost twice as much in England as it did in France, so although each country was supposed to import sugar only from its own colonies, a lot found its way across the Channel. So did other items barred for the protection of British industry. Smugglers operated right across the Atlantic, with Newfoundland serving as a clearing-house where ships from Europe could exchange wine and salt for tobacco brought there by settlers from Virginia, who were evading their own export duty.

The warehouses of the smuggling industry were coastal inns and churches, its merchants were local landowners, and the men who distributed the goods ashore ran private armies. Wool was the chief unofficial export, smuggled out by "owlers," while tea and brandy were the main duty-free imports. Distilleries sprang up on the French shore to supply the English smuggling trade. In some cases more imports passed surreptitiously across deserted beaches than went through the regular ports. In 1745 there were claims that more than three quarters of Britain's tea was being smuggled in and that twenty thousand professional smugglers were at work in Kent and Sussex alone. They often carried on their trade openly, because loyalty and terror ensured that no one would ever testify against them, and magistrates or jurymen who were themselves engaged in the trade would not convict them. On the northern coast of Cornwall, cross-country from Cawsand, some parishioners asked their parson if there were any sins that God would never forgive. When he asked what they had in mind, they replied:

> Why, sir, we thought that if a man should find out where run goods was deposited, and should inform the gauger, that such a villain was too bad for mercy.

Britain's American colonists were taxed less heavily than their compatriots at home, and they evaded much of what was due by smuggling along the American seaboard and across the Atlantic. The flame of independence in Massachusetts was lit in 1761 when the lawyer James Otis opposed the grant of a search warrant to a customs officer of Salem. Boston relied on smuggled molasses for the making of rum, and there was consternation when the British government promised a higher rate of prize money to its customs officers to make them more diligent. In 1772 the customs vessel *Gaspee* was boarded and burnt in Narragansett Bay, and the next year the Boston Tea Party caused the British to blockade the port and detonate the revolution.

The destruction of 342 chests of tea by men with blackened faces who tipped them into Boston harbour was not provoked, as some imagine, by punitive British taxes on the tea. On the contrary, the government in London had reduced the duty and arranged for the British East India Company to supply the Americans with cut-price tea from surplus stocks. The tea was far too cheap! It undercut the smugglers who brought in illicit tea from the Dutch East India Company. Of course, for Samuel Adams, the Lenin of the American Revolution, liberty had no need for logic, and even a smarter administration than Lord North's could have done nothing right in the eyes of the Sons of Liberty. In that sense there may have been more to the revolution than concern for smugglers' profits.

The first community to suffer in Britain's war against its own smugglers was Guernsey, in the Channel Islands. Centrally placed, and an entrepôt since pre-Roman times, it was an ideal centre for distributing goods. In 1767 the British government imposed a Custom House at Peter Port, and sent an armed schooner and cutter to arrest smuggling boats. Although these scarcely bothered the Guernsey smugglers, the French king seized the chance to declare Roscoff and Fécamp free ports. Many smuggling merchants decamped with their rich businesses from Guernsey to Roscoff.

During the French Revolution, English smugglers helped aristocrats to escape across the Channel, and their trading activities went on all through the wars that followed. Napoleon received gold and newspapers from England, and French brandy and silk continued to arrive in England. The English smugglers maintained a wartime colony in northern France, first at Dunkirk and then at Gravelines. They claimed to bring intelligence to England, but they also carried French spies. Suspicions that they had helped the French cause more than the English may have encouraged the attack on them that followed Napoleon's defeat.

In 1815 the navy was sent to seal the shores of Kent and Sussex, and found it harder than the blockade of Brest. A new enforcement service was created, but it did not impress anyone at first. Recruits had to be ignorant of their shoreline, because local men were presumed to have relatives among the smugglers. Henry Shore quoted an old Cornishman:

I can mind, when a boy, many a time seeing the six-oared galley at Polperro going off to board the cutters, the men going floppity-flop with their oars, one after the after, just like a lot of ploughboys.

By 1829 the service was being called the Coastguard, and requiring seagoing experience in its recruits. "Run goods" then had to cross three barriers: revenue cutters and their patrolling boats, the coast-guards watching the beaches, and a mobile mounted guard that could seize the goods once they were ashore. Vigilance was keenest on the moonless nights favoured by smugglers.

Who guarded the guardians? Bribes were commonplace, and women could easily distract the coastguards when a run was in progress. A zealous officer at Lulworth in Dorset was simply murdered. The revenue men were often drunk on seized brandy, and in 1832 the entire crew of the revenue cutter *Nimble* was dismissed from the service when she was found running her own cargo of spirits from the Channel Islands to Devon.

A smuggler could in theory be hanged if caught with a mask on or a blackened face. Convicted smugglers might be sent to serve five years in the navy, where they won quick promotion as excellent seamen. Captured boats of the smugglers were sawn into two or three pieces. Just having a crew larger than necessary for your craft made you a suspect. Any rowing boat with more than six oars was automatically forfeit, and every man aboard might be fined £40. Because the smugglers developed huge headsails to elude the revenue cutters, a sailing boat would be seized if her bowsprit was more than two thirds of the length of the hull.

Pilot boats that went into the Channel to meet ships and deliver or retrieve pilots, could easily accept goods over the side. *Ant* of Cowes was a pilot cutter found to have built-in hiding places under her gravel ballast. Boats purpose-built for smuggling had false bottoms, hollow keels, hollow booms, and hollow spars. They could alter their appearance overnight by changing to sails of a different colour and cut, and at least one smuggling boat carried the burgee of the Royal Yacht Club. You could make ropes out of tobacco, and cover tubs of brandy with cement to look like stones. Tubs made up into rafts could be set loose to drift ashore on the tide. Or you might weight the tubs and sink them on the sea bed, where your fishermen friends would retrieve them. In bad weather in mid-Channel, a string of tubs served as a sea anchor, lightening the boat and holding her head to wind.

Ghosts, too, were part of the smugglers' craft. Resurrection Jackman was a Brixham man who turned up as his own ghost at his own funeral. He frightened away the officers who suspected, correctly, that the coffin contained untaxed brandy. Other smugglers chased off inquisitive folk on dark nights by pretending to be spirits of the dead. Churchyards, for instance, had to be kept clear after dark for the safe transport of liquor and tobacco, and if any sceptic watched to check the stories of ghosts, a little play-acting would see him off.

By the early 1840s officials had become more efficient, and lower duties cut the smugglers' profits even when they escaped detection. Cawsand's fleet was crippled by capture, shipwreck, and the loss of too many valuable cargoes. But smuggling never stopped.

When the gunrunner Erskine Childers passed this way at night in July 1914 he ran into the navy engaged in manoeuvres off Plymouth. The lights of warships towered around the yacht. A destroyer came racing straight at them, and swerved just in time. How the cargo of smuggled guns must have rattled as the destroyer's bow wave swept under the yacht! Childers would have feared for his boat's safety, knowing she was overladen. Presumably the destroyer reported the presence of a yacht, but there was no further investigation, and *Asgard* went on her way down the Cornish coast, towards Ireland.

An Irish yachtswoman, Cecily Lefort, helped the British secret services in World War II when cross-Channel smuggling routes between Cornwall and the Breton coast were used to put spies and saboteurs ashore in occupied Europe and bring out escapers. At first, submarines ferried agents across the Channel, but the navy hated risking them, so the secret services gathered flotillas of Breton fishing boats and British torpedo boats and gunboats, based in Cornwall's Helford River. When the Special Operations Executive created an escape line called VAR in the winter and spring of 1943–44 Mrs. Lefort said that she owned a villa at Saint-Cast near Saint-Malo and suggested the beach below it as a suitable landing place. She handed over an ancient Irish ring, and an officer who parachuted into Brittany to reconnoitre the beaches showed it to the maid at the villa as a sign. Mrs. Lefort later went to France herself as a courier and died in a German prison camp.

Just like the old smugglers, secret agents would cross to France in their gunboats at the dark of the Moon. To leave Cornwall as unobtrusively as possible, they went aboard the mother ship of a regular gunboat flotilla in Falmouth harbour, masquerading as commandos on leave visiting naval friends. A gunboat from Helford quietly collected them there. The special antennas for navigation and communication that she carried would be explained away to the curious as hush-hush radio research. "When are you going to do something dangerous like the other boys?" one Helford wife demanded of her gunboat husband.

In keeping with the best smuggling practices, the landing in Brittany was timed so that a rising tide would erase footprints from the beach. Approaching the shore, the gunboat stopped her main engines and went in slowly, to minimize noise and phosphorescence. She anchored to a grass rope, and a sailor stood in the bows with a hatchet, ready to cut it if the enemy appeared.

A discreet signal, either a Morse letter on a flashlamp or a luminescent ball uncovered in the hand, announced the presence of friends on the beach. One officer would go in alone to make sure that they were not German guards. The tender that went to the beach used time-honoured muffled oars, and sailors carried the agents through the surf so that they would not be stained with salt water. For the escapers waiting to embark, total silence was the rule. At first light, one of the shore party would check the beach for any telltale traces of the landing.

Every yacht coming to an English port from abroad is supposed to fly a yellow flag, report her arrival, and be visited by a customs officer. This means a big effort by the customs service, especially at the height of the cruising season, and the officers get plenty of exercise clambering on and off yachts. Not every yacht with a middle-class crew is as innocent as she looks. A British high court judge had to resign in 1983 after he was caught carrying a classic cargo of spirits and tobacco in the motor yacht *Papyrus* from Guernsey to Ramsgate. Another Channel yacht, *Escapade of Torbay,* was arrested that year on a cannabis run to the Welsh coast after four years of successful operations. The gang turned out to be a medley of real-estate managers, photographers, an engineer, and a professional drug trafficker from the Netherlands. The reception arrangements included inflatable boats to ferry the drugs from the yacht to the shore, and cars with secret compartments for carrying them inland. In this heavily criminal side of the business, huge profits are still available to smugglers for a short voyage. On *Escapade*'s last trip the street value of her three tons of cannabis was put at £6 million. In the following year the schooner *Sir Robert Gordon* was shadowed up the Channel and seized on the Essex coast, with nearly twice as much cannabis. Perhaps more typical of modern smuggling was the discovery in 1985 of £14 million worth of heroin hidden in a ship from Thailand docking at Southampton.

Those policemen who want to flood the market with cheap drugs and obliterate the criminals' profits may have a case. The old brandy smugglers called themselves free traders, and the free-trade policies of nineteenth-century governments undermined their business more thoroughly than any eyestrained coastguard. The number of contraband and dutiable items went down from more than a thousand in 1815, to less than thirty in 1822, and the duties diminished. The moral seems to be that laws create lawbreakers. With the decline of smuggling on the open coasts, the role of the coastguard changed. Nowadays the customs service is the operational foe of the smuggler, and Her Majesty's Coastguard is entirely dedicated to the saving of life at sea.

The collapse of large-scale smuggling was disastrous for the economy of southern England. A report from Sussex in the 1830s said, "The putting down of smuggling is the ruin of the coast." The villages of the Channel shore were saved from destitution only by the railway and the Seaside Age. The steam trains to Cornwall followed Brunel's bridge across the Tamar River, completed in 1859. Cornish men and women learnt to be polite to the foreigners from England, cook their breakfasts, and flatter the fashionable artists who came to paint their "pretty" villages. The sons of smugglers found themselves carrying trippers on joy rides around the bay.

A branch line brought visitors to the old twin ports of Looe, either side of a river mouth eight miles west of Plymouth Sound. A century and a half ago three successive chief officers of the Looe Coastguard were sacked for collusion with the local smugglers. Nowadays you can scarcely move in the narrow streets in summer, as tourists swarm up the cliffs on the western side, or pile into boats for a trip to the smugglers' Looe Island half a mile offshore.

Polperro, slotted into the cliffs three miles west of Looe, is the very model of a smuggling village. The nearer headland, with a small white lighthouse, is called Spy House Point. The harbour, 150 metres wide, dries out, and at low tide sightseeing launches lie toppled on the mud. The occasional visiting yacht leans against the harbour wall, among the smugglers' cottages, although she might be better off lying to one of the mooring buoys outside. Cruising yachts, as Erskine Childers well knew, have this in common with the smugglers of yore: they sail unpredictably from harbour to harbour, ignoring the main shipping routes.

Polperro, remember, was where the revenue men were said to row like ploughboys. Here, and all along England's south coast, the locals titillate visitors with reminders of the heyday of free trade. The inns and coves and caves are real enough, but don't mistake these basking days of summer for smugglers' weather. The best time for a run was a dirty, starless night in midwinter, when the rocks fountained with spray and the revenue men collapsed over their oars from exhaustion and hypothermia.

Cornwall's principal harbours lie on a succession of fault lines slanting to the northwest, parallel to Plymouth's Lynher fault. The Cornish rivers flow chiefly towards the English Channel, and although they may skip from one fault to another, their main estuaries emerge close to the faults at Looe, Fowey, and Falmouth—all important ports in their day. The great cracks lie at short intervals, and our ketch passes Fowey while Looe Island is still plainly in view, just eight sea miles astern.

Fowey, which rhymes with Troy, takes its name from the Celtic word for beech trees. The port is well tucked into its estuary, but a ruined church on the eastern headland and a lighthouse on the west show the way in. This line has excellent harbours at both ends of it: Padstow on Cornwall's northern coast and Fowey in the south. Between the Fowey River and Padstow's Camel River there is a couple of hours' walk across the watershed, and that was a route for early travellers and traders between the Irish Sea and the English Channel, which avoided going around Land's End. One traveller was an Irish missionary saint on his way to Brittany in the sixth century A.D. Saint Samson landed in Padstow harbour, crossed Cornwall, and embarked for Brittany in the Fowey estuary, probably at Golant, five kilometres upstream, which has a Church of St. Samson. On the far side of the English Channel he landed in the Rance estuary and made his way to Dol, to become one of Brittany's most famous saints.

Religion provided Cornish seafarers with a valuable passenger trade in the Middle Ages. Pilgrim ships from Fowey and other ports set off across Biscay to the Celtic-Christian supershrine of Saint James of the Milky Way, or Santiago de Compostela, near Spain's northwestern corner. A reason for choosing a Fowey ship would have been in hope of immunity from attack by the piratical "gallants" of Fowey.

It seems a modest place now, with a population of little more than two thousand, but Fowey formerly ruled the western Channel. An impression of the relative importance of various ports in the Middle Ages comes from the tally of ships gathered by the English during the attack on France that led to the fall of Calais. London, for example, sent twenty-seven ships, Dartmouth thirty-one, Plymouth twenty-six, and Fowey forty-seven ships. Piracy apart, legitimate trade in pilgrims, metals, and imported wine help to account for some of Fowey's standing. Needless to say, the descendants of pirates were prominent in the illegal tobacco and brandy trades in the eighteenth and nineteenth centuries.

By the early twentieth century Fowey was home for a famous company of trading schooners owned by John Stephens and his associates. Many of the ships had *Little* in their names—*Little Pet, Little Wonder, Little Gem,* and so on. Basil Greenhill relates how Stephens in his old age would go and watch the repair and maintenance of his ships to make sure that after the caulking the green-painted bottoms were perfectly smooth. These were fast vessels, and would often overtake far larger, full-rigged ships during their transatlantic voyages to fetch fish from Newfoundland for the European market. Crews of the big ships would watch in awe when, in the mountainous seas of a North Atlantic gale, *Little Secret* or *Little Mystery* would cross their bows, racing along under scraps of sail, lee gunwale under water, with oilskin-clad figures lashed to the wheel.

The smallest of the fleet, *Isabella,* a converted Brixham trawler, was 24 metres long (75.8 feet) and when fully laden her freeboard amidship was scarcely more than 40 centimetres (1.4 feet). Yet in the year 1900, with a crew of four including the skipper, she sailed from Fowey to Spain, then eight times across the Atlantic, and back to Fowey, all in less than eight months. Atlantic crossings from North America to Europe often took less than eleven days. Only in the era of high-tech multihulls have the racing yachtsmen begun to match such fast sailing.

The Stephens fleet of Fowey was the last pure sailing merchant fleet in Britain, and its barquentine *Waterwitch* was the last square-rigged ship in commercial operation. After losing eleven schooners to the U-boats in World War I, the business kept going in a small way until 1935, when John Stephens's son Edward died. Greenhill tells how *Waterwitch* and the schooner *Jane Banks* were laid up side by side on the mud of Par harbour, with blue bands painted around them to mourn the death of the shipowner.

Earthy Assets

Nature's gifts to the Duchy of Cornwall are peculiar. When Gondwanaland collided with Brittany 300 million years ago, Cornwall
was a thick mass of mud that accumulated for a million centuries
on a sea bed between Brittany and Wales. When the crust broke
under the impact, the piece carrying what is now the West Country
was pushed northwestward, up and over the adjacent territory,
and the mud was incorporated in a broad mountain chain. The
fierce grinding of the pieces of crust heated the deep-lying rock
to make a long pool of molten rock paralleling the present coastline. Plumes welled up through the compacted mud, and froze
into domes of granite. That was 290 million years ago, and the
granite still lay deep in the roots of the Hercynian mountains. But
Cornwall, like Brittany, has been above sea level most of the time
since then, and prolonged erosion has laid the granite bare.

As a result, Cornwall is a slate-grey lump of congealed mud
punctured by granite domes still warm from the ancient collision.
It lacks the geological variety of the Saxon counties farther east.
The old mud made amorphous mudstone, layered shale, and hardened slate. These rocks compose most of the coast. The higher
hills have ledges 130 metres above sea level, cut by the sea when
Cornwall was awash 5 million years ago. Since then the land has
bobbed up. As the sea attacked the present shoreline, the softer
material was eroded into bays and cover, while the harder lumps
survived in capes like Gribbin Head, which slopes into the sea
ahead of us with a tall red and white daymark on top of it.

The soil is thin and unproductive, in spite of Cornwall's moist and sunny climate. The ground is badly drained, and when it is not steep and craggy it is often waterlogged, fit only for rough pasture. Dairy farming has been subsidized in recent decades, but on the whole the people of Cornwall and western Devon have had to look to the sea and the granite for their livelihoods. When they were not pirating and smuggling they were leading the Industrial Revolution.

Half a dozen granite domes form a ragged line from Devon's high Dartmoor to low-lying Scilly off Land's End. Beyond the islands of Scilly a major fault defining an underwater boundary of England has carried a seventh dome away towards Ireland. The domes rise from a continuous block of deep-lying granite that runs the length of Cornwall. The granite is rich in metal ores that occupy a tracery of veins. Tin and tungsten ores fill the cracks in the granite nearest to the hot cores of the domes, while other ores solidified in cooler regions towards the edges: copper, uranium,

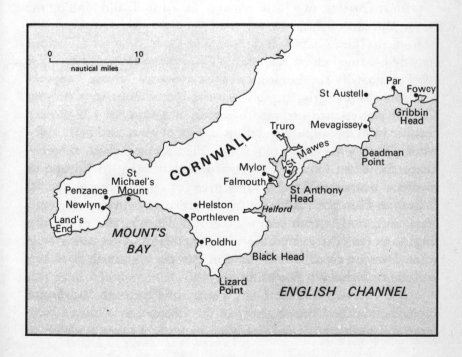

nickel, cobalt, silver, lead, zinc, and iron. Of these, the tin and copper were the most important. Cornwall's tin was famous in pre-Roman times, and western Devon had the world's largest copper mine in the nineteenth century. But the extraction of kaolin, a form of thoroughly decomposed granite, has made the most obvious change in the Cornish landscape.

Beyond Gribbin Head, in St. Austell Bay, an extraordinary scene opens up. Man-made hills rise behind the shore, and they look weirdly luminous in the afternoon mist. These are the spoil heaps of the kaolin industry, and they stand on the St. Austell granite dome. The harbour of Par lies in the corner behind Gribbin Head. It dries out when the tide goes down, but it manages to handle 1800-ton ships, and more than half a million tons of kaolin a year. The bigger ships use Fowey, where a 17,000-ton kaolin carrier astonished the fishermen in 1984. Fowey and Par also deliver kaolin in slurry form to purpose-built tankers. Little Charlestown, at the western end of St. Austell Bay, offers a wet dock, built for the copper industry, but now handling kaolin ships.

Near Charlestown is the town of St. Austell, and high on the hill to the east of the town are the large flat-topped headquarters of English China Clays. The reason why this product of a Cornish hillside is named china clay after a country on the far side of the world, and why the English call their crockery "china," appears in a story from early in the Industrial Revolution. In A.D. 500, Chinese potters had invented porcelain as a superior self-glazing ceramic with the solidity and translucency of glass, and beautifully white. They used clay from a hill called Kauling (high ridge)—hence the word kaolin. Porcelain found its way to Europe in medieval times, and local potters tried for centuries to imitate it. Italians in Florence made artificial porcelain by mixing clay and glass. In the eighteenth century German, French, and eventually English potters discovered the secret ingredient of genuine chinaware. Dresden china was the first in Europe; Plymouth porcelain was the first china in England, in 1768.

The chemist William Cookworthy of Plymouth had found kaolin beside the Cornish shore of the Channel in Mount's Bay, some sixty kilometres west of here, in 1746. Two years later he came upon bigger deposits near St. Austell. The other ingredient of porcelain is china stone, also found in Cornwall. When news of these sensational discoveries leaked out, Josiah Wedgwood and other famous pottery magnates hurried to Cornwall to secure their supplies of china clay. Nowadays only about one eighth of the output of kaolin ends up in ceramics. By far the largest use is in papermaking, and smaller quantities go to the paint and plastics industries. Some of the Cornish kaolin finds its way onto women's faces, in cosmetics, or into the stomachs of sufferers of diarrhoea.

The geological key to the formation of kaolin is to be found in the uranium mines, just east of St. Austell. Early in this century Marie Curie came to Cornwall from France. At St. Stephen, six kilometres east of St. Austell, she set up a laboratory for extracting radium from the uranium ore. The uranium and other radioactive materials present in the granite drove the natural kaolin-making process. Heat generated within the granite by radioactivity kept hot fresh water circulating underground through cracks in the rocks. The water leached metals out of the rocks, redepositing them elsewhere, and gradually destroyed the granite. The colour changed from brown to white, until what was left was a loose mixture of quartz, mica, and kaolin. Colin Bristow, chief geologist of English China Clays, thinks the process is still going on, 290 million years after the granite froze.

The kaolin pits are large holes in the ground, with man-made rivers sweeping a slurry of clay down to the bottom. One pit covers 130 hectares (325 acres) and is 80 metres deep. The rivers are created by high-pressure hoses attacking the walls of the pit. A long sequence of operations removes the quartz sand and mica, and then refines, grades, blends, and dries the finished kaolin. Beside the port of Par the chimneys of a drying plant vent steam into the Channel breeze. The local children call it the cloud factory.

Every million tons of kaolin produced creates 8 million tons of waste, which goes by conveyors or trucks onto sand tips. Until 1973 much of the mica was allowed to run away, making the rivers and the sea of St. Austell Bay a milky white, but now the mica accumulates in pools. The high tips were originally regarded as an eyesore, but they became a tourist attraction, advertised as the "Cornish Alps" or "Mountains of the Moon." The scenery is changing rapidly, because English China Clays now employs thirty people in landscaping the man-made hills. Some conical mounds have been beheaded, and the latest tips make lower elongated prisms. Left to itself, nature slowly colonized the old tips with heather, gorse, and eventually shrubs. The newer tips are seeded with clover and ryegrass, and a herd of hardy Soay sheep from Scotland tramples the ground and grazes the grass. Vegetables grow on the dried-out mica pools.

The chief hazard between Plymouth and Falmouth is the Deadman. This headland, known more politely as Dodman Point, has Jacuzzis of rough water off it, caused by underwater rocks. The Deadman looks like a reclining death mask with an up-turned nose, and a brow 111 metres high. The light behind it puts the near cheek in shadow, giving the Deadman a doom-laden look. The stone cross on the extremity is not calculated to allay anxiety.

Falmouth harbour's lighthouse on St. Anthony Head has beckoned many a clipper ship into port after voyages from the other side of the world. In the middle of the entrance there is a troublesome Black Rock. On the far side, Pendennis Point has a castle built four centuries ago to guard the approaches to the harbour. Once inside, the sailor can turn right to St. Mawes, or left into Falmouth itself.

The pirates of the Killigrew family built and named Falmouth town in the seventeenth century. Before then, towns farther up the rivers had the trade, Pendennis and St. Mawes possessed the castles, and the Tudor naval dockyard was at Mylor. But Falmouth's harbour, the most westerly of any great size, was an excellent base for preying on shipping at the entrance to the English Channel. The seafarers of Falmouth then found more respectable work as transatlantic mailmen.

If you had an urgent message for the American colonies, you did not want it beating to and fro for weeks in a ship trying to go down-Channel from London or Portsmouth in the teeth of the prevailing winds, and exposed to attack by the French *corsaires*. So you sent it by mounted courier overland to Cornwall, and dispatched it by the appropriate Falmouth packet boat. Starting as mail packet station with a service to Lisbon in 1688, Falmouth acquired worldwide fame as a communications centre.

As in any postal service, there were complaints about slow deliveries. Everyone understood the vagaries of the weather, but it made no sense that the fast Falmouth packet boats sometimes took two weeks longer to sail to America than colonial merchant ships leaving England at the same time. In the 1760s a postmaster in Philadelphia, Benjamin Franklin by name, was of a scientific cast of mind, and he discovered the explanation from a Nantucket whaling skipper. He said he had sometimes met the westbound Falmouth packets navigating in the Gulf Stream against a contrary current of two or three knots. "We advised them to cross it," the skipper said, "but they were too wise to be counselled by simple American fishermen." Franklin had an oceanographic chart of the Atlantic prepared, depicting the course of the Gulf Stream, and sent the chart to Falmouth for the enlightenment of the packet skippers. They declined to be counselled by a colonial postman, either. What made it sillier was that the Spanish had known about the Gulf Stream for 250 years.

Steam packet ships were undismayed by head winds in the Channel, and they destroyed Falmouth's privileges in respect of mails in the mid-nineteenth century, but what steam took away the electric telegraph restored. As long as most oceanic cargoes travelled by clipper ship, this harbour continued as a communications centre for owners and captains. "Falmouth for orders" was the frequent instruction to ships leaving other continents to come to Europe. From here the ships could be redirected to Scotland or the Mediterranean before they committed themselves to the one-way weather valve of the English Channel. As a result, this harbour, like the Downs at the other end of the south coast, was crowded with great sailing ships at anchor, waiting for instructions or a fair wind.

Cutters with red sails make a fine sight, racing at the entrance to the Helford River in lumpy seas left by last night's strong winds. To continue westward from Falmouth, the ketch must first steer southward to round the Lizard peninsula, passing the Helford entrance and the Manacles, a group of rocks strewn inconveniently in the path of ships leaving or entering Falmouth harbour. The name comes from the Celtic *Men Eglos,* or "church rocks," and they are a favourite spot for skin divers hunting for wrecks.

The steep headland that first looms up ahead is not the Lizard Point but its companion, Black Head. It is as pure a lump of scrambled serpentine as you will see anywhere. On the shore below the hillside village of Coverack, the rocks are studded with crystals of olivine. This peninsula is one of the oddest places on Earth for a geologist. Tourists who visit the Lizard by land are offered knicknacks made of green, red, blue, or black serpentine, a soapy kind of rock. The southern end of the peninsula is a seventy-square-kilometre mound of serpentine. The rocks at the water's edge are typically slate, while the southernmost tip, Lizard Point, is a small lump of granite two hundred metres wide. But Black Head is serpentine, and so is a multicoloured stretch of coast to the west of the Lizard Point.

Serpentine is material that originally bled from the planet's interior, during a brief mismatch between the moving plates of the Earth's outer shell, perhaps 170 million years ago. This opened a wound many kilometres deep, through which rose up not basalt but the mother of basalt—olivine, alias peridot. Chemical reactions with water have altered it into serpentine of mottled colours, like a reptile's skin, which inspired the name serpentine, but did not give rise to the apparently reptilian name of the peninsula. Lizard is a Celtic word for "high court."

When Lizard Point and its lighthouse come into view beyond Black Head, they look suitably dignified. The famous headland is fairly high—about sixty metres—and precipitous at its southern tip. Lizard Point is the most southerly place in Britain and for Atlantic voyagers was often the equivalent of the white cliffs of Dover for the cross-Channel traveller: the last sight of England or the first. If you just want to watch the ships go by, the Lizard is a good spot to stand on a clear day. By bleeding where it did, the Earth gave the local people a valued asset, and I don't mean the serpentine.

. Wrecking is another of Cornwall's traditional industries, and the Lizard its chief workshop. The word "wrecking" suggests the deliberate luring of ships to disaster, but it usually meant waiting for the ships to wreck themselves. To a Cornishman, wrecks were always a part of the natural bounty of the sea, along with the pilchards, the seaweed, and flotsam washed up by the tide. And the inhabitants of the Lizard were outraged when the first lighthouse was kindled on Lizard Point.

The motives of John Killigrew, who erected the beacon in 1619, were not humanitarian. As one of the piratical Killigrews of Falmouth, he wanted the authority to stop every ship and charge dues for the benefit of the light. Killigrew was no friend of the villagers, and he brushed their protests against the lighthouse aside: "They have been so long used to reap purchase by the calamity of the ruin of shipping as they claim it hereditary." This remark wins the English Channel's first prize for humbug. Shortly before Killigrew's lighthouse first broadcast its feeble firelight into the December night, he had seized by force the silver of a Spanish treasure ship cast on the rocks off Lizard Point.

More powerful than the Cornish villagers were the Trinity Brethren of London, who objected to private enterprise in the matter of lighthouses and had the Lizard fire extinguished for twenty years. Restored in 1640, the Lizard light has burned ever since, and saved innumerable lives. The concentrated shipping around the Lizard nevertheless ensured a steady supply of wrecks. Ships had reasons for coming close, to save distance and time, and to make sure of the ship's position after crossing the Atlantic. Lizard Point was also a signal station, so ships expecting orders had to sail near enough to exchange messages by signal flags.

Richard Larn and Clive Carter, the authors of *Cornish Shipwrecks,* say that the Lizard has been the scene of many more wrecks than any other point on England's south coast. If a sailing ship was caught in a bay in an onshore wind and fighting to get out, the people would gather on the clifftops like vultures. As Larn and Carter describe it:

It was not uncommon for a ship to sail back and forth in this manner for days at a time, the spectators ashore moving along the coast in sympathy; men staying away from work to watch, the children from school.

These authors rightly stress the heroic efforts of Cornish lifeboatmen and fishermen in trying to save the lives of crews and passengers in wrecked ships, not least by the men of Cadgwith, in the Lizard lifeboat. They also say that no one was ever convicted of deliberate wrecking. But I wonder how a prosecutor could prove ill-intent if someone lighted a bonfire on a clifftop that might be mistaken for the Lizard light? Certainly Trinity House ruled that no Cornishman should be allowed to man the St. Agnes lighthouse in Scilly, after one of them had let a ship from Virginia wreck herself when the light was out, and then helped himself to the cargo.

Plenty of real jagged rocks lie off Lizard Point, and the taller ones are topped with the guano of the sea birds. A Dutch ocean-racing yacht coming the other way has just put her spinnaker up, but the wind can hardly lift it, and the keen young men are moving backward on the tide that is carrying our ketch around the Lizard. The land curves away to the north into Mount's Bay, the last large hollow in England. Sea, sky, and land are just different shades of light grey today, but as the cliffs become lower, wraiths appear in the air above the Lizard peninsula. They are the dishes of a satellite ground station, firing phone calls, TV shows, and the intercontinental chatter of computers through the Cornish sky.

This is a fitting place for them, and not only because it is close to the home of the Falmouth packets. On the shore just beyond Mullion Cove, where the serpentine comes to an end, the Victorian hotel at Poldhu was chosen by a young Italian in 1901 for the most sensational experiment in the history of radio science. Guglielmo Marconi's motives were strictly commercial. He had already sent signals across the Dover Strait from South Foreland to Boulogne, and flashed the results of the 1899 America's Cup races at Newport, Rhode Island, to newspapers in New York. But the Lizard was the stage for the decisive test of his "wireless telegraph": the transmission of a radio signal across the Atlantic Ocean.

It was obviously impossible. The top physicists of the day knew that radio waves travelled in straight lines, so that the signals would shoot off at a tangent into space. Marconi erected masts on the Lizard to carry his transmitting antenna. On December 12, 1901, the crude spark generator repeatedly sent out three short pulses—*S* in Morse Code. Almost instantaneously, they registered in a receiver at St. John's, Newfoundland.

That is the cosmetic version of the story. What really happened was more interesting. Marconi's original aim was two-way wireless telegraphy between the Lizard and Cape Cod, Massachusetts. The signals were to be registered on Morse Code printers. Imposing masts, sixty metres tall and arranged in rings sixty metres in diameter, arose on the two sides of the Atlantic to support the antennas. The Lizard masts stood just behind the hotel. On September 15 an English Channel gale toppled them; a few weeks later, the winds of Cape Cod wrought the same result. The inhabitants of Cornwall and Massachusetts, who knew more than most about the art of staying masts, must have chuckled over the wreckage.

In desperation, Marconi improvised a one-way test. He rigged a makeshift transmitting antenna on the Lizard between two better-supported masts. He then hurried off by steamer to Newfoundland, with balloons and kites for flying the receiving antenna. On Signal Hill at St. John's all was confusion. The blustery winter weather made the flying of the antenna difficult. Static blotted out the continuously repeated Morse *S* from Cornwall. Any signal was too feeble to actuate the printer, so we only have Marconi's word for it that, now and again, he and his assistant heard the faint *dot-dot-dot*. As the weather worsened, Marconi knew he had failed to achieve a convincing demonstration.

What saved his reputation was the Anglo-American Telegraph Company asserting its monopoly rights in Newfoundland. They ordered Marconi to stop his experiment, and this gave him an excuse for deficient data. The newspapers announced that the experiment had succeeded, and Marconi went to New York City to organize a celebration at the Waldorf. Distinguished guests hesitated to accept the invitation until Thomas Edison said he believed Marconi's story. Thanks to the lash-up on the Lizard peninsula, radio was decisively launched on the international stage. Luckily, the experiment was correct in principle. "An unexpected bonus on the part of Providence," one physicist called the ionospheric mirror in the sky that reflected intercontinental radio signals back towards the Earth.

A gravel beach with a lake behind it marks the old entrance to Helston—a river mouth now reduced to a culvert. In early medieval times Helston was an important port, but by the thirteenth century the bar was becoming troublesome to ships. Helston continued as a centre of the tin industry, and it developed strong links with the rescue services. The rocket-fired rope for lifesavers was invented there, and the Royal Navy's rescue helicopters now operate from nearby Culdrose. At Porthleven, the surviving fishing port north of the lake, where erosion of the cliff has caused part of a house to fall into the sea, a fifty-ton boulder on the shore is known locally as the Giant's Rock. It is a piece of rock transported all the way from northern Scotland, and is a prize exhibit for those who argue that ice sheets and glaciers helped to shape the Channel shore.

Mount's Bay stretches from the Lizard all around the northern horizon to Gwennap Head, near Land's End. The bay takes its name from St. Michael's Mount, a shrunken mirror image of Mont Saint-Michel, across the English Channel in the corner of the Gulf of Saint-Malo. In the eleventh century the monks from Mont Saint-Michel founded a monastery here. It became a target for pilgrimages, like its counterpart on the French side. The package tour for pious travellers in the Middle Ages took them cross-Channel to visit Saint Michael in both places. A castle now tops the granite cone on the Protestant side of the water.

Newlyn and Mousehole break through the haze on the port bow. They are fishing ports on the western side of Mount's Bay, which makes a funnel leading to Penzance, a couple of miles beyond the Mount. Penzance means "holy cape" in Celtic. You will find megalithic tombs and circles on the granite of this extremity of Britain, matching those of Brittany and Ireland, and telling of nautical connections four thousand years ago or more. The Mount itself was famous among the ancient Greeks as a tin emporium.

Every visitor to Mount's Bay soon discovers that you need to take a boat to reach St. Michael's Mount at high water, but you can walk to it from the town of Marazion when the tide is low. It was the same long before the birth of Christ. The Greek explorer Pytheas, who visited Cornwall around 300 B.C., is quoted as saying:

> They beat the metal into half cylinders and carry it to a certain island lying off Britain, called Ictis. During the ebb tide the space between dries out, and they carry abundant tin over into this island in their wagons. [Trans. adapted from H. O'N. Henken.]

Long before the southerner Pytheas came this way, seafarers were carrying the Cornish tin northward. Emrys Bowen, an archaeologist and historical geographer, has explained that the first people to exploit these deposits in making tin bronze lived in Ireland, where smiths of the Beaker era were fashioning bronze axes and daggers before 1500 B.C. As Ireland had no tin workings of its own, they must have fetched the metal by sea from Cornwall or Brittany. From later in the Bronze Age, archaeologists have discovered a hoard of tin ore at Treviskey in Cornwall. It consists of small black pebbles, of the kind recovered by "streamers" in later millennia, from the beds of streams flowing out of the tin-ore districts.

The Tartessians, people living in southwestern Spain, ventured into the Atlantic before 500 B.C., and brought back tin from northwestern Spain and southern Brittany. Then came the Phoenicians and Carthaginians, who liked to cut out the middleman and were soon fetching their own tin from the Atlantic shores. The tin exports from Cornwall to the Mediterranean began in the sixth century B.C., when the Carthaginian navy prevented Greek ships from reaching the Atlantic. From St. Michael's Mount, tin went by sea across the Chops of the Channel, past Ushant, and around to the Loire River. From there it travelled by sea, river, and road to the Greek colony of Massilia (modern Marseilles) on the Mediterranean shore.

In Julius Caesar's time, the seafarers who carried the tin from St. Michael's Mount to the Loire River were almost certainly the Veneti of western Brittany. After the Roman galleys destroyed their fleet in 56 B.C. Spain became the chief supplier of tin to the Roman empire. So Cornwall's tin industry had its ups and downs. In the Middle Ages pewter, which is hardened tin, became popular in Europe, and the stannaries of the West Country flourished. By that time the miners were working underground, following the veins in the granite. They were as rowdy as their piratical seagoing cousins, and spent their hard-earned spare time drinking and gambling, wrestling and wrecking. The last great mining age in the West Country came with the Industrial Revolution, and cushioned the economy during the decline of smuggling. The boom began with copper, before 1800, and continued with tin, especially after the invention of tin cans for food preservation in the 1830s.

West Country engineers were already leaders in technology. At Dartmouth in Devon, early in the eighteenth century, a middle-aged blacksmith called Thomas Newcomen knew of the miners' difficulties with underground water, so he set about using steam to drive pumps more effectively than horses. Denis Papin in France, and Thomas Savery, another Devonian, had made primitive devices employing steam, but Newcomen developed the world's first piston-driven engine. Many Newcomen engines went into Cornish mines, and the chimneys of the pumping houses, scattered across the moors, became the emblem of the mining industry. Later, some miners preferred a more economical engine devised by James Watt of Glasgow.

Britain's Industrial Revolution was mainly powered by water mills in its early phases, and the cumbersome steam engines remained a rarity. The man who launched the real age of steam was a barely literate mining engineer born twenty kilometres from St. Michael's Mount. His name was Richard Trevithick. He saw that Watt's famous engine was hobbled by its use of low-pressure steam. High-pressure steam made possible a much more compact and efficient machine. By 1797, when he was twenty-six, Trevithick had turned the idea into a fully practical engine hoisting ore up the shaft of a Cornish mine. In 1801 he drove a steam-powered car up a Cornish hill, demonstrated the world's first railroad locomotive in Wales in 1804, and had a paddle-wheel barge steaming along with a high-pressure engine in 1805. He did not forget his original purpose, and Trevithick's "Cornish pumping engine," twice as efficient as Watt's, became the equipment of choice in the mining industry. Despite the fears of boiler explosions, everyone adopted Trevithick's high-pressure steam in the end. Piston-engined steamships, and the turbine ships and the motor vessels that followed, altered the seascapes of Cornwall beyond recognition.

Ships brought cheaper metal from other continents—African copper, Malaysian tin—which crippled the West Country mines. Many miners emigrated, and you will find plenty of Cornish names in the Colorado telephone directories. Cornwall still produces about one per cent of the world's tin from modernized mines, and the reserves are worth billions of dollars. But on most of the moors and cliffs the mine chimneys stand smokeless, as the menhirs of the Industrial Revolution.

The heirs of Trevithick have not run out of ideas. From the Camborne School of Mines, which overlooks the place where Trevithick tested his steam engines, a team led by Tony Batchelor has set out to turn Cornwall into a boiler for the water of the English Channel. Underground, Cornwall is the hottest place in England, and the tin miners suffered abominably. The radioactivity in the granite, and the uplift and erosion that laid bare the vertebrae of the West Country, have provided hot rock close to the surface. On the granite domes the rate of flow of heat out of the ground is comparable with what you will find near volcanoes. Batchelor tells his visitors: "You are standing on granite twenty-seven kilometres deep which contains the energy equivalent of all Britain's coal reserves."

Other countries have power stations running on natural steam, but the granite of Cornwall is largely dry, so here you must inject your own water. Batchelor and his team took possession of an abandoned stone quarry in a granite moor north of the Lizard peninsula, between Falmouth and Helston. In 1982 they bored holes two kilometres deep, and shattered the rock between them by explosives and high-pressure water. Then they pumped cold water down one hole and recovered hot water from the other. The basic demonstration was accomplished, but there was a big snag. The continuing pressure of Africa against Europe produces strong forces underground, pushing to the northwest, and these make the granite liable to crack. The rock split downward from the ends of the boreholes.

The granite under that quarry is the most thoroughly monitored piece of the Earth's crust. Sensitive seismometers, coordinated by an elaborate computing system, record every creak and groan deep underground. By the end of 1984 the team had bored a third hole, penetrating six hundred metres below the first two and passing through the cracked zone. In principle, it could recover hot water percolating downward through the region, but its purpose was scientific—to confirm that the cracking was not due to a pre-existing fault, and to test ways of opening water channels without causing them to crack in that uncontrolled fashion. One idea is to use a sticky fluid, akin to wallpaper paste, to force pathways through the rock.

The coast may sprout new structures housing the heat exchangers and turbogenerators of geothermal power plants. They would not be very obvious, because the borehole heads and steam turbines can be mounted underground. The Camborne team's design study visualizes a fifty-megawatt plant standing on the Cornish shore where the granite comes close to the sea. Every second it would dispatch a ton of English Channel water five or six kilometres underground, to be turned into high-pressure steam at two hundred degrees centigrade. Batchelor thinks that a dry-rock geothermal station could produce electric power at about the same price as a coal-fired station. It might supply local industry directly, from a pollution-free, renewable source. Think of the energy needs of the kaolin quarrymen working in the other granite dome of St. Austell.

This subterranean heat has many other uses besides power

generation. Shallower boreholes could supply heat for green-houses, fish farms, domestic hot water, and so on. And about eighty per cent of the Earth's land surface is, in Batchelor's opinion, a potential source of geothermal power. If Cornwall's dry-rock experiments succeed, they may transform energy policies as thoroughly as Trevithick's inventions did.

Towards Bishop Rock

Beyond Nationhood

At this Atlantic corner of Britain and Europe, the English and French are intruders in a Celtic world, where the old midsummer festival is still celebrated on May 8 each year with Furry Dances at the lost port of Helston across Mount's Bay. But the Cornish people are more thoroughly assimilated by the English than the Welsh or the Scots are, or the Bretons across the Channel by the French. The most violent and successful assertion of Celtic nationhood has been by the Irish, starting with the Irish Volunteers to whom Erskine Childers and Conor O'Brien were running guns in July 1914.

On the western side of Mount's Bay, a sea mile and a half from Penzance, our ketch passes a buoy marking the Low Lee rock. This is where you pick up the pilot, if you need one for getting into Penzance or the neighbouring fishing port of Newlyn. By the modern system it is an east cardinal buoy, black-yellow-black, but it was striped in black and white when O'Brien came out of the mist. *Kelpie* had entered Mount's Bay on the fifth morning after leaving the Ruytingen light vessel with her consignment of arms. Her crew was seriously short of bread. They could not heat the oven without the risk of exploding their cargo, and they were living on the remains of a black loaf obtained from the tug *Gladiator* in exchange for a bottle of whisky. The day had broken under a thin, luminous fog, with the Manacles buoy tolling astern of *Kelpie,* and as she rounded the Lizard the fog closed in.

O'Brien showed his worth as a smuggler and navigator when

he decided to take advantage of the fog to slip ashore for bread. He had walked along this coast some months earlier. By what an Englishman might call fine Irish logic, the fact that the walk was also in fog made it seem all the more helpful to the task of finding a safe anchorage. O'Brien wrote later:

> I do not attempt to explain my method of navigation, but in time a black-and-white striped buoy drifted into sight. I was so convinced that I had seen such a buoy from the hill above Mouse-hole that I set a course as from Low Lee towards Newlyn, and soon a schooner at anchor loomed up. I gave her a berth of a little more than the visibility at the time—we were quite safely invisible from the pier-head—lowered the kedge noiselessly, put a compass into the dinghy and sent her away to find Penzance, and bread, and newspapers. . . . And at nightfall we drifted away again into the fog.

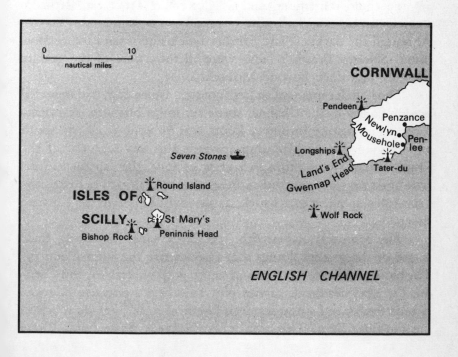

Nationalism may be the only universal religion in the modern world, but human motives reach beyond it. Lifeboatmen pay no attention to what national ensign a ship in distress may be flying. If other human beings are in danger of losing their lives, the lifeboatmen will risk their own lives by going out in any kind of weather to try to save them. They are strong and healthy people, but otherwise nothing out of the ordinary, and anyone with a low opinion of human nature should think about them. As if to prove to cynics that the risks are real, every so often a lifeboat is lost.

On Penlee Point, behind the Low Lee rock, a slipway runs down to the water from the red door of a lifeboat house. On a Saturday night, December 19, 1981, the door opened and the lifeboat *Solomon Browne* slid into the raging waters of Mount's Bay. Her eight-man crew came from the picture-book fishing village of Mousehole, guarded by a craggy island just south of Penlee Point. One crew member, Charlie Greenhaugh, was a pub owner who two days before had ceremoniously switched on Mousehole's Christmas lights. But this was the worst night that anyone could remember, and as Coxswain Trevelyan Richards steered past the village, the lifeboat pitched in mountainous waves. Although the darkness and driving rain made it hard to see anything, *Solomon Browne*'s crew were all too aware of the granite presence that starts beyond Mousehole.

The Dutch captain of an Irish coaster, *Union Star,* had reported engine failure in the Channel some six miles offshore. A storm-force wind gusting to ninety knots was blowing from the south and driving the disabled ship towards this last segment of the English coast. In addition to a crew of four, the captain had his wife and two teenage stepdaughters aboard. The waves tossed the 1400-ton ship like a matchstick, as she drifted close to the Cornish shore.

The peninsula of Penwith, the Celtic name for Land's End, is one of the granite domes that characterize the West Country. The blocky cliffs are terraced and heavy with vegetables, and Carn-du, the next headland, carries pine trees and a pinnacle of rock. A mile farther on, a neat modern lighthouse on Tater-du glints in the morning light. This was where *Solomon Browne* and *Union*

Star came to their fatal rendezvous, with Tater-du's flashes, three every fifteen seconds, lighting the wild night like a strobe. The low cliffs have a fringe of shallows and granite rubble around them. A British naval helicopter from Culdrose, piloted by Russell Smith of the U.S. Navy, tried repeatedly to rescue the people aboard *Union Star,* but the weather made it impossible. The ship was close to the shore near Tater-du by the time the lifeboat reached her.

As Coxswain Richards tried to manoeuvre alongside, a huge wave lifted the lifeboat and smashed her down on the coaster's deck. The boat slithered back into the sea. At another attempt, the same thing happened again. Still the lifeboat did not give up. She went in once more, and slammed hard against *Union Star's* side. This visit gave four of the coaster's people the chance to jump aboard the lifeboat. It was already a gold-medal rescue, but there were still four others aboard the coaster, and the rocky shore was only fifty metres away. When last seen, the lifeboat was turning as if for another attempt. A wave overwhelmed the coaster and pitched her on the shore. The lights of the lifeboat disappeared. Victims and rescuers died together in the frenzied sea.

Daylight found *Union Star* upside down at the foot of the cliffs west of Tater-du. Lifeboats from Lizard and Scilly and many local fishing boats were searching the area. Mousehole was already in mourning, but one of the widows told the bishop of Truro "My husband warned me three weeks ago that this might happen, and that if it did I was not to make a fuss."

Another lifeboat was sent at once to Newlyn to provide temporary cover in Mount's Bay, while fresh volunteers from Mousehole began immediate training for the lifeboat that very soon replaced *Solomon Browne.* Charlie Greenhaugh's Christmas lights were switched on again in Mousehole.

Prince Peter Kropotkin, the Russian explorer and anarchist who took refuge in England at the end of the nineteenth century, pointed to the British lifeboat service as the perfect example of anarchism in action. The middle-class ladies who organize coffee mornings and charity concerts to raise money for the Royal National Lifeboat Institution might be appalled to hear that, but Kropotkin had a point. Coxswains command the lifeboats, so anarchism need not mean indiscipline, but the crew are all volunteers who train and risk their lives because they choose to, not because they are bullied or bribed. For a coastal community to have a lifeboat station is a matter of privilege and pride; it is their boat, and local people man it and run it. Fund-raising, the design of boats and equipment, and certain practicalities of search and rescue procedures are coordinated at the headquarters at Poole in Dorset, but the "National" in the RNLI's title only means nationwide, and nothing governmental. Since 1824 the organization has been run entirely on donations from the public, and makes no charge for its services.

Amid the world's rampant nationalism, and the concentration of power in the hands of governments, there are always tendencies the other way. Whether you want to call their work anarchism or just decentralization, the lifeboatmen are a telling example to set alongside the Bretons across the water who took on the operators of *Amoco Cadiz*. With stubborn, honest people like these around, there seems to be hope for our species.

From southward of the Runnel Stone buoy, Land's End becomes visible about four miles to the northwest, beyond the barren Gwennap Head, with a white hotel above the cliffs at England's extremity. The granite sprawls under the sea, and the Longships lighthouse stands on a group of rocks a mile offshore.

Off Land's End, the ghosts of Childers and O'Brien turn right for Ireland. Without sighting each other, the gun-laden *Asgard* and *Kelpie* both rounded the Longships early on July 18, 1914. After marking time in bad weather for a week, *Asgard* entered Howth harbour near Dublin at the appointed time of noon on July 26. A deliberate rumour that arms were being landed far away to the south lured away a British warship standing guard in Dublin Bay. Mary Spring Rice wore a red skirt as a signal to the Irish Volunteers concealed around the harbour. The guns were handed ashore quickly enough to be pointed at the coastguards when they came to investigate. O'Brien successfully transferred *Kelpie*'s cargo to another Irish yacht.

Asgard slipped away to Wales, where Erskine and Molly Childers left her. A week after that World War I broke out and—the irony of it!—Childers and O'Brien were soon both wearing the uniform of the British navy, which they had deceived on their gun-running expedition. Childers used his knowledge of German waters to navigate the lead aircraft in the first naval air attack, on Cuxhaven on December 25, 1914. By 1922, disillusioned by the half-baked form of Home Rule granted to Ireland, Childers was working as a propagandist for the Irish Republican Army. He was betrayed to the soldiers of the Irish Free State and executed by an Irish firing squad. *Asgard* outlived Childers, but *Kelpie* did not. O'Brien killed her (his own verb) in 1921 while sailing her single-handed; his alarm clock failed to wake him and the boat hit the coast of Scotland. The smuggling of guns to militant Irishmen has never ceased.

Our own course is set towards the off-lying islands of Scilly. Ushant lies less than a hundred miles away, somewhat east of south. Apart from the occasional fishing boat, scarcely a ship is to be seen at this crossroads where traffic from the Bristol Channel and the Irish Sea meets the English Channel traffic. A solitary tanker is southbound in the shipping lane between Scilly and the mainland. A helicopter scoots past with passengers from Penzance, serving as the modern sailor's equivalent of a migrating bird and pointing the way to Scilly.

The English Channel is shaped like a megaphone, and it is the Channel of English, by which the language has been broadcast around the Earth. Besides the colonists who went to North America, a fleet of eleven ships outward bound from Portsmouth in May 1787 took English convicts to Australia, the first of 160,000 forcibly transported to that continent over a period of eighty years. In 1806 English settlers followed the Dutch to South Africa, and the New Zealand Company dispatched its first ship *Tory* from Plymouth in 1839. Even China was subdued by the British sailing ships. By 1914 the British empire and commonwealth held sway over a quarter of mankind, and, in addition, an American empire extended to the Philippines. Great injury was done to native populations, but with their language the English also exported certain ideas about justice, democracy, and science. These helped to undermine the empires. In the process, liberal values became the norm worldwide, so that even repressive states must now pretend to have elections and fair trials.

The generations of seafarers who headed out past Land's End bequeathed an unfair advantage to everyone whose native language is English. In this linguistic and cultural sense, the struggle for world domination was settled a long time ago, by the storm-beaten ships tacking about off Ushant to keep Napoleon's fleet bottled up in Brest. If the Celtic sea god Manannan, who has all the world's treasures in his bag, would grant me just one wish about nationhood, it would be this: that the English-speaking peoples should realize how sweeping their cultural victory is. It will be tragic if they hazard what they have gained by persisting in geopolitical games that violate their own ideals. How can the Russians or the Nicaraguans conceivably succeed where Napoleon failed? Kaiser Wilhelm and Adolf Hitler were far too late, and only a nuclear war can now prevent the tongue of Francis Drake's mother becoming the language of the planet.

That is nothing to be complacent about, even linguistically. Seaspeak, like the language of air traffic control, may be a forerunner of a new discipline in English, after centuries of creative free-for-all. The language may now face a long period of austerity, because languages that become too ambiguous have to change. Non-native speakers using radios and computers quickly spot the ambiguities, and they have no sentimental attachment to the niceties of English or its informalities and bizarre spellings. Perhaps the foreigners will make of World English a new and even more powerful tongue, and send it back up the English Channel, along with the ocean swell.

The biggest island of Scilly, St. Mary's, appears ahead, and other islands scattered beyond it. They are the flooded summit of a lump of granite, and the channels separating the islands are shallow. When their smuggling was stamped out, the tough Scilly islanders turned improbably to gardening, exploiting the mild oceanic climate to supply London with flowers out of season. After St. Mary's, an old white lighthouse, now disused, rises plainly from the almost treeless St. Agnes island. A procession of small islands and rocks accompanies us westward. Gannet Island looks like a fort.

With the Western Rocks close to windward and eighty metres of water under her, our ketch *Charmed* is out of the English Channel. Two miles to the north, the Bishop Rock lighthouse is a great grey tower balanced on a small rock and whitened with salt on its western side. For seafarers approaching from the Atlantic, Bishop Rock is the English equivalent of the lights of Ushant. Astern, in the hazy sunshine, Scilly appears as a string of granite humps the colour of milk chocolate, fading across the water.

Here the ghosts of the Pilgrim Fathers disappear into the Atlantic. They were near Scilly twice, in fact, because *Mayflower* and *Speedwell* first came this way twenty days after sailing in high hopes from Southampton. They had spent half that time in Dartmouth trying to cure leaks in *Speedwell,* but once past Land's End they found she was taking in water again. After hours of debate in the Atlantic swell, Captain Jones in *Mayflower* agreed to escort Captain Reynolds in *Speedwell* back to Plymouth. There the leaky ship was left behind, together with some of the passengers. "And thus, like Gideon's army, this small number was divided," observed their chronicler, William Bradford.

That was why Plymouth became the Pilgrims' final port of departure. Greybeards on the waterfront who had sailed with Drake shook their heads as they watched *Mayflower* set off for the North Atlantic with passengers aboard, so late in the year. She left in a "fine small gale" and she passed Scilly at her second attempt on September 17, 1620. It was to be a horrible voyage, with plenty of bad weather to compound the usual discomforts of wetness, seasickness, and cramped quarters.

Mayflower made her landfall at Cap Cod, far to the north of the Hudson River, where the colonists had meant to go. Attempting to head south, the ship ran into broken water, and Captain Jones turned back. On the morning of November 21 he anchored in the shelter of the hook of Cap Cod. The Pilgrims' troubles had just begun, as the wisest among them knew. Bradford described the scene:

For summer being done, all things stand upon them with a weatherbeaten face, and the whole country, full of woods and thickets, represented a wild and savage hue . . . What could now sustain them but the spirit of God and his grace? May not and ought not the children of these fathers rightly say: "Our fathers were Englishmen which came over this great ocean, and were ready to perish in this wilderness."

More than a month passed in surveying the coasts until *Mayflower* came to anchor at Plymouth, Massachusetts; and then a couple of months more, with Pilgrims and Indians observing one another suspiciously, before an Indian approached boldly and said "Welcome" in English.

Sources and Further Reading

The following selection of sources, by chapters, cannot adequately acknowledge the many individuals, museums, books, almanacs, atlases, charts, maps, encyclopaedias, journals, and newspapers consulted. Books in English recommended for further general reading are marked*.

1. Towards Ushant: WORLD'S BEND

*E. G. Bowen, *Britain and the Western Seaways*, Thames & Hudson, 1972.
J. Cogné and M. Slausky (eds.), *Géologie de l'Europe*, Mémoire du BRGM No. 108, BRGM, 1980. (In French.)
S. Hugill, *Shanties from the Seven Seas*, Routledge & Kegan Paul, 1984.
Hydrographer of the Navy (UK), *Channel Pilot*, HM Stationery Office, 1977.
G. Le Scouëzec, *Guide de la Bretagne Mystérieuse*, Editions Princesse, 1979. (In French.)
J. Prunieras, interview, 1984, on the Service des phares et balises, and Ushant light structure.
P. Ziegler, chapter in *Petroleum Geology of the Continental Shelf of North-West Europe*, Institute of Petroleum (London), 1981.

2. Towards Brest: FIT FOR AN ADMIRAL?

A. Autran and J. Dercourt (eds.), *Evolutions géologiques de la France*, Mémoire du BRGM No. 107, BRGM, 1980. (In French.)
N. Calder, *Nuclear Nightmares*, Viking, 1979.
W. S. Churchill, *The Second World War*, Cassell, 1948–1954.
*D. Howarth, *Trafalgar: The Nelson Touch*, Collins, 1969.

*E. H. Jenkins, *A History of the French Navy*, Macdonald & Jane's, 1973.

A. T. Mahan, *The Influence of Sea Power upon the French Revolution and Empire, 1793–1820* (two vols.), Sampson Low, Marston, 1893.

E. P. Von der Posten, *The German Navy in World War Two*, Barker, 1970.

H. Wickliffe Rose, *Brittany Patrol*, Norton, 1937.

3. *Towards Roscoff:* ACCIDENTAL OIL

Amoco Cadiz: Le combat continue, Syndicat mixte de protection et de conservation du littoral nord-ouest de la Bretagne, 1983. (In French.)

A. Arzel, interview, 1984, on *Amoco Cadiz*.

S. Durand (ed.), *Bretagne*, Guides Géologiques Régionaux, Masson, 1977.

*D. Fairhall and P. Jordan, *Black Tide Rising: The Wreck of the Amoco Cadiz*, Deutsch, 1980.

Y. Fouéré, *Problemes bretons du temps présent*, Les Editions d'Organisation, 1982. (In French.) Also interview, 1984, on Breton nationalism.

*Guides Vertes, *Bretagne*, Michelin, 1979. (In French; also available in English.)

E. R. Gundlach and others, *Science*, Vol. 221, 1983, p. 122, on the fate of *Amoco Cadiz* oil.

R. D. Pingree, interview, 1984, on tidal mixing.

M. Robson, *French Pilot*, Vol. 2, Nautical Publishing Co., 1979.

4. *Towards Bréhat:* SOMEONE ELSE'S STONES

Autran and Dercourt: see reference, Chapter 2.

A. Berthelsen, in D. A. Galson and S. Mueller (eds.), *First Workshop on the European Geotraverse*, European Science Foundation, 1984.

R. Coatantiec, interview, 1984, on Ploumanac'h wreck.

P.-R. Giot, *Barnenez, Carn, Guennoc*, Ouest-France, 1980. (In French.)

F. Giron, *Le Point*, September 26, 1983, p. 118, on Ploumanac'h wreck. (In French.)

R. L. Merritt and A. S. Thom, *Archaeological Journal*, Vol. 137, 1980, p. 27, on menhirs.

*P. Phillips, *The Prehistory of Europe*, Allen Lane, 1980.

C. Renfrew (ed.), *The Megalithic Monuments of Europe*, Thames & Hudson, 1981; also interview, 1984.

A. J. and E. Southward, *New Scientist*, April 10, 1975, on sea urchins; also interview, 1984.

Y. Toutain, interview and correspondence, 1984, on Ploumanac'h life-boat.

5. *Towards the Rance River:* THE TIDES OF SAINT-MALO

K. Adlard Coles, *North Brittany Pilot*, Adlard Coles, 1972.
S. Durand: see reference, Chapter 3.
S. B. C. Eyre, *Henry VII*, Methuen, 1972.
*E. H. Jenkins: see reference, Chapter 2.
*K. Spence, *Brittany and the Bretons*, Gollancz, 1978.
Usine Marémotrice de la Rance, *Prévisions*, periodical.

6. *Towards Guernsey:* NEVER A BARRIER

*J. Caesar, *The Conquest of Gaul*, trs. S. A. Handford, Penguin, 1951.
Cruising Association Handbook, Cruising Association (London), 1981.
B. W. Cunliffe, *Oxford Journal of Archaeology*, Vol. 1, 1982, p. 39, on prehistoric trade; also interview, 1984.
M. Dean, interviews, 1984–1985, on historic wrecks.
I. Kinnes, *Les Fouaillages and the Megalithic Monuments of Guernsey*, Ampersand Press (Channel Islands), 1983; also interview, 1984.
L. Langouët (director), *Fouilles Sous Marines à Saint-Malo*, Centre Regional Archéologique d'Alet, 1978. (In French.) Also interview, 1984.
S. McGrail, *Oxford Journal of Archaeology*, Vol. 2, 1983, p. 299, on prehistoric navigation.
*S. Macready and F. H. Thompson (eds.), *Cross-Channel Trade between Gaul and Britain in the Pre-Roman Iron Age*, Society of Antiquaries of London, 1984.
K. Muckelroy, *Proceedings of the Prehistoric Society*, Vol. 47, 1981, p. 275, on Bronze Age shipping.
K. Oatley, *New Scientist*, Vol. 64, 1974, p. 863, on navigation without instruments; also interview, 1984.
M. Robson, *Channel Islands Pilot*, Nautical Publishing Co., 1979.
A. G. Sherratt, *The Ashmolean*, No. 1, 1982, p. 12, on early ships.
*E. G. R. Taylor, *The Haven-Finding Art*, Hollis & Carter, 1956.
D. W. Waters, *The Rutters of the Sea*, Yale University Press, 1967.

7. *Towards Barfleur:* ELEANOR'S EMPIRE

K. Adlard Coles, *Channel Harbours and Anchorages*, Nautical Publishing Co., 1974.

J. T. Appleby, *The Troubled Reign of King Stephen*, Bell, 1969.

E. Halley, *Journal of the Paramore 1699–1701*, British Museum Add MSS 30368.

R. Hargreaves, *The Narrow Seas*, Sidgwick & Jackson, 1959.

Hydrographer of the Navy (UK): *Tidal Stream Atlases* (various), HM Stationery Office, various dates.

E. H. Jenkins: see reference, Chapter 2.

S. Malin, interview, 1984, on Halley's geomagnetic studies.

*D. Seward, *Eleanor of Aquitaine*, David & Charles, 1978.

*N. J. W. Thrower (ed.), *The Three Voyages of Edmond Halley in the Paramore 1698–1701*, Hakluyt Society, 1981.

William of Malmesbury, *Chronicle of the Kings of the English*, c. 1125, quoted on the loss of the White Ship in G. Uden and R. Cooper, *A Dictionary of British Ships and Seamen*, Allen Lane/Kestrel, 1980.

8. *Towards Saint-Vaast-la-Hougue:* ROOKE'S BONFIRE

A. Bryant, *Samuel Pepys: The Saviour of the Navy*, Cambridge University Press, 1938.

E. Delmar-Morgan (revised by M. Brackenbury), *Normandy Harbours and Pilotage*, Adlard Coles, 1982.

*J. Haswell, *James II: Soldier and Sailor*, Hamilton, 1972.

E. H. Jenkins: see reference, Chapter 2.

C. Lloyd, *Sea Fights Under Sail*, Collins, 1970.

E. Rieth, interview, 1984, on historic wrecks.

9. *Towards Ouistreham:* THE BEACHES OF NORMANDY

J. D. Bernal, Actes du Congrès de Caen, Association Française pour l'Avancement des Sciences, 1955, on scientific work for D-Day.

F. Doré and others (eds.), *Normandie*, Guides Géologiques Régionaux, Masson, 1977. (In French.)

T. F. Gaskell, interview, 1984, on scientific work for D-Day.

*Guides Vertes, *Normandy*, Michelin, 1974.

M. Harrison, *Mulberry: The Return in Triumph*, W. H. Allen, 1965.

*J. Keegan, *Six Armies in Normandy*, Cape, 1979.

B. Strutton and M. Pearson, *The Secret Invaders*, Hodder & Stoughton, 1958.

*W. Tute and others, *D-Day*, Sidgwick & Jackson, 1974.

S. Wavell, *Guardian*, May 12, 1984, on the Angel of Hermanville.

10. *Towards the Seine River:* HEIRS OF THE VIKINGS

Bayeux Tapestry. (In Latin.)

Deutscher Forschungsdienst, No. 1, 1980, on the origin of tennis, work of H. Gillmeister.

F. Doré: see reference, Chapter 9.

J. J. Duffau, *French Channel Ports,* French Chamber of Commerce (London), 1982.

A. Horne, *To Lose a Battle: France 1940,* Little, Brown, 1969.

*D. Howarth, *1066: The Year of the Conquest,* Viking, 1978.

W. B. Lockwood, *A Panorama of Indo-European Languages,* Hutchinson, 1972.

M. Magnusson, *Vikings!,* BBC, 1980.

J. A. Williamson, *The English Channel,* Collins, 1951.

11. *Towards Boulogne:* URANIUM RIVER

J. Caesar: see reference, Chapter 6.

C. Delattre (ed.), *Région du Nord,* Guides Géologiques Régionaux, Masson, 1973. (In French.)

Electricité de France, *Les échos de Paluel,* No. 11, 1984. (In French.)

D. Fishlock, *Financial Times,* November 23, 1984, on French nuclear industry.

French Delegation, *Statement by France,* General Conference of the International Atomic Energy Agency, Vienna, 1984.

Guides Vertes, *Nord de la France,* Michelin, 1977. (In French.)

Hydrographer of the Navy (UK), *Dover Strait Pilot,* HM Stationery Office, 1982.

G. A. Kellaway, interview, 1984, on dry valleys.

S. McGrail: see reference, Chapter 6.

C. Seillier and others, *Histoire de Boulogne-sur-Mer,* Presses Universitaires de Lille, 1983. (In French.) Also C. Seillier, interview, 1984.

Suetonius, *The Twelve Caesars,* trs. R. Graves, Penguin, 1957.

12. *Towards Gris-Nez:* PETROLEUM RIVER

J. Arthur, interview, 1984, on cross-Channel ferries.

A. N. Cockcroft, *Collision Statistics,* Doc. NAV 26/4/1, Intergovernmental Maritime Consultative Organization, 1981.

B. Hayman, interview, 1984, on Seaspeak.

International Association of Lighthouse Authorities, IALA Maritime Buoyage System, IALA, Paris, 1980.

I. D. Irving, *Journal of Navigation*, January 1982, p. 224, on crossing courses.

C. W. Koburger, *Safety at Sea*, April 1984, p. 10, on shipping-lane problems.

K. Lucas, "Trinity House," lecture to Cruising Association (London), 1983.

P. Marchand, interview, 1984, on traffic surveillance at CROSS Gris-Nez.

N. F. Matthews, interview, 1984, on International Association of Lighthouse Authorities.

*N. Mostert, *Supership*, revised edition, Penguin, 1975.

R. D. Pingree, interview, 1984, on sand ridges.

F. Weeks and others, *Seaspeak Reference Manual*, Pergamon, 1983.

*R. Woodman, *Keepers of the Sea*, Dalton of Lavenham, 1983, on Trinity House.

13. Towards Calais: THE DAM AND THE TUNNEL

J. P. Auffret and others, *La Manche Orientale: paléovallées et bancs sableux*, 1982. (Geological map with explanations in French and English.)

D. Fishlock, *Financial Times*, August 20, 1979, November 6, 1979, and June 6, 1984, on power link.

Franco-British Channel Link Financing Group, *Finance for a Fixed Channel Link*, Midland Bank and National Westminster Bank, London, 1984.

G. R. M. Garratt, *One Hundred Years of Submarine Cables*, HM Stationery Office, 1956.

P. Howard, "The French Connection," lecture at Institution of Electrical Engineers, 1984.

C. Melville, *Disaster*, Vol. 5, 1981, p. 369, on the historical seismicity of England.

A. Muir Wood, "Tunnelling the Channel—Why Not?" lecture at British Association for the Advancement of Science, 1984.

R. Muir Wood, "British Earthquakes," lecture at British Association for the Advancement of Science, 1984.

A. J. Smith, *Marine Geology*, Vol. 64, 1985, p. 65, on a catastrophic origin for the palaeovalleys; also interview, 1984.

J. Vogt (ed.), *Les tremblements de terre en France*, BRGM, 1979. (In French.)

*T. Whiteside, *The Tunnel Under the Channel*, Hart-Davis, 1962.

14. Fogbound in Calais: DIFFERENT KINDS OF MADNESS

N. Edmonds, *Late Late Breakfast Show*, BBC-TV, September 1, 1984.

M. Grosser, *Technology Review*, May/June, 1981, on *Gossamer Albatross*.

J. Kington and B. Kington, *Geographical Magazine,* November 1983, on Blanchard flight.

G. Orwell, "England Your England," in *Selected Essays,* Penguin, 1957.

Voltaire, *Lettres Philosophiques,* ed. F. A. Taylor, Blackwell, 1946. (In French.)

*Voltaire, *Letters on England,* trs. L. Tancock, Penguin, 1980. (Translation and commentary on *Lettres Philosophiques.*)

Voltaire, *Candide,* trs. J. Butt, Penguin, 1947.

*T. Zeldin, *The French,* Collins, 1983.

15. *Towards De Panne:* WHO WON THE ARMADA FIGHT?

*F. Braudel, *The Perspective of the World,* trs. Siân Reynolds, Harper & Row, 1984.

K. S. Douglas and others, *A Meteorological Study of July to October 1558: The Spanish Armada Storms,* Climatic Research Unit, University of East Anglia, 1978.

Guides Vertes, *Belgique, Luxembourg,* Michelin, 1981. (In French.)

*D. Howarth, *The Voyage of the Armada,* Collins, 1981.

*G. Mattingly, *The Defeat of the Spanish Armada,* Cape, 1959.

16. *Towards South Goodwin:* ESCAPE OF AN ARMY

E. Childers, *The Riddle of the Sands,* reprinted Hart-Davis, 1955.

W. S. Churchill: see reference, Chapter 2.

*L. Deighton, *Fighter,* Cape, 1977.

D. Divine, *The Nine Days of Dunkirk,* Faber, 1959.

A. Horne: see reference, Chapter 10.

*W. Lord, *The Miracle of Dunkirk,* Viking, 1982.

C. O'Brien, *From Three Yachts: A Cruiser's Outlook,* Arnold, 1928.

H. Popham and R. Popham, *A Thirst for the Sea: The Sailing Adventures of Erskine Childers,* Stanford Maritime, 1979.

E. P. Von der Posten: see reference, Chapter 2.

R. Watson Watt, *Three Steps to Victory,* Odhams, 1957.

R. Wheatley, *Operation Sea Lion,* Clarendon Press, 1958.

17. *Towards Dover:* ECHOES IN THE SAND

C. G. Carter, *Forgotten Ports of England,* Evans, 1951.

D. Defoe, *The Storm,* London, 1704.

E. Eckwall, *The Concise Oxford Dictionary of English Place Names,* Oxford University Press, 1960.

*J. Eddison, *The World of the Changing Coastline*, Faber & Faber, 1979.
M. Redknap and M. Fleming, *World Archaeology*, Vol. 16, 1985, p. 312, on Goodwins Archaeological Survey.
T. Smollett, *Travels through France and Italy*, Lehmann, 1949.
M. J. Tucker and K. Dyer, interviews, 1983, on waves and beaches.
R. Woodman: see reference, Chapter 12.

18. *Towards Hastings:* WRECK OF A DUTCHMAN

F. Braudel: see reference, Chapter 15.
B. W. Cunliffe, *Britannia*, Vol. 11, 1980, p. 227, on Lympne.
R. W. Gallois and F. H. Edmunds, *The Wealden District*, HM Stationery Office, 1965.
*P. Marsden, *The Wreck of the Amsterdam*, revised edition, Hutchinson, 1985.
P. Marsden, *International Journal of Nautical Archaeology and Underwater Exploration*, Vol. 7, 1978, p. 133, on *Amsterdam*'s treasure.
F. H. Thompson (ed.), *Archaeology and Coastal Change*, Society of Antiquaries of London, 1980.
*J. A. Williamson: see reference, Chapter 10.

19. *Towards Brighton:* THE SEASIDE AGE

J. Boardman and N. Ellis, geological field trip, 1983.
Ruth Manning-Sanders, *Seaside England*, Batsford, 1951.
A. J. F. Smith, *Beside the Seaside*, Allen & Unwin, 1972.
*University of Sussex Geography Editorial Committee, *Sussex: Environment, Landscape and Society*, Alan Sutton, 1983.

20. *Towards Selsey:* GREEN AND PLEASANT LAND

W. Blake, *Poetry and Prose*, ed. G. Keynes, Random House, 1948.
B. W. Cunliffe, *Iron Age Communities in Britain*, Routledge & Kegan Paul, 1978.
E. Eckwall: see reference, Chapter 17.
D. Hill and M. Jesson (eds.), *The Iron Age and Its Hill-Forts*, Southampton University Archaeological Society, 1971.
*W. G. Hoskins, *The Making of the English Landscape*, Hodder & Stoughton, 1955.
R. A. Pelham, "The Concept of Wessex," in F. J. Monkhouse (ed.), *A Survey of Southampton*, British Association for the Advancement of Science, 1964.

University of Sussex Geography Editorial Committee: see reference, Chapter 19.
J. A. Williamson: see reference, Chapter 10.
*M. Wood, *In Search of the Dark Ages,* BBC, 1981.

21. *Towards the Solent:* POMP OF YESTERDAY

*K. Caffrey, *The Mayflower,* Deutsch, 1975.
M. Drummond and P. Rodhouse, *The Yachtsman's Naturalist,* Angus & Robertson, 1980.
E. W. H. Gifford and co-authors, papers at Florida Institute of Technology, Conference on the Design, Construction, and Operation of Commercial Fishing Vessels, 1984.
D. Hearst, *The Guardian,* July 20, 1984, on *Mary Rose* burial.
A. J. Holland, *Ships of British Oak,* David & Charles, 1971.
*P. Kemp, *The Oxford Companion to Ships and the Sea,* Oxford University Press, 1976.
P. Padfield, *An Agony of Collisions,* Hodder & Stoughton, 1966.
C. Palmer, *Yachting Monthly,* Vol. 144, 1984, p. 1388, on rigs trials.
L. Purves, *The Tatler,* July/August 1983, on Royal Yacht Squadron.
*M. Rule, *The Mary Rose,* Windward, 1983.

22. *Towards Weymouth Bay:* THE SOURCE OF THE OIL

G. Boillot and M. Rioult (eds.), *La Manche,* BRGM/CNEXO, 1974. (Geological map with explanations in French and English.)
F. Cowper, *Sailing Tours,* Part II, Nore to Tresco, 1909; reprinted, Ashford Press, 1985.
B. W. Cunliffe: see reference, Chapter 6.
K. Dunham and A. J. Smith (organizers), "A Discussion on the Geology of the English Channel," *Philosophical Transactions of the Royal Society of London,* Vol. 279, 1975, p. 1.
R. Freethy, *The Naturalist's Guide to the British Coastline,* David & Charles, 1983.
T. F. Gaskell, interview, 1984, on geophysical exploration.
*M. Green, *The Art of Coarse Cruising,* Hutchinson, 1976.
P. Hinde, "The Development of the Wytch Farm Oilfield," lecture at Institution of Gas Engineers, London, 1980.
K. McDonald, *Diver,* Vol. 27, 1982, No. 11, p. 20, on Needles wrecks.
D. H. Matthews, interview, 1984, on deep seismic studies.
R. Muir Wood, interview, 1985, on structural evolution of the Channel.

A. J. Smith and D. Curry in Dunham and Smith, 1975.
A. J. Smith, *Annales de la Société Géologique du Nord,* Vol. 103, 1984, p. 253, on structural evolution of the Channel.
R. Stonely, *Journal of the Geological Society of London,* Vol. 139, 1982, p. 543, on Wessex basin.
P. Ziegler: see reference, Chapter 1.

23. Towards Brixham: SLINGERS AND FISHERMEN

L. Cottrell, *The Great Invasion,* Evans, 1958, on Roman conquest of Britain.
B. W. Cunliffe, interview, 1984.
G. S. P. Freeman-Granville, *Atlas of British History,* Rex Collings, 1979.
T. Hardy, *The Well-Beloved,* introduced by J. Hillis-Miller, Macmillan, 1960.
D. Hill and M. Jesson (eds.), *The Iron Age and Its Hill-Forts,* Southampton University Archaeological Society, 1971.
Hydrographer of the Navy (UK): see reference, Chapter 1.
T. Nashe (1598), quoted in M. Mason and others (eds.), *The British Seafarer,* Hutchinson/BBC, 1980.
National Fisheries Museum, Brixham, on history of fisheries.
R. D. Pingree and L. Maddock, *Marine Geology,* Vol. 32, 1979, p. 269, on tidal effects of headlands; also R. D. Pingree, interview, 1984, on tidal effects on marine life.
A. J. Southward, *Nature,* Vol. 785, 1980, p. 361, on the Channel as an unstable ecosystem; also interview, 1984.
E. W. White, *British Fishing-Boats and Coastal Craft,* HM Stationery Office, 1950.

24. Towards Plymouth: THE DRAKE PHENOMENON

M. Bacon in Dunham and Smith, 1975, on Start Point Thrust: see reference, Chapter 22.
E. D. S. Bradford, *Drake,* Hodder & Stoughton, 1965.
F. Braudel: see reference, Chapter 15.
*A. Calder, *Revolutionary Empire,* Cape, 1981.
G. Chaucer, *The Canterbury Tales,* trs. N. Coghill, Penguin, 1960.
E. Eckwall: see reference, Chapter 17.
E. A. Edmonds and others, *British Regional Geology: South-West England,* HM Stationery Office, 1975.
D. Fishlock, *Financial Times,* October 14, 1981, on "open-heart surgery" for nuclear submarines.

R. Hakluyt, *Voyages and Discoveries,* edited and introduced by J. Beeching, Penguin, 1972.

G. A. Kellaway and others, in Dunham and Smith, 1975, on traces of glaciation: see reference, Chapter 22.

*J. H. Parry, *The Age of Reconnaissance,* Cardinal, 1973.

D. W. Waters, *The Art of Navigation in England in Elizabethan and Early Stuart Times,* Hollis & Carter, 1958.

J. A. Williamson: see reference, Chapter 18.

25. *Towards Fowey:* FREE TRADERS

M. R. D. Foot, *SOE in France,* HM Stationery Office, 1966.

M. R. D. Foot and J. M. Langley, *MI9,* Bodley Head, 1979.

*B. Greenhill, *The Merchant Schooners* (two vols.), David & Charles, 1968.

J. Hadfield (ed.), *The New Shell Guide to England,* Joseph, 1981.

R. Hargreaves: see reference, Chapter 7.

S. E. Morison, *The Oxford History of the American People,* Oxford University Press, 1965.

*D. Phillipson, *Smuggling,* David & Charles, 1973.

H. N. Shore, *Smuggling Days and Smuggling Ways,* Cassell, 1892.

R. Woodman: see reference, Chapter 12.

26. *Towards Penzance:* EARTHY ASSETS

M. Allaby, *New Scientist,* April 2, 1983, on reclamation of clay tips.

A. S. Batchelor, interview, 1985, on hot dry rocks.

E. G. Bowen: see reference, Chapter 1.

C. Bristow, *Geology of China Clay in Cornwall,* Wheal Martyn Museum, undated; also interview, 1985.

J. F. Dewey, *Journal of the Geological Society of London,* Vol. 139, 1982, p. 371, on plate tectonics and the British Isles.

E. A. Edmonds and others: see reference, Chapter 24.

B. Franklin, *Transactions of the American Philosophical Society,* Vol. 2, 1786, on Gulf Stream.

W. P. Jolly, *Marconi,* Constable, 1972.

*R. Larn and C. Carter, *Cornish Shipwrecks,* Pan, 1969.

27. *Towards Bishop Rock:* BEYOND NATIONHOOD

W. Bradford, *Of Plimouth Plantation,* Wright & Potter, Boston, 1899.

K. Caffrey: see reference, Chapter 21.

P. Howarth, *The Life-Boat Story,* Routledge & Kegan Paul, 1957.
Royal National Lifeboat Institution, *The Lifeboat,* Vol. 48, 1982, Nos. 479 and 480, on the Penlee disaster.
P. Kropotkin, Mutual Aid, Heinemann, 1904.
C. O'Brien: see reference, Chapter 16.
H. Popham and R. Popham: see reference, Chapter 16.

Index